Fishing North Carolina

Also By Mike Marsh

Inshore Angler: Coastal Carolina's Small Boat Fishing Guide
Offshore Angler: Carolina's Mackerel Boat Fishing Guide
Quest for the Limit: Carolina Hunting Adventures

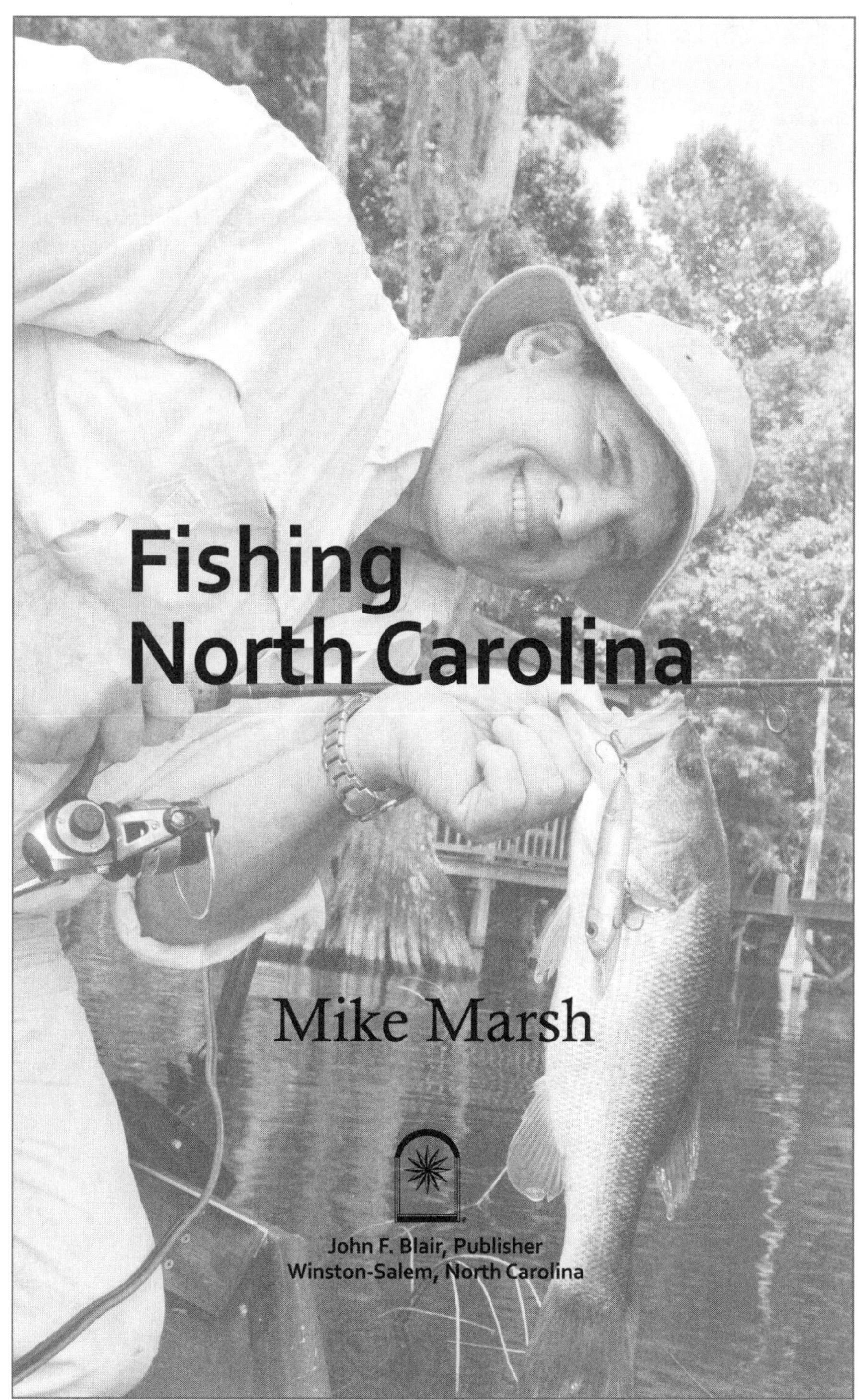

Fishing North Carolina

Mike Marsh

John F. Blair, Publisher
Winston-Salem, North Carolina

1406 Plaza Drive
Winston-Salem, North Carolina 27103
www.blairpub.com

Manufactured in the Canada

All photographs by Mike Marsh or Carol Marsh

Cover photograph:
The author with Largemouth bass, Lake Waccamaw
Photo by Carol Marsh

Library of Congress Cataloging-in-Publication Data

Marsh, Mike, 1953-
Fishing North Carolina / by Mike Marsh.
p. cm.
Includes index.
ISBN-13: 978-0-89587-396-5 (alk. paper)
ISBN-10: 0-89587-396-6 (alk. paper)
ISBN-13: 978-0-89587-397-2 (ebook)
1. Fishing—North Carolina—Guidebooks. 2. North Carolina—Guidebooks. I. Title.
SH531.M377 2011
799.109756—dc22

2010047821

To Justin and Carol

Contents

Preface

Fishing North Carolina is the culmination of many years of background research and on-the-water personal fishing experience. So many other anglers and biologists have been involved that it would be impossible to name them all. This book is really the result of a community effort involving many experts on every aspect of the state's legendary fishing.

No one angler could possibly know everything about fishing, even for a single water body or a single species. But every angler is an expert at something when it comes to fishing on his home waters. Such local experts and fishing guides were generous in providing me detailed information, often agreeing to take me fishing after a chance meeting at a boat ramp or following a single telephone call.

Sometimes, the species list for a certain destination proved a mystery. When I didn't manage to catch what sources said should be in the water, I turned to the biologists of the North Carolina Wildlife Resources Commission for an incredible amount of accurate information. They identified species that were abundant or absent and named specific locations that offered some of the best fishing in their districts. I found many surprises. Biologists at the North Carolina Division of Marine Fisheries also provided information about various saltwater fish species and locations for catching them. Park rangers, superintendents, and staffers provided much of this book's information about fishing in municipal reservoirs. Some of these small water bodies offer surprisingly good fishing.

It is guaranteed that some of the places identified in this book as excellent places to catch fish will raise the eyebrows of anglers who live right around the corner but have never considered fishing them. Conversely, some anglers may decide against driving to certain destinations once they learn through this book that better fishing opportunities may lie an equal distance away.

Anglers have different reasons for fishing different bodies of water. Some places are ideal for bringing children and families, others offer amenities like camping or hiking, and others boast some of the most spectacular scenery on planet earth. All such aspects of the best fishing destinations are discussed in detail in the following pages.

My son, Justin Marsh, served a summer internship away from his studies at the University of North Carolina at Charlotte to help me find and sort the background information and maps for many of the fishing destinations. My wife, Carol Marsh, spent many of her vacations traveling with me and conducting field research. We often fished a different water body every day—and sometimes two or three—from our trusty johnboat. At times, it was an exhausting schedule. But it sure was fun. We fish together as a family whenever we can. Sharing a day on the water has proven a joyful experience, forming bonds and creating memories that will last our lifetimes. Fishing together has helped make us a family.

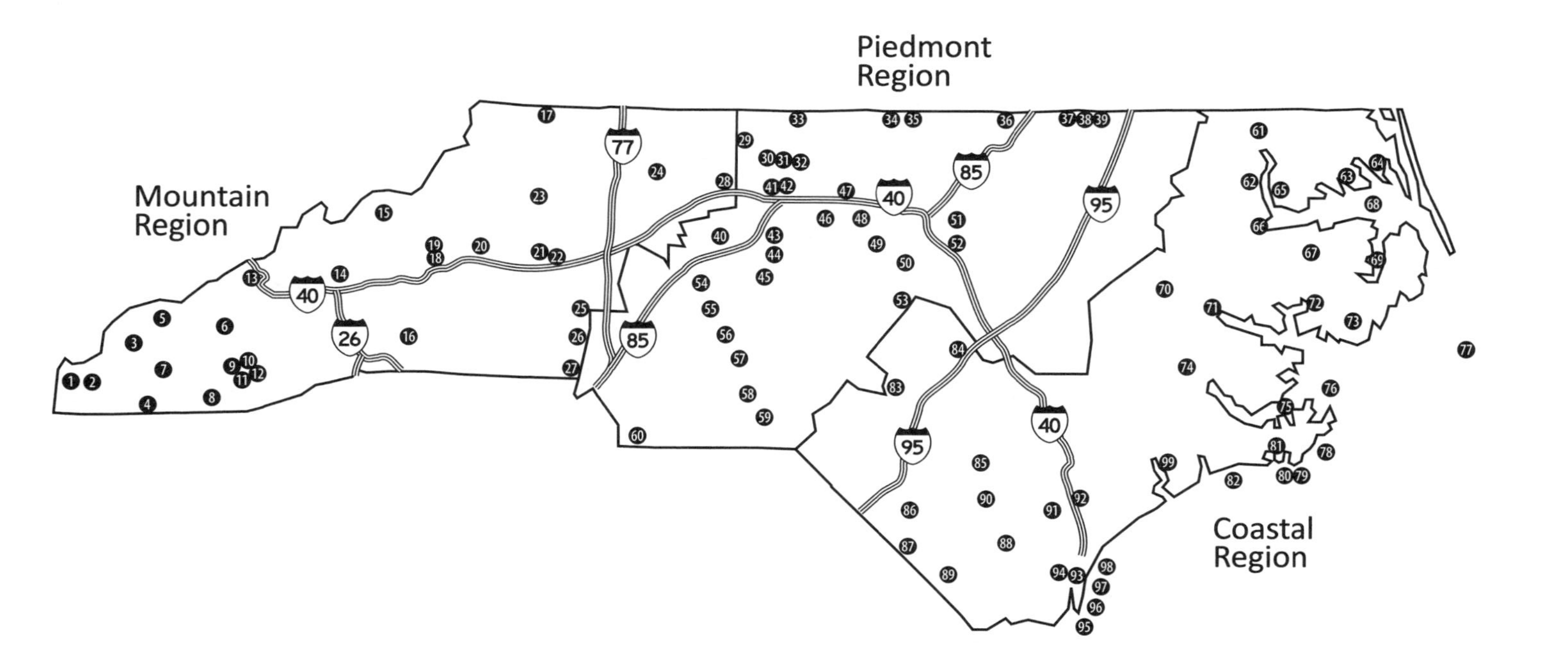
Mountain Region
Piedmont Region
Coastal Region
40
26
77
85
95

Introduction

Few states have the sheer number of fishing opportunities North Carolina offers its anglers. The state's internal waters include streams, rivers, ponds, lakes, and sounds. North Carolina also has one of the longest Atlantic Ocean coastlines of all the states.

Encompassing a land area of 48,711 square miles, a water area of 5,107 square miles, and a total area of 53,818 square miles, it's an enormous state that boasts more water bodies than any angler can fish in a lifetime. Driving across the state from the mountains to the sea can take more than eight hours. Driving from the South Carolina line to the Virginia line can take more than five hours. Everywhere in between are scores of waters that hold an incredible variety and abundance of game fish.

The number of recreational fishermen of all license types in North Carolina is about 1.2 million. Since the state has a total population of 9.4 million, that means one out of every eight citizens goes fishing. Angling is therefore one of the most popular types of outdoor recreation. It is also extremely important to the state's economy because of the many businesses it supports, along with the state tax revenues and license fees that anglers and boaters contribute.

Beginning in the high mountain streams, anglers catch brook, rainbow, and brown trout. As rivers grow from these tiny streams, smallmouth bass, muskellunge, rock bass, bullhead, and channel catfish begin to appear. In the mountain lakes, anglers catch walleye, trout, smallmouth bass, muskellunge, largemouth bass, white crappie, bullhead, and flathead catfish. The species composition increases as the water grows warmer through the foothills, where blue catfish, spotted bass, striped bass, white bass, and white perch become angler favorites.

Anglers in the Piedmont lakes and rivers see a decline in smallmouth bass and spotted bass in favor of largemouth bass and black crappie, which start mixing with white crappie. Downstream into the coastal plain, yellow perch, chain pickerel, bowfin, and gar are native species that increase the fish diversity. Native black crappie eventually take precedence over white crappie in coastal rivers. The constant fish from the mountains to the sea are the many sunfish species, which occur almost anywhere there is water and thrill anglers of all ages.

In the brackish zones, anglers catch migratory striped bass, white perch, and shad. Speckled trout, red drum, and flounder are added to the species mix as the salinity increases in the coastal sounds and rivers. Tarpon and giant red drum mix with black drum, sharks, rays, and other saltwater fish in the sounds and coastal rivers.

Along the beaches, surf anglers and pier fishermen catch every saltwater fish except offshore species such as marlin, dolphin, yellowfin tuna, wahoo, grouper, and snapper. Some of the most popular fish along the beaches are spot, croaker, Spanish mackerel, king mackerel, flounder, sheepshead, whiting, speckled trout, gray trout, red drum, and pompano. The sites in this book end at the waters along the beaches and the fishing piers.

The boundaries for the Mountain, Piedmont, and Coastal regions in this book are not based on the technical geographic boundaries for the three regions. Instead, they are based on the North Carolina Wildlife Resources Commission's wildlife districts. Each region has three wildlife districts, for a total of nine wildlife districts. These districts were established in the 1940s for the purpose of managing similar fish and wildlife habitats within each of the districts and regions, with the borders of the districts and regions following county lines. To avoid confusion and conflict with the commission's wildlife districts, this book's maps show the same regions as the maps on the commission's website.

Fishing North Carolina is intended as a resource for anglers driving to its various destinations, perhaps while towing a small- to medium-sized boat or with a kayak or canoe tied to the car roof. For more on the state's saltwater fishing opportunities, consult this author's other books, *Inshore Angler: Coastal Carolina's Small Boat Fishing Guide* and *Offshore Angler: Carolina's Mackerel Boat Fishing Guide*.

How to Use This Guide

The "Fish Species of North Carolina" chapter is divided into sections covering freshwater species and saltwater species. The smaller sections covering the individual species provide information about North Carolina's most popular game fish. The more anglers know about particular species, the better they become at locating and catching them. These sections offer basic information about the types of waters in which the fish are found, their habits, and the best ways of presenting baits or lures for catching them. The species are grouped by the methods anglers will most likely use to catch them. For example, the sunfish species are grouped together because many of them occupy the same waters and are likely to be caught in combination using the same methods. A **Best bets** section appears at the end of each species listing. Each destination in the **Best bets** section has been selected because it is a popular and consistent place for anglers to catch the species. For fish that are not abundant, it gives sites where anglers are most likely to catch them.

Following the chapter on fish species is a brief "Special State Fishing Programs" chapter intended to make newcomers aware of state programs and to inform experts who might catch a record or award-winning fish on how to go about having it recognized. There have been many would-be records that were not properly documented because the anglers didn't have such information beforehand.

The bulk of the book is taken up by the 100 site listings stretching from the mountains to the coast. Each site listing begins with basic information including the key species found in the water body, a short overview of the site, the best ways to fish the water, and the best times of year to fish.

The **Description** section covers special features and historical information.

The **Fishing** section provides the information needed to plan a successful fishing trip. It covers the best ways to catch particular species and the best places in the water body to begin fishing.

The ***N.C. A-G* grid** is the location of the reference grid where the site is found in the *DeLorme North Carolina Atlas and Gazetteer*. The references are approximate. Some sites fall on the confluence lines of more than one grid, so they are covered on more than one page of the *N.C. A-G*. The *DeLorme North Carolina Atlas and Gazetteer* is available in tackle shops, discount stores, and bookstores statewide or directly from DeLorme Mapping, P.O. Box 298, Yarmouth, Maine 04096; call 800-561-5105 or visit www.delorme.com.

The **General information** section covers special rules and regulations, special licenses, opening and closing dates and hours, launch or fishing fees, boat rentals, on-site tackle shops, navigation hazards, fish consumption advisories, and other information anglers should know before traveling to the site.

The **Nearest camping** section tells where to find campgrounds close to the site. These are usually public campgrounds in state and federal parks. In places where no public campgrounds are available, some privately run campgrounds are included.

Directions are given from the nearest major highway, population center, or landmark. For many sites, a site map is also provided. For large sites such as reservoirs, rivers, and sounds that have multiple access points, the map provides a selection of access points covering most of the site. After looking over the site map to scout the general location, anglers can consult other sources including maps and government agency websites to find the locations of additional ramps and fishing facilities. Private facilities are shown where public access is limited or unavailable.

Locator maps are also provided. These are broken down into the Mountain

Region, the Piedmont Region, and the Coastal Region. These in turn are broken down along county lines and roughly along the transitions where the fishing conditions and species composition begin to change from cold-water freshwater fish in the mountains to warm-water freshwater fish in the Piedmont and warm-water freshwater, brackish-water, and saltwater fish on the coast.

Last comes an appendix containing important contact information for the state and federal agencies, county and town departments, ranger offices, visitor centers, power companies, public and private parks, refuges, marinas, campgrounds, and piers discussed throughout the book.

Weather

North Carolina's weather varies from temperate to subtropical, depending upon elevation and latitude. In the mountains, winter snowfall is frequent. But along the state's southern coast, snow events are rare. In the Piedmont, a couple of snowfalls occur annually, along with some freezing rain events. Cold weather keeps many fishermen indoors. But it shouldn't because many cold-water species bite best in winter. In cold conditions, anglers must be very careful to keep from falling into the water. Hypothermia and drowning can cause winter fishing fatalities.

Hot weather can be just as difficult. Locating lakes and rivers that offer the shade of trees or bridges and fishing at night are good tactics for dealing with the heat of summer. It is not unusual for North Carolina anglers to endure strings of summer days with temperatures ranging from the low 90s to the low 100s. Summer days can be 10 degrees cooler in the mountains than at the coast. In summer, anglers should bring plenty of water and ice for staying cool.

Of all the weather events that prevent anglers from fishing, strong winds are the worst. In the mountains, winds of 10 to 15 miles per hour are considered strong. On the coast, anglers often fish in winds that blow twice that speed across flat terrain with nothing to block them. Fishing early in the day is a common tactic on the coast, where land and sea breezes rise and set with the sun.

At the coast, tropical storms and hurricanes can destroy fishing opportunities by closing boat ramps, blowing down boat docks and fishing piers, temporarily closing large expanses of coastal water to boating until they are checked for safe navigation, and creating fish kills through oxygen depletion that decimate coastal river fish populations. But angling infrastructure and fish populations can be restored. Residents of the coast are used to dealing with tropical events. Coastal fish species evolved to survive these events as well. When the wind is blowing too hard for safe boating, anglers can always pursue options such as fishing from the bank, the shore, or a pier.

Summer thunderstorms can build swiftly from otherwise clear skies. Anglers should stay tuned in to radios when unsettled weather is forecast. Strong winds, driving rains, lightning, and tornadoes accompany thunderstorms. The only safe way for anglers to avoid lightning strikes is to get their boats off the water.

Other Safety Precautions

Whether wading or boating, anglers must always be careful not to fall into the water. Drowning fatalities are rare, but they do occur every year. Anglers should wear personal flotation devices at all times. Under state laws, children are required to wear them when aboard boats. Another way to prevent accidental drownings and other mishaps is to share a fishing trip with at least one friend.

North Carolina anglers have an extremely high incidence of skin cancer because there is virtually no time of year they can't be outside pursuing their sport. Anglers should wear hats, long-sleeved shirts, long pants, and sunscreen. A roof or canvas cover on a boat can also help stave off the effects of the summer sun. The other way to reduce sun exposure is to fish early or late in the day or at night.

Insects and ticks are widespread hazards. While mosquitoes, biting flies, and gnats are usually nothing more than irritations, ticks carry deadly and disabling diseases. Wasps pose a hazard to anglers fishing lakes and rivers when lures become stuck in overhanging bushes where the insects have nests. Anglers should wear protective clothing and use chemical repellents when these pests are in the fishing area. Biting bugs have prematurely ended many fishing trips.

Poisonous snakes live in most areas of the state. Anglers should use caution when launching, walking the shoreline, wading the shallows, and retrieving lures stuck in shoreline structure. Cottonmouths are common in coastal rivers. Copperheads and rattlesnakes occur statewide. North Carolina is among the top states in the nation for the number of humans bitten by poisonous snakes each year. Anglers should be aware of their surroundings and never attempt to pick up or otherwise bother snakes that may be venomous.

Many species of fish have sharp teeth. Rays even have stingers. Anglers should learn to identify dangerous fish, to handle and subdue them carefully using towels or gloves, and to remove hooks or lures with long-nosed pliers or other de-hooking devices. Sharp spines and gill covers also pose hazards because they can puncture or cut hands and fingers. Hooks themselves are dangerous, whether in fish that have been boated or while dangling unprotected from rods. Knives, gaffs, and other pointed tools also pose dangers. Such gear should be safely stowed when not in use. All marine wounds should be cleaned, disinfected, and dressed quickly, since water and fish harbor an amazing assortment of bacteria and other pathogens. Anglers should always keep a first-aid kit handy.

All gear required by law must be aboard any boat. In addition, boaters should have along maps, extra fuel, radios, strobe lights, and other safety gear.

With regard to boats, there is no such thing as having too much safety gear.

The United States Coast Guard and the North Carolina Wildlife Resources Commission (NCWRC) regulate boating safety. Boating anglers should familiarize themselves with the regulations of these agencies, including accident-reporting requirements. The way to prevent boating accidents is through constant alertness.

The state has issued several fish consumption advisories for metals and chemicals. Anglers should consult the NCWRC's website or regulations digest or contact the North Carolina Department of Health and Human Services (NCDHHS) for listed species and waters.

Access

The boating access areas in this book are by no means the only ones at many of the sites. In addition to the numerous other NCWRC and power company boating access areas, many private marinas allow launching for a small fee. There are also many municipal ramps and places to launch at bridges and road rights of way.

Walk-in access is available at many places where road rights of way and bridges touch water bodies. Anglers should always respect private property when wading streams or portaging canoes to get to rivers, lakes, and streams.

The NCWRC maintains public fishing areas across the state. These access areas have piers and other amenities, including handicapped-accessible fishing areas.

See the appendix for contact information regarding fishing areas and ramps maintained by the NCWRC, various other state and federal agencies, and power companies.

Fish Species of North Carolina

Freshwater Species

Black Bass

Several bass species inhabit North Carolina waters, including smallmouth bass, rock bass, spotted bass, and largemouth bass. While all of these fish may be found in combination in overlapping waters, one species typically dominates a certain water body.

The smallmouth bass (*Micropterus dolomieu*) is one of the most highly sought game fish of the mountains. It has a bronze or brown back and sides, leading to the nickname "bronzeback." The jawbone does not extend behind the rear edge of the eye. The two dorsal fins are connected. Smallmouth bass can top 10 pounds but usually weigh one to three pounds. They are found in clear, swift, rocky streams and clear mountain lakes. The easternmost waters they inhabit in North Carolina are thought to be the Uwharrie and Dan rivers.

Rock bass (*Ambloplites rupestris*) are common catches in the deep pools of clear, rocky, and sandy streams. They are chunkier in appearance than smallmouth bass and have a dark olive to black coloration. The scales have dark spots, and the eye has a red rim, leading to the nickname "redeye bass."

Spotted bass (*Micropterus punctulatus*) are common in the foothills transition zone between the mountains and the Piedmont. Stocked statewide, the fish may supplant largemouth bass in many rivers and lakes. It has evenly arranged spots in alternating rows below a dark lateral line. The two dorsal fins are connected. While spotted bass can weigh eight pounds, most weigh one to four pounds.

Largemouth bass (*Micropterus salmoides*) are found in warmer waters than the other bass species, which extends their range through the Piedmont all the way to the coastal rivers and lakes. They are nonnative to North Carolina but have been stocked statewide. The jawbone extends to the back of the eye, and the two dorsal fins are nearly separated, allowing them to be easily identified among the black bass species. Largemouth bass can weigh 20 pounds, but most weigh between one and six pounds. They thrive in the quiet, warm waters of streams, lakes, ponds, and rivers. They prefer heavy vegetation, deadfalls, stumps, and brush.

Techniques

Casting: All black bass species will attack the same types of lures. The most fun type of fishing is topwater fishing. Bass strike topwater walk-the-dog lures, buzzbaits, poppers, chugging lures, rubber frogs, and floating plastic worms. The best bet is casting topwater lures early or late in the day near cover areas. Pockets in pad beds, the edges of grass beds, stump fields, rocky or clay banks, sand bars, docks, and any other places with anomalies are likely to draw strikes. Topwater action is best in spring and fall. Spinnerbaits are also very productive because they can be fished in almost any type of cover. Anglers cast spinnerbaits to reach beneath overhanging cover such as docks and tree limbs. They also work well when cast to the edges of aquatic vegetation beds or rocky areas. In streams and rivers, inline spinners and floating crankbaits work well. Soft plastic lures shaped like worms, flukes, and lizards rigged with weights to make them slither or jump along the bottom work well in almost any situation except swiftly flowing water. Crankbaits are all-around favorites. They can run shallow or deep, with rattles or without, to attract bass from great depths or great distances. Bouncing a crankbait off woody cover, rocks, or the bottom of a lake is a classic way to draw a strike from a lethargic bass.

Bait fishing: Since bass love minnows and crayfish, these two baits are mainstays of the fishing. Anglers can buy shiners and goldfish for use as bass bait. They also catch the various shad species to use as bait. Live sunfish and perch can be used. A big gob of night crawlers will also catch bass as long as other fish don't beat the bass to the bait. Crayfish work best for the cold-water bass species in mountain lakes and streams. Some of the biggest bass are fooled by live baits. Live baits are usually fished on float rigs cast to likely fish-holding cover. They are especially effective when fished in tight places where a lure can't be easily retrieved, such as in flooded timber or beneath docks. Live baits can also be trolled or drifted. They are popular for bass fishing from public bank- or pier-fishing areas.

Fly casting: Fly casting is an exciting way to catch all bass species. The most popular fly is the popping bug, which makes a loud pop and creates a bubble wake when the line is pulled hard and fast. Other good flies include the slider, which doesn't have a concave face like the popper, and floating mouse and frog imitations. Fly-fishing is popular among anglers who fish ponds from small boats, who wade or drift-fish mountain rivers, or who wade-fish the sandy-bottomed coastal lakes.

Best bets for smallmouth bass: Hiwassee Lake (site 2), Lake Santeetlah (site 3), Fontana Lake (site 5), Tuckasegee River (site 6), Lake Glenville (site 8), Pigeon River/Waterville Lake (site 13), Toe River System (site 15), New River (site 17)

Best bets for spotted bass: Chatuge Lake (site 4), Lake Norman (site 25), Mountain Island Lake (site 26), Upper Cape Fear River (site 90)

Best bets for largemouth bass: Randleman Regional Reservoir (site 43), Lake Lucas (site 44), B. Everett Jordan Lake (site 50), Harris Reservoir (site 53), High Rock Lake (site 54), Lake Tillery (site 57), Chowan River (site 62), Lake Phelps (site 67), Sutton Lake (site 91)

Best bets for rock bass: Tuckasegee River (site 6), Nantahala Lake/Nantahala River (site 7), Toe River System (site 15), New River (site 17)

Striped Bass

The striped bass species include striped bass (*Morone saxatilis*), white bass (*Morone chrysops*), striped bass–white bass hybrids (*Morone saxatilis* x *M. chrysops*) or "Bodie bass," and white perch (*Morone americana*). All species are anadromous, migrating from salt water to fresh water to spawn. But all of these species also have landlocked populations.

Stripers are heavy bodied and have an underlapping jaw. Their coloration is dark green to gray on the back, silver on the sides, and white on the belly. Seven or eight usually unbroken longitudinal stripes give the fish its name; it is alternately known as the striper or rockfish. Stripers can top 60 pounds, but most weigh less than 20 pounds.

White bass are silver with faint horizontal stripes. The two dorsal fins are only slightly separated. A single tooth patch on the tongue identifies them.

Hybrids have seven or eight black broken stripes. The profile of the hybrid is deeper than that of the striper. Hybrids can weigh 20 pounds but usually weigh less than 10 pounds.

White perch are less streamlined than white bass and lose their stripes as they mature.

Techniques

Casting: Topwater lures, jigs, spoons, and crankbaits work well for all the striped bass species. It's a matter of matching the size of the lure to the size of the baitfish and the fish. Casting poppers to points or to surfacing schools is a good tactic. Anytime a school is working the surface, a lipless vibration lure or jig is a good bet when cast beyond the school and reeled fast. A jig works well when cast to a deep or shallow school. Trolling a stickbait or crankbait is a good bet for deeper fish. Jigging or casting a spoon is also a good tactic when the fish are deep or when they are surfacing for only a short time before scattering or submerging.

Bait fishing: Live minnows and shad are good bets for striped bass. For white bass, shiners and small shad are good choices. For hybrids, chicken liver, shrimp, and minnows make good baits. White perch anglers use small shiners and worms.

Best bets for striped bass: Dan River (site 33), John H. Kerr Reservoir (site 36), Roanoke River (site 39), High Rock Lake (site 54), Upper Neuse and Trent Rivers (site 74), Cape Hatteras National Seashore (site 77)

Best bets for white bass: Lake Norman (site 25), Badin Lake (site 56), Lake Tillery (site 57)

Best bets for hybrids: Lake Thom-A-Lex (site 40), Oak Hollow Lake (site 41)

Best bets for white perch: Lake Norman (site 25), Mountain Island Lake (site 26), Lake Wylie (site 27), Lake Tillery (site 57), Pasquotank River (site 64), Lake Waccamaw (site 88)

CATFISH

Native catfish include brown (*Ameiurus nebulosus*), yellow (*Ameiurus natalis*), and black (*Ameiurus melas*) bullheads and white catfish (*Ameiurus catus*). Nonnative catfish include channel (*Ictalurus punctatus*), blue (*Ictalurus furcatus*), and flathead catfish (*Pylodictis olivaris*). Catfish are distinctive, thanks to their slick skins, whiskers, and sharp fin spines. They are found statewide. In waters where they were once common, many native species have been displaced by channel, blue, and flathead catfish. Catfish are primarily bottom feeders. What works for catching one can catch the other species as well. Bullheads typically weigh only a pound or two but can reach five pounds or more. White catfish can top 20 pounds but usually weigh five pounds or less. Channel catfish can weigh 20 pounds; fish of up to 10 pounds are common. Blue and flathead catfish can top 100 pounds; 30-pounders are common.

Techniques

Bait fishing: Catfish are living tongues, sensing their food with "whiskers" (more accurately called barbels) and other sensory organs in their skin. Commercial stinkbaits, dough baits, and dip baits that are applied to a sponge work well for all catfish. Cut fish, chicken liver, shrimp, worms, live minnows, cut and live eels, and clams are all great catfish baits. Bullheads love worms. White catfish and blue catfish feed on shad and other small baitfish. Flathead catfish anglers prefer fishing with live sunfish, shad, or eels when specifically targeting these large catfish. For the biggest catfish, saltwater pier tackle is used. But for smaller species, bass rods and reels work well. The bait is typically fished on the bottom, but float rigs can be effective in ponds and shallow rivers. Catfish are among the most popular species for bank and pier fishing at public parks. They are widely stocked through the NCWRC's Community Fishing Program.

Best bets for channel catfish: Graham-Mebane Lake (site 47), Sutton Lake (site 91)

Best bet for white catfish: B. Everett Jordan Lake (site 50)

Best bets for blue catfish: Badin Lake (site 56), Blewett Falls Lake (site 59), Upper Cape Fear River (site 90), Lower Cape Fear River (site 93)

Best bets for flathead catfish: Badin Lake (site 56), Blewett Falls Lake (site 59), Lumber River (site 86), Upper Cape Fear River (site 90), Sutton Lake (site 91), Lower Cape Fear River (site 93)

Crappie

The black crappie (*Pomoxis nigromaculatus*) is indigenous to rivers of the coastal plain, but the white crappie (*Pomoxis annularis*) has been widely stocked. The black crappie is darker and has black spots all over the body. The white crappie is silvery with vertical bars. Although both species may inhabit the same lakes, the white crappie is predominant in the colder reservoirs, while the black crappie is dominant in many Piedmont and coastal lakes. Both species can attain weights exceeding four pounds but typically weigh up to two pounds.

Techniques

Casting: Beetle grub spinnerbaits, inline spinners, and jigs dressed with hair, feathers, or soft plastic trailers are the best bets for crappie. Ultralight spinning or spincast tackle is the ticket to casting into the thick cover where they hide. Casting along shoreline cover and docks is the best way to catch them.

Bait fishing: Crappie strike small minnows and red worms. Fixed-depth float rigs work well when the fish are shallow in spring, while sliding float rigs and split-shot rigs are better when the fish are deep in summer. Small gold wire hooks that are easily bent for retrieval from structure are the best bets for crappie fishing. A combination of jigs, some rigged with live baits and some with grubs, can be used for trolling the channels and shoreline contours with great success.

Best bets for crappie: Hyco Lake (site 34), B. Everett Jordan Lake (site 50), Falls Lake (site 51), Harris Reservoir (site 53), High Rock Lake (site 54), Cashie, Middle, and Eastmost Rivers (site 66)

PIKE

North Carolina has two pike large enough to be classified as game fish.

The larger of the two is the muskellunge (*Esox masquinongy*), or "muskie," which has been called "the fish of 10,000 casts" because it can be exhausting work to catch one. It is a fierce predator that feeds primarily on suckers and other fish. It has a very long, relatively narrow body that is dark green along the top with vertical bars. Black spots are present on the fins and tail. Duckbill-like jaws studded with sharp teeth are a dead giveaway. The fish inhabits large pools in mountain rivers, streams, and lakes, especially those with overhanging trees or timber that has fallen into the water and rocky drop-offs or ledges. Muskie can sometimes top 60 pounds, but fish of less than 30 pounds are most common.

The other large pike is the chain pickerel (*Esox niger*), or "jackfish," which usually attacks baits and lures intended for other fish. Compared to muskellunge, chain pickerel are small, weighing one to four pounds, though jackfish of nine pounds have been landed. Nonetheless, they are great game fish. Common in coastal rivers, lakes, and streams, they also occur in some Piedmont lakes. Their ice-pick teeth don't typically cut lines. The fish is named for the chain-mail-like markings on its flanks.

A third pike is the redfin pickerel (*Esox americanus*), which shares the same waters as the chain pickerel. It has red fins and dark vertical bands on its flanks. A common catch in some waters, it seldom exceeds a foot in length or a pound in weight. Techniques for catching redfin pickerel are the same as those for catching chain pickerel.

MUSKELLUNGE

Techniques

Casting: Muskellunge anglers use stout baitcasting rigs spooled with 80- to 130-pound superbraid lines. Wire leaders are also necessary to prevent cutoffs from the sharp teeth. A muskie strike can be savage or subtle, depending on the mood of the fish. The angler can often see a fish following a lure up to the boat, only to dart away at the last second. When muskie fishing, the angler should set the hook hard at every tiny tap he feels. If a fish does "show" and follows the lure to the boat, the angler uses the rod to move the lure in a figure-eight pattern to entice the fish to strike. If the fish moves away, the angler keeps working the area for as long as an hour with other lures to try to induce a strike. Large spinnerbaits, stickbaits, swimbaits, and topwater chugging lures are the best bets for muskie fishing. The more noise or vibration, the greater the odds a muskie will mistake a lure for injured prey. Muskie often strike lures cast for bass or trolled for other species, leading to most anglers' first encounters with the fish.

Bait fishing: Few North Carolina muskellunge anglers intentionally target the fish by using live baits. However, a live sucker is the best bait throughout the muskie's range.

Fly casting: Large 10- to 12-weight rods are necessary to cast large streamers and poppers all day long. The best flies are large and light.

Best bets for muskellunge: French Broad River (site 14), Toe River System (site 15), Lake James (site 18)

Chain Pickerel

Techniques

Casting: Chain pickerel strike the same spinners and crankbaits intended for bass and crappie.

Bait fishing: The best bait for chain pickerel is a live shiner fished on a float rig.

Fly casting: Chain pickerel will strike spoon flies, minnow imitations, and poppers intended for other species such as bass and sunfish.

Best bets for chain pickerel: Mayo Reservoir (site 35), Rhodes Pond (site 84), Northeast Cape Fear River (site 92)

Perch

Yellow perch (*Perca flavescens*) are residents of coastal rivers, streams, millponds, and lakes. Also called "raccoon perch" and "redfin perch" for the stripes on their backs and their often brilliant fins, these fish thrive in acidic waters. Yellow perch are bright yellow on the belly and greenish or dark above with yellow to red-orange fins. Most yellow perch weigh less than one pound, but they can grow to four pounds.

Walleye (*Stizostedion vitreum*) are golden brown with a white belly. Their large, glassy eyes and long, sharp teeth identify them. They can weigh 15 pounds but typically weigh only one or two pounds. Walleye are residents of cold, deep lakes and dam tailraces.

Techniques

Casting: Yellow perch and walleye both strike spinners and small crankbaits, whether they are cast or trolled. They form large schools. If one fish strikes, anglers toss out a marker and continue fishing the area. Yellow perch, walleye, and the baitfish on which they feed can be found with an electronic depthfinder. Once on top of a school of perch, anglers use jigs or spoons to catch large numbers of fish.

Bait fishing: Live minnows and worms should be fished with enough weight to get the bait down to the fish. Drifting or slow-trolling the bait just above the bottom is a good tactic.

Best bets for yellow perch: Lake Phelps (site 67), White Lake (site 85), Lake Waccamaw (site 88), Waccamaw River (site 89)

Best bets for walleye: Hiwassee Lake (site 2), Fontana Lake (site 5), Lake Gaston (site 37)

Shad

American or "white" shad (*Alosa sapidissima*) is the larger of the two shad species and hickory shad (*Alosa mediocris*) the smaller. The hickory shad weighs only a pound or two. It has a lower jaw that is longer than the upper and a series of spots behind the head. The American shad can weigh more than six pounds and has a single spot behind the head. The fish can be found in combination in some rivers, but one species or the other is usually the main species in a particular river.

Techniques

Casting: Shad are anadromous fish. The best time to catch them is during their spring spawning run up the rivers. The curious thing about these fish is that they do not eat any animal matter but strike small jigs and spoons. Small jigs called "darts" that have tiny tufts of hair dressing their hooks are the traditional lures. But lead-head jigs with tiny curly-tailed grubs and small silver or gold spoons also work well. Ultralight spinning tackle allows anglers to get the most fight out of these sporty fish.

Fly casting: Fly-fishing for shad is gaining in popularity. Anglers use jigs and darts, casting them with intermediate or sinking fly lines to get the lures down to the fish in the river currents.

Best bets for shad: Roanoke River (site 39), Tar River (site 70), Lower Cape Fear River (site 93)

SUNFISH

Sunfish are abundant but can become hybridized to the extent that they are difficult to identify. The main sunfish species include bluegill or "bream" (*Lepomis macrochirus*), redear (*Lepomis microlophus*), redbreast (*Lepomis auritus*), green (*Lepomis cyanellus*), warmouth (*Lepomis gulosus*), spotted (*Lepomis punctatus*), pumpkinseed (*Lepomis gibbosis*), and flier (*Centrarchus macropterus*). The bluegill is probably the most widespread, followed by redbreast and redear. These three species may be found in all fresh waters of the state except the coldest mountain streams.

The bluegill takes its name from its dark gill cover.

The redbreast earns its nickname of "robin" from its bright red or orange belly, which is especially prominent during the spring spawning period. Redbreast sunfish prefer rivers from the mountains to the coast that have clear water, but they are also found in lakes and ponds.

The redear gets its nickname of "shellcracker" because it feeds primarily on mollusks.

Green sunfish are found primarily in mountain rivers.

Warmouth sunfish lurk in the tannin-stained waters of coastal millponds, beaver ponds, and streams.

Spotted sunfish, indigenous to the rivers of the Southern coastal plain, earn their nickname of "stumpknocker" from their habit of guarding a particular stump or cypress knee.

The pumpkinseed takes its name from its body shape, which is similar to that of a pumpkinseed. Pumpkinseed sunfish occur in the slow-moving rivers and natural lakes of the coast. Their habit of staying in or near grass beds in lakes leads to their nickname of "grass perch."

The flier looks something like a black crappie but is more compact and has darker sides with dots, rather than the silver, speckled sides of a crappie. When hooked, the flier doesn't give much of a fight. Rather, it "flies" across the water. Anglers say catching one is like reeling in a wet leaf. The flier lives in the dark, acidic waters of oxbows, millponds, and beaver ponds along the coast.

Sunfish can weigh from a few ounces to two pounds. A few weigh as much as four pounds.

Techniques

Casting: Sunfish are suckers for beetle grub spinners, inline spinners, and small jigs. Ultralight tackle gets the most out of these sporty little fish.

Bait fishing: Sunfish baits include red worms, night crawlers, worms, crickets, and shrimp. A popular option is float fishing, in which an angler on a pier or bank uses a rig tied to a cane pole or telescoping fiberglass pole to poke the bait back into pockets of vegetation or cover or beyond snags. Bottom fishing with a split shot to hold the bait on the bottom is popular in slow-moving streams. Shellcracker are most likely to strike worms fished on the bottom. Warmouth sunfish readily strike minnows intended for bass and crappie.

Fly casting: Fly casting for sunfish is extremely popular. The best bet is a popping bug or slider cast at dawn or dusk. But when the fish are deeper in early spring and fall or on the beds in early summer, a rubber grub or sponge-body ant or spider fished beneath the surface is deadly for sunfish.

Best bets for sunfish: bluegill, Chowan River (site 62); **redear**, Lake Wylie (site 27); **redbreast**, Lumber River (site 86); **green**, Toe River System (site 15); **warmouth**, Northeast Cape Fear River (site 92); **spotted**, Waccamaw River (site 89); **flier**, Lumber River (site 86)

Trout

Trout are cold-water fish, which means they don't survive water temperatures above 70 degrees and require much colder water to spawn successfully. Trout are stocked throughout their range, which includes the streams, lakes, and rivers in the Mountain Region. There are many designations of trout waters, such as "hatchery-supported" and "delayed harvest." Anglers must become familiar with the trout-fishing designations and regulations before fishing any designated waters. In the many undesignated waters, trout may be caught by any method and retained in accordance with the established creel limits. Trout fishermen should refer to the NCWRC's *Regulations Digest* and *North Carolina Trout Fishing Maps*, available by calling the NCWRC or visiting the website.

Trout species include brook, rainbow, and brown.

Brook trout (*Salvelinus fontinalis*) are the native trout of the North Carolina mountains. They have been supplanted or joined by rainbow trout (*Oncorhynchus *mykiss*) and brown trout (*Salmo trutta*) in many places. However, the NCWRC has initiated a brook trout restoration project on a few experimental streams with a goal of eliminating nonnative trout and other fish species. Brook trout seldom exceed two pounds but can grow as large as 15 pounds. Their coloration runs from dark green to slate gray on the back and sides. The sides have a few red spots with blue halos surrounding them. All of the fins except the dorsal fin have white edges.

Rainbow trout have a pink or red stripe down the center of the side. This coloration is typically brighter in fish spawned in the wild than in hatchery-raised fish. They have many black spots on the back, dorsal, and anal fins. Rainbow trout can attain weights of more than 32 pounds but rarely grow larger than five pounds.

Brown trout have olive brown sides with red spots surrounded by blue halos from the head to the tail. The tail fin is nearly square. Brown trout can attain weights of 40 pounds but rarely grow larger than five pounds.

Some large specimens—especially brown trout—have come from relatively tiny streams. But the largest trout usually grow in lakes and large rivers.

Techniques

Casting: Many anglers fish for trout with ultralight spinning and spincasting rods and reels. Monofilament lines from two to eight pounds are popular. The smaller, less visible lines are used for small streams and light lures and the heavier lines for larger water and heavier lures. Tiny inline spinners and small, floating minnow-imitating stickbaits are very popular. When casting artificial lures, anglers should work slowly upstream, casting to pockets behind rocks and below the riffles or casting upstream and working the lures downstream into these holding areas. In some lakes, trolling deep-diving crankbaits also works well for catching trout.

Bait fishing: Crayfish, crickets, worms, fly larvae, corn, salmon eggs, and scented artificial bait "eggs" impregnated with enzymes work well for catching trout. Float-fishing works well in some of the broad, calm stretches, especially at many hatchery-supported waters with designated fishing areas. Most anglers fish with bottom rigs, which consist of a small wire hook and a split shot just large enough to keep the bait moving slowly along the bottom. The artificial "egg" baits are good for this application because they float off the bottom and are very durable.

Fly casting: Fly casting is the only legal way to fish some waters but can certainly be used on any of the other designated waters with equal effectiveness. Fly casting has advantages over other methods, especially when a fly hatch is in progress. Small streams can be a lot of trouble to fly-fish, but they can also be the most productive. It's amazing how many ways anglers find to get their flies into deep pockets of water in mountain streams. Sometimes, this doesn't even involve casting, but rather sneaking to the water, hiding behind boulders, and dangling a fly from a rod threaded through the tree limbs. But stalking the fish yields results. Trout can be extremely easily spooked. They are disturbed by footfalls and other vibrations, as well as shadows and bottom sediments if they are moving downstream. Wading anglers find fly casting much easier in larger waters, where they encounter less overhanging cover to snag lines. Dry flies work extremely well. Dedicated fly-fishermen tie flies to match the hatch. Fishing with nymph and other wet-fly patterns is also popular. Anglers allow the wet flies to drift along, perhaps with the use of a strike indicator tied to the line above the nymph. Fly patterns that mimic many terrestrial insects, larvae, and minnows also work well in certain instances.

Best bets for trout: Nantahala Lake/Nantahala River (site 7), French Broad River (site 14), Toe River System (site 15), Lake Lure (site 16), Linville River (site 19)

Saltwater Species

Bonito

False albacore (*Euthynnus alletteratus*), or "little tunny," and Atlantic bonito (*Sarda sarda*) are fast-swimming members of the tuna family. They are also referred to as spotted bonito and striped bonito. The false albacore is identified by its lack of teeth, its shiny sides and belly with inconsistent swirled markings, and the spots on its flanks. The Atlantic bonito has sharp teeth and longitudinal stripes on its sides. These fish form large schools at inlets and nearshore reefs.

Techniques

Casting: The small tuna species readily strike spoons, poppers, jigs, and lures. Anglers sight-cast to schools of surfacing fish chasing baitfish. Trolling with lures and spoons also works well. These fish run from less than a pound to more than 20 pounds. Most weigh five to 12 pounds.

Fly casting: Fly casting is a popular way to catch these fish. Baitfish patterns and poppers work well.

Best bets for bonito: Cape Lookout National Seashore (site 78), Beaufort Inlet (site 79), Masonboro Inlet (site 98)

Striped Bass

Striped bass (*Morone saxitilis*) is the same species as that found in fresh water. The fish are identified by their robust size, silvery bodies, and seven or eight longitudinal stripes. Caught in the ocean and in coastal rivers and sounds, they can weigh more than 70 pounds, though most weigh one to 20 pounds.

Techniques

Casting: Anglers use a variety of lures to catch stripers. The fish often school on top, where they strike poppers, jigs, spoons, and lures. Trolling with spoons and diving lures is a popular way to catch them.

Bait fishing: Striped bass strike live menhaden, eel, mullet, and shad fished on float rigs and bottom rigs. They also strike cut baits fished in the surf. Heavy rods are required to cast heavy surf sinkers long distances.

Best bets for striped bass: Albemarle Sound (site 68), Cape Hatteras National Seashore (site 77)

BLUEFISH

Bluefish (*Pomatomus saltatrix*) are found anywhere salt water is present, often running far inshore in the rivers and sounds. The smaller members of the species are called "tailors" for the way they snip the tails of baits and soft lures. The larger fish are called "choppers" for the way their teeth slice up their prey. The coloration is steely blue on the sides and back, transitioning to a silvery belly. Most bluefish weigh one to four pounds, but they can weigh more than 30 pounds.

Techniques

Casting: Bluefish are among the easiest to catch of all saltwater game fish. They are caught from ocean fishing piers, by anglers in boats, and by surf fishermen. Hard plastic and metal lures are the best bets for surviving repeated strikes. A wire leader is necessary for preventing cutoffs. Spoons, jigs, poppers, and diving lures work well for bluefish. Trolling spoons, jigs, or diving lures also work well.

Bait fishing: Bluefish strike shrimp or any type of cut or live fish. Some anglers catch big bluefish by drifting with float rigs or trolling with unweighted lines baited with live mullet or menhaden.

Fly casting: Fly fishermen catch bluefish using a variety of patterns. The harder resin-bodied flies survive more battles than those tied with less durable materials. Poppers work well for catching bluefish.

Best bets for bluefish: Cape Hatteras National Seashore (site 77), Cape Lookout National Seashore (site 78), Beaufort Inlet (site 79), Lower Cape Fear River (site

93), Fort Fisher (site 95), Freeman Park (site 96), Masonboro Island (site 97), Masonboro Inlet (site 98), ocean fishing piers (site 100)

Cobia

Cobia (*Rachycentron canadum*) resemble flathead catfish. They have a brown back and a light belly. Cobia can weigh more than 100 pounds. Thirty- to 50-pounders are common. Cobia orient to navigation markers and are also attracted to floating objects like boats.

Techniques

Casting: Anglers sight-fish for cobia, spotting them as they cruise near inlets or circle navigation buoys. Large soft plastics resembling eels fished on jig heads and rubber tube eels are the best bets for sight-fishing.

Bait fishing: Anglers pitch live or frozen baitfish to catch visible cobia. Slow-trolling a live or dead baitfish near an inlet or nearshore structure may also draw a strike. Float rigs and balloon rigs with a balloon substituted for a hard float also work well for live-bait fishing. Anglers also fish with blue crabs, cut fish, and live baits on the bottom of navigation channels. Cobia fishermen use trolley rigs to catch the fish from ocean piers.

Best bets for cobia: Cape Hatteras National Seashore (site 77), Cape Lookout National Seashore (site 78), Beaufort Inlet (site 79), Masonboro Inlet (site 98), ocean fishing piers (site 100)

Spot

Spot (*Leiostomus xanthurus*) are named for the dark spot just behind the head. Spot weigh a few ounces and seldom exceed one pound. They are found in coastal rivers, navigation channels, and the surf.

Techniques

Bait fishing: No other fish brings more anglers to the coast than spot. Spot are caught from fishing piers and the surf by anglers fishing with bottom rigs. Multiple-hook rigs are used. Most have two hooks, though some have more. Each hook is baited with a piece of bloodworm, an artificial bloodworm strip, or fresh shrimp.

Atlantic Croaker

Croaker (*Micropogonias undulatus*) are caught along with spot because they inhabit the same waters. The techniques and places to catch them are similar to those for catching spot.

Whiting

Whiting species—also called sea mullet, Virginia mullet, and kingfish—consist of the Gulf kingfish (*Menticirrhus littoralis*), the northern kingfish (*Menticirrhus saxitilis*), and the southern kingfish (*Menticirrhus americanus*). These small, tasty, elongated fish with small chin barbels seldom weigh more than a pound or two. They are caught using the same techniques and in the same places as spot and croaker.

Best bets for spot, croaker, and whiting: Pamlico Sound (site 76), Cape Hatteras National Seashore (site 77), Cape Lookout National Seashore (site 78), Bogue Sound (site 82), Lower Cape Fear River (site 93), Fort Fisher (site 95), Freeman Park (site 96), Masonboro Island (site 97), ocean fishing piers (site 100)

Black Drum

Black drum (*Pogonias cromis*), the largest members of the croaker family, are named for their dark coloration and the drumming sounds their internal organs make. The juvenile fish have dark vertical bands on silvery flanks. In adult fish, the stripes disappear and the overall color changes to a dark bronze. The fish have a black cast when dead or dying. Their chin barbels help them find prey in the murky waters of rivers and sounds. But they also migrate long distances in the ocean. They can attain weights exceeding 100 pounds, but most weigh from one pound to 15 pounds.

Techniques

Casting: Black drum strike lures resembling shrimp and crabs. Soft plastic jigs are the best bets. Adult fish may strike these baits but are not as aggressive as juveniles in striking lures. The best places to fish are shell beds, riprap areas, boat docks, and bridge pilings.

Bait fishing: Black drum feed primarily on crustaceans, making fiddler crabs, mole crabs, and blue crabs prime baits. The bait is fished on the bottom near hard structure. But bait fishing also works at ocean fishing piers and in the surf.

Best bets for black drum: Cape Hatteras National Seashore (site 77), Cape Lookout National Seashore (site 78), Fort Macon (site 80), Bogue Sound (site 82), Lower Cape Fear River (site 93), Fort Fisher (site 95), New River (site 99), ocean fishing piers (site 100)

Red Drum

The red drum (*Sciaenops ocellatus*) is North Carolina's state saltwater fish. It is widely available in all saltwater areas, from brackish coastal rivers and sounds to the Atlantic Ocean. The fish is named for its red coloration and its eyelike spot, or sometimes several of them, at the base of the tail, as well as for the drumming sound made by its internal organs. It is also called spottail, channel bass, puppy drum, and redfish. Juvenile red drum, or puppy drum, stay in the sounds and rivers until four years of age and about 32 inches in length, when they head to the ocean. Thereafter, the fish return to Pamlico Sound only to spawn in summer. Red drum can top 90 pounds, but most weigh less than 15 pounds.

Techniques

Casting: Red drum anglers use many lures to catch puppy drum. The favorites include spoons, jigs, minnow imitations, and jigs tipped with soft plastic trailers. Sometimes, anglers spot the spottails before fishing. Other times, they work shoreline cover like docks, riprap, and sea walls. Oyster beds and grass beds also hold redfish. A topwater lure worked over flooded tidal-grass beds can draw explosive strikes.

Bait fishing: Red drum will eat almost any type of marine life. Anglers use live and cut fish, squid, crabs, and shrimp to catch them. Baits can be fished on the bottom or on float rigs. During summer, huge red drum move into Pamlico Sound, where anglers fish for them at night using bottom rigs and large chunks of cut fish. Surf fishing for red drum is extremely popular.

Fly casting: Fly-fishing for red drum has grown in popularity. While poling or wading through the marshes, anglers watch for the fish or for muddy water and grass stems moving on the flats where they are feeding. Approaching a red drum is one of the most exciting events in shallow-water fishing. The fish are incredibly wary and swim away at the slightest bump or shadow. Flies resembling small crabs, shrimp, and minnows are the best bets for red drum. A spoon-fly is a traditional style of fly used to catch the fish.

Best bets for red drum: Lower Neuse River (site 75), Pamlico Sound (site 76), Cape Hatteras National Seashore (site 77), Cape Lookout National Seashore (site

78), Beaufort Inlet (site 79), Newport River (site 81), Bogue Sound (site 82), Lower Cape Fear River (site 93), Fort Fisher (site 95), Freeman Park (site 96), Masonboro Island (site 97), Masonboro Inlet (site 98), ocean fishing piers (site 100)

Flounder

Southern (*Paralichthys lethostigma*), summer (*Paralichthys dentatus*), and Gulf flounder (*Paralichthys albigutta*) are North Carolina's main flounder species. Southern flounder have indistinct markings, while summer flounder have a five-spot pattern of eyelike spots and Gulf flounder have a three-spot pattern of eyelike spots. Southern flounder are found primarily at inlets and inshore waters, summer flounder at nearshore hard bottoms, surf, inlets, and piers, and Gulf flounder on offshore sandy bottoms. All three species can achieve weights of 10 pounds, but most specimens weigh one to three pounds. Flounder have both eyes on the top of the head, white undersides, and dark topsides.

Techniques

Casting: Spinning rigs and baitcasting outfits both have their flounder-fishing fans. Flounder strike anything that looks like a minnow. Jigs rigged with scented soft plastic trailers are the best bet. Flounder prefer structure such as oyster reefs and grass beds but can be caught anywhere in salt water or brackish water.

Bait fishing: Flounder strike minnows best but also strike shrimp, squid, and strips of fish. The best techniques include anchoring near likely structure and casting a bottom rig or drifting on the tide at an inlet or coastal river with the bait dragging along the bottom. Some anglers keep their boat motors in gear to maneuver the baits, trolling them along the bottom.

Best bets for flounder: Lower Neuse River (site 75), Pamlico Sound (site 76), Cape Hatteras National Seashore (site 77), Cape Lookout National Seashore (site 78), Beaufort Inlet (site 79), Bogue Sound (site 82), Lower Cape Fear River (site 93), Fort Fisher (site 95), Freeman Park (site 96), Masonboro Island (site 97), Masonboro Inlet (site 98), ocean fishing piers (site 100)

Florida Pompano

The Florida pompano (*Trachinotus carolinus*) is silver with yellow coloration on the throat and underside. The dorsal fin is dark. It averages a pound in weight but can weigh eight pounds. It is one of the best eating fish.

Techniques

Bait fishing: Pompano are caught from the surf, at inlets and navigation channels, and from ocean piers. The techniques are the same as for spot and croaker. The best baits are shrimp and mole crabs.

Best bets for pompano: Cape Hatteras National Seashore (site 77), Cape Lookout National Seashore (site 78), Beaufort Inlet (site 79), Lower Cape Fear River (site 93), Fort Fisher (site 95), Freeman Park (site 96), Masonboro Island (site 97), Masonboro Inlet (site 98), ocean fishing piers (site 100)

King Mackerel

The king mackerel (*Scromberomorus cavalla*) has an elongated body that is silver with a greenish to bluish iridescence. The lateral line dips sharply, while the lateral line of a Spanish mackerel does not. King mackerel, or "kings," run in large schools. They are caught from ocean piers and by anglers fishing nearshore waters in boats. King mackerel can weigh 80 pounds, but most weigh 25 pounds or less.

Techniques

Casting: King mackerel are caught with jigs, spoons, and crankbaits. Trolling these lures is a great way to catch kings.

Bait fishing: Live-bait techniques for many other species of game fish came about as a result of the efforts of king mackerel anglers, especially tournament fishermen. Purses for king tournaments run into millions of dollars annually. The standard tactic is slow-trolling live menhaden or other baitfish over structure such as natural ledges and artificial reefs. The rig, a wire leader with two or more treble hooks, can have a skirt or other attractor. Dead baits can be used, but they don't attract the largest kings. Trolley-rigging live baits at ocean piers is a standard king mackerel tactic. High-capacity conventional trolling reels are the best bets for live-bait fishing.

Best bets for king mackerel: Cape Hatteras National Seashore (site 77), Cape Lookout National Seashore (site 78), Beaufort Inlet (site 79), Masonboro Inlet (site 98), ocean fishing piers (site 100)

Spanish Mackerel

Spanish mackerel (*Scromberomorus maculatus*) form huge schools at reefs, inlet bars, and jetties and often enter coastal rivers and sounds. They have a dark spot on the forward part of the dorsal fin, and the lateral line does not have a pronounced dip. The fish is usually covered with gold spots and has a green back and silvery sides. Spanish mackerel can weigh more than seven pounds, but most weigh only one to three pounds.

Techniques

Casting: Anglers spot the fish first, then cast spoons, jigs, and hard plastic lures. One of the best ways to catch them is to cast a metal-tube jerk lure from a fishing pier at dawn or dusk. The lure is designed with a slanting face that forms a projecting "chin," which helps it dig into the water when fished from an elevated pier.

Bait fishing: Live menhaden and mullet are used for catching Spanish mackerel at inlets, along jetties, and at artificial reefs. The rig is a modified king mackerel rig with a single treble hook and a short wire leader. The baits are drifted or trolled.

Fly casting: Fly-fishing techniques for Spanish mackerel are the same as those for false albacore, Atlantic bonito, and bluefish.

Best bets for Spanish mackerel: Cape Hatteras National Seashore (site 77), Cape Lookout National Seashore (site 78), Beaufort Inlet (site 79), Masonboro Inlet (site 98), ocean fishing piers (site 100)

Sheepshead

Sheepshead (*Archosargus probatocephalus*) are named for their massive teeth, which resemble those of sheep. The fish have dark vertical stripes. They range in weight from less than a pound to more than 10 pounds. A few top 20 pounds.

Techniques

Bait fishing: Sheepshead are legendary for their soft strikes. Since sheepshead feed on shellfish, small sand fiddler crabs are one of the top baits. The crabs are hooked with a single hook rig and dropped beside pilings. It helps to scrape some oysters and barnacles from the pilings during low tide to attract the fish. To survive the powerful teeth, a small, stout hook is needed, along with a sinker just heavy enough to hold the bait stationary. The best places to fish include bridge pilings, dock pilings, and ocean fishing pier pilings.

Best bets for sheepshead: Bogue Sound (site 82), Lower Cape Fear River (site 93), Fort Fisher (site 95), ocean fishing piers (site 100)

TARPON

The tarpon (*Megalops atlanticus*) is one of the largest and hardest-fighting inshore game fish, exhibiting spectacular leaps when hooked. Tarpon can be caught from coastal rivers and sounds, from piers, and from boats trolling along the beaches. Surf fishermen hook tarpon but seldom land them. Most tarpon weigh 70 to 100 pounds, but they can top 200 pounds.

Techniques

Bait fishing: Tarpon strike live and dead fish and crabs. The baits are fished on the bottom and spread in a pattern that will cover as much water as possible. Chumming with ground fish and fish chunks helps attract tarpon to the baits. Tarpon strike live baits fished on trolley rigs from ocean fishing piers.

Best bets for tarpon: Lower Neuse River (site 75), Pamlico Sound (site 76), Cape Lookout National Seashore (site 78), Lower Cape Fear River (site 93)

SPOTTED SEATROUT

Spotted seatrout (*Cynoscion nebulosus*), or "speckled trout," are one of the top saltwater game fish of inshore waters. The fish are gray to silver and covered with black spots. They have a large mouth with prominent teeth. They are caught from ocean piers, from the surf, and at hard structure such as inlet jetties, docks, sea walls, and oyster beds. While "specks" can achieve 10 pounds, most weigh one to four pounds.

Techniques

Casting: Speckled trout anglers probably rely on lures more than any other saltwater fishermen. Notoriously finicky, specks change color preference on a whim and can disappear suddenly from areas of former abundance. Jigs with scented soft plastic trailers and hard plastic minnow-imitating lures are the top choices for specks. But some exciting action occurs when specks strike topwater walk-the-dog lures.

Bait fishing: Live shrimp are the favorite bait for catching specks. But the fish also strike mud minnows, menhaden, small croakers and pinfish, and mullet. The baits can be fished on float rigs or bottom rigs.

Best bets for spotted seatrout: Pamlico and Pungo Rivers (site 71), Swanquarter National Wildlife Refuge (site 72), Upper Neuse and Trent Rivers (site 74), Lower Neuse River (site 75), Pamlico Sound (site 76), Cape Hatteras National Seashore (site 77), Cape Lookout National Seashore (site 78), Beaufort Inlet (site 79), Fort Macon (site 80), Newport River (site 81), Bogue Sound (site 82), Lower Cape Fear River (site 93), Fort Fisher (site 95), Masonboro Inlet (site 98), ocean fishing piers (site 100)

Special State Fishing Programs

The NCWRC's Fishing Tackle Loaner Program operates in the same way as a library. Anglers who register at participating parks receive a tackle loaner ID card, which allows them to check out rods and reels. Anglers under 18 years of age must have a parent or guardian complete the registration form. After returning loaner rods and reels to the park office, first-time participants under 16 years of age receive a free mini tackle box containing hooks, bobbers, sinkers, and a fish stringer. Several of the sites detailed in *Fishing North Carolina* participate in the Fishing Tackle Loaner Program, among them Lake Higgins (site 30), Lake Brandt (site 31), Oak Hollow Lake (site 41), High Point Lake (site 42), Randleman Regional Reservoir (site 43), Lake Mackintosh (site 46), and Graham-Mebane Lake (site 47).

The NCWRC's Community Fishing Program (CFP) sometimes operates in conjunction with the Fishing Tackle Loaner Program. More than 40 lakes, usually located in county and city parks, receive monthly stockings from April through September of channel catfish grown to catchable size in an NCWRC hatchery. Some sites have handicapped-accessible fishing piers and solar-powered fish feeders. The goal of these CFP sites is to allow people with limited time and budgets to have fishing opportunities nearby. Since the CFP sites are parks, other amenities also make them attractive fishing destinations for families with children. One site detailed in *Fishing North Carolina* participates in the CFP: the Pee Dee River (site 58).

The NCWRC's North Carolina Angler Recognition Program (NCARP) gives anglers an opportunity to catch and release or retain trophy fish and have their fishing skills recognized. Anglers catching fish that exceed a certain size can apply to the commission's Division of Inland Fisheries for NCARP recognition. The Division of Inland Fisheries sends these accomplished anglers NCARP certificates featuring color reproductions of the fish by wildlife artist and former commission fisheries biologist Duane Raver. NCARP also has a Master Angler award program, which awards a Master Angler certificate and patch to anglers who catch six trophy-sized fish of the same species or of six different species. NCARP application forms are available from bait-and-tackle shops, sporting goods stores, wildlife cooperator agents, and the NCWRC website.

The NCWRC's North Carolina State Record Fish Program keeps all-tackle records of common freshwater game fish caught in North Carolina waters. To qualify for state-record recognition, a fish must have been caught on hook and line in a sporting manner. The angler must provide the common name of the fish, its weight on certified scales, its length from nose to tip of tail, its girth, the date caught, the location of the catch, the name and address of a witness to the weighing, and the name and address of the angler. If there is no witness to the catch, an affidavit is required. Fish from state-boundary waters shared by North Carolina and an adjacent state must have been caught in the North Carolina portion. The fish must be weighed on scales certified by the North Carolina Department of Agriculture. The fish should be frozen or otherwise preserved until identified by a qualified expert from the Division of Inland Fisheries. All information must be in written form, and the angler must sign his name and provide a full side-view photo of the fish.

The North Carolina Division of Marine Fisheries (NCDMF) holds an annual saltwater tournament. Anglers catching saltwater fish of a certain size, determined by weight or length, can receive a citation recognizing the catch. Everyone is eligible except charter-boat captains, crewmen of for-hire boats, and anyone who offers fish for sale. Weigh masters and their employees are eligible for awards, provided a witness signs verification. Eligible waters include the Atlantic Ocean and all North Carolina sounds, estuaries, and surf. All fish must be caught on hook and line and landed or brought to gaff or net by the angler. No electric or hydraulic equipment is allowed. Fish must be weighed at an official weigh station. Each fish must be recorded on an official application form signed by the angler and an official weigh master. For a fish to qualify under release rules, the angler or mate must touch the fish or the leader. The released-fish application must be completed with the exception of length and weight. (The length must be recorded for false albacore, amberjack, Atlantic bonito, barracuda, cobia, black drum, jack crevalle, king mackerel, shark, striped bass, gray trout, speckled trout, and red drum.) A witness must sign the release citation application.

The NCDMF also maintains a State Record Saltwater Fish Program. Following the procedures for the Saltwater Tournament Program should be adequate to qualify the fish for a state record if it surpasses the weight of the previous state-record fish of that species. State-record fish are measured by weight only.

For more information on special state fishing programs, see the appendix listing for the NCWRC. For locations of weigh stations and for a list of state-record saltwater fish, see the appendix listing for the NCDMF.

Mountain Region

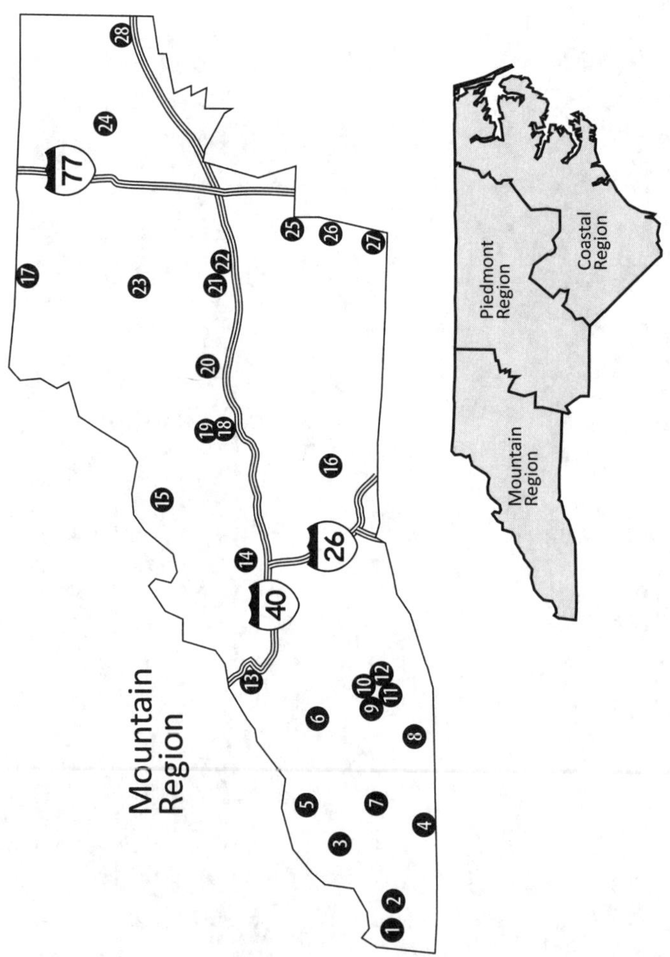

|| Previous page: Cedar Cliff Lake

1 Apalachia Lake

Key species: Bluegill sunfish

Overview: Apalachia Lake is a small, deep, cool-water mountain lake. Although the dam was built primarily to generate hydropower, the reservoir also provides a beautiful site for fishing, canoeing, hiking, and primitive camping. Located adjacent to Nantahala National Forest, the reservoir has little private shoreline development and no commercial recreation facilities.

Best way to fish: Boat

Best time to fish: April through October

Description: The construction of Apalachia Dam was completed in 1943. The dam is 150 feet high and stretches 1,308 feet across the Hiwassee River. The surface elevation of the reservoir is approximately 1,280 feet. The lake level can fluctuate down to about 1,272 feet. The lake is 9.8 miles long and has 31 miles of shoreline and approximately 1,070 acres of water surface. It collects rainfall from a 1,018-square-mile watershed.

The fishing: Because of the reservoir's isolation, relatively few fishermen use it, though a significant amount of rafting and fishing takes place downstream. While this is not a particularly fertile lake, those who enjoy solitude and gorgeous scenery can fish for bluegill sunfish here. A few bass also live in the lake.

N.C. A-G grid: 30, A-1

General information: NCWRC fishing regulations apply.

Nearest camping: Hanging Dog Campground is east of the lake in the Tusquitee Ranger District of Nantahala National Forest. The campground has flush toilets and running water but no hot showers. See the appendix for information on national forest campgrounds.

Directions: To reach the NCWRC's Apalachia Boating Access Area from U.S. 64/U.S. 74 west of Murphy, travel west on N.C. 294 for 8.4 miles, turn right on S.R. 1314 (TVA Hiwassee Dam Access Road), drive 4.7 miles, and turn left on Powerhouse Road. Travel 0.6 mile and turn left into the access area.

2 Hiwassee Lake

Key species: Smallmouth bass, spotted bass, largemouth bass, black crappie, walleye, panfish, channel catfish, flathead catfish

Overview: Hiwassee Lake was created by and is managed by the TVA. Like other lakes in the TVA system, Hiwassee's primary purpose is to provide hydroelectric power. It is also used for flood control. The shoreline is almost entirely surrounded by Nantahala National Forest. The lake was created by damming the Hiwassee, Nottely, and Valley rivers. It is upstream of Apalachia Lake.

Best way to fish: Boat

Best time to fish: April through November

Description: Hiwassee Lake is 22 miles long and has 6,090 acres of surface area and 163 miles of shoreline. Its depth exceeds 200 feet in places. Built in 1935, the dam is 1,376 feet long and 307 feet high. The elevation of the water surface is approximately 1,400 feet. It can decline by as much as 60 feet in the winter months.

The fishing: The lake's banks are steep, and its water is deep. These two factors can make finding fish difficult. The quality of the fishing depends on the forage base of blueback herring. Anglers must find the baitfish to locate the predatory fish. A 10-pound smallmouth bass caught here in 1951 is the state record. A state-record striper also caught here is an anomaly, since it likely made its way into the lake from upstream waters. Stripers are not stocked in Hiwassee.

The best place to fish is the upstream end, where the Hiwassee River enters the lake. In mountain lakes, the upstream end is typically the more fertile. The fertile areas attract the herring that make up the forage base for game-fish species, which include channel catfish, flathead catfish, bass, and crappie.

While other game fish are present, the biggest draw at Hiwassee is its excellent walleye fishing. Vertical jigging is the best tactic for walleye. Anglers use electronic depthfinders to identify the areas where walleye feed on baitfish. Good areas are located along the steep banks and the points. Because of the good forage base, anglers catch walleye weighing seven to eight pounds. It will not be surprising if the lake produces a state record.

Hiwassee also offers good fishing for smallmouth, spotted, and largemouth bass. The smallmouth bass are concentrated toward the dam, the spotted bass in the middle, and the largemouth bass in the upper end. Crappie anglers have their best luck in the upper end, where the water has its highest fertility.

An occasional large flathead catfish is caught from the lake. Most catfish anglers fish on the bottom using commercial baits, worms, or liver. But big flatheads are caught with live minnows or panfish.

N.C. A-G grid: 30, A-2

General information: NCWRC fishing regulations apply.

Nearest camping: Hanging Dog Campground is east of the lake in the Tusquitee Ranger District of Nantahala National Forest. The campground has flush toilets and running water but no hot showers. See the appendix for information about national forest campgrounds.

Directions: From the intersection of Peachtree, Valley River, Hiwassee, and Tennessee streets in Murphy, travel Tennessee Street, which becomes Joe Brown Highway outside the city limits. After 4.3 miles, turn left on Hanging Dog Road (S.R. 1447) and travel 1.8 miles to the access area, located at the end of the road.

3 Lake Santeetlah

Key species: Largemouth bass, smallmouth bass, panfish, walleye, yellow perch

Overview: A dam built across the Cheoah River created Lake Santeetlah in 1928. The lake is located in Graham County. It serves as a major water-control reservoir for four lakes owned and operated by the Tapoco Division of Alcoa Power Generating, Inc. It is also used to generate hydropower. The TVA has control over all the

Carol Marsh used a crankbait to catch this largemouth bass from Lake Santeetlah.

lake releases and water levels throughout the Tennessee Valley river system, including Lake Santeetlah.

Best ways to fish: Powerboat, kayak, canoe. Some bank and pier fishing is available at the USFS recreation areas.

Best times to fish: The cold months are best for walleye fishing. The bass fishing is best in spring, summer, and fall. Trout may be caught any time of year.

Description: The elevation of the lake surface is approximately 1,812 feet but fluctuates substantially. Lake Santeetlah has 79 miles of shoreline, of which 23 percent has the potential for commercial and residential development. Nantahala National Forest adjoins the remaining shoreline. The lake has 2,881 acres of surface area. It has exceptionally clear water but is fertile enough to offer good fishing.

The fishing: Smallmouth bass orient to the steep points and along the river channel drop-offs. In cool weather, spinners, crankbaits, and topwater lures work well. Live baits such as shiners work well any time of year and are the top baits for crappie fishing in the backs of the coves in spring. In summer, the best bet is a tube jig fished in 20 to 45 feet of water on a very light line.

Threadfin and gizzard shad form a forage base in the lake, so anything that looks like a small baitfish is a good choice. The smallmouth bass may be suspended in water as deep as 130 feet in the middle of winter and during the hottest days of summer, when dissolved oxygen levels are low. At those times, jigging with ice-fishing jigs or metal spoons can work well. Downriggers and planers can be put to good use for these deepwater fishing opportunities and for catching trout as well.

In spring and fall, smallmouth and largemouth bass may be found schooling on top, where they feed on shad. Topwater lures such as poppers and buzzbaits will catch schooling bass, especially early and late in the day. Another good bet for jump-fishing schooling bass is a casting spoon; silver is the best color. Soft plastics worked along steep points and deep ledges will catch lots of bass. Crankbaits and spinnerbaits also work well when the fish are in shallower water.

Besides minnows, other natural baits such as crickets and worms work well

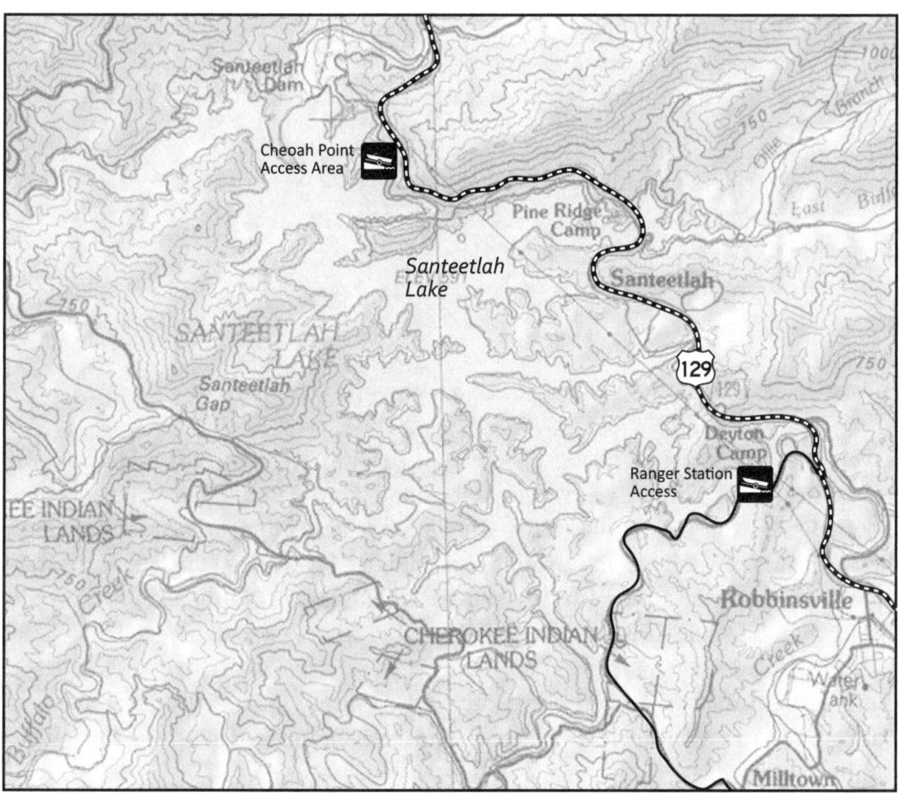

for catching panfish, bass, walleye, and yellow perch. Using fishing worms and stinkbaits on the bottom at night is a good way to catch catfish.

N.C. A-G grid: 50, A-3

General information: NCWRC fishing regulations apply. A North Carolina Department of Health and Human Services limited consumption advisory is in effect for walleye, due to elevated mercury levels. See the appendix for contact information for the NCDHHS.

Nearest camping: Private marinas with rental boats are available, as are bed-and-breakfast lodgings. More than 50 primitive campsites are located around the lake on USFS property. The sites are available without fees or permits. Nearby USFS campgrounds include Cheoah Point, Horse Cove, and Rattler Ford. Cheoah Point Recreation Area, located on the lakeshore, has a beach, fishing and swimming areas, picnic facilities, and restrooms. Horse Cove, located on Big Santeetlah Creek, has toilets but no showers. Rattler Ford is a group campground with showers and toilets.

Directions: To reach Cheoah Point Recreation Area from Robbinsville, travel north on U.S. 129 for 5 miles to the junction with S.R. 1145. Turn left and drive 1.5 miles to the campground and boat ramp.

4 Chatuge Lake

Key species: Largemouth bass, spotted bass, hybrid bass, crappie

Overview: Construction of the TVA's Chatuge Dam began in 1941 and was completed in 1942. Chatuge Lake was used for flood control until 1954, when a hydropower generation facility was built. The lake's waters are nearly equally divided between Georgia and North Carolina. Located in Clay County, the lake surrounds some peninsulas and islands that are part of Nantahala National Forest on the North Carolina side. It was named for a nearby Cherokee settlement.

Best ways to fish: Chatuge Lake can be fished from a boat or from the bank at Jackrabbit Mountain Recreation Area. Downstream in the Hiwassee River, wade fishing is popular.

Best time to fish: May through October

Description: The dam is 144 feet high and extends 2,850 feet across the Hiwassee River. The lake has 6,840 acres of surface area and 80 miles of shoreline. It is 13 miles long. The water level is approximately 1,926 above sea level. It can fluctuate nine feet in an average year.

The fishing: Blueback herring support a good fishery for bass. Since the water is very clear, fishing deep areas and using light lines is the preferred method. The main species is spotted bass, but a few largemouth bass are also present, as well as some crappie and panfish. The fishing can be excellent but is subject to fluctuations. Spotted bass appear to have supplanted other bass species in the lake. Chatuge offers excellent fishing for spotted bass and the potential for catching largemouth bass weighing more than six pounds. For bass, topwater lures, spinnerbaits, crankbaits, and soft plastics work well.

The crappie fishing can be fair to good. A lot of work is required to find the fish. Anglers have good luck fishing for crappie with minnows and jigs along any shoreline cover. Trolling with jigs in the early spring helps locate schools of fish. The crappie fishing is best in the spring. Trolling or using live baits is the best way to catch hybrid bass, which have been stocked experimentally by Georgia biologists to see how they fare.

N.C. A-G grid: 50, C-3

General information: NCWRC fishing rules and regulations apply. A reciprocal license agreement is in effect with Georgia. Anyone possessing a North Carolina fishing license may fish the Georgia side of Chatuge Lake, including any tributaries accessible from the lake by boat.

Nearest camping: Jackrabbit Mountain Campground, located on Chatuge Lake, is in the Tusquitee Ranger District.

Directions: To reach Jackrabbit Mountain Recreation Area from Hayesville, travel east on U.S. 64 for 4.7 miles, turn right on N.C. 175, drive 2.5 miles, turn right on Jackrabbit Campground Road (S.R. 1155), and travel 1.4 miles to the campground. Boating access areas are located at the campground and at the end of the road.

To reach Ledford's Chapel Boating Access Area, travel east on U.S. 64 for 3.1 miles from Hayesville, turn right on Ledford Chapel Road (S.R. 1151), and drive 0.9 mile to the end of the road.

5 Fontana Lake

Key species: Smallmouth bass, largemouth bass, spotted bass, flathead catfish, channel catfish, walleye, crappie

Overview: Fontana Lake, owned by the Tennessee Valley Authority (TVA), is located in the Great Smoky Mountains west of Bryson City. It has spectacular mountain scenery with limited shoreline development because the United States Forest Service (USFS) and the National Park Service own more than 90 percent of the land surrounding the lake. Nantahala National Forest and Great Smoky Mountains National Park offer a variety of recreational opportunities including hiking, biking, horseback riding, hunting, and wildlife viewing. The lake offers spectacular views when the surrounding forest shows fall colors.

Best ways to fish: Boat, shoreline

Best time to fish: February through October, though something is biting all year. Walleye fishing is the top draw.

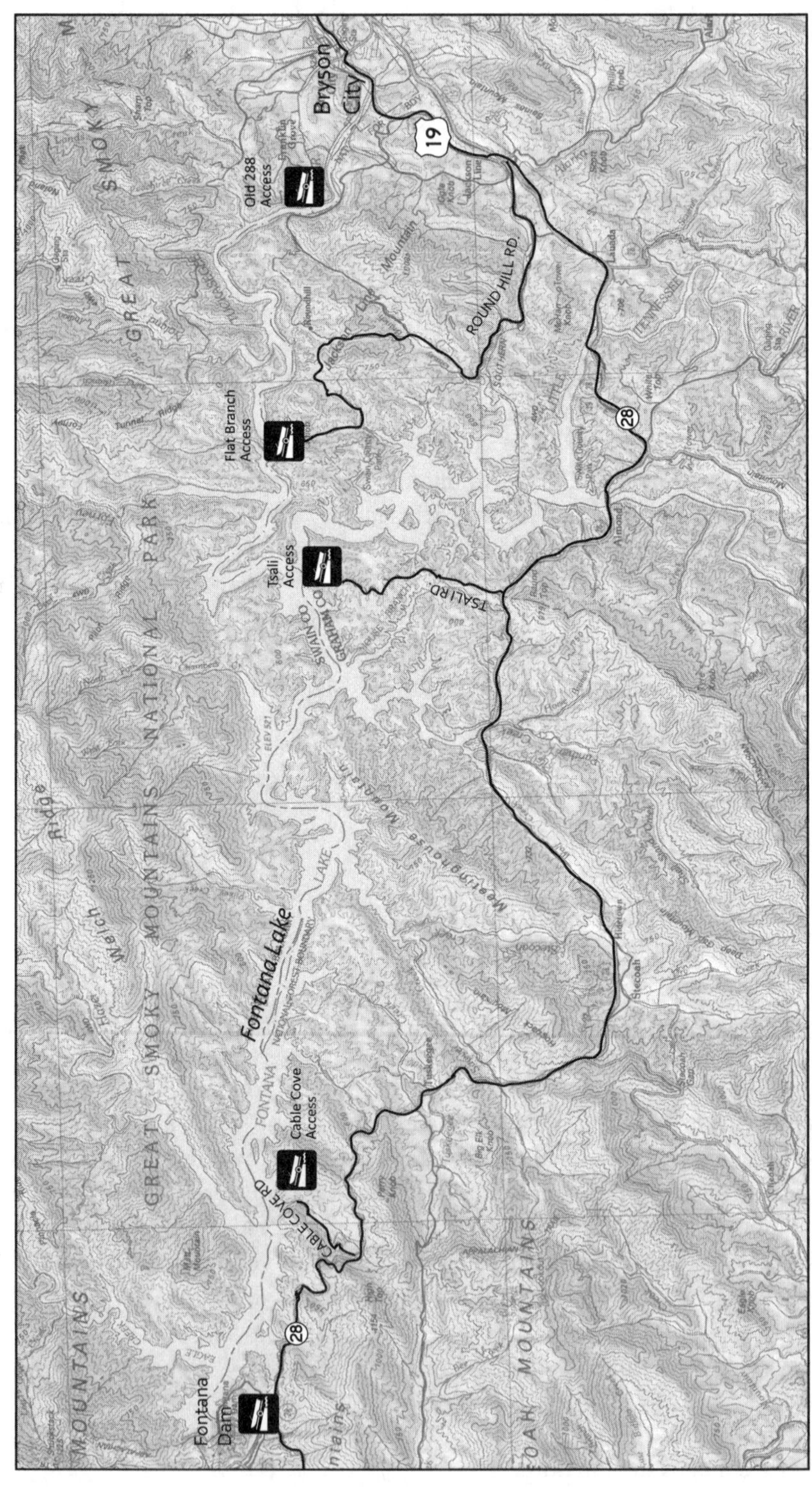
Fontana Dam
Cable Cove Access
CABLE COVE RD
Fontana Lake
FONTANA
LAKE
Tsali Access
TSALI RD.
Flat Branch Access
Old 288 Access
ROUND HILL RD.
Bryson City
19
28
28
GREAT SMOKY MOUNTAINS NATIONAL PARK
GREAT SMOKY MOUNTAINS
MOUNTAINS
Welch Ridge
Meetinghouse Mountain
SWAIN CO
GRAHAM CO
Stecoah
Almond
Turkey Ridge

Description: Fontana Lake covers 11,700 acres. It is 29 miles long and has over 240 miles of shoreline. In places, its depth exceeds 400 feet. The Tennessee and Tuckasegee rivers feed the lake, creating unusually fertile conditions that result in excellent fishing. Fontana Lake has been called one of the best-kept secrets in the South because of its excellent cold-water fishing.

The fishing: The bottom is relatively free of woody cover, due to its age and timber-clearing operations before the lake was filled. Sometimes, the lake is impacted by severe declines in water level. These fluctuations reveal areas of shoreline cover to anglers cruising the lake during low-water conditions. Most ramps are accessible even during low-water periods. The lake is very clear.

Smallmouth bass orient tightly to the natural shoreline cover, which includes rock outcrops, steep drop-offs, rocky points, and woody cover. Anglers using spinnerbaits, crankbaits, tube jigs, and soft plastic lures have excellent success casting to visible structure. In February, smallmouth bass enter the shallow ends of coves and the upper portions of the water column along the steeper and deeper places. In warm weather, smallmouth bass head for deeper water and are sometimes caught by walleye fishermen trolling the deep channels.

Tube jigs are great lures for catching smallmouth bass all year because the fish have a hearty appetite for crayfish. For summer fishing, using tube jigs takes patience because the fish may be in water depths of 35 feet or greater. When they are in the shallows early in the year, topwater lures, spinnerbaits, crankbaits, and soft plastics are all great choices.

The Little Tennessee and Tuckasegee river arms are the best places for catching largemouth bass. Largemouth bite best in spring and fall, April and September being the prime months. The lake's clear, deep water dictates fishing with finesse using small soft plastic lures and jigs. The best topwater action occurs early and late in the day. Crankbaits are the best choice when the sun is high.

Fontana has one of the best walleye densities of any mountain lake. But the fish don't get as big as at Hiwassee Lake. They bite best during cold weather, but good walleye fishermen are able to catch them all year. The fish form large schools as they attack schools of baitfish. Some of the best fishing occurs along the red banks where the wave action muddies the water. The muddy water can concentrate walleye as late as May. Walleye also form large schools in the creek channels at depths of 10 to 20 feet or more. Trolling deep-diving crankbaits and spoons and jigging with jigs dressed with bucktail or plastic trailers are standard walleye fishing tactics. Casting small jigs and crankbaits into the fast-flowing river headwaters is another great tactic for walleye. In the headwaters, walleye are caught in combination with other fish.

Anglers catch some rainbow trout while trolling for walleye. Other action occurs at the dam, where anglers catch some very large trout using live minnows for bait.

Crappie are present. The upper end of the lake is the best place to fish for them. But a lack of structure and water fluctuations can make them difficult to locate. The best bet is fishing in the spring, and the best place to find them is at fallen trees extending into the water. Other tactics for locating schools of crappie include trolling or drifting with live minnows and jigs.

N.C. A-G grid: 29, D-4

General information: Fontana Lake is classified as undesignated trout water. The North Carolina Department of Health and Human Services (NCDHHS) has issued a limited-consumption advisory for walleye due to elevated mercury levels.

Nearest camping: Camping facilities are available in Great Smoky Mountains National Park. Deep Creek Campground is the closest to Fontana Lake. The USFS maintains Tsali and Cable Cove recreation areas, which offer shoreline fishing, boating access, camping, hiking, and horseback trails. Many private campgrounds with boat ramps and marinas are also located around the lake.

Directions: To reach Tsali Recreation Area, travel U.S. 74 West from Bryson City. After U.S. 74 merges with N.C. 28, continue approximately 5 miles. Turn right on S.R. 1286. The ramp is at the end of the road.

To reach Cable Cove Recreation Area, travel west along N.C. 28 for 8.2 miles from the junction with N.C. 143. Turn right on S.R. 1287. The ramp is at the end of the road.

To reach the Swain (Old 288) ramp, travel 0.2 mile on S.R. 1323 from Bryson City and turn left on S.R. 1321 (Bryson Walk), which is designated Old 288 outside the city limits. Travel 1.6 miles and turn left, continuing on Old 288. Drive 0.8 mile to the ramp, located at the end of the road.

To reach Swain (Flat Branch) Boating Access Area, travel U.S. 19 South for 1.1 miles from Bryson City and turn right on Old U.S. 19 (S.R. 1320). Drive 0.1 mile and turn right on S.R. 1311 (Buckner Branch Road). After 3.1 miles, turn right on S.R. 1312 (Round Hill Road). Travel 2.8 miles and turn right on S.R. 1313 (Greasy Branch Road). Drive 3.1 miles to the access area, located at the end of the road.

6 Tuckasegee River

Key species: Mountain trout, smallmouth bass

Overview: The Tuckasegee River begins in Pisgah National Forest west of Brevard in Jackson County and flows 50 miles northwest past Cullowhee, Whittier, and Bryson City, where it enters Fontana Lake. A dam in the upper West Fork forms Thorpe Reservoir. Dams along the East Fork form Cedar Cliff, Bear Creek, Wolf Creek, and Tanasee reservoirs. The river's name likely comes from a Cherokee Indian village, Tsiksitsi, which once stood on the bank. The name means "crawling terrapin," after the sluggish movement of the waters. The slow waters are unusual for a mountain river, making the Tuckasegee ideal for fishing.

Best ways to fish: Wading, drift boat

Best time to fish: April through November

Description: The dam discharges and the high elevation of the upper river segments create some of the best trout fishing in the nation. Brook, brown, and rainbow trout are stocked in the river by the NCWRC.

The lower elevations of the river have warmer water, creating an excellent smallmouth bass fishery.

The fishing: Fly-fishing is popular for trout and smallmouth bass. Dry flies and nymphs work well for trout, while popping bugs are the best bet for catching smallmouth bass and rock bass. The best smallmouth fishing is downstream of Dillsboro.

For baitcasting and spinning rigs, inline spinnerbaits work well for trout and smallmouth bass where and when multiple-hook lures are legal. Anglers should become familiar with the designated trout waters along certain stretches of the Tuckasegee and its tributaries that have special regulations for artificial lures and live-bait prohibitions. Topwater lures, stickbaits, tube jigs, and small soft plastic worms also work well for smallmouth bass.

Natural baits can be used for catching trout from certain designated waters during the open seasons. Scented baits, salmon eggs, corn, and worms are popular.

N.C. A-G grid: 29, D-6

General information: Many sections of the river can be waded with ease, but anglers should be careful of the deep holes, the rolling cobbles, and the rocky bottom, which can be slippery. Good access is available all along the river from the adjoining public lands, but some of the riverbank is privately owned. The various sections of designated trout water are marked with signs. The Tuckasegee has several types of trout water, including delayed harvest, hatchery-supported, and undesignated trout water. In the upper reaches, many feeder streams are designated as wild trout water or catch-and-release trout water. The NCWRC special trout-fishing license applies for designated trout waters and seasons. Certain seasons and bag limits are applicable for all designated and undesignated trout waters, wherever they occur.

For information on stream designations, size limits, bag limits, and open seasons for mountain trout fishing, consult the *North Carolina Inland Fishing, Hunting, and Trapping* and the *North Carolina Trout Fishing Maps* booklets available from the NCWRC.

Nearest camping: Many private campgrounds are nearby, as is Deep Creek Campground in Great Smoky Mountains National Park.

Directions: Swain County maintains a boating access area at the community of Ela on U.S. 19.

7 Nantahala Lake/Nantahala River

Key species: Walleye, sunfish, trout, smallmouth bass

Overview: Nantahala Lake is in Macon County. This reservoir is regulated and maintained by Duke Energy for hydropower generation. Nantahala National Forest comprises 85 percent of the lake's shoreline. The lake and river are located in the Nantahala Ranger District. The Cherokees christened the river gorge Nantahala, meaning "land of the middle sun," because its sides are so steep that only the noonday sun penetrates to the bottom. Nantahala Power and Light Company (now Duke Energy) impounded the lake by damming the river in 1956. From Nantahala Lake, the river flows 8.5 miles north to Fontana Lake.

Best ways to fish: Powerboats and kayaks are popular craft for fishing the lake. Nantahala Gorge is a popular whitewater rafting area. As many as 250,000 people visit the gorge each year, making it one of the most popular National Forest Service recreation areas in the nation. Anglers have good luck bank fishing or wading in the river gorge.

Best times to fish: Fishing is good all year in the lake. Anglers will find the river productive during the trout seasons in spring, summer, and fall.

Description: Nantahala Lake has 1,606 acres of surface area. The lake is 3,012 feet above sea level.

The fishing: Nantahala Lake is nutrient poor, as are most lakes in the state's western mountains. But the lake is unique because it is the only place in North Carolina where kokanee salmon are found. Native to the western United States, the fish was stocked in Nantahala Lake in the mid-1960s by the NCWRC in an attempt to establish it as a forage fish for predator fish in the lake. This stock has since become a favorite target for anglers. Kokanee salmon can weigh as much as three to five pounds. Anglers catch them by casting spoons and spinners. The walleye fishing is best during the cold months. Anglers have good luck catching smallmouth bass and panfish in the warm months. The lake has deep, clear water, so deep jigging and working deep-diving crankbaits on the lake points are good ways to catch smallmouth bass and walleye. Another way to catch smallmouth bass in any water depth is with soft plastic lures such as worms and tube jigs. Trolling for walleye in the mouths of the coves also works well. But anglers won't catch as many walleye in Nantahala as in some other lakes. The lake's main attractions for anglers are its relatively low number of boaters, its breathtaking scenery, and its kokanee salmon. Rock bass have been stocked in the river system.

N.C. A-G grid: 51, B-4

General information: The Nantahala Gorge, located below Nantahala Lake, has both hatchery-supported and delayed-harvest trout waters and excellent fishing. Feeder streams to the lake and river located in Nantahala National Forest are designated as wild trout water. A mountain trout–fishing license is required for catching trout from all of these designated waters.

Nearest camping: Primitive camping is allowed on National Forest Service lands except where signs prohibit it. The USFS's Appletree Group Campground is located near the lake and the river. Many private lodgings and campgrounds are also available in the river gorge. In addition, the USFS campgrounds at Fontana Lake can be used for fishing trips to Nantahala Lake.

Directions: To reach the NCWRC's Choga Road Boating Access Area, follow S.R. 1505 (Junaluska Road) for 6.3 miles from the junction with U.S. 19 Business at Andrews. Turn right on S.R. 1657 (Big Choga Road), travel 3.3 miles, and turn left to the access area.

To reach the NCWRC's Rocky Branch Boating Access Area from U.S. 19

in the Nantahala Gorge, follow S.R. 1310 (Wayah Road) for 11.9 miles and turn right onto the access area road.

The USFS's Appletree Group Campground is the nearest public campground to Nantahala Lake and the river.

8 Lake Glenville (Thorpe Reservoir)

Key species: Smallmouth bass, largemouth bass, walleye, trout

Overview: Located in a beautiful mountain forest, Lake Glenville, formerly Thorpe Reservoir, was renamed in 2001 as part of the relicensing process for the hydroelectric power plant. On some maps, it is still called Thorpe Reservoir. The name was changed to establish a better identity for the community of Glenville on the lake's eastern shoreline. At an elevation of 3,942 feet, this is the highest lake east of the Mississippi River. Duke Energy owns Lake Glenville.

Best way to fish: Boat

Best time to fish: March through September

Description: Lake Glenville has 1,462 acres of surface area and approximately 26 miles of shoreline. Its deepest point is 165 feet. It has four islands, five waterfalls, and a moderate amount of shoreline development. The lake is located on the West Fork of the Tuckasegee River.

The fishing: Walleye fishermen have good luck in the highly oxygenated water below the cascading waterfalls. The best walleye fishing occurs while the fish are schooling from mid- to late March through sometime in April. The best time to catch walleye is at dusk, when shining a flashlight into the water may reveal their eye reflections in the clear water.

At the waterfalls and the creek mouths near them, walleye strike medium-depth diving stickbaits and three-inch crawdad colored jigs. Jigs are the best lures for casting beneath overhanging limbs. During the summer when the fish are deeper, walleye anglers make some nice catches by trolling deep-diving lures across the main lake points.

Smallmouth bass are suckers for live minnows on weightless lines at all types of structure. Deep-diving lures cast or trolled across the numerous points are also good bets. Anglers should stay 20 to 25 feet away from the banks while trolling, allowing their lures to bounce over the submerged points in passing. Smallmouth

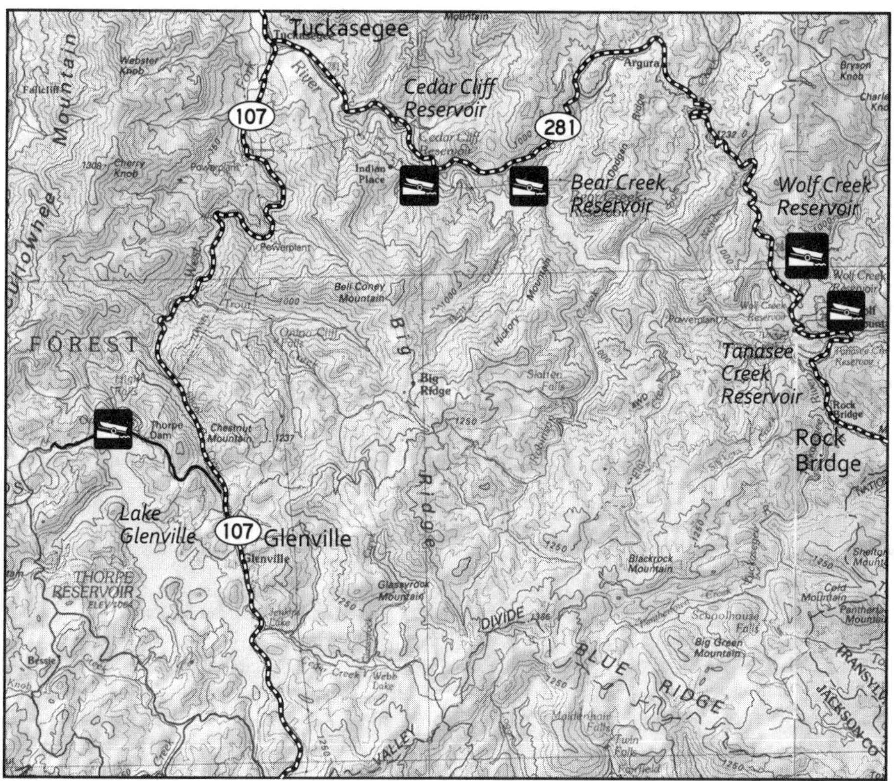

bass form surface schools beginning in May, then continue schooling throughout the summer. When they are feeding on baitfish at the surface, a small walk-the-dog lure is an excellent choice for catching them. But the big fish usually feed below the surface. To catch them, anglers should cast deep-diving lures.

Largemouth bass strike soft plastic lures cast to downed trees, boat docks, and stumps. Sometimes, the topwater action is also good; twitch baits and walk-the-dog lures are the best bets. The best time of year to catch largemouth bass is in the spring before tourists churn up the lake around Memorial Day. The best largemouth bass fishing is early and late in the day.

The banks are steep and the water deep, so bass anglers should be patient while working downed trees with soft plastic lures or jigs. The best tactic is to work the top of the tree away from the bank, then move slowly to the trunk, then the root system, so as to avoid spooking the fish in the clear water.

Glenville has lots of boat traffic. The wakes can create heavy mud lines. The best bet at these times is casting a spinnerbait into the mud line and reeling it into the clear water, where bass working the clear edge of the mud line will strike.

Glenville occasionally produces some exceptionally large brown trout and rainbow trout. In winter, when trout are in shallow water, they strike

Lake Glenville is one of the most beautiful mountain lakes yet one of the least known among fishermen. Mike Marsh casts for bass along a rock outcrop in Lake Glenville.

minnow-imitating stickbaits. In summer, when the trout head deep, anglers troll for them using lead core lines rigged with red-and-white spoons.

N.C. A-G grid: 52, D-1

General information: Canoe and kayak rentals and camping are available from private concerns at Lake Glenville. Since the lake is classified as undesignated trout water, the NCWRC special trout-fishing license is not required, but other regulations for undesignated trout water apply.

Nearest camping: Jackson County's Ralph J. Andrews Campground has full facilities for RVs and primitive camping. It also offers opportunities for picnicking and hiking, as well as a boat ramp. See the appendix for contact information.

Directions: To reach the NCWRC's Power House Boating Access Area, travel south on N.C. 107 for 8.2 miles from the junction with N.C. 281 South at Tuckasegee. Turn right on S.R. 1157 (Pine Circle Road) and drive 1.3 miles to the access area road, on the left.

9 Cedar Cliff Reservoir

Key species: Largemouth bass, trout, panfish

Overview: Cedar Cliff Reservoir is a hydroelectric power generation lake on the East Fork of the Tuckasegee River. Owned by Duke Energy, it is the farthest downstream of several small lakes on the East Fork.

Best ways to fish: Boat, canoe, kayak

Best time to fish: April through October

Description: Cedar Cliff Reservoir is a 121-acre lake with steep banks. It is located at an elevation of 2,330 feet and has approximately 4.5 miles of shoreline. The water typically is clear and cold.

The fishing: Bass anglers using jigs, minnows, and deep-diving plugs have some success. Small, two- to four-inch soft plastic worms are the ticket for largemouth bass. Some smallmouth bass may also be in the lake. Anglers should fish worms on light lines rigged with a split shot on the line ahead of the lure or on a small jig head. Soft plastics should be fished with a slow, steady retrieve along the bottom. Although Cedar Cliff Reservoir is not stocked with trout, they do make it downstream from the lakes above, where trout are stocked by the NCWRC.

Tube jigs are a good choice for bass in the cold months. Topwater lures will catch bass in the summer. For best success, anglers should fish the grass beds in spring when the bass are spawning. Jigs, topwater lures, and spinnerbaits work well when the fish are in the grass beds.

For trout and panfish, spinners and natural baits are the best choices.

N.C. A-G grid: 52, D-2

General information: NCWRC fishing regulations apply. The lake has no facilities except for Cedar Cliff Access Area. The special trout-fishing license is not necessary because Cedar Cliff Reservoir is not stocked with trout. Undesignated trout water regulations apply.

Nearest camping: Singing Waters Camping Resort in Tuckasegee is a nearby private full-service facility. See the appendix for contact information.

Directions: Travel south on N.C. 107 for 0.1 mile from the junction with N.C. 281 South, turn left on S.R.1135 (Shook Cove Road), and drive 3.3 miles. The access area is on the left.

10 Bear Creek Reservoir

Key species: Largemouth bass, walleye, trout

Overview: As a small, secluded mountain lake, Bear Creek Reservoir is easy to overlook. Nevertheless, it is the largest lake on the East Fork of the Tuckasegee River. Its size doesn't mean it can't offer good fishing. Bear Creek Reservoir is a hydroelectric power generation lake owned by Duke Energy. Built by damming the East Fork in the 1950s, it is located upstream of Cedar Cliff Reservoir and downstream of Wolf Creek Reservoir and Tanasee Creek Reservoir.

Best way to fish: Boat

Best time to fish: April through October

Description: Bear Creek Reservoir covers 476 surface acres and has 13.5 miles of shoreline. It has some shoreline development, which offers fish extra cover. The lake is 160 feet deep at the dam and is as shallow as 50 to 60 feet at the upstream end.

The fishing: For catching Bear Creek Reservoir's walleye, anglers use jigs, minnows, and deep-diving plugs. Live earthworms rigged on jig heads may also entice walleye.

For largemouth bass, soft plastic worms are the winning ticket under most conditions. Anglers should fish soft plastics on very light lines, casting them among the rocks and woody cover in the shallow water at the backs of coves, along the shoreline, and in the high, submerged humps that indicate tree stumps left from timber-harvesting operations before the lake was filled. The large amount of woody cover makes Bear Creek one of the best small mountain lakes for bass fishing. A large island is a key feature of the lake. It creates excellent bass habitat along its slopes and steep drop-offs.

Tube jigs are a good choice for bass in the winter and early spring. Topwater lures will catch both bass species at dawn and dusk in spring and fall. The best bets for topwater action, especially in April and May when the fish are spawning, are the grass beds and woody cover in the shallows at the upper ends of the creeks. Deep-diving crankbaits are good bets in the warm months, especially during the middle of the day. Clear water conditions can create difficult fishing in hot weather when the sun is high. A spinnerbait is the go-to lure for bass at all times of year because it can be fished in any type of cover and at any depth.

Bear Creek Reservoir hosts some great brown and rainbow trout fishing. For catching trout, most anglers use inline spinners and natural baits. Trout numbers are highest near the mouths of the feeder streams. In spring, anglers watch for dimples at the water surface created by feeding trout. Casting spoons to the dimples can result in hookups with exceptionally large trout.

N.C. A-G grid: 52, D-2

General information: NCWRC fishing regulations apply. Bear Creek, designated as hatchery-supported trout water, is stocked regularly by the NCWRC. Anglers must possess the special trout-fishing license and adhere to the special rules and seasons for hatchery-supported trout water.

Nearest camping: Singing Waters Camping Resort in Tuckasegee is a nearby private full-service campground. See the appendix for contact information.

Directions: Travel south on N.C. 281 (Canada Road) for 4.1 miles from the junction with N.C. 107 South at Tuckasegee and turn right onto the access area road. Drive 0.6 mile to the access area, located at the end of the road.

11 Wolf Creek Reservoir

Key species: Largemouth bass, trout, panfish

Overview: Located in Jackson County, Wolf Creek Reservoir is a small, secluded mountain lake and is therefore easy to overlook. But its size doesn't mean it can't offer good fishing. Wolf Creek Reservoir is a hydroelectric power generating lake owned by Duke Energy. Built by damming the East Fork of the Tuckasegee River in the 1950s, it is located upstream of Bear Creek Reservoir and downstream of Tanasee Creek Reservoir.

Best way to fish: Boat

Best time to fish: February through October

Description: Wolf Creek Reservoir is 176 acres in area and has 6.9 miles of undeveloped shoreline. Its surface elevation is 3,080 feet. The dam is 810 feet long and 175 feet high.

The fishing: Wolf Creek Reservoir, like the other upper Tuckasegee River lakes, is not heavily fished because of its remoteness. But people who know about this mountain treasure enjoy vacations at the lake and take advantage of the fishing. Many homes with boat docks are along the shoreline.

While the stocked trout attract the most attention from fishermen, the lake also offers excellent bass fishing. Trolling small inline spinners and jigs in dark colors is a great way to catch bass and trout. Trout fishing is best around the sandy sections of the lake and near the mouths of feeder streams.

Bass anglers catch fish by casting lures to the bank edges, rocky ledges, and visible woody structure. In January and February, casting soft plastics or topwater lures in the backs of coves is a great way to catch bass. In summer, jigging deeper water with tube jigs in crawdad colors brings the most success. The best bass-fishing months are April and May.

The lake is very clear, which can create problems for bass fishermen. The hydrilla beds on the lake bottom can foul lures, but they also attract bass and panfish. Anglers must take care to avoid spooking largemouth bass by casting from long distances away from any structure. The best largemouth bass fishing occurs during times of low light penetration at dawn and dusk and on overcast days. Because of the clear water, lightweight monofilament lines and small lures are best for bass fishing.

Lure color is important in clear mountain lakes. Light shades of green and brown with black flecks seem to work best for Wolf Creek Reservoir largemouth bass.

The trout fishing is best around the sandy sections of the lake and near the mouths of the feeder streams.

Some large bluegill sunfish are caught at Wolf Creek Reservoir. The best lures for them are small beetle grub spinners. Best live baits are worms and crickets.

N.C. A-G grid: 52, D-2

General information: Wolf Creek Reservoir is designated as hatchery-supported trout water, so a special trout license is required. All other NCWRC licenses and regulations apply.

Nearest camping: Singing Waters Camping Resort in Tuckasegee is a nearby private full-service campground. See the appendix for contact information.

Directions: To reach the NCWRC's Wolf Creek Boating Access Area, travel south on N.C. 281 for 12.7 miles from Tuckasegee and turn left on S.R. 1758 (Wolf Pen Road).

12 Tanasee Creek Reservoir

Key species: Largemouth bass, trout

Overview: Tanasee Creek Reservoir is a small, secluded mountain lake and is therefore easy to overlook. It is the smallest lake in the East Fork of the Tuckasegee River, but its size doesn't mean it can't offer good fishing. Tanasee Creek Reservoir is a hydroelectric power generating lake owned by Duke Energy. Built by damming the East Fork in the 1950s, it is located upstream of Wolf Creek Reservoir.

Best ways to fish: Boat, bank

Best time to fish: April through October

Description: Tanasee Creek Reservoir has 40 acres of surface area and little shoreline development. The Tanasee Creek Dam is 385 feet long and 140 feet high.

The fishing: The fishing is similar to that at the Wolf Creek and Bear Creek reservoirs. Small soft plastic worms, tube jigs, and spinners on light lines are best for bass. Spinners are the ticket for trout.

N.C. A-G grid: 52, D-2

General information: NCWRC fishing regulations apply. Tanasee Creek Reservoir is designated as hatchery-supported trout water and is stocked regularly by the NCWRC. Anglers must possess the special trout-fishing license and adhere to special rules and seasons for hatchery-supported trout water. Large outboard motors are not allowed.

Nearest camping: Singing Waters Camping Resort in Tuckasegee is a nearby private full-service campground. See the appendix for contact information.

Directions: To get to the Tanasee Creek Reservoir Boating Access Area, travel

N.C. 281 South from Tuckasegee for 14.5 miles. Access is on the right, before crossing the Tanasee Creek Bridge.

13 Pigeon River / Waterville Lake

Key species: Smallmouth bass, mountain trout

Overview: The Pigeon River suffered for many years from pollution created by a paper mill. But it has become much cleaner in recent years, to the point that it is now an excellent fishing location. Located in Haywood County, the river flows into Tennessee not far downstream of Waterville Lake. The lake was created by the construction of Walters Dam across the Pigeon River in 1930. The lake and dam are used for hydropower generation.

Best ways to fish: Wading, bank, float tube, kayak, canoe, small johnboat

Best time to fish: April through November

Description: The two dozen miles of the Pigeon River from the confluence of the East Fork and the West Fork to Waterville Lake run through mostly private lands, as do the lower reaches of both forks. However, state roads paralleling the river and several bridge crossings provide access from public rights of way. Parking areas are easy to identify from long use.

N.C. 215 and Lake Logan Road provide the best access to the West Fork, while U.S. 276 and Old Cruise Road provide the best access to the East Fork. The roads parallel the streams along the lower stretches, making several crossings.

Upstream of Canton, N.C. 215, N.C. 110, and the crossroads between them provide access to the Pigeon River. At Canton, several roads offer river access. Downstream of Canton, access is available in Clyde and off N.C. 209 and Panther Creek Road. Several miles downstream of Hepco, the river forms Waterville Lake. The lake has no formal access and is therefore not heavily fished. But bank fishing is possible in some areas. Parking is available at the powerhouse.

The fishing: Smallmouth bass are abundant in the Pigeon River. Some spotted bass and panfish are also present. Rainbow, brook, and brown trout are abundant in several stretches. Successful anglers fish the main river channel and the forks by casting small crankbaits, topwater lures, inline spinners, spinnerbaits, jigs, flies, and popping bugs. Live baits are also popular where and when they are legal.

At some locations, it is possible to fish the river by launching a small johnboat.

But most anglers cast from the bank or wade. Smallmouth anglers can catch dozens of fish in one day. For fishing the bypass channel downstream of the Waterville Lake powerhouse, anglers must use extreme caution because water releases during power generation operations fill the channel. Waterville Lake offers fishing for smallmouth bass.

N.C. A-G grid: 30, D-2

General information: Much of the West Fork along N.C. 215 is hatchery-supported trout water. Feeder streams in that section are designated as wild trout water. Check out the NCWRC website for exact locations of designated trout waters and public access points. In addition to a general fishing license, a special mountain trout license is required for trout fishing in designated waters.

Nearest camping: Great Smoky Mountains National Park's Big Creek Campground and Cataloochee Campground are nearby. The park's Cosby Campground has the most extensive facilities. It is located in Tennessee.

Directions: The Pigeon River covers a good deal of territory in Haywood County. Most of its fishing areas are easily accessible from roads exiting I-40 between Canton and the North Carolina–Tennessee line. The most direct way to reach Cataloochee Campground is to turn off I-40 at Exit 20. Travel 0.2 mile on U.S. 276, turn right on Cove Creek Road, and follow the signs 11 miles into Cataloochee Valley.

14 French Broad River

Key species: Smallmouth bass, brown trout, brook trout, rainbow trout, muskellunge, catfish

Overview: The French Broad River is the third-oldest river in the world and the largest watercourse in western North Carolina. The river offers a wide variety of fishing opportunities. It flowed through French territory during colonial times and was named the French Broad to differentiate it from the Broad River.

The water quality was degraded during the first part of the industrial age. Forest clearing degraded it as well. It has since been restored into a premier recreational waterway. The river is generally deep and broad but has rapids and shallows as well. Many fishing guides and outfitters stake their reputations on producing fish from the river for their clients.

Best ways to fish: The French Broad may be accessed by small craft like kayaks and rafts, as well as by wading and using float tubes. Fly rods and spinning rigs are the most popular gear for fishing the river.

Best times to fish: Trout fishing is available all year, depending on the trout water designation. The winter months offer good trout fishing, while the warm months produce excellent smallmouth bass and muskie fishing.

Description: The French Broad River runs approximately 70 miles in western North Carolina from its beginning at a 50-foot waterfall west of Rosman in Transylvania County to the Tennessee border. But its total length including areas outside North Carolina is approximately 200 miles. From its headwaters, the French Broad flows north through Brevard, Asheville, and Hot Springs and ultimately into Tennessee, where it forms the Tennessee River. The French Broad's watershed includes 4,136 miles of other rivers and streams in eight North Carolina counties.

The fishing: The best trout fishing occurs upstream of Brevard. The best fishing for smallmouth bass is between Asheville and the state line. Muskie anglers have the best luck from Brevard to the state line. The best fishing for catfish occurs downstream of Hot Springs.

The main channel of the river is too warm and turbid for sustaining many trout. Most of the major tributaries begin in the higher elevations within Pisgah National Forest. Dozens of these upper tributaries hold wild trout including rainbow, brown, and brook trout.

Several miles of the upper river are designated as hatchery-supported trout waters. Wild trout waters occur at Looking Glass Creek and Avery Creek along U.S. 276 and flow into the Davidson River, a tributary of the French Broad. These creeks offer excellent wild trout fishing. The best wild trout stream may be the South Mills River. Most sections of these three watercourses have difficult access, which appeals to many wild trout anglers because it decreases fishing pressure. The South Mills River is accessible off N.C. 280 via South Mills River Trail, which runs beside the river for approximately 12 miles. It has excellent brown and rainbow trout fishing. Anglers fishing with spinning lures and weighted flies have excellent luck.

Delayed-harvest trout waters include the North Mills River, Big Laurel Creek, Shelton Laurel Creek, and the East Fork of the French Broad. Big Laurel and Shelton Laurel creeks may be accessed along N.C. 208, N.C. 212, and U.S. 25/U.S. 70.

Good access to the North Mills River is available inside the national forest from North Mills River Road and F.R. 1206. Spinners, small jigs, and flies work well in the delayed-harvest trout water sections.

Catch-and-release trout waters include 10 miles of the Davidson River and some of its tributaries, as well as the more-difficult-to-access Carter Creek. The

Davidson River is legendary among fly fishermen on the special catch-and-release section because trout numbers and sizes are exceptional. The best access to the Davidson River is along U.S. 276 and F.R. 475.

Carter Creek is smaller than the Davidson River. It is accessible from Craggy Gardens Road, which is off the Blue Ridge Parkway. Ultralight spinners and jigs are the best bets. The smallest-sized fly rods may be used for flipping nymphs and dry flies into tight places.

Sections designated wild trout/natural bait waters include the North Fork of the French Broad and Spillcorn Creek, a tributary of Big Laurel Creek. Access to the North Fork is moderate to difficult. N.C. 215 provides access points. The North Fork downstream of S.R. 1326 is classified as wild trout/natural bait waters. Upstream on Pisgah National Forest land, it is designated as wild trout waters. Worms, crickets, and fish eggs are popular natural baits. Artificial scented eggs are popular as well.

Hatchery-supported trout waters in the French Broad drainage include part of the Davidson River, as well as the French Broad from the forks of the river downstream for several miles. The Davidson is heavily stocked with trout, making it a popular destination. The Davidson River's hatchery-supported section runs from Avery Creek to the Ecusta water intake. Access points are along U.S. 276. Wading is popular along the Davidson's hatchery-supported section. Successful anglers use spinners and natural baits.

Other tributaries classified as hatchery-supported trout waters include the Swannanoa River, the West Fork of the French Broad, and Big Ivy Creek. The French Broad is designated as hatchery-supported trout waters from the forks to the U.S. 276 bridge.

Smallmouth fishing is extremely popular and productive in the main river channel. Wading, tubing, kayaking, and floating are all good techniques for accessing the bass fishing. Fly rods and spinning rods are popular. In the spring and fall, spinnerbaits and floating, shallow-running stickbaits or small crankbaits work well. In the summer, topwater lures and popping bugs catch lots of fish. Tube jigs and other soft plastics will catch smallmouth bass at any time they are biting.

Big muskellunge may be found in the long, flat stretches and deep holes. Downed trees, rock slides, ledges, and any other heavy cover or structure may hold these large predators. Muskie fishermen have good success using large swimbaits, topwater lures, and spinnerbaits.

Anglers catch catfish with commercial stinkbaits, worms, and liver fished on the bottom in deep holes. Panfish and smallmouth bass are often caught by anglers casting small spinners, worms, and crickets.

N.C. A-G grid: 31, D-5

General information: A special mountain trout license is required for fishing designated trout waters. Trout water designations are subject to change, so anglers should check regulations annually and watch for signs along the banks. All other NCWRC rules and regulations apply.

Nearest camping: The Pisgah Ranger District operates Rocky Bluff Campground, which is located on Spring Creek, a tributary of the lower French Broad River.

Directions: To reach the campground and the French Broad and Spring Creek access areas from Asheville, follow U.S. 19/U.S. 23 North to Marshall and exit right onto U.S. 25/U.S. 70. Follow U.S. 25/U.S. 70 through Marshall and Walnut Gap to the intersection with N.C. 208. Turn left and continue on U.S. 25/U.S. 70 to Hot Springs. To access the lower French Broad River, turn right on S.R. 1304 and travel to Murray Branch Recreation Area. To access Spring Creek, drive U.S. 25/U.S. 70 through Hot Springs, turn left on N.C. 209, and follow it to Rocky Bluff Campground, on the left.

15 Toe River System

Key species: Mountain trout, muskellunge, smallmouth bass, sunfish, catfish

Overview: The South Toe River begins in Yancey County on the east slope of Mount Mitchell near Mount Mitchell State Park and the Blue Ridge Parkway. The South Toe flows northward to join the North Toe River near Micaville. The North Toe begins near Newland and flows westward through Avery and Mitchell counties to form the boundary between Mitchell and Yancey counties. Below the confluence of the North Toe and the South Toe, the river becomes known as the Toe River, though many maps still call it the North Toe. The Toe River continues westward to its confluence with the Cane River north of Burnsville, where it becomes the Nolichucky River. The Toe River system offers many areas of outstanding scenic beauty.

Best ways to fish: Bank, wading, float tube, raft, kayak

Best times to fish: Although the Toe River system provides fishing opportunities any time of year, most anglers fish in the spring, summer, and fall. The highest water levels occur during spring. Trout anglers fish during the open seasons on designated trout waters.

Guide Scott Cunningham caught this Toe River smallmouth bass using a popping bug cast on fly tackle.

Description: The Toe River system consists of rocky, shallow rivers and streams with bars, boulders, and low-gradient and high-gradient beds. The streambed gradient and the rise and fall of water levels from snowmelt and rainfall determine the depth and swiftness of the current. Rolling cobbles, slick boulders, and fast currents call for careful foot placement and good boating skills. But anglers will also find numerous roadside bank access areas near pools and bars that offer good footing and excellent fishing. Water level and streambed gradient dictate whether or not the river can be safely floated or waded.

The fishing: The rivers and streams within the Toe River system support a variety of fishing opportunities, including back-country trout fishing and excellent smallmouth bass fishing. Rock bass, catfish, and panfish are also present. Some exceptionally large trout are occasionally caught from the middle section of the South Toe, and large smallmouth bass are caught routinely from the North Toe, Toe, and Nolichucky rivers. Trout are stocked into the upper end of the South Toe and in the North Toe from its headwaters to the Mitchell County line. For catching smallmouth bass and rock bass, anglers prefer using light spinning tackle to cast inline spinners, jigs, topwater lures, and stickbaits. Popping bugs fished with fly tackle are also a top choice for catching bass. Depending on the NCWRC trout water classifications, trout can be caught with bait, flies, or small spinners. Native bullhead and channel catfish strike commercial dough baits or night crawlers fished on the bottom. Anglers catch panfish right along with the various larger game fish species by using popping bugs, flies, spinners, and natural bait. A few anglers take advantage of the NCWRC's stocking of 70 muskellunge each year between the Penland bridge and Poplar.

N.C. A-G grid: 32, A-1

General information: See the appendix for TVA stream-flow data. Anglers should check the NCWRC trout regulations annually because they can change. The South Toe River has multiple designations of trout water, including a popular hatchery-supported section along N.C. 80. Other South Toe designations include a catch-and-release single-hook/artificial-fly section in Pisgah National Forest near the Blue Ridge Parkway and catch-and-release single-hook/artificial-lure sections for Upper Creek and Lower Creek near Mount Mitchell. Many South Toe feeder streams are also designated as wild trout waters. The North Toe River in Avery County is designated as hatchery-supported water. Many of the feeder streams along it are designated as wild trout waters. After flowing into Mitchell County, a short segment of the North Toe carries a hatchery-supported designation until degraded habitat downstream results in the river's becoming undesignated water for the rest of its length, including the Nolichucky. Many of the Nolichucky's feeder streams in Pisgah National Forest are designated as wild trout waters. The hatchery-supported and undesignated trout water sections of the North Toe and the Nolichucky offer some good fishing for trout, smallmouth bass, panfish, and catfish. Anglers have access from private and public river landings and road rights of way. The Nolichucky has a steep gradient and whitewater conditions. The Cane River has a hatchery-supported section along N.C. 197 south of Burnsville.

Nearest camping: The USFS's Carolina Hemlock and Black Mountain campgrounds offer overnight camping for trailers and tents. Sites are available for a fee on a first-come, first-served basis.

Carolina Hemlock Campground is located on N.C. 80 about 3.8 miles north of Busick. It is open from April 15 through October 31. Float tubes are available for rent. The campground has 29 tent or RV sites and four tent sites. Flush toilets are available, but showers and RV hookups are not. The campground offers a hiking trail and bank fishing.

To reach Black Mountain Campground from Busick, travel north on N.C. 80 for 0.7 mile to the campground sign at South Toe River Road (F.R. 472/S.R. 1205). Bear left on South Toe Road and drive 2.5 miles to the campground. It has two tent sites, 46 combination tent and RV sites, a waste station, showers, flush toilets, and three trails offering a total of 9.5 miles of hiking.

Primitive camping is allowed on USFS land throughout the Toe River area except where signs are posted and where primitive campsites have been designated along major forest service roads to protect water quality and other natural resources.

Directions: To reach the South Toe River from Asheville, follow U.S. 19/U.S. 23 North to Mars Hill and exit left onto U.S. 19. Follow U.S. 19 through Burnsville. Approximately 4 miles outside Burnsville, turn right on N.C. 80 in the town of Micaville. Drive south on N.C. 80 past Mount Mitchell Golf Course, then bear immediately right on F.R. 472, which follows the South Toe to its headwaters. Upper and Lower creeks are marked along this road.

To reach the South Toe from the Blue Ridge Parkway, turn onto F.R. 472 near Milepost 344 and N.C. 80.

To reach the South Toe from I-40, take Exit 72 (the Old Fort exit). Follow U.S. 70 to its intersection with N.C. 80. Turn left on N.C. 80 and follow it under the Blue Ridge Parkway to Mount Mitchell Golf Course. Bear left on F.R. 472.

To reach the USFS's Chestoa Boat Launch on the Nolichucky River, travel north from Asheville on U.S. 19/U.S. 23. Take Exit 12 and drive 12 miles into Tennessee; U.S. 19/U.S. 23 becomes I-181 at the state line. Turn right at the bottom of the ramp, then left at the T intersection. Drive 2.4 miles from the T intersection, then turn right on Chestoa Road. Travel 1 mile and cross the Nolichucky River bridge, then turn right on Jones Branch Road. Nolichucky Gorge Campground is located 1.1 miles down Jones Branch Road, and Chestoa Boat Launch is another 0.2 mile farther.

To reach the USFS's Poplar Boat Launch from Burnsville, travel N.C. 197 North to Poplar and turn onto Cross Pond Mill Bridge Road.

16 Lake Lure

Key species: Rainbow trout, brown trout, largemouth bass, smallmouth bass, crappie, white bass, catfish, sunfish

Overview: Lake Lure was constructed as an integral part of a private resort in 1927. The town of Lake Lure now manages the lake as a trust. The lake is fed by the Broad River, also called the Rocky Broad. The Lake Lure Dam generates power for the town. The excess electricity generated is sold to Duke Energy. Lake Lure has been called one of the most beautiful man-made lakes in the world, thanks to its spectacular mountain scenery in the vicinity of Chimney Rock.

Best ways to fish: Boat, private dock

Best time to fish: Fish may not be retained during the first three months of the year. Good fishing occurs year-round.

Description: Lake Lure has 726 acres of surface area and 27 miles of shoreline. It is approximately 104 feet deep and has a surface elevation of 990 feet. The shoreline is highly developed.

The fishing: Trout and all of the bass species strike inline spinners, topwater lures, and crankbaits. Bass anglers also have good luck by fishing with tube jigs and spinnerbaits. Anglers have good opportunities for catching schooling white bass by trolling when they are deep or by sight-casting when they are seen feeding at the surface. Docks are excellent places to fish for crappie and bass. Steep drop-offs and rock outcrops also offer plenty of fish-holding structure, especially for largemouth and smallmouth bass. The lake has an excellent crappie population. It is routinely stocked with several species of fish, with an emphasis on trout species. The Broad River is classified as hatchery-supported trout water for several miles upstream. Downstream of the dam, the river is popular for tubing. It also offers some fishing opportunities. The river flow velocity is light when power is not being generated.

N.C. A-G grid: 54, B-2

General information: Around December 1 each year, the town stocks the lake with fish that do not reproduce well. Most years, this stocking includes approximately 1,400 two-pound rainbow trout. Crappie and other species are sometimes stocked as well. NCWRC creel limits apply for all game fish kept from Lake Lure. The fishing is managed through a cooperative agreement with the NCWRC. A prohibition against keeping fish is in effect from December 1 through March 31 each year. During that time, anglers must use artificial lures with single hooks, and the hooks must be barbless; no fishing with live, natural, or prepared baits is allowed. A special permit from the town is required for all boats.

See the appendix for Lake Lure Dam discharge information.

Nearest camping: See the appendix for contact information for Lake Lure RV Park and Campground.

Directions: From Asheville, travel I-26 East to Exit 49B (the Bat Cave/Chimney Rock/Lake Lure/U.S. 64 exit). Travel east approximately 13 miles on U.S. 64 to the intersection with U.S. 74A in Bat Cave. Turn right on U.S. 74A and drive 4 miles to the Lake Lure Municipal Center/Town Hall.

17 New River

Key species: Smallmouth bass, rock bass, trout, muskellunge, flathead catfish, panfish

Overview: The New River is believed to be one of the oldest rivers in North America. Dedicated as a National Scenic River in 1976, it is the centerpiece of New River State Park. Its waters are slow and placid compared to those of most other high-elevation rivers. Its views of hillsides, pasturelands, and meadows are extraordinary. Although it has the same name as the New River of coastal Onslow County, it is an entirely different river.

Best ways to fish: Canoe, bank, float tube

Best time to fish: February through November

Description: Located in Ashe County, the North Fork New River and the South Fork New River converge to form the New River near Jefferson. The New flows north through Alleghany County into Virginia, crossing back into and then out of North Carolina again near Sparta.

The fishing: Buzzbaits and popping bugs work well for catching smallmouth bass and rock bass in summer. In spring and fall, spinnerbaits and Texas-rigged soft plastic jerk baits work well for catching bass. Floating crankbaits that resemble minnows or crawfish are good bets any time of year. The best smallmouth fishing occurs along the lower reaches of the river, especially below the forks. Nevertheless, smallmouth bass from a pound or two all the way up to five pounds are present throughout the river system. Smallmouth bass prefer to hang out in eddies created downstream of the bars and rocks in the river channel, along the undercut banks, and where any woody structure is located. Redbreast sunfish can be caught with worms, crickets, small spinnerbaits, and inline spinners. A good way to catch panfish is to cast for them downstream of the sand bars along the edges of the river when they bed in April, May, and June. Anglers fishing with live sunfish and shiners have good luck catching flathead catfish; casting live baits to bank cover is the best bet. Muskie anglers toss big spinnerbaits, buzzbaits, and surface plugs near downed trees and logjams and above rock ledges below the steep banks. A muskie could be lurking anywhere that deep, calm water and hard structure are found.

N.C. A-G grid: 14, A-2

General information: NCWRC fishing regulations apply. Panthers Creek, Cranberry Creek, Nathans Creek, Peak Creek, and Roan Creek are tributaries of the South Fork New River designated as hatchery-supported trout waters. Trout Lake on Peak Creek has a delayed-harvest designation. The main river channels are undesignated waters.

Nearest camping: Four recreation and access areas totaling 1,800 acres in New River State Park provide opportunities for camping, fishing, picnicking, and canoeing. Visitors may leave their vehicles and launch canoes at Wagoner Road Access Area, located at River Mile 26, at U.S. 221 Access Area, located at River Mile 15, and at Kings Creek Access Area, located at River Mile 7. All vehicles must register for overnight parking. Canoes may also be launched from several bridges and roadways that cross the river. Parts of the river are suitable for tubing at times. The park office offers tube and canoe rentals.

Each recreation area has a canoe-in primitive campground with tables and grills. Wagoner Road Access Area offers nine primitive campsites and bathroom facilities with hot showers. Campers may park and carry their supplies 250 yards to the campsite or canoe downstream to a takeout ramp at the campground. At U.S. 221 Access Area, campers must either walk or canoe to the 15 primitive campsites. Bathroom facilities with hot showers are nearby. Alleghany County Access Area has eight canoe campsites and is accessible only by canoe. It offers pit toilets and a pump for drinking water. Campers must sign in at the registration boxes or with a park ranger. A modest fee is charged for camping.

Directions: From Jefferson, follow N.C. 88 East. Travel across the New River bridge and turn left on Wagoner Access Road (S.R. 1590), which leads to the park office.

U.S. 221 Access Area is located eight miles northeast of Jefferson off U.S. 221. From the park office, travel back out the entrance to Wagoner Baptist Church, turn right on N.C. 88 West, drive to U.S. 221/N.C. 16 North, turn right, and go approximately 4.7 miles to Tom Fowler Road. Turn right and travel 1.3 miles to the stop sign. Turn left on U.S. 221 and drive 2.6 miles to the entrance, on the right.

To reach Kings Creek Access Area from the park office, drive back out to Wagoner Baptist Church, turn right on N.C. 88 West, then turn right on U.S. 221/N.C. 16 North and follow it to Overpass Ramp Road. Turn right, then turn right at the end of the ramp and continue to Chestnut Hill Road. Turn right, drive to George McMillian Road, turn left, and travel to Kings Creek Road. Cross the river and turn right. Kings Creek Access Area is on the left. Park signs are located at all the major turns.

Alleghany County Access Area, at River Mile 1, and other state park properties may be reached only by canoe.

18 Lake James

Mike Marsh and guide Jesse Buchanan with a Lake James muskie.

Key species: Largemouth bass, smallmouth bass, sunfish, crappie, muskellunge, walleye, bullhead catfish, white catfish

Overview: The Linville, Paddy Creek, and Catawba dams impound the Catawba and Linville rivers to form the 6,510-acre Lake James, which serves as a reservoir to provide hydropower for Duke Energy. The lake has 150 miles of shoreline. A canal connects the impounded waters of the Catawba River and Paddy Creek, which form a confluence. Some of the shoreline has been developed, but the lake still offers spectacular scenery.

Best ways to fish: Powerboat, canoe, bank

Best time to fish: Something is biting all year, but the best fishing occurs from February through October.

Description: Lake James is a large, relatively clear mountain lake. But it has fairly high fertility in its Catawba River arm and therefore produces an abundance of game fish. High winds can make fishing precarious on the main body of the lake. Many private and public boating access areas provide options for fishermen to launch their boats and fish in places that are out of the wind. The high relief of the surrounding mountain terrain helps block the wind. Duke Energy maintains six access areas on the lake.

The fishing: Lake James has a bipolar personality in terms of water quality and fish population densities. The Catawba River arm is fertile, boasting an abundance of largemouth bass and a reputation for producing big muskellunge. While largemouth bass achieve the best numbers and largest sizes in the upper Catawba arm, the lake produces heavyweight smallmouth bass in the Linville arm and the lower Catawba arm. Nevertheless, both species may be caught from either arm.

The large game fish feed on gizzard and threadfin shad. Anglers use jigging spoons and spinnerbaits when the fish are feeding on the shad schools. Bass can suspend with the baitfish schools at 20 feet, then suddenly move to shallow flats, following the food source as it migrates according to light penetration or temperature change. Stickbaits and spinnerbaits work well when the fish move into the shallows.

Spring is the best time to catch bass in the shallow water in the backs of coves. Topwater lures, soft plastic lures, and buzzbaits will hang plenty of bass when they are in the pre-spawning and spawning modes. The smallmouth bass bite best in January and February, while the largemouth bass feed more actively in March, April, and May. Both species turn on again in the fall. October is a great fishing month.

Small lures including plastic worms, rubber jigs, and tube jigs work well when bass are feeding on baitfish jammed against the vertical rockfaces in summer, fall, and winter. Upstream in the rivers where woody cover is plentiful, anglers have good luck by casting soft plastic lures, crankbaits, and spinnerbaits beneath the overhanging limbs and into the tops of trees that have fallen into the water due to bank erosion.

To catch muskellunge, anglers cast large twitchbaits, crankbaits, spinnerbaits, and swimbaits in the upper Catawba River arm. Muskies hang out around overhanging limbs and downed trees and along the sheer drop-offs that have ledges projecting from the rock cliffs at depths of 15 to 25 feet. Muskie anglers find the best fishing where the river narrows and they can cast to both sides with ease.

Walleye anglers prefer the clearer waters of the Linville arm, but the fish are also present in the murkier Catawba arm. The best months for walleye are January and February, though they can be caught at any time of year. In February, the fish move into shallow water. During other times, they can be spotted with a depthfinder. Once a baitfish school with walleye marks has been located, fishermen use jigs tipped with minnows or drop minnows on weighted rigs down to the level of the baitfish schools. Jigging while drifting and slow-trolling live minnows are the two most effective methods for catching walleye. A jigging spoon is the best lure when walleye are in deep water.

The crappie bite best from late March through early May. In March and April, they suspend at the cove mouths, forming large schools as they feed ravenously while preparing to spawn. Anglers trolling or dropping live minnows on weighted rigs and jigs catch large numbers of the tasty fish at that time. In April and May, anglers catch crappie in the backs of coves when they move into woody or standing cover to spawn. Jigs, small spinnerbaits, and minnows fished on float rigs are the best bets when crappie enter the shallows.

N.C. A-G grid: 33, C-5

General information: NCWRC rules and regulations apply.

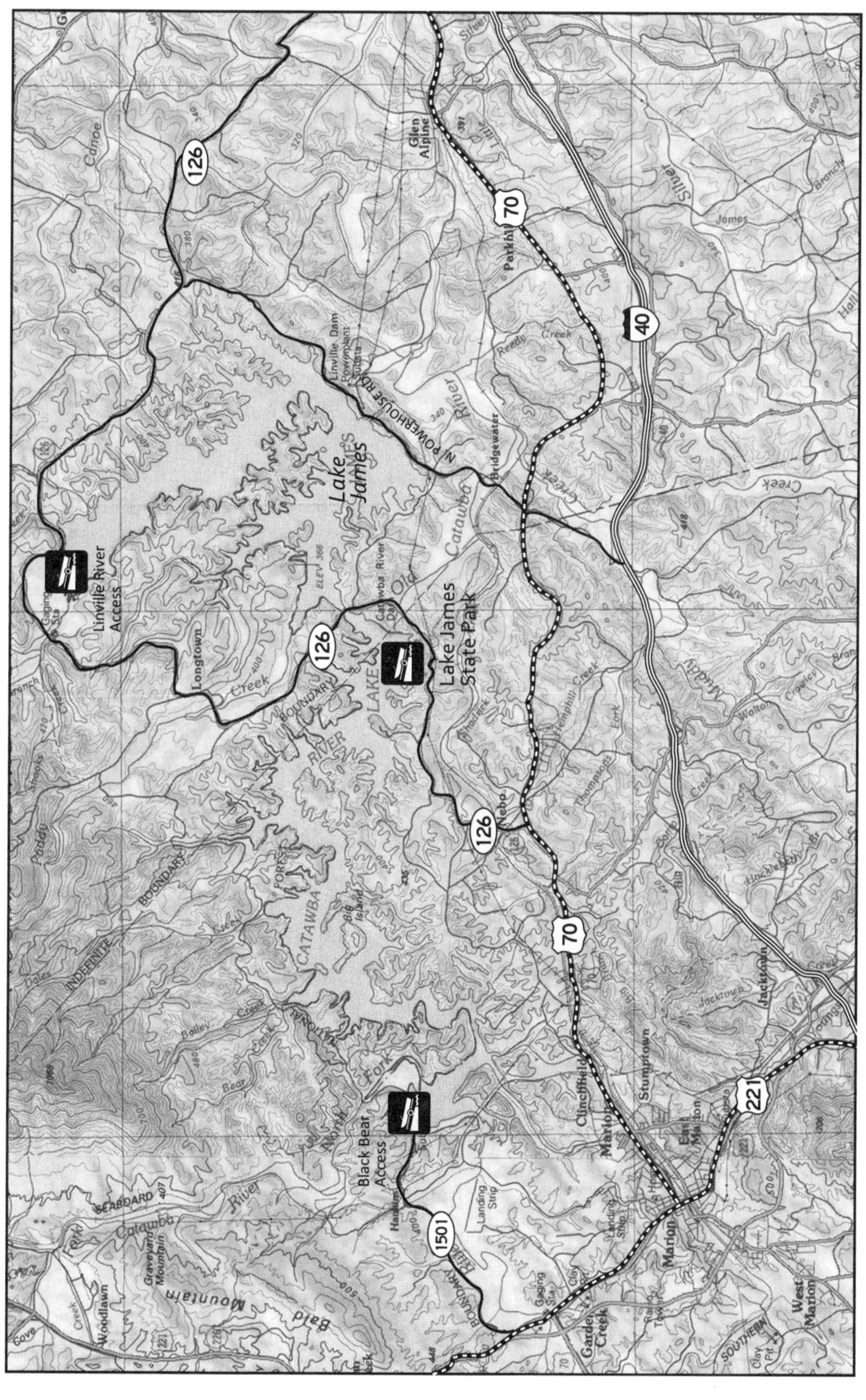

Linville River Access
Lake James
Lake James State Park
Black Bear Access
Linville Dam Powerplant
N POWERHOUSE RD
Catawba River
Glen Alpine
Bridgewater
Nebo
Marion
East Marion
West Marion
Clinchfield
Stumptown
Jacktown
Woodlawn
Longtown
Big Island
126
70
40
221
1501

Nearest camping: Lake James State Park has 20 walk-in campsites but no electric services. Each site has a fire circle, a picnic table, and tent space. Drinking water, restrooms, shower facilities, and firewood are available. The campground is open from March 15 through November 30. Canoe rentals are available.

Directions: Lake James State Park is located in Burke and McDowell counties 5 miles northeast of Marion on N.C. 126. From I-40, take the Nebo/Lake James exit (Exit 90) and head north for 0.5 mile. Turn right on Harmony Grove Road and follow it for 2 miles to a stoplight. Travel straight across the intersection and past Nebo Elementary School to a stop sign. Turn right on N.C. 126 and follow the signs for 2.3 miles to the park entrance, on the left.

To reach Linville River Boating Access Area from I-40, travel north on Jamestown Road for 2.7 miles. Turn left on N.C. 126 West, travel 10.6 miles, and turn left into the access area.

To reach Black Bear Boating Access Area from I-40, take the exit for N.C. 226/U.S. 221 and drive north for 6.7 miles. Turn right at the traffic light, go 50 yards, turn left on Hankins Road, and travel 2.5 miles to the access area, on the right.

19 Linville River

Key species: Mountain trout, smallmouth bass

Overview: Located in Burke County, the 12,000-acre Linville Gorge Wilderness Area of Pisgah National Forest has some spectacular scenery at high elevations. The river falls more than 2,000 feet in 12 miles before entering Lake James. The rim elevations of the gorge range from 1,300 feet to 4,040 feet. The sides are so steep that the gorge is often called "the Grand Canyon of the East." Below Lake James is a short stretch of the Linville River before its confluence with the Catawba River.

Best ways to fish: Wading, bank

Best time to fish: April through October

Description: Formed by Jonas Ridge on the east and Linville Mountain on the west, Linville Gorge is bisected by the Linville River, which drops into the valley below. The odd rock formations on Jonas Ridge include Sitting Bear, Hawksbill,

These rainbow trout were caught from the Linville River. Rainbow trout are among the most popular game fish in mountain lakes and streams.

Table Rock, and the Chimneys. The stretch of water below the Lake James powerhouse is much tamer, for those who would rather forgo the wilderness experience. The rugged Linville River Trail offers steep slopes, rocky footing, and thick vegetation.

The fishing: The river is classified as hatchery-supported trout water, so anglers can fish with whatever they like, including natural baits, lures, or flies. The trout fishing in the Linville Gorge section is extremely good. Anglers use small spinners, flies, and live or natural baits with excellent success. Anglers should be in good physical condition because the hiking trails down to the river are steep and the bottom is slick and rocky. Some hardy anglers fish the river with nothing more than wading shoes on their feet in July. The water is still extremely cold even in summer. Anglers carry lightweight chest waders for fishing the longer stretches of the river. The best fishing often occurs just at dark on hot summer days.

Downstream of the Lake James powerhouse, Bridgewater Fishing Area is located on the final portion of the Linville River. This short stretch is classified as hatchery-supported trout water. Bridgewater Fishing Area has a generous parking area, a fishing trail, and a handicapped-accessible fishing pier.

N.C. A-G grid: 33, B-4

General information: Linville Gorge is in the USFS's Grandfather Ranger District. See the appendix for contact information. Fishermen should check in with the rangers and let them know they are going into the gorge. A good place to contact rangers is at the Linville Falls Visitor Center, which is open April 15 through November 1 from 9 A.M. to 5 P.M. Maps are available at the visitor center.

The stretch of the Linville River downstream of the Lake James powerhouse is subject to water releases through the power-generating facility. This water fills the riverbed and can make conditions hazardous for fishermen. Times and dates of water discharges can be obtained by calling the Bridgewater Plant Hydrogeneration Schedule Information Line at 828-584-1451. Information is available three days in advance but can vary due to certain conditions. An alarm sounds before any release is made from the powerhouse.

Nearest camping: A permit is required to camp overnight in Linville Gorge on Fridays, Saturdays, Sundays, and holidays between May 1 and October 31. No more than 10 campers are allowed per group. The maximum length of stay is three days and two nights.

Directions: To reach the eastern section of Linville Gorge from Marion, take U.S. 221 North to N.C. 183 at Linville Falls. Turn right on N.C. 183, continue to N.C. 181, turn right (south), travel 3 miles, and turn right on F.R. 210 (Gingercake Road). At the first fork, turn left and continue through the Gingercake Acres housing development. Continue approximately 2 miles to the first parking area for Devils Hole Trail. The second parking area, for Hawksbill Trail, is approximately 1 mile from Devils Hole; the parking area is on the left and the trail on the right. The third parking area, for Spence Ridge Trail and North Table Rock Trail, is approximately 1 mile beyond Hawksbill Trail. Continue 1 mile to the first intersection and turn right beyond the Outward Bound School sign. Bear to the right and stay on this road through several switchbacks to Table Rock Picnic Area.

To reach the western section of Linville Gorge from Marion, take N.C. 221 North to N.C. 183. Turn right on N.C. 183 and continue 1 mile to Old N.C. 105 (Kistler Memorial Highway). Trailheads and parking lots accessing the western section of the gorge lead off Kistler Memorial Highway. To reach this highway via N.C. 126 from Marion, travel U.S. 70 East to Nebo, continue on N.C. 126 across Lake James, drive 8 miles, then turn left on Kistler Memorial Highway. This gravel road is very rough in places. Two-wheel-drive vehicles are not recommended.

To reach the NCWRC's Bridgewater Fishing Area from I-40, take Exit 94 (the Dysartsville exit) and travel north on S.R. 1129. After approximately 0.5 mile, turn left at the stop sign onto U.S. 70. Travel approximately 1.5 miles, turn right on S.R. 1233, drive approximately 2.5 miles along the Lake James Dam, and turn right on S.R. 1223. Continue 0.5 mile to the parking area.

20 Lake Rhodhiss

Key species: Brown trout, largemouth bass, crappie, sunfish, catfish, muskellunge, walleye, white perch

Overview: Duke Energy owns and operates Lake Rhodhiss, which was constructed in 1925 for hydropower generation by damming the Catawba River. Most of the lake is located in Burke County, but the northeastern part is in Caldwell County. Although this is one of the state's most fertile mountain lakes, its relatively small size, riverlike narrowness, and heavy shoreline development keep it off many anglers' lists of destinations. The lake's sandy bottom gives it clear blue water, in contrast to the clay-bottomed lakes in the Catawba chain, which have dark or muddy water. Duke Energy has retained approximately 20 miles of shoreline in a natural state, providing impressive scenery.

Best way to fish: Boat

Best times to fish: Lake Rhodhiss offers excellent fishing year-round. Stripers and crappie are active in the cold months, while other fish species are active in the warm months.

Description: Lake Rhodhiss has an elevation of 991 feet. It covers 3,515 acres and has more than 90 miles of shoreline. It is approximately 10 miles in length.

The fishing: One of the most fertile lakes in the Catawba chain, Lake Rhodhiss produces more species and numbers of fish than many of the better-known lakes. Rhodhiss boasts bigger striped bass than most other lakes, but the spawning run occurs as late as May or June, since its waters are colder than those of other Catawba River lakes. Anglers catch striped bass by trolling, casting crankbaits and jigs, and fishing live baits. The gizzard shad, threadfin shad, and sunfish in the lake create an abundant forage base. Anglers use shad and shiners for striper baits.

Largemouth bass are plentiful and grow large. Anglers use deep-diving crankbaits across the rockfaces and man-made shoreline structure to catch bass. But soft plastics such as tube jigs, jigs with skirts or trailers, and Carolina-rigged plastic worms and lizards also attract plenty of strikes when pitched around the hard structure.

Crappie are abundant and sought-after. Most anglers catch them near boat docks and at standing woody cover and submerged fallen trees. Panfish and catfish are also plentiful. Anglers fishing from boat docks catch them by using natural baits.

The only special-regulation trout water designation in the state occurs from just below Muddy Creek on the Catawba River to the city of Morganton's water intake dam at the head of Lake Rhodhiss. This special section of the Catawba is stocked and managed to produce trophy-sized brown trout. Brown trout from stockings into the Catawba occasionally make their way into Lake Rhodhiss.

The lake once had a substantial white bass fishery. But illegal and/or unintentional angler stockings of white perch have all but eliminated white bass fishing opportunities.

N.C. A-G grid: 33, C-7

General information: NCWRC fishing regulations apply at Lake Rhodhiss. No other special rules or regulations are in effect.

Nearest camping: Boone Fork Recreation Area in the Grandfather Ranger District of Pisgah National Forest has 14 tent campsites with grills, tables, and primitive toilets but no running water. Campsites are available on a first-come, first-served basis year-round. A small fee is charged.

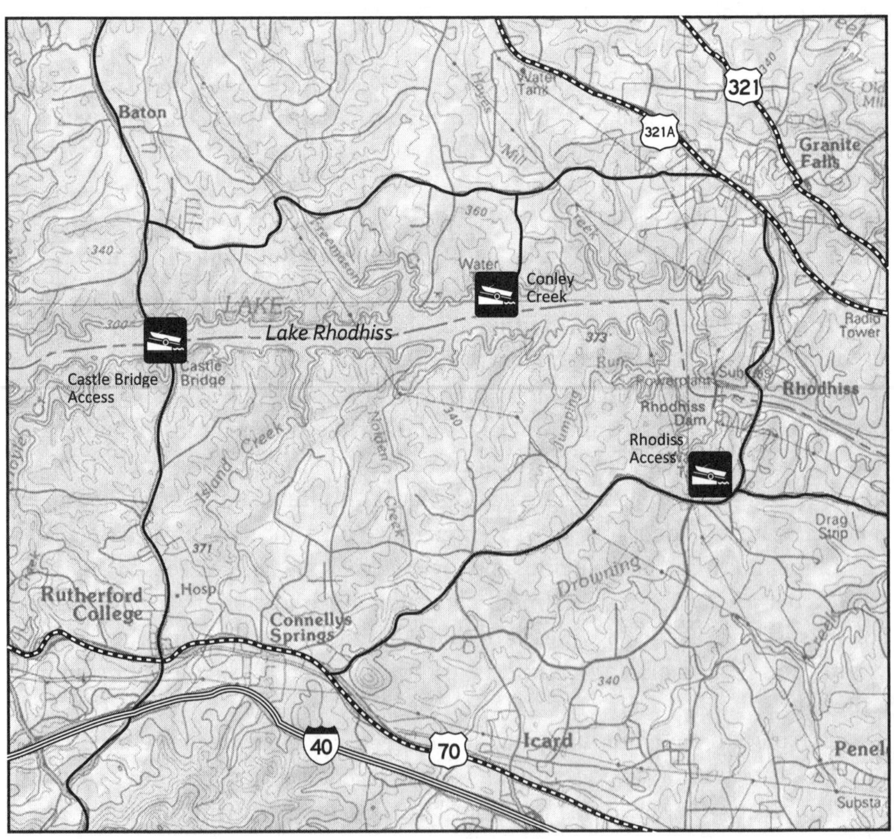

To reach Boone Fork Recreation Area from Lenoir, travel N.C. 90 West for 4 miles to a sign for the recreation area. Turn right at the sign onto Mulberry Creek Drive and go 4.5 miles. Turn right on Boone Fork Road and drive 2 miles to the campground.

Directions: Lake Rhodhiss has six boating access areas, some of which offer picnic facilities and hiking trails. These access areas are owned and maintained cooperatively by the NCWRC and Duke Energy. To reach John's River Access Area, take Exit 103 off I-40, follow U.S. 64 East for 0.8 mile, and turn left on Truck Road (U.S. 64 East). Travel 3.7 miles, turn left on N.C. 18 North, and drive 2.4 miles. The access area is on the right. To reach Castle Bridge Boating Access Area, take Exit 113 off I-40 and travel north on Rutherford College Road for 4.7 miles. Turn right on Dry Pond Road, drive 3.2 miles, turn right on Waterworks Road, and go 1 mile to the access area, located at the end of the road.

21 Lake Hickory

Key species: Largemouth bass, smallmouth bass, striped bass, channel catfish, crappie, walleye

Overview: Lake Hickory was created in 1927 upon the completion of Oxford Dam across the Catawba River. The dam is 122 feet high and has an overall length of 1,200 feet. Its spillway section is 550 feet long. Lake Hickory was named after the city of Hickory, located just south of the lake. The lake has 4,223 acres of surface area and 105 miles of shoreline. The full-pond elevation is 935 feet. Lake Hickory is a source of water for Hickory and Longview. It is also used by Duke Energy for hydropower generation.

Best ways to fish: Boat, bank, dock

Best times to fish: Good fishing for the black bass species is available all year. Stripers and walleye offer good winter fishing.

Description: Lake Hickory is a narrow lake with heavy shoreline development. Submerged woody structure is limited because of the lake's age. Much of the original woody cover has deteriorated.

The fishing: While Lake Hickory has low numbers of smallmouth bass, it is one of the mountain region's top largemouth bass lakes in terms of numbers of fish. Its largemouth bass are healthy and exhibit an average growth rate. Plenty of three- to four-pound largemouth bass are available; an occasional fish weighs six pounds or more. Most anglers cast to shoreline cover. Docks and cut-and-cabled trees provide bass the best structure. Lake Hickory has few of the primary or secondary points and other familiar topographic features that anglers see at most other lakes. But the deepwater structures, consisting of underwater peaks and valleys, are good places to fish. The lake is popular for nighttime bass fishing because the water is usually very clear.

The crappie fishing is lackluster. The lake's crappie population has been in decline since the 1990s. Biologists believe this could be caused by illegal or inadvertent angler introductions of alewife and white perch, which eat crappie eggs and compete with crappie for forage. Most crappie anglers catch the fish from docks that have submerged evergreen trees beneath them. The NCWRC has stocked crappie fingerlings in an experiment to determine if the population can be improved.

The lake offers excellent fishing for channel catfish weighing 10 pounds or more. Most catfish anglers fish at night. The lake also has excellent striper fishing. Good numbers of stripers weighing up to 15 pounds are available, and catching a 20- or 30-pounder is a possibility. Although Lake Hickory has excellent fishing potential for walleye, anglers have not taken advantage of the opportunity as they have in some of the lakes at higher elevations. Biologists have found fat walleye weighing up to six pounds in their sampling runs. Walleye mix with stripers in winter, schooling at the main lake points and deep flats. Walleye feed on the same forage fish as striped bass and can be caught with the same lures. Trolling and jigging are the best bets for both fish in winter. Live minnows are also good baits. Panfish anglers find excellent fishing for redear sunfish, also known as shellcrackers.

N.C. A-G grid: 34, C-2

General information: Duke Energy, in cooperation with the NCWRC, provides five public access areas on the lake—the Gunpowder, Lovelady, Wittenburg, Dusty Ridge, and Oxford access areas. Other acess areas are operated by Catawba County, the city of Hickory, and private concerns. Several public access areas offer fishing facilities, restrooms, and picnic shelters. Besides boating access areas, visitors will find a hiking trail and canoe rental service at River Bend Park and a hiking trail and playground at Glen C. Hilton Park. Both of these parks are operated by Catawba County.

Nearest camping: See the appendix for contact information for Lake Hickory RV Resort.

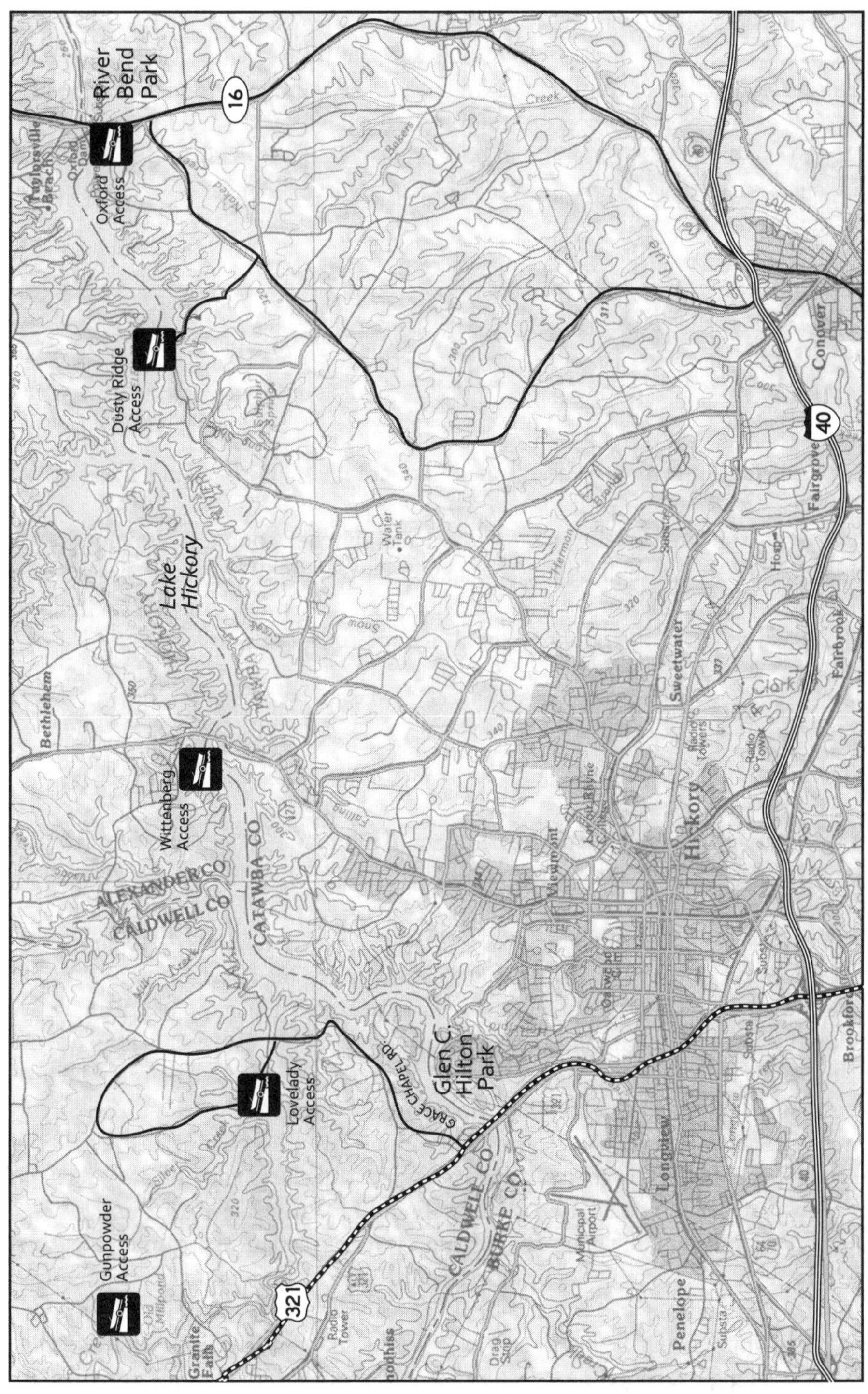
Gunpowder Access
Lovelady Access
Glen C. Hilton Park
GRACE CHAPEL RD.
Wittenberg Access
Lake Hickory
Dusty Ridge Access
Oxford Access
River Bend Park
16
321
40
ALEXANDER CO
CALDWELL CO
CATAWBA CO
BURKE CO
Bethlehem
Hickory
Longview
Conover
Fairgrove
Sweetwater
Penelope
Municipal Airport
Granite Falls

Directions: To reach Oxford Access Area from I-40, take Exit 131, travel north on N.C. 16 for 7.6 miles, turn left on St. Peters Church Road, go 0.1 mile, then turn right on Claude Road. Continue 0.4 mile and turn right on the access area road.

To reach Lovelady Access Area from I-40, take Exit 123 and follow U.S. 321 North for 4.4 miles. Turn right on Grace Chapel Church Road (S.R. 1758), travel 2.8 miles, turn left on Hurricane Hill Road, and drive 0.8 mile to the access area, on the right.

22 Lookout Shoals Lake

Key species: Largemouth bass, striped bass, crappie, sunfish, channel catfish

Overview: Located in Alexander, Catawba, and Iredell counties, Lookout Shoals Lake is one of the smallest lakes owned by Duke Energy. It isn't much wider in most places than the former Catawba River channel. It was formed in 1915 upon the construction of the Lookout Shoals hydroelectric station.

Best ways to fish: Bank, boat

Best time to fish: April through May

Description: Lookout Shoals Lake has approximately 1,305 acres of surface area and 37 miles of shoreline. Its full-pond elevation is 838 feet.

The fishing: Lookout Shoals Lake is not high on most anglers' destination lists. However, two fishing opportunities make traveling to the lake worthwhile. While the crappie population is not extremely high, anglers catch crappie well above average in size. Jigs and minnows are the tickets to crappie. The best fishing is from late March through early May. The most exciting fishing opportunity in the lake occurs in April or May when the stripers make their spawning runs. The fish do not reproduce successfully, yet they still run upstream in the river channel all the way to the dam. Anglers catch striped bass by casting lures and jigs from the bank downstream of the Lake Hickory dam (Oxford Dam). Catawba County's River Bend Park offers public bank-fishing opportunities just downstream of the dam. The stripers at Lookout Shoals are generally larger than those in other mountain and foothills lakes.

Largemouth anglers have good luck casting soft plastic worms, jigs, and spinnerbaits along the shoreline structure. During spring and fall, topwater lures are also good bets.

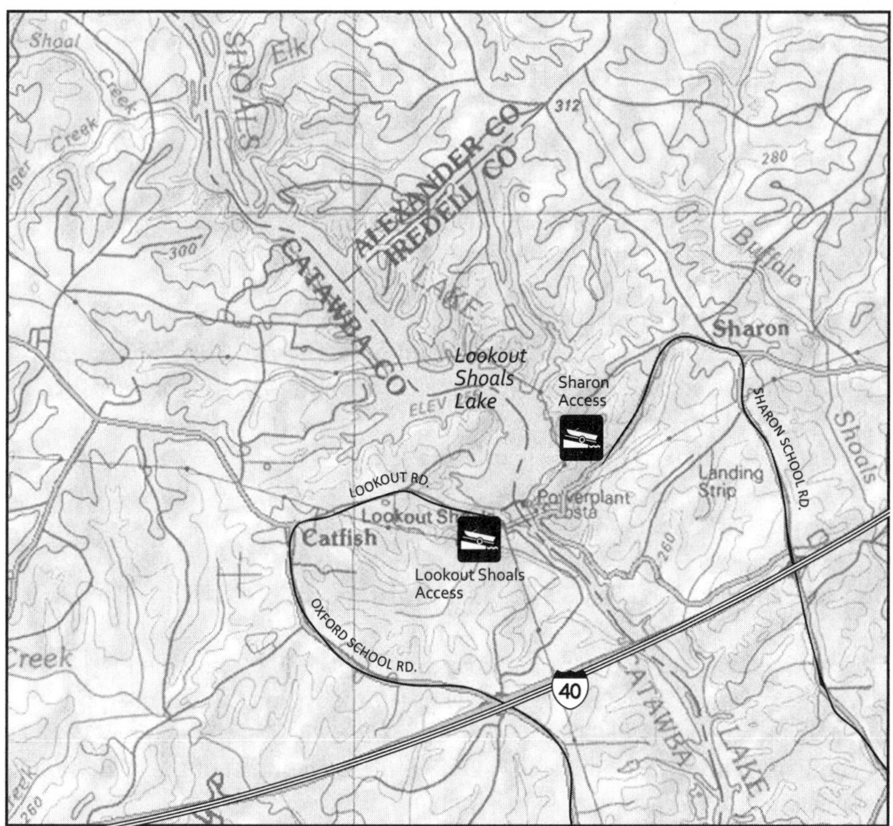

N.C. A-G grid: 34, C-4

General information: Lookouts Shoals Lake has had some problems with exotic vegetation such as elodea and parrot feather over the years. Grass carp have been introduced and seem to be curtailing the vegetation problems. But anglers have also found the best bass fishing when emergent weeds are present in the lake. Lookout Shoals anglers should therefore be on the lookout for beds of surviving vegetation because they are likely to attract largemouth bass.

Nearest camping: See the appendix for contact information for Indian Springs Campground.

Directions: Duke Energy maintains Sharon and Lookout Shoals access areas in cooperation with the NCWRC. To reach Lookout Shoals Access Area from I-40, take Exit 138 and travel east for 2.3 miles on N.C. 10 (Oxford School Road). Turn right on S.R. 1006, drive 1.3 miles, and turn left into the access area.

23 W. Kerr Scott Reservoir

Key species: Largemouth bass, smallmouth bass, spotted bass, hybrid striped bass, striped bass, crappie, sunfish, channel catfish

Overview: W. Kerr Scott Dam is located on the Yadkin River upstream of Wilkesboro in Wilkes County. The United States Army Corps of Engineers (COE) constructed the lake in 1962 for controlling devastating floods such as those in 1899, 1916, and 1940. The reservoir is also used for fish and wildlife management, recreation, and water supply purposes.

Best ways to fish: Boat, dock

Best time to fish: Good fishing is available year-round.

Description: The earthen dam has an elevation of 1,107 feet, which is 148 feet above the streambed. The reservoir extends 9.7 miles along the river. At the normal pool elevation of 1,030 feet, the reservoir covers 1,475 acres and has 55 miles of shoreline. The mean pool depth is 28 feet; the deepest part of the lake near the dam measures 65 feet.

The fishing: A forage base of blueback herring and gizzard shad helps create excellent fishing for game fish species. The lake has been stocked with many game fish and forage fish species. Improvements in fish habitat also aid angling success. Christmas tree bundles, gravel spawning beds, wooden pallets, and hardwood treetops have been placed in the lake as fish attractors. Cut-and-cabled trees also extend into the water from the shoreline. In addition, private docks create shelter for fish. Several fishing areas are located at the COE recreation areas around the lake. Some stretches of shoreline have been kept in their natural state.

The best smallmouth bass fishing is in the Yadkin River arm, though smallmouth bass occur throughout the lake. Spotted bass may be more abundant than largemouth bass. Spots are more aggressive but do not achieve the size of largemouth bass. The lake is nutrient poor compared to Badin and Tuckertown lakes. Its water is very clear. The lack of nutrients keeps bass and other fish populations at lower numbers than in the other Yadkin lakes. But plenty of quality-sized fish are still to be had.

Most anglers fish for bass with deep-diving crankbaits, casting them along the deepwater points and over the deep structure areas provided by submerged hills and cliffs. But jigs also work well in the deep structure. Because of its many deepwater structure areas, this is a good lake for winter bass fishing, especially for smallmouth.

In spring, summer, and fall, largemouth and spotted bass strike soft plastic worms and lizards, spinnerbaits, and topwater lures cast along the shoreline areas with downed trees and in the dips in the shoreline and coves.

Anglers catch catfish from boats or the banks using worms and chicken liver. Hybrid stripers also strike chicken liver, along with jigs, live shad and shiners, crankbaits, topwater plugs, and trolling lures.

Striped bass have been stocked as an experimental fish to determine whether they or hybrids are the better species for the lake. If stripers exhibit better growth and survival rates than hybrids, the NCWRC may stock them instead of hybrids in the future.

Most of the lake's crappie are rather small and grow slowly. But catching a crappie weighing three pounds is a possibility. In early spring, the clay banks are good places to fish for crappie with jigs and small beetle grub spinnerbaits. As the water warms, the fish move into the cover areas. Anglers find concentrations of crappie at the cut-and-cabled trees and the Christmas tree reefs established and maintained by the COE. A few docks may also hold crappie, but most of the lake's shoreline is undeveloped. When the fish move into the cover, anglers fishing with live minnows and jigs have the best success.

N.C. A-G grid: 34, A-2

General information: Fishing is permitted throughout the reservoir with the exception of a restricted safety zone near the dam. Of the 14 recreation areas around the lake, seven have boat ramps. A fee is charged for launching boats at COE ramps; some of the ramps are closed at night. Boat ramps are located at the Bandits Roost, Boomer Park, Fort Hamby, Keowee, Dam Site, and Smitheys Creek recreation areas and at Wilkes Skyline Marina. Public fishing docks are located at the Bandits Roost and Warrior Creek recreation areas. Fish-cleaning stations are located at the Blood Creek, Keowee, and Tailwater recreation areas. Most of the recreation areas have playgrounds and picnic shelters.

Nearest camping: Campsites are available at several of the COE recreation areas, including Bandits Roost, Fort Hamby, and Warrior Creek. Dump stations, electricity, and group camping facilities are offered.

Directions: From Wilkesboro, travel 5 miles west on N.C. 268.

24 Yadkin River

Key species: Spotted bass, largemouth bass, smallmouth bass, redbreast sunfish, catfish

Overview: The Yadkin River begins in the mountains at 3,600 feet near Blowing Rock and flows southeast toward Lenoir, then northeast through Ferguson into W. Kerr Scott Reservoir. Downstream of the reservoir, the river flows between North Wilkesboro and Wilkesboro and through Pilot Mountain State Park before turning south and flowing west of Winston-Salem and entering the Piedmont. The Yadkin forms a confluence with the South Yadkin River near Salisbury. Downstream of Salisbury, the Yadkin becomes High Rock, Tuckertown, and Badin lakes. Downstream of Badin Lake at Lake Tillery, the Uwharrie River forms a confluence with the Yadkin, after which it is called the Pee Dee River. The Pee Dee flows through Blewett Falls Lake and into South Carolina below the Blewett Falls Dam.

Best ways to fish: Bank, kayak, raft, johnboat

Best time to fish: April through October

Description: The Yadkin River is swift flowing and shallow at its upper elevations and slows to moderate whitewater or lazy water in its lower elevations. It is very tame in the stretches where it serves as the headwaters of the various lakes in the Yadkin chain. The river has lots of rocks and boulders and very muddy water during peak flow conditions in winter and early spring.

The fishing: Most anglers take advantage of the warm, stable water conditions in late spring, summer, and early fall. Fishermen catch more spotted bass than other bass species. Most bass are caught between W. Kerr Scott Dam and Idols Dam near the Forsyth County–Davidson County line. Smallmouth bass prefer the rocky areas, while largemouth bass prefer deep holes with sluggish water. Spotted bass are caught all along this stretch of the river. Bass anglers have excellent luck using topwater lures, soft plastic lures, crankbaits, and spinnerbaits. The bass fishing is best in spring when the water warms and the fish begin to spawn. Redbreast sunfish bite best in April, May, and June, then again in September and October.

To catch panfish, anglers cast popping bugs with fly rods or small spinnerbaits with ultralight tackle. Natural baits such as worms, minnows, and crickets are also popular for catching panfish and crappie.

Anglers catch catfish by fishing at night during the summer months. Bank fishing for catfish is popular. Dough baits, liver, and night crawlers are good bets for catfish. In the headwaters and tailraces of the lakes, live and cut shad and panfish are the top catfish baits. Flathead catfish occur mainly downstream of Idols Dam. Although bullhead catfish are the primary catfish species upstream of the dam, flathead catfish have also been caught there, posing a threat to the native catfish.

N.C. A-G grid: 16, C-2

General information: The Yadkin River Trail runs 165 miles from near W. Kerr Scott Dam to York Hill near the headwaters of High Rock Lake. Passing through five lakes, it is the longest river trail with developed access in North Carolina's trail system. Its creation in 1985 was coordinated by the North Carolina Division of Parks and Recreation with the cooperation of several agencies.

Nearest camping: Pilot Mountain State Park has 49 campsites for tents and trailers. Each site has a tent pad, a table, and a grill. Drinking water and hot showers are available, but no hookups are provided. Campsites are offered on a first-come, first-served basis for a modest fee. The campground is open from March 15 through November 30. Canoe access and bank fishing are available on the two-mile stretch of the Yadkin within Pilot Mountain State Park.

Directions: Pilot Mountain State Park is located in Surry and Yadkin counties 24 miles north of Winston-Salem and 14 miles south of Mount Airy. From U.S. 52, take the Pilot Mountain State Park exit and travel west into the Mountain Section of the park. The North River Section is in Surry County 10 miles from the Mountain Section. From U.S. 52, take the Pinnacle exit and follow the signs to Horne Creek Farm. The park entrance is 0.4 mile past the farm. The South River Section is in Yadkin County 20 miles from the Mountain Section. Take N.C. 67 to East Bend. From Main Street, turn right on Fairground Road. Turn right on Shady Grove Church Road, then turn right on Shoals Road and follow it to the park.

25 Lake Norman

Key species: Striped bass, largemouth bass, spotted bass, white bass, white perch, panfish, crappie, catfish

Overview: Located in Catawba, Lincoln, Iredell, and Mecklenburg counties, Lake Norman was constructed and filled between 1959 and 1964. Built in conjunction with the construction of Cowans Ford Dam on the Catawba River, it is owned and operated by Duke Energy to supply cooling water for the Marshall steam-electric plant and the McGuire nuclear power plant, as well as for hydroelectric power generation at the Cowans Ford plant. It was named for a former Duke Power president, Norman Cocke. The lake also serves as a water supply for surrounding counties and municipalities. It is a muddy lake with steep sides, as is typical of foothills lakes. Weekend boat traffic stirs up the bank mud, which then subsides through the week, making for better fishing on weekdays. The lake has heavy shoreline development, though a few stretches of natural bank remain. Lake Norman State Park has 13 miles of undeveloped shoreline and some outstanding foothills scenery in spring and fall. The flood plain of the Catawba River at the lake's headwaters also has some undeveloped stretches of shoreline.

Best ways to fish: Boat, private dock, bank

Best times to fish: Something is biting at Lake Norman year-round. In the dead of winter, fishing is best at the Hot Hole, the anglers' name for the discharge area of cooling water from the Marshall steam-electric plant. The best times for bass fishing are March through June, September, and October. Crappie fishing is excellent from March through May. Striper fishing is good all year long; the fish go deeper during the hot months of summer.

Description: Lake Norman is 34 miles long and has 520 miles of shoreline and

White perch are prolific and widespread in North Carolina lakes and coastal rivers. This one fell for a trolled vibration lure.

a surface area of more than 32,510 acres. The full-pond elevation is 760 feet. The lake is used for flood control, which often results in wide fluctuations in water level. The maximum drawdown usually occurs in winter. Although the lake has little vegetated shoreline cover as a result of water-level fluctuations, some emergent vegetation has survived and becomes flooded at the backs of the creeks and coves during spring and summer. The lake has extensive shoreline development. Many waterfront residents remove erosion-felled trees and place riprap to prevent erosion by wave action from boat wakes. Docks and piers provide some of the best cover for fish, since many owners place evergreen trees beneath their docks to attract panfish, crappie, and bass.

The fishing: Lake Norman is stocked by the NCWRC with striped bass, which provide one of the top fishing opportunities. In spring, stripers run upstream to the Lookout Shoals Dam to spawn. Anglers with knowledge of the hazards in the Catawba River downstream of the dam find excellent striper fishing in the rocky channel. In spring, the river is a good place for casting soft plastics and stickbaits. At other times of year, striper anglers catch the fish by trolling. The best topwater opportunities on the main lake body occur during the cold months, often when a skim of ice is on the water. Anglers should watch the sea gulls. Wherever they are feeding on baitfish, stripers are sure to be feeding below. Topwater poppers and soft plastic or bucktail jigs are popular striper lures. Deep-diving lures are best for trolling. Some anglers drift live baits for stripers along the former river channel. Shad species are abundant and can be caught with a cast net to use as bait. Gizzard shad is a top bait choice.

White bass were once abundant and grew very large, but biologists fear these popular game fish will all but disappear from Lake Norman because of intentional illegal stockings of white perch by fishermen. White perch may also create a decline in the abundance of crappie and other game fish because of competition for the same forage species, as well as predation on eggs. White perch may initially grow large but have the potential to overpopulate and become too stunted to attract interest from fishermen. White perch and white bass often school together at the surface. At other times, anglers can locate schools by using electronic depthfinders. Schooling fish will strike trolled or cast spoons, spinners, jigs, and surface poppers.

Lake Norman is a top crappie fishing destination. Most anglers catch crappie from beneath the boat docks. Live minnows and small feather or tube jigs are the best bets. Largemouth bass are abundant in Lake Norman but do not achieve the large sizes they do in Piedmont reservoirs. Spotted bass are extremely abundant.

Lake Norman holds several species of catfish. Blue catfish have overshadowed the other catfish species. Native bullhead catfish have greatly decreased in abundance since the introduction of flathead catfish, which have an appetite for bullhead catfish above all other species. But some impressive catches of all catfish

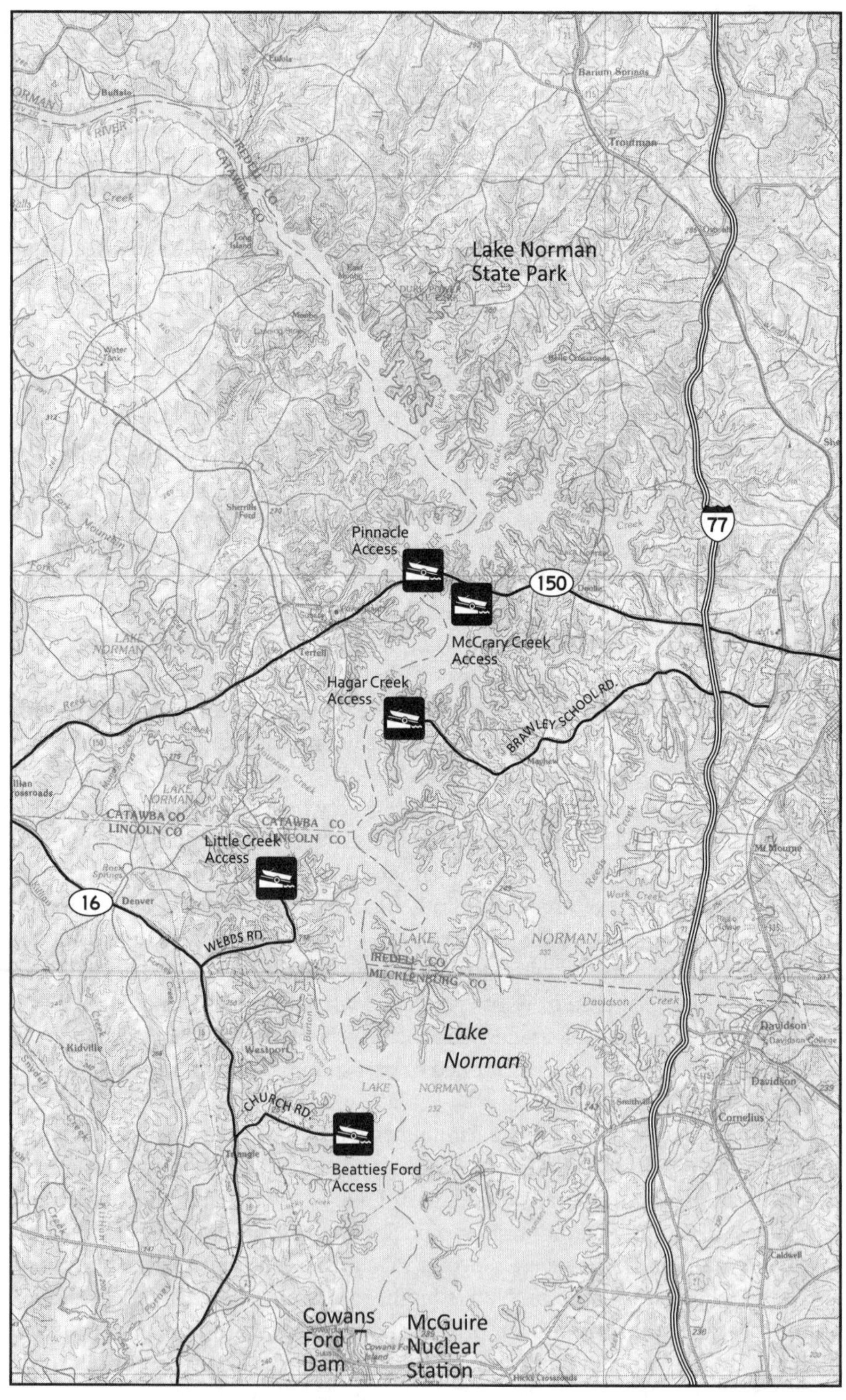
Lake Norman
State Park
Pinnacle
Access
McCrary Creek
Access
150
77
Hagar Creek
Access
BRAWLEY SCHOOL RD.
Little Creek
Access
16
WEBBS RD
Lake
Norman
CHURCH RD.
Beatties Ford
Access
Cowans
Ford
Dam
McGuire
Nuclear
Station
Troutman
Barium Springs
Denver
Westport
Davidson
Cornelius
CATAWBA CO
LINCOLN CO
IREDELL CO
MECKLENBURG CO

species are still made at the lake. Catfish anglers use live or cut shad and panfish for bait. The lake also has a tremendous population of common carp, which offer fishing and bowfishing opportunities in spring when they enter the shallow waters to spawn. Carp strike canned corn, dough baits, and worms.

N.C. A-G grid: 57, A-5

General information: NCWRC rules and regulations apply. Public-access areas are operated by Duke Energy and the NCWRC.

Nearest camping: Lake Norman State Park was created through a partnership between Duke Energy and the North Carolina Division of Parks and Recreation. Along its shoreline are two bank-fishing areas and eight public boating access areas with facilities for launching powerboats. Bank fishing is not allowed in other areas of the park. Thirty-three individual tent pads are available on a first-come, first-served basis at the family campground, which is open from March 15 through November 30. The group tent camping area, open from April through November, has drinking water and restrooms. The community building can be leased for a fee. Pedal boats and canoes are available for rent. Other recreational activities at the park include hiking and swimming.

Directions: To reach the Duke Energy/NCWRC Pinnacle Access Area from I-77, take Exit 36 and travel N.C. 150 for 4.4 miles. Turn right into the entrance road just before crossing Lake Norman on the N.C. 150 bridge. Other access areas are located at Long Island, Hager Creek, McCrary Creek, Beatties Ford, and Little Creek.

26 Mountain Island Lake

Key species: Striped bass, largemouth bass, spotted bass, crappie, catfish, white perch, white bass

Overview: Mountain Island Lake was built in 1924 for producing hydropower at Duke Energy's Mountain Island hydroelectric station. Although relatively small, the lake serves as the water supply for a million citizens of Mount Holly, Gastonia, and Charlotte-Mecklenburg. It has shoreline in Mecklenburg, Lincoln, and Gaston counties. The high island near the dam is called Mountain Island by local anglers but is also known as Big Island. Mecklenburg County's Latta Plantation Park, Cowan's Ford Wildlife Refuge, and Mountain Island Educational

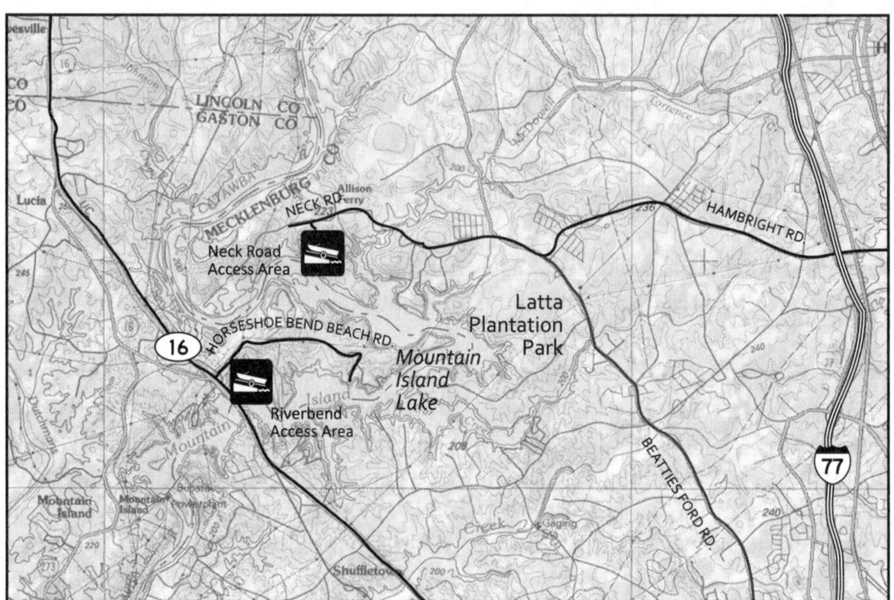

State Forest preserve some of the lake's shoreline in its natural state. But shoreline development is abundant. The lake level can change rapidly; it may fluctuate 10 feet.

Best ways to fish: Boat, bank

Best time to fish: February through October

Description: Mountain Island Lake encompasses 3,261 acres and has 61 miles of shoreline. It has an average depth of 17.7 feet and a maximum depth of 58.4 feet near the dam. The full-pond elevation is 647.5 feet.

The fishing: Mountain Island Lake's deep, clear water offers excellent fishing for many species. The lake fishes like a river in its narrow upper reaches but like a deep lake near the dam. Spotted and largemouth bass anglers catch lots of fish by casting spinnerbaits, crankbaits, and soft plastics along the shoreline cover and the steep drop-offs beginning in the spring; April and May are the peak bass-fishing months. The backs of the coves offer excellent fishing during the spawn. As summer progresses, bass anglers fish the river channel because the cool water from the Lake Norman Dam keeps the bass active. Spotted bass are more prevalent at the lower end of the lake, while largemouth bass dominate the upper end of the lake in its riverlike areas. The lake has plenty of shoreline structure for holding bass, including boat docks, rock outcrops, fallen trees, deep channels, and shallow bars.

Striped bass and crappie anglers have good luck year-round where the Catawba River channel enters the upstream end of the lake. For catching stripers, anglers use live shad, drifting or trolling them in the deep areas. For catching crappie, anglers cast along the shoreline in spring using live minnows or jigs. Trolling the deep areas using jigs works well for catching crappie during the months on either side of the peak spawn, which occurs from late March through mid-May.

The best catfish action occurs in the lower end of the river channel where it enters the lake. Catfish anglers also have good luck at Mountain Island Tailrace Fishing Area. Anglers fishing from private boat docks at night also catch lots of catfish. Cut or live baits work well for catfish.

White perch and white bass offer anglers a chance at smaller schooling fish. Trolling small spinners and crankbaits is a good tactic for catching not only these but many other species as well.

N.C. A-G grid: 57, B-5

General information: NCWRC rules and regulations apply. The two public access ramps are operated by Duke Energy and the NCWRC. Picnicking, hiking, and horseback riding are offered at Latta Plantation Park; see the appendix for contact information. Mountain Island Tailrace Fishing Area, located off N.C. 273 at the end of Mountain Island Dam Road, allows bank anglers fishing opportunities.

Nearest camping: Camping is offered at Lake Norman State Park but is not allowed on the islands or the shoreline.

Directions: To reach Riverbend Boating Access Area from I-85 near Charlotte, take Exit 36 and follow N.C. 16 North for 8.7 miles. After crossing Mountain Island Lake, turn right on Horseshoe Bend Beach Road (S.R. 1912). Travel 0.2 mile and turn right onto the access area road.

To reach Neck Road Boating Access Area from I-85 near Charlotte, take Exit 34 and follow N.C. 27 East (Mount Holly–Huntersville Road) toward Huntersville for 4 miles. Turn left on Beatties Ford Road (S.R. 2074), drive 3.1 miles, turn left on Neck Road, and go 0.8 mile to the access area, on the left.

27 Lake Wylie

Key species: Largemouth bass, catfish, crappie, white perch, panfish

Overview: Lake Wylie was named after Dr. W. Gil Wylie, who organized the Catawba Power Company, a predecessor of Duke Energy. The oldest lake on the Catawba River, it was created in 1904 by a dam near Fort Mill, South Carolina. When the dam was rebuilt in 1924, the lake's surface area expanded to approximately 13,443 acres. Lake Wylie has 325 miles of shoreline and a length of 32 miles from the Mountain Island Dam upstream to the Wylie Dam downstream. In addition to supporting the Wylie hydroelectric station, the lake supports the Allen steam station and the Catawba nuclear station with cooling water and provides a dependable water supply for Belmont and Rock Hill. The full-pond elevation at Lake Wylie is approximately 569 feet. The average depth is 23 feet and the maximum depth 94 feet.

Best ways to fish: Boat, dock

Best time to fish: March through October

Description: Lake Wylie has a highly developed shoreline but still boasts a few stretches of forest along its banks. It has the clay banks and rocky points of what is essentially a widened river channel. Lots of long points, submerged stumps, and rocky underwater hills are present. Long, winding creeks with dips and deep pockets enhance the fish habitat and fishing opportunities. The water is not as clear as that of the lakes on the upper stretches of the Catawba River. Boat docks and erosion-felled trees add to the shoreline cover. Aquatic vegetation is absent.

The fishing: Lake Wylie's turbid water is likely the reason for its excellent population of gizzard shad, which serve as the forage base for most game fish species. Its dingy water means the lake is fertile.

The fishing for largemouth and spotted bass is excellent. In early spring, spinnerbaits and crankbaits cast along the shoreline work well for catching bass. As the water heats up, soft plastic lures and topwater plugs become reliable bass producers. In April and May, the best action occurs during full moons when spawning is taking place. Anglers use trolling motors to move slowly along the banks to spot the bedding bass. Plastic lizards and crawdads and rubber jigs cast to the beds typically catch the biggest bass of the year. A noisy topwater lure such as a buzzbait will get a bedding bass's attention if one of the more subtle bottom-bumping lures won't draw a strike. Most bass anglers use highly visible lure colors for best success in the dark water. Schooling bass offer extra sport in spring and summer. Beaver Dam Creek and Armstrong Bridge are the places to watch for surface-feeding schools. Anglers should be on the lookout for surface activity at other locations early and late in the day. Propeller lures and chugging plugs are the best bets for catching schooling bass.

The lake has a reputation for producing heavy stringers of crappie. But white perch may be crowding out the crappie. For catching crappie, most anglers cast float rigs baited with minnows to any shoreline structure. Soft plastic tube jigs are also good bets. Many property owners place evergreen trees beneath their docks to attract crappie.

White perch anglers spot the schools feeding at the surface or find them in deeper water by using electronic depthfinders. Jigs, spinners, spoons, minnows, and worms are good bets for white perch. Some anglers also use Sabiki rigs, consisting of a half-dozen tiny, gold-hooked feather jigs rigged in tandem. These rigs were designed to catch baitfish in saltwater environments, but what is a white perch but another baitfish? Multiple perch catches are possible when a Sabiki rig is dropped into a white perch school.

Panfish anglers have excellent luck catching shellcrackers (redear sunfish). These fish can be used as bait for catching flathead catfish or kept for the pan. The best way to catch them is by baiting a float rig with a piece of shrimp or a worm and casting it near a boat dock or other shoreline cover. Shellcrackers and other panfish also bed in the backs of the sandy-bottomed coves.

Catfish anglers enjoy excellent luck at Lake Wylie. The feeder creeks are the best bets for blue catfish, especially during flows from spring runoff and following summer thunderstorms. Mill Creek and Paw Creek are good bets for blue catfish; fishing near the upstream dam is also a good bet. Channel catfish inhabit the deep holes in the creek channel bends and the Catawba River channel. Flathead catfish move from these same deepwater areas into the shallows to feed on panfish at night. The best baits for channel cats include commercial stinkbaits and shrimp. Fresh-cut shad and panfish baits are the best bets for blues. Live shad and panfish work best for catching flathead catfish. The catfish bite is good day and night; the rule of thumb is to fish deep during the day and shallow at night. During summer, most anglers prefer catching catfish at night. The hot-water discharge from the Allen plant creates an excellent year-round bank-fishing opportunity for catfish at Allen Fishing Access Area off Canal Road.

N.C. A-G grid: 57, B-5

General information: NCWRC rules and regulations apply. Duke Energy provides six public boating access areas. Many private boating access areas and marinas are also located around the lake. Allen Fishing Access Area is operated in cooperation with the NCWRC and the South Carolina Department of Natural Resources. Since portions of Lake Wylie are located in North and South Carolina, fishermen are advised to obtain proper licenses and to adhere to fishing creel limits for both states' sections of the lake.

Nearest camping: Several private campgrounds are located at the lake. Crowders Mountain State Park is about 15 miles west of Lake Wylie at Gastonia. It offers group camping and individual tent pads. Grills, picnic tables, drinking water, and pit toilets are available. Activities at the park include hiking, rock climbing, and fishing and canoeing on a nine-acre lake.

Directions: To reach South Point Boating Access Area from I-85, take the N.C. 273 South exit, travel 6.1 miles to S.R. 2525 (South Point Road), and follow S.R. 2525 for 2.2 miles to the access area.

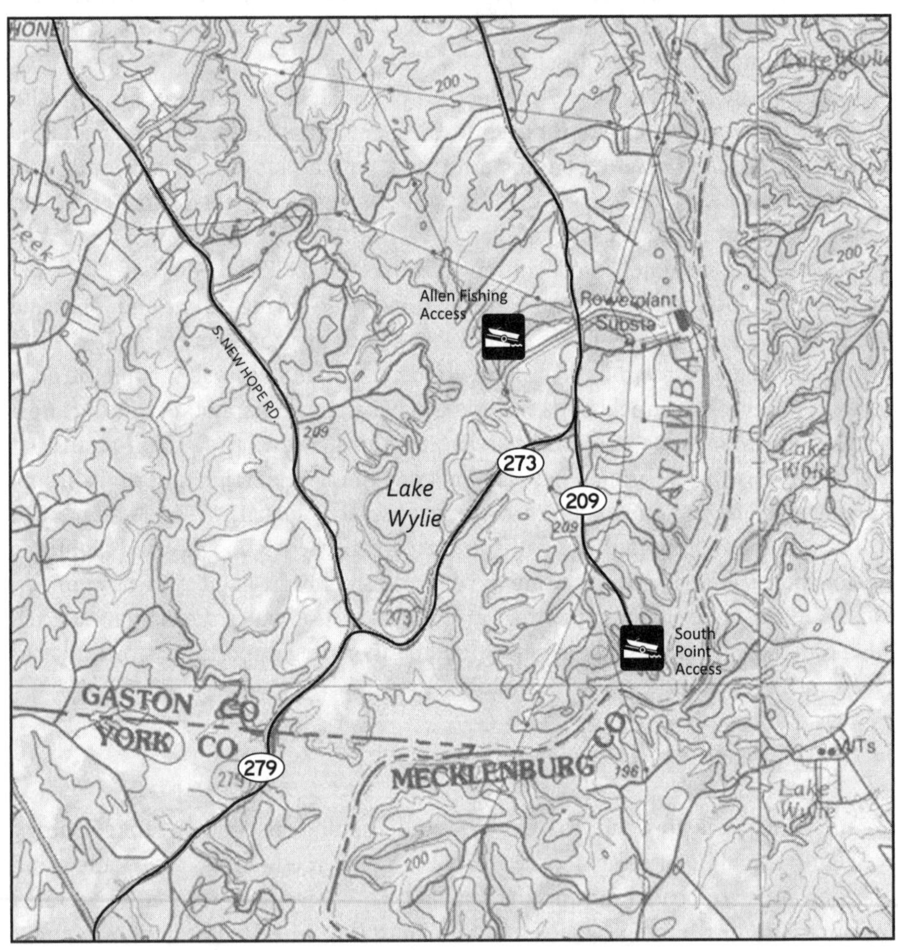

28 Salem Lake

Key species: Hybrid bass, largemouth bass, catfish, crappie, sunfish, carp, white perch

Overview: Salem Lake is a short drive from downtown Winston-Salem. Surrounded by a park, it offers a quiet retreat from city life. The lake has a limit on powerboat engine size. It is used for municipal water supply.

Best ways to fish: Kayak, canoe, powerboat, pier

Best times to fish: Spring and summer

Description: Salem Lake is a 365-acre lake formed by Salem Lake Dam. The lake's elevation is 797 feet. The lake level rises and falls in response to rainfall and water-supply demands. One of the park's amenities is a 6.9-mile walking trail.

The fishing: Salem Lake is stocked with several species of game fish and boasts some of the best trophy largemouth bass fishing in the state. The lake-record largemouth weighed 11 pounds, 14 ounces. Bass at or near 10 pounds have been caught here since the record was established in 1968. Bass fishermen use crankbaits and spinnerbaits in the spring. Once the water heats up, they cast soft plastic worms to the grass beds, stumps, and other woody cover. Anglers fishing for catfish with live sunfish have caught some exceptionally large bass.

Anglers also catch some huge catfish weighing more than 55 pounds. The lake has flathead, blue, and channel catfish, all of which can be caught from the fishing pier. Live sunfish and chicken liver make excellent catfish baits. The lake has a good population of channel catfish, which strike worms, minnows, liver, and shrimp.

The hybrid bass fishing is superior for such a small lake. Salem Lake produces hybrids as heavy as 15 pounds. Catfish anglers land hybrids incidentally while using chicken liver as bait. Some anglers therefore target hybrids with chicken liver. Another good way to catch hybrids is by trolling with crankbaits or stickbaits.

N.C. A-G grid: 36, A-4

General information: Salem Lake has a 300-foot fishing pier. Bank fishing is not allowed. Boats with engines greater than 50 horsepower must have the propellers removed prior to launching; they can be removed by personnel at the fishing station. Salem Lake operates on a schedule according to the time of year. It is open for the longest hours during summer. The full-service tackle shop offers canoe and johnboat rentals. Fees are charged for launching, docking, and fishing. The lake hosts pier- and boat-fishing tournaments for bass and catfish.

The lake will be closed for dam reconstruction in 2011 and is scheduled to reopen in 2012. See the appendix for contact information for Salem Lake Fishing Station and Winston-Salem Recreation and Parks.

Nearest camping: Camping is not allowed at Salem Lake.

Directions: To reach Salem Lake Boating Access from I-40 east of Winston Salem, take Exit 195 toward N.C. 109. Turn right on N.C. 109, drive 0.2 mile, and turn right on East Clemmonsville Road. Go 0.6 mile, turn right on Waughtown Street, and travel 1.3 miles to Salem Lake Road. Turn left and follow Salem Lake Road to the access, located at the end of the road.

Piedmont Region

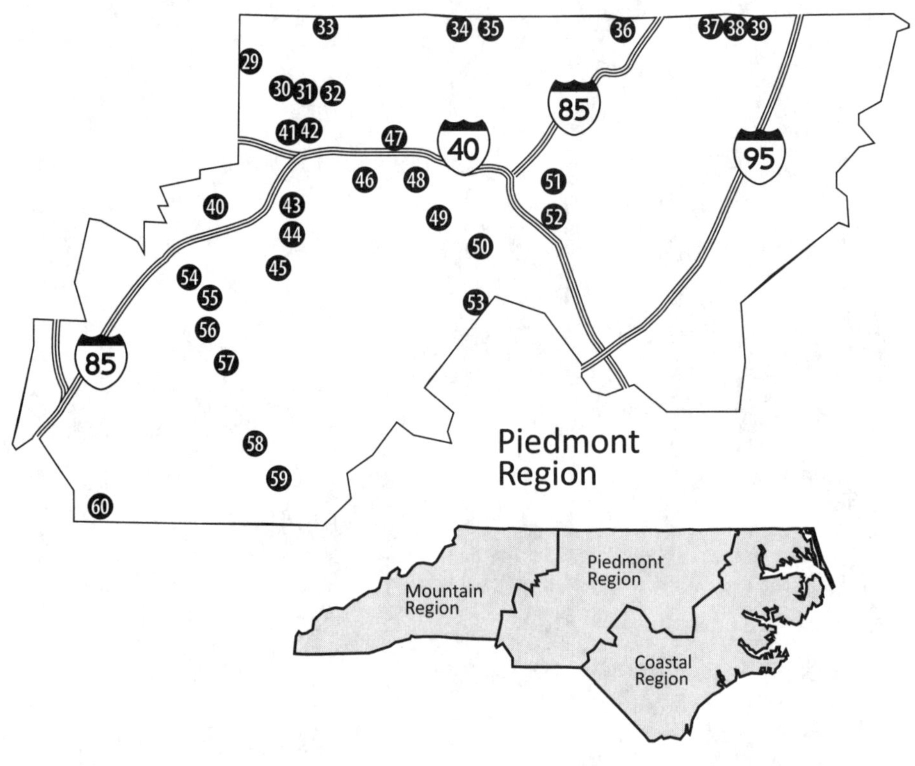

|| Previous page: Carol Marsh caught this largemouth bass from Randleman Regional Reservoir.

29 Belews Lake

Key species: Largemouth bass, crappie, blue catfish, channel catfish, sunfish

Overview: Completed in 1973, Belews Lake has a surface area of 3,863 acres and a shoreline of approximately 88 miles. The lake was created to provide cooling water for the Belews Creek steam station. Belews Lake is located in Rockingham, Stokes, and Forsyth counties.

Best way to fish: Boat

Best time to fish: March through October, though the hot-water discharge from the Belews Creek steam station keeps fish active during the winter months

Description: A rolled earthwork dam with a concrete spillway across Belews Creek impounds Belews Lake. Drawdown of the lake occurs only when necessary to maintain a minimum discharge flowing into the Dan River. The water surface elevation is 721 feet above sea level.

The fishing: Fly ash from the Belews Creek steam station led to selenium poisoning in Belews Lake. But fish have been returning to the lake since cleanup efforts began in the mid-1990s. The best opportunities for landing catfish occur upstream in the many creeks that are tributaries of Belews Lake. Catfish are also caught in Belews Creek downstream of the dam. Largemouth bass are present, but low fertility has led to low growth rates and low numbers. Most largemouth bass weigh from one to three pounds. The water is exceptionally clear, so most largemouth bass are caught from deep structure, primarily dead standing timber and stumps. Deep-fishing lures including weighted soft plastics and jigs are the best bets for bass. The "hot hole" produces bass and catfish year-round.

N.C. A-G grid: 17, C-5

General information: NCWRC fishing rules and regulations apply. A limited fish consumption advisory is in effect because of selenium poisoning. See the appendix for contact information for the NCDHHS regarding fish consumption advisories and for regulations pertaining to power company lakes.

Nearest camping: See the appendix for contact information for Carolina Camp-in and Marina and Humphrey's Ridge Family Campground. See the appendix entry for Duke Energy for maps of these campground locations.

Directions: To reach Piney Bluff Boating Access Area from U.S. 158 near Stokesdale, follow N.C. 65 West. The access area is on the left.

To reach Pine Hall Boating Access Area from N.C. 311 near Pine Hall, drive south on Pine Hall Road (S.R.1904) toward Belews Lake. The access area is on the left.

30 Lake Higgins

Key species: Largemouth bass, crappie, sunfish, catfish, chain pickerel

Overview: Lake Higgins is a water-supply reservoir for the city of Greensboro. It was built in 1956 and named after a former city councilman, Vic Higgins, who served from 1955 to 1957.

Best ways to fish: Boat, pier, kayak, canoe

Best time to fish: April through October

Description: Formed by an earthen dam, Lake Higgins covers 226 acres. It is part of a system of lakes north of Greensboro. The marina offers canoe and kayak rentals and has a scenic nature trail.

The fishing: Lake Higgins is stocked with catfish and other species, making it one of the best fishing lakes in the Greensboro area, despite its small size. Six-pound bass can be caught from the lake. Occasionally, a much larger fish is landed. Severe drawdowns can hurt the fishing temporarily. But the low water results in good fishing later because predatory fish eat stunted prey species at those times and also because nutrients are released when the water level returns to normal. Higgins is best known for its catfish and crappie fishing. Lots of big chain pickerel make the fishing unusual for a Piedmont lake. All three Greensboro city lakes (Higgins, Townsend, and Brandt) hold fishing tournaments. The nearby Taylor Turner Hatchery Pond is used to nurture catfish and trout.

N.C. A-G grid: 17, D-6

General information: Lake Higgins is open all year. Hours of operation vary according to the season. All NCWRC regulations apply. Rowboats, kayaks, and canoes are available for rent.

Nearest camping: Overnight camping is not permitted.

Directions: To reach Lake Higgins Marina from U.S. 220 (Battleground Avenue), turn west on Hamburg Mill Road (S.R. 2135) and travel 0.4 mile to the access, on the left.

31 Lake Brandt

Key species: Largemouth bass, white crappie, channel catfish, bream

Overview: Lake Brandt was built in 1925, then raised to its present level in 1958. It is named in honor of Leon Brandt, who served as mayor of Greensboro in 1907 and 1908. The lake is located on Lake Brandt Road two miles north of the city limits.

Best ways to fish: Kayak, canoe, boat

Best time to fish: April through October

Description: Lake Brandt is an 816-acre municipal reservoir.

The fishing: Lake Brandt offers some exceptional largemouth bass fishing for its size. It is one of the best bass-fishing lakes in the north-central Piedmont. Anglers can actually expect to catch bass weighing five pounds and have a chance to catch one weighing 10 pounds. The pristine shoreline attracts many local anglers, who fish from bass boats and johnboats. The best spots for fishing are the points and drop-offs. But during most years, the stable water level results in pad beds that offer shade for bass and cover for prey species. Spinnerbaits and crankbaits work well along the shoreline structure and points. Soft plastics and topwater lures are good choices for fishing the pad beds.

White crappie congregate along the shoreline structure and in the backs of the coves wherever they find brushy or woody cover. The best months to catch them are March and April. Most crappie anglers use minnows for bait. Bluegill sunfish are common. Small beetle grub spinners, worms, and crickets are the best bets for bluegills. This is a better lake than either Higgins or Townsend for catching crappie and bass.

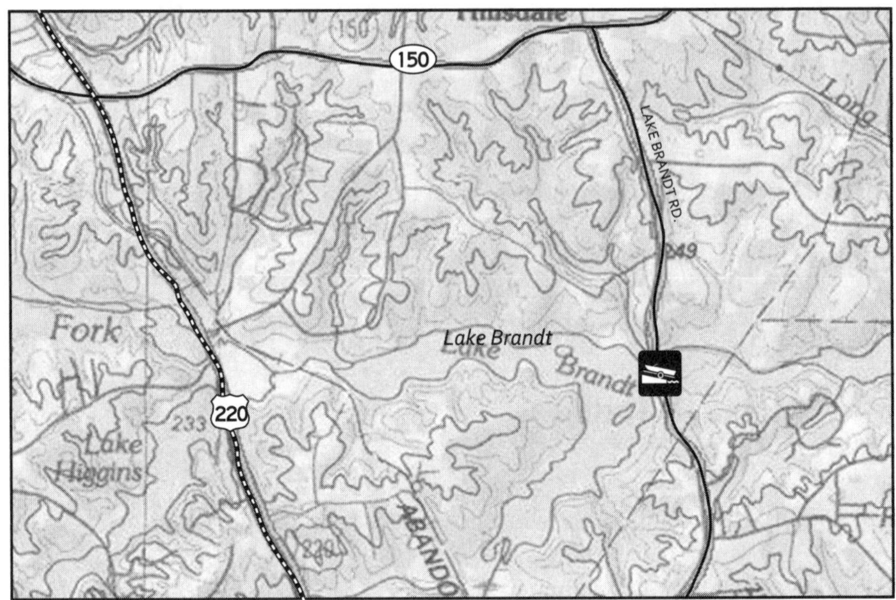

N.C. A-G grid: 17, D-7

General information: Lake Brandt is a municipal reservoir boasting amenities such as canoe and kayak rentals, hiking trails, and pier fishing. Shelters are available for rent for family or event gatherings. The park opens and closes at different times, depending on the month; it is closed on Tuesdays. All boats must be off the water within 15 minutes of the designated closing time. A fee is charged for launching private boats. The nearby Lake Brandt Greenway offers some remarkably scenic hiking. See the appendix for contact information for Lake Brandt Marina and to obtain fishing and boating access information.

Nearest camping: Camping is not allowed at Lake Brandt.

Directions: To reach Lake Brant Marina from N.C. 150 near Hillsdale, drive south for 2.3 miles on Lake Brandt Road. The marina is on the right.

32 Lake Townsend

Key species: Largemouth bass, hybrid bass, catfish, crappie

Overview: Lake Townsend offers boat and pier fishing, pleasure boating, and sailing. Rowboats, kayaks, and sailboats are available for rent. A large boat ramp for private boat launching and another ramp for small sailboats are offered.

Best ways to fish: Powerboat, canoe, kayak, pier

Best time to fish: April through October. The best bass fishing occurs in early May.

Description: Lake Townsend was named in honor of James R. Townsend, city manager of Greensboro from 1947 to 1961. Encompassing 1,542 surface acres, it is the largest of Greensboro's municipal reservoirs. The lake is adjacent to the Bryan Park Complex and Golf Course off U.S. 29 North. It was built and opened for recreation in 1969.

The fishing: Standing structure such as power line supports and bridge pilings are where anglers will find the best fishing. Deep-running crankbaits are the best bets for catching Lake Townsend's bass, which grow quite large. Bass of up to five pounds are not uncommon, and a 10-pounder is possible. This is the place to go if you don't want many bass but want the fish you do catch to be exceptionally large.

Although crappie are in the lake, the fishing for them is not good. For catching crappie, most anglers use minnows, but jigs also work. After white perch colonized the lake in the 1990s, the crappie fishing drastically declined. The perch overpopulated the lake and became stunted.

To catch channel catfish, most anglers use worms or liver as bait. Anglers

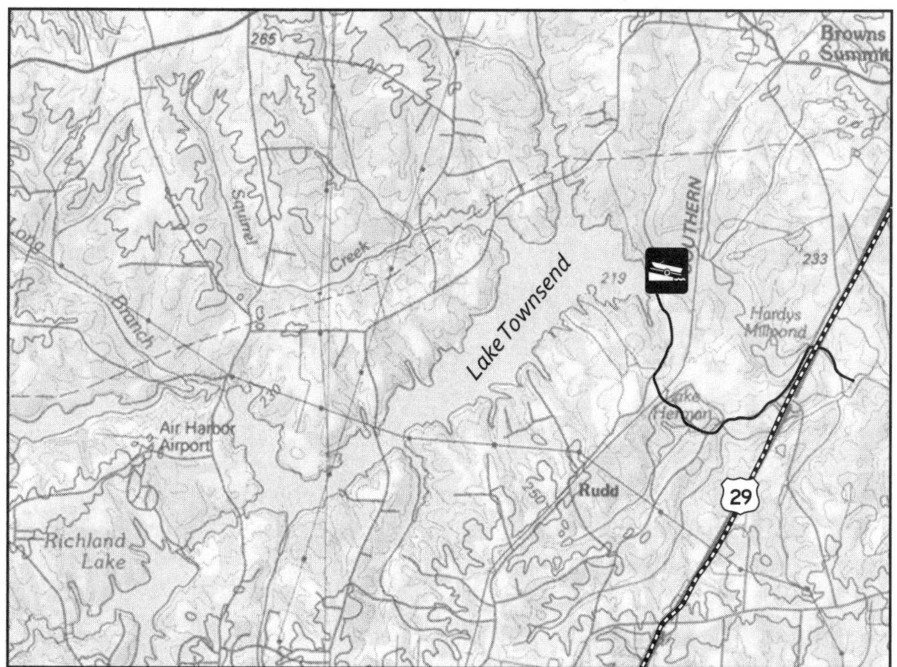

catch hybrid bass (Bodie bass) with live minnows and liver, often while fishing for other species such as catfish and panfish. At dawn and dusk during spring and fall, hybrid bass feed at the surface, where anglers can catch them with small poppers, spoons, and vibration lures. Trolling with spinners or small crankbaits is another method for catching hybrid bass.

N.C. A-G grid: 17, D-7

General information: The hours of operation for Lake Townsend vary throughout the year. The park is closed on Wednesdays. A fee is charged for launching private boats. Canoe and kayak rentals are offered. See the appendix for contact information for Lake Townsend Marina.

Nearest camping: Camping is not allowed at Lake Townsend.

Directions: To reach Lake Townsend Marina from U.S. 29, take the Summit Avenue exit. Turn left on Summit Avenue, travel 0.6 mile, turn right on Bryan Park Road, drive 0.6 mile, and turn right on Townsend Road.

33 Dan River

Key species: Largemouth bass, smallmouth bass, panfish, catfish, white bass, striped bass, some trout in the upper reaches

Overview: The Dan River begins in the Appalachian Mountains and meanders through North Carolina and Virginia. Ample fishing opportunities await anglers along the length of the river before it enters John H. Kerr Reservoir.

Best ways to fish: Shore, boat, kayak, canoe, wading

Best time to fish: The spring months

Description: The Dan River begins near Buffalo Knob in Patrick County, Virginia, and eventually flows to the Roanoke River in Halifax, Virginia. It was most likely named after the early Saura chief Danapaha.

The fishing: The upper reaches of the river provide trout-fishing opportunities, while the lower sections have excellent striped bass fishing during spring. A section of the Dan before it crosses the Virginia line into Stokes County is designated as hatchery-supported trout waters.

During spring, striped bass migrate upstream from John H. Kerr Reservoir to spawn. Anglers fishing with bucktail lures from the bank or from boats catch large numbers of big striped bass. Many bank-fishing opportunities are available in the state parks. Striped bass draw more anglers to the river than any other fish. The river is rocky in many stretches and can have steep gradients. Aluminum johnboats, canoes, and kayaks are popular.

Canoeing from Milton, North Carolina, to Danville, Virginia, yields some topnotch white bass fishing. Poppers, spinners, and small crankbaits work best for catching white bass.

The river has excellent fishing for catfish from the banks or from anchored boats. Live panfish, cut baits, live shad, minnows, shrimp, chicken liver, and worms make great catfish baits.

For smallmouth and largemouth bass, popping bugs fished with fly rods, topwater lures, spinnerbaits, stickbaits, and soft plastics work well. The Dan is among the best smallmouth rivers in North Carolina and Virginia.

N.C. A-G grid: 16, B-3

General information: A reciprocal licensing agreement exists between the NCWRC and the Virginia Department of Game and Inland Fisheries. The agreement covers the Dan River east of the Brantley steam plant dam, the Staunton River east of the U.S. 360 bridge, and Kerr and Gaston reservoirs and their tributaries accessible by boat. The U.S. 360 bridge is the first bridge crossing the Staunton River upstream of John H. Kerr Reservoir. The agreement also covers the portion of the New between the confluence of the river's North and South forks in Alleghany County, North Carolina, and the confluence of the New and Little rivers in Grayson County, Virginia. All NCWRC regulations apply.

For information on stream designations, size limits, bag limits, and open seasons for mountain trout fishing, consult the *North Carolina Inland Fishing, Hunting, and Trapping* and *North Carolina Trout Fishing Maps* booklets available from the NCWRC.

Nearest camping: Camping opportunities are available along the Dan. Hanging Rock State Park offers primitive camping near Danbury, North Carolina.

Directions: To reach Hanging Rock Access Area from Danbury, travel 2.75 miles northwest on N.C. 89, turn left on Flinchum Road (S.R. 1487), and drive 0.35 mile to the parking area and access.

To reach the NCWRC's Eden Boating Access Area from Eden, follow N.C. 87 South and turn left on Bethlehem Church Road (S.R. 2039). The access area is on the left.

34 Hyco Lake

Key species: Largemouth bass, white crappie, sunfish, bream, catfish

Overview: Hyco Lake is located in Person and Caswell counties in the north-central part of the state near Roxboro, North Carolina, and Danville, Virginia. The lake was constructed in the early 1960s by Carolina Power and Light, now Progress Energy, to supply cooling water to the Roxboro steam electric plant. An earthen dam near McGehee's Mill impounds the lake. The name Hyco is a shortened version of Hicotaminy, the Native American name for the area. Hyco is now the name of the lake, the dam, and the river leaving the lake.

Best way to fish: Boat

Best times to fish: Winter, spring, and fall. The winter fishing is exceptional for a Piedmont lake.

Description: Hyco Lake covers 3,750 acres and has 120 miles of shoreline. Constructed on the Hyco River, the lake has three main tributaries: North Hyco Creek, South Hyco Creek, and Cobbs Creek. The After Bay Reservoir stays warm during winter, making it a good fishing spot in the cold months. The After Bay is used to provide a guaranteed minimum flow for the river downstream, which is regulated by a spillway.

The fishing: The best fishing at Hyco Lake is for largemouth bass. Largemouth weighing more than five pounds are routinely caught. Anglers fish shoreline cover including docks, downed trees, points, and drop-offs. The water is deep and relatively clear. Soft plastic worms fished near the boat docks are the best bet. But crankbaits, spinnerbaits, and soft plastics are good bets, too. The topwater action is fair in spring and fall. The abundant crappie offer good fishing. Boat docks with brush beneath them and woody shoreline cover are the best bets for crappie. The bridge pilings in the After Bay are good structure for holding crappie in the winter months. The biggest problem in fishing Hyco and the After Bay is low summer water levels that can expose bars. The problem is amplified during drought conditions. During low-water periods, some steep, rocky areas still offer shoreline targets for bass casting.

In Hyco's upper half, where three creeks feed into the lake, fish growth and abundance are excellent. But downstream of the power plant toward the dam, the fishing is not as good. The lake gets very open and clear at the lower end, and

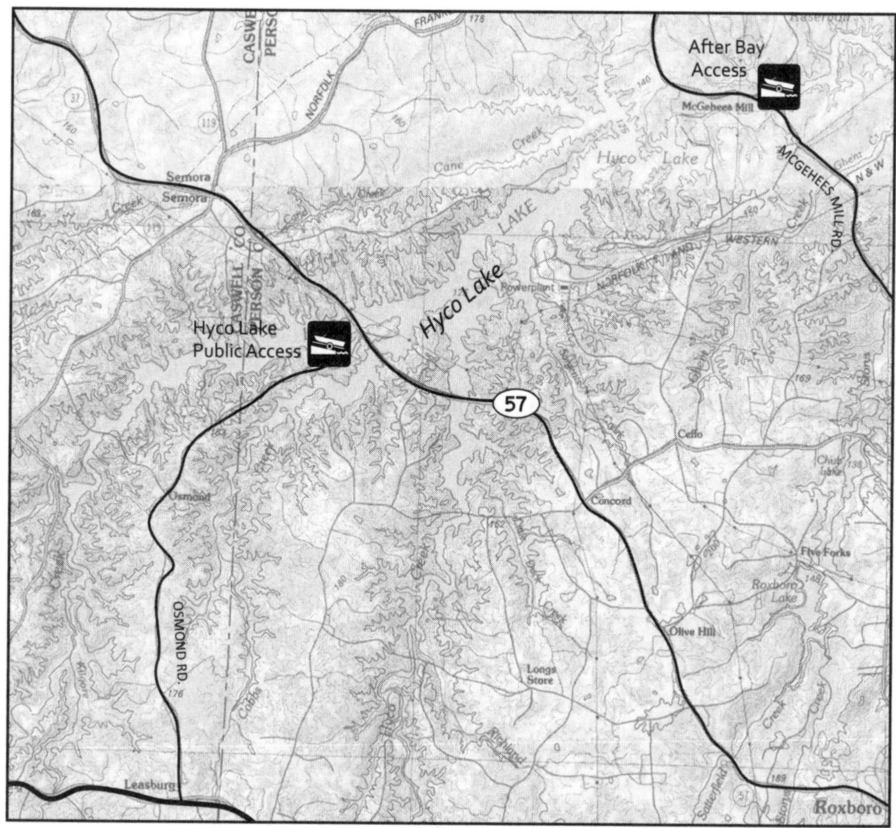

the bass grow thinner and become less abundant. All three creeks offer excellent fishing; the best success is found in South Hyco and Cobbs creeks. The crappie fishing is excellent; anglers will find plenty of keeper-sized crappie. Two species of tilapia—blue Nile and red belly tilapia—are in the lake. These exotic fish can be seen in the backs of the coves in spring, when they make very large spawning beds. Tilapia guard their young inside their mouths and are very dominant fish. They entered the lake when they escaped during a caged research project and survive because of the warm discharge from the power plant. The fish feed on aquatic vegetation and are therefore unlikely catches by hook-and-line anglers.

Night fishermen catch bullhead and channel cats from docks. Flathead catfish have also been documented in the lake.

N.C. A-G grid: 19, B-6

General information: The biggest draw for anglers is a water temperature that drops no lower then the mid-50s because of the discharge from power plant operations. A limited consumption advisory for Hyco Lake fish is in effect because of selenium. See the appendix for contact information for NCDHHS fish consumption advisories, NCWRC regulations, and the Person County Lake Authority.

Nearest camping: Cabins, campsites, and RV parking are available at Hyco Lake Public Access Area. See the appendix for contact information.

Directions: To reach Hyco Lake Public Access Area from Roxboro, travel west on U.S. 158 to Leasburg, turn right on Solomon Lea Road (S.R. 1561), and continue on Kelly Brewer Road (S.R. 1313) to the area access. No maintained boat ramp is available for access to the After Bay. However, the former asphalt roadbed enters the lake at both sides of the McGehee's Mill Road bridge. Johnboats and bass boats can be launched from the road ends; anglers should watch out for broken asphalt.

35 Mayo Reservoir

Key species: Largemouth bass, black crappie, chain pickerel, sunfish, catfish

Overview: Located in Person County, Mayo Reservoir was built by Carolina Power and Light, now Progress Energy, to provide cooling water for its Roxboro plant, which is the 10th-largest coal-fired plant in the United States. The lake was named for William Mayo, an English engineer who was largely responsible for surveying the nearby North Carolina–Virginia border.

Best ways to fish: Powerboat, kayak, canoe

Best times to fish: Spring and fall

Description: Mayo Reservoir covers approximately 2,613 acres and has about 85 miles of shoreline.

The fishing: The main reason to fish at Mayo is its beauty. Permanent docks are not allowed at the reservoir, so a principal habitat type that attracts crappie and largemouth bass at its sister lake, Hyco, is absent. Also, the lake level remains constant. While the lack of shoreline cover and of varying water levels may create pristine vistas, they also cause reduced fishing opportunities when compared to those at Hyco.

The most interesting fish in Mayo is the chain pickerel. The hydrilla beds are full of these toothy predators, which are not usually found in such large numbers

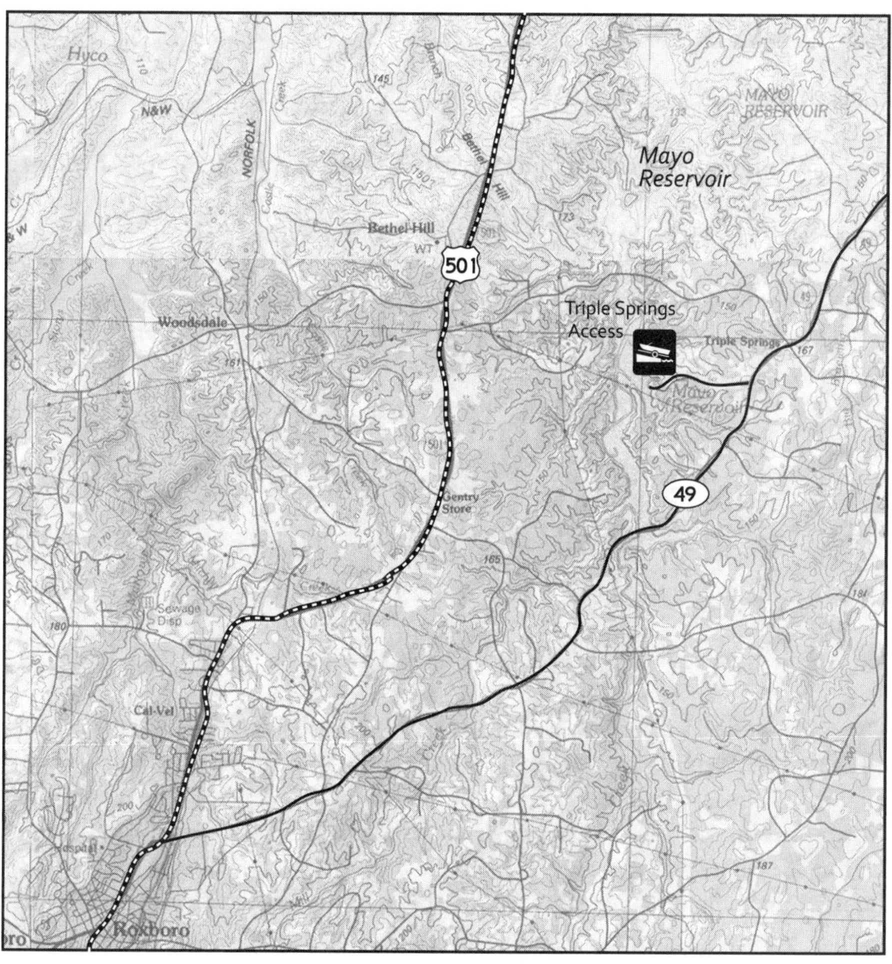

in Piedmont lakes. Bass and crappie also orient to the hydrilla beds. Thanks to the stable water level, pad beds are located in the backs of the coves. Chain pickerel, or jackfish, strike any lure intended for bass but will also strike minnows intended for crappie.

Some of the lake's largemouth bass reach impressive sizes. Growth rates for bass are above average for a Piedmont reservoir. But anglers don't catch many outsized bass. The lake doesn't have much nutrient inflow and is very clear. Therefore, using light-colored lures and light lines help bass anglers catch fish. They cast along the shoreline using soft plastics, crankbaits, and topwater lures. Some fallen trees in the water provide good bass cover. The former creek channels also offer good bass fishing, especially when the fish move to deep water in the summer.

Crappie anglers troll or drift along the edges using minnows and jigs for bait. The crappie fishing is average; it is best in the spring. Sunfish anglers use worms, crickets, and small spinners. Catfish anglers use worms and chicken liver.

N.C. A-G grid: 19, B-7

General information: All NCWRC regulations apply.

Nearest camping: Located on the eastern end of the lake, the 120-acre Mayo Lake Park offers rental cabins, campsites, and RV hookups. For more information, see the appendix entry for Person County Recreation, Arts, and Parks.

Directions: To reach Triple Springs Access Area from U.S. 501 at Roxboro, travel north on N.C. 49 for 9 miles, then turn left on Neals Store Road (S.R. 1515). Drive 1 mile to the access area.

36 John H. Kerr Reservoir (Buggs Island Lake)

Key species: Striped bass, largemouth bass, crappie, sunfish, catfish

Overview: John H. Kerr Reservoir, also called Buggs Island Lake, was constructed in the 1950s primarily to provide flood control and support hydropower generation. The reservoir has shoreline in Granville, Vance, and Warren counties in North Carolina and Mecklenburg, Charlotte, and Halifax counties in Virginia. During the early stages of construction, the project was called Buggs Island Lake. Located immediately downstream from the dam, Buggs Island was named after Samuel Bugg, an 18th-century pioneer. Congress changed the name of the project to John H. Kerr Dam and Reservoir in 1951. John H. Kerr was a congressman from North Carolina who was instrumental in the authorization of the construction.

Best way to fish: Boat

Best time to fish: Year-round

Description: The Corps of Engineers operates the 50,000-acre reservoir and oversees an additional 50,000 acres of surrounding land. John H. Kerr Dam is 332 feet above sea level. The reservoir is fed primarily by the Roanoke and Dan rivers and has over 800 miles of shoreline.

The fishing: Kerr Lake has excellent fishing for largemouth bass, striped bass, and black crappie.

For largemouth bass, any popular lure type will work at certain times. But the lake level can fluctuate substantially. When it is high, especially during the spring, anglers use deep-fishing methods. Good methods for high water include bumping deep-diving crankbaits off woody cover and submerged hills, tossing spinnerbaits into the flooded grass and other bank cover, including floating docks and boathouses, and jigging any stumps or timber with a rubber jig or jig-n-pork rind. Muddy water during flood conditions dictates the use of lures that make lots of noise and are brightly colored. Spinnerbaits with hammered blades, lipless vibration crankbaits, and soft plastics with rattle chambers work best for bass when the water is stained. During normal lake levels, the topwater action is excellent; buzzbaits, walk-the-dog lures, and propeller lures are the best bets. Schooling bass may appear at the surface. Anglers catch them with surface poppers and spoons. A soft plastic is a good bet at any time the water temperature is warm.

The lake's striped bass fishing is fabled. Most striper fishermen catch shad with cast nets for use as live striper bait. Live shad are drifted or trolled with sideplaners or on weightless lines, lead-core lines, weighted lines, or downriggers. The trick with live baits is spreading them in a wide pattern. They should be spread from side to side as well as up and down in the water column. An electronic depthfinder is an important piece of equipment for locating baitfish schools and striped bass feeding on them; once the proper presentation depth is found, the fishing depth of the live baits is adjusted accordingly. Stripers head upstream in the rivers that feed the lake during their spring spawning run. However, anglers who follow them must use caution when entering the river channel because the water has some dangerously shallow areas. When striped bass spread throughout the lake during the warm months, anglers locate them by trolling with deep-diving plugs along the channel edges and points. Once they locate a school, they can use a metal jigging spoon, a bucktail jig, or a jig with a plastic trailer. In cool weather, striped bass may chase shad to the surface. Some of the best topwater action occurs when a skim of ice covers the water. Sea gulls can tip anglers off to the locations of striper schools in winter.

Although crappie fishermen have good luck all year, the best fishing comes during late winter and early spring. In February and March, crappie stage before they spawn, congregating at the deepwater areas in the mouths of the coves. As warmer weather arrives and the fish begin to spawn by April, crappie move into the woody cover at the backs of the coves, to boat docks with brush beneath them, to fish attractors, and to other cover. Using an electric trolling rig to troll along the bank contours and creek channels while employing small jigs is a very effective technique. Casting live minnows on float rigs to visible cover and fish attractors is another good tactic. Throughout the summer, night fishermen use lights to attract crappie to bridge pilings and lighted docks, where they catch them using jigs and minnows.

The lake produces huge blue catfish and flathead catfish, which have overshadowed the smaller channel catfish. Cut and live shad are the best baits for blue

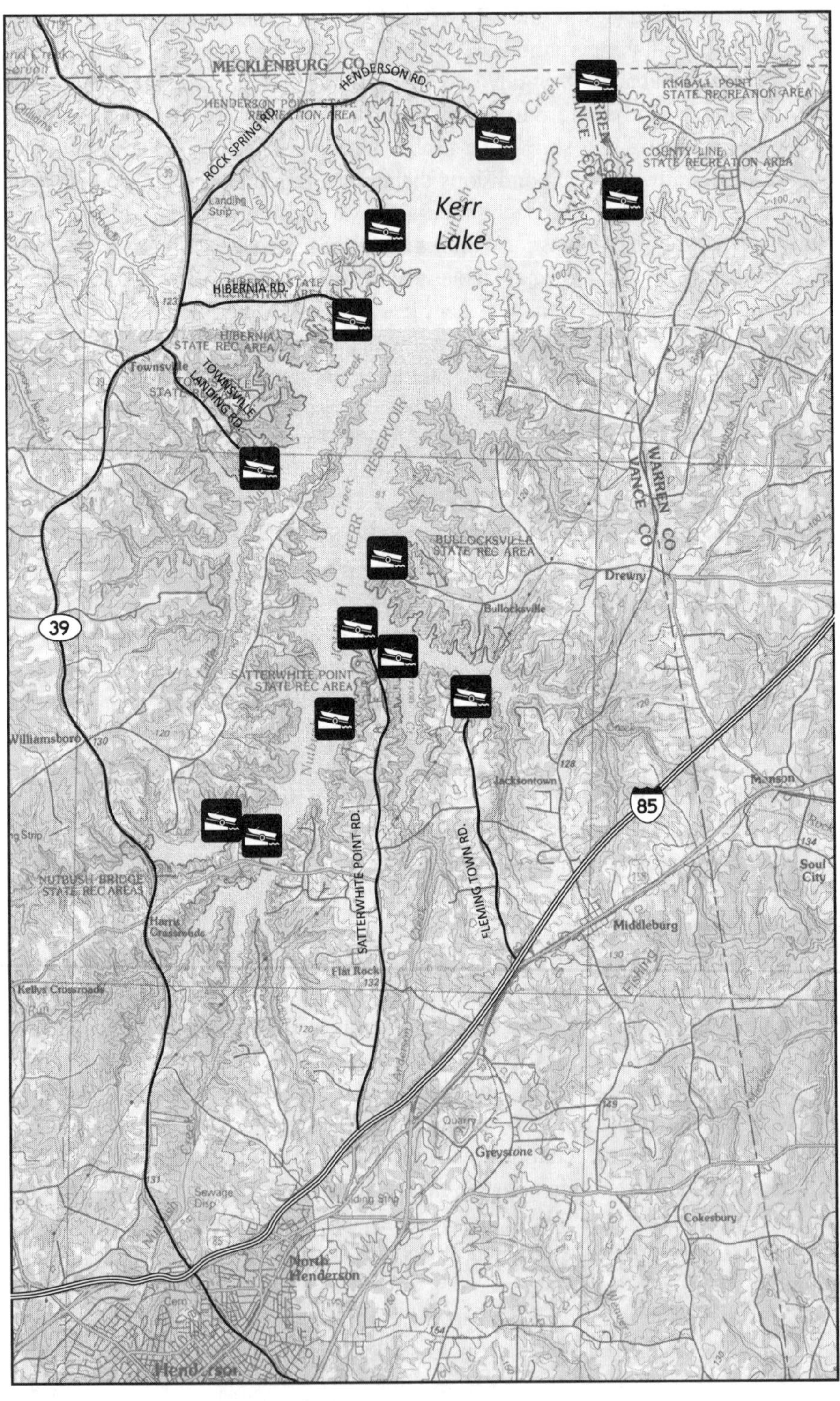
MECKLENBURG CO
HENDERSON RD.
HENDERSON POINT STATE RECREATION AREA
ROCK SPRING RD.
KIMBALL POINT STATE RECREATION AREA
COUNTY LINE STATE RECREATION AREA
Kerr Lake
Landing Strip
HIBERNIA RD.
HIBERNIA STATE REC AREA
Townsville
TOWNSVILLE LANDING RD.
KERR RESERVOIR
WARREN CO
VANCE CO
BULLOCKSVILLE STATE REC AREA
Drewry
Bullocksville
39
SATTERWHITE POINT STATE REC AREA
Williamsboro
Jacksontown
Manson
85
Soul City
NUTBUSH BRIDGE STATE REC AREAS
SATTERWHITE POINT RD.
FLEMING TOWN RD.
Middleburg
Harris Crossroads
Flat Rock
Kellys Crossroads
Quarry
Greystone
Sewage Disp
Cokesbury
North Henderson
Henderson

catfish. Live shad and sunfish are the best baits for flathead catfish. Channel cats aren't picky and will eat cut fish, minnows, shrimp, liver, and worms. Most fishing for cats is done at night. Catfish bite all year long. Flatheads tend to favor areas with lots of cover, while blue cats stick to the deep holes and channel bends of former watercourses. Anglers fishing from the shore or from boat docks at night catch channel cats. The main river channels entering the lake are great places to catch the large catfish species. Fishing the river channels from an anchored boat is a popular method. But drifting or trolling baits slowly along the bottom is also a good catfish tactic.

N.C. A-G grid: 21, B-5

General information: The entire John H. Kerr Reservoir can be fished by anyone possessing a North Carolina fishing license. For more information, consult the NCWRC regulations regarding reciprocal license agreements with Virginia.

Nearest camping: North Carolina's Satterwhite Point Park has facilities for camping and boat launching. The many camping locations around John H. Kerr Reservoir are operated by the Corps of Engineers and the North Carolina and Virginia state parks.

Directions: To reach Satterwhite Point Park Boat Access Area from I-85, take Exit 217 near the town of Henderson and follow Satterwhite Point Road (S.R. 1319) for 6 miles to the park.

To reach Hibernia State Recreation Area Boating Access from I-85, take Exit 214, follow N.C. 39 North for 13 miles to Hibernia Road (S.R. 1347), turn right, and travel 2 miles to the access area.

37 Lake Gaston

Key species: Striped bass, rock bass, largemouth bass, crappie, sunfish, blue catfish, channel catfish, walleye, white perch

Overview: Lake Gaston begins downstream of the dam at John H. Kerr Reservoir. In turn, Lake Gaston supplies water to Roanoke Rapids Lake, located immediately downstream. Lake Gaston is owned by Dominion Resources, and its water is used for producing hydroelectric power. Lake Gaston has shoreline in Halifax, Warren, and Northampton counties in North Carolina and Mecklenburg and Brunswick counties in Virginia.

Best way to fish: Boat

Best times to fish: Spring, summer, fall

Description: Virginia Electric and Power Company constructed Lake Gaston by damming the Roanoke River in 1963. The lake is about 35 miles long, covers more than 20,300 acres, and has 350 miles of shoreline. The carefully controlled water level fluctuates less than two feet annually.

The fishing: Lake Gaston has a good population of largemouth bass. In spring, the bass move to the backs of the coves and shoreline sand bars as they prepare to spawn. Once spawning begins, their beds are visible in the clear water. Jigs, buzzbaits, and soft plastics including worms, lizards, and crawfish entice bass to strike when they are in the shallows or on the beds. In summer, the bass move to deeper water, but soft plastic lizards, worms, and jigs are still good bets for fishing the lake edges. Cool water coming off the dam at Kerr Lake keeps the bass fairly active all summer, so topwater lures work well for catching them at dawn and dusk. Rocks, docks, underwater humps and stumps, and weed beds are the best bass-holding cover in summer and fall. Casting a floating worm or rubber frog to the pockets and edges is a good tactic when fishing the weed beds. Dropping a soft plastic worm or lizard into a pocket or letting it fall slowly with a lightweight sinker from the edge of a bed is another good tactic. The edges of the hydrilla beds can also be fished with crankbaits or spinnerbaits, but the resulting fouled hooks and spinners may become frustrating. Hydrilla, the main waterweed in Lake Gaston, is the subject of ongoing control measures including herbicide applications and grass carp introductions. It is both a curse and a blessing, since it makes navigation difficult but provides excellent cover for predators and baitfish in older lakes such as Gaston, where other cover is in short supply.

The striped bass fishing is good all year. The cold months are the best time to find them in tight schools. Trolling with deep- or shallow-running stickbaits while watching a depthfinder is the best way to locate stripers. Once a strike occurs, or when the depthfinder screen shows the location of a school of stripers, dropping a jig or spoon into them usually turns the trick. Live minnows or shad also work well for catching stripers. In fall and winter, fishing a topwater chugging lure at one of the island points is a good way to catch stripers.

Crappie and white perch feed on the same baitfish schools as stripers. Trolling with small spinners or crankbaits and jigging with spoons or small jigs are the top tactics for catching these schooling fish. In spring, crappie congregate along the shoreline cover, especially at boat docks, where anglers catch them by fishing with float rigs baited with live minnows. Casting a small beetle grub spinnerbait, inline spinner, or tube jig along the shoreline or near the hydrilla beds is another good way to catch crappie or sunfish.

Anglers catch blue catfish weighing more than 60 pounds from Lake Gaston. Live and cut shad and sunfish are the best baits. The best places to fish are the edges, ledges, and deep holes along the former river channel. The river channel runs as deep as 40 feet and has sheer drop-offs and submerged timber areas that hold big blue cats.

The walleye bite best in winter; January is usually the peak month for catching them. But they are also caught incidentally at any time of year by anglers fishing with live or dead baits on or near the bottom. They may also strike trolled stickbaits at any time of year. Walleye are present throughout the lake. However, anglers targeting them should fish the deep areas, including the river channel and the area upstream of Lake Gaston Dam. The cold temperature of the water entering Lake Gaston from the dam at John H. Kerr Reservoir also attracts schools of walleye at the upstream end of the lake. Walleye anglers spot the fish with depthfinders or locate them by trolling small, deep-diving crankbaits. Once a school of biting walleye is located, the best way to target them is by trolling a night crawler rigged on a worm harness with a forward spinner or a live minnow. Drifting a live minnow or night crawler on a single hook rig weighted with a split shot or on a jig head works well for walleye.

N.C. A-G grid: 22, A-1

General information: The reciprocal fishing agreement with Virginia covers the

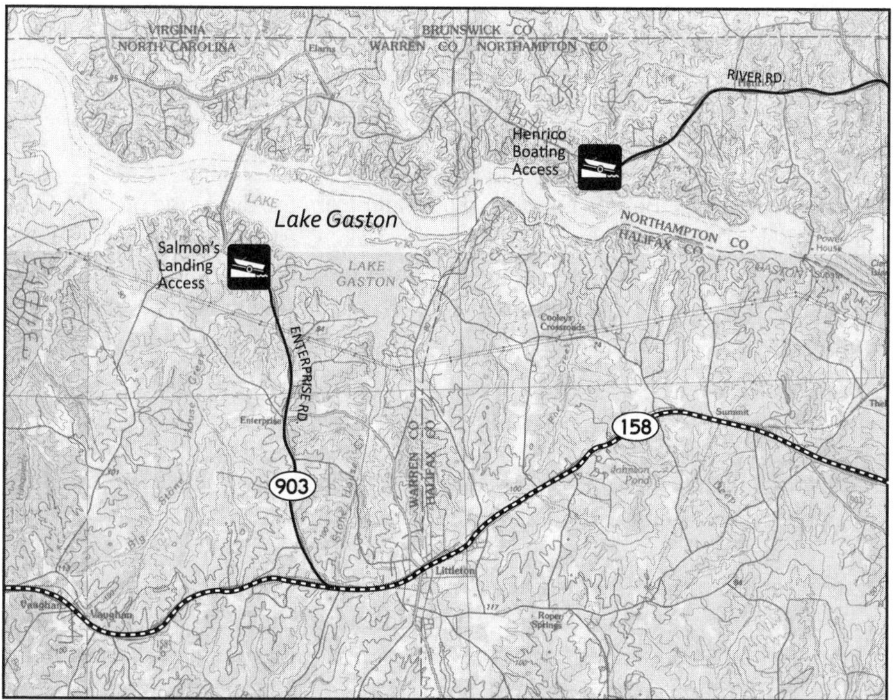

Dan River east of the dam at the Brantley steam plant, the Staunton River east of the U.S. 360 bridge, Kerr and Gaston reservoirs, and any of their tributaries that can be accessed by boat. The U.S. 360 bridge is the first bridge crossing the Staunton River upstream of John H. Kerr Reservoir. The agreement also covers the portion of the New River between the confluence of its North and South forks in North Carolina's Alleghany County and the confluence of the New River and the Little River in Virginia's Grayson County. The North Carolina Division of Health and Human Services has issued a fish consumption advisory because of elevated mercury levels. See the appendix for information about NCDHHS fish consumption advisories.

Nearest camping: See the appendix for contact information for Lake Gaston Campground and other privately owned campgrounds.

Directions: To reach Salmon's Landing Boating Access Area from U.S. 158, follow Enterprise Road (S.R. 1357) to the junction with Salmon's Landing Road (S.R. 1371). The access area is at the end of Salmon's Landing Road.

To reach Henrico Boating Access Area from Lake Gaston, travel north on N.C. 46 (Lawrenceville Road), turn left on River Road (S.R. 1214), and drive 5.5 miles. The access area is on the left.

38 Roanoke Rapids Lake

Key species: Striped bass, largemouth bass, crappie, sunfish, catfish

Overview: Roanoke Rapids Lake is fed by water from the discharge of Lake Gaston. Roanoke Rapids Lake was built prior to Lake Gaston and also has a stable water level. It receives less angler attention than Lake Gaston but has some good fishing opportunities. Roanoke Rapids Lake has shoreline in Halifax and Northampton counties in North Carolina.

Best way to fish: Boat

Best times to fish: The striped bass fishing is at its best in spring and summer. The largemouth bass fishing is good in spring, summer, and fall.

Description: Roanoke Rapids Lake is impounded by a concrete dam built on a rock foundation. The hydroelectric dam, constructed in 1955, has a maximum height of 172 feet above sea level. The lake is eight miles long, has a maximum width of 1.25 miles, and covers 4,600 acres. It has 47 miles of shoreline.

The fishing: Roanoke Rapids Lake has been stocked with various species of game fish and therefore offers ample fishing opportunities. It is a small lake with no shoreline development. Most anglers fish the larger Lake Gaston upstream or the Roanoke River downstream. The best place to catch largemouth bass is along the rocky shoreline and at the hydrilla beds. Anglers use topwater lures including floating worms, propeller lures, and buzzbaits. The water is very clear, and its level is stable. Anglers should be careful in the shallows because of the rocky bottom.

Striped bass strike live or cut shad fished in the deep water near the lake's dam. Topwater chugging lures will also entice them early and late in the day when cast to the rocky points.

The lake also has crappie and sunfish. Most anglers use minnows for crappie and worms or crickets for sunfish. The best places to fish are along the edges of the hydrilla beds and at any woody shoreline cover. Roanoke Rapids Lake is also a good place to catch shad for transporting to other lakes and the Roanoke River to use as striper bait.

N.C. A-G grid: 22, A-3

General information: The reciprocal fishing agreement with Virginia covers the Dan River east of the dam at the Brantley steam plant, the Staunton River east of the U.S. 360 bridge, and Kerr and Gaston reservoirs and any of their tributaries that are accessible by boat. The U.S. 360 bridge is the first bridge across the Staunton River upstream of John H. Kerr Reservoir. The agreement also covers the portion of the New River between the confluence of its North and South forks

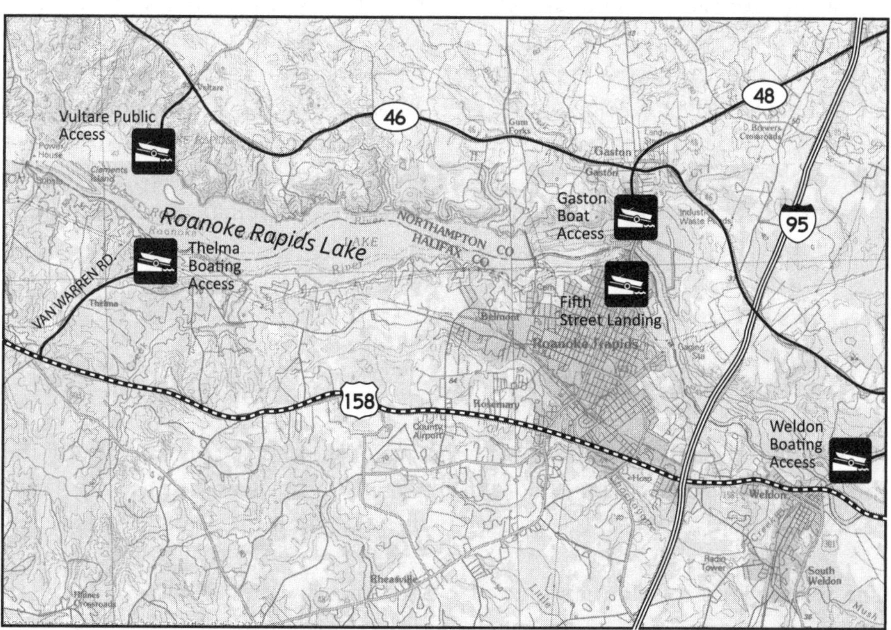

in North Carolina's Alleghany County and the confluence of the New River and the Little River in Virginia's Grayson County.

Nearest camping: Camping is available at several privately run campgrounds and at Medoc Mountain State Park; see the appendix for contact information.

Directions: To reach Fifth Street Landing Public Access Area in Roanoke Rapids from N.C. 48 (Gaston Road), travel west on Fifth Street. The access area is at the end of the road.

To reach Vultare Public Access Area from N.C. 46 West, turn right on Old Gaston Road (S.R. 1213). The access area is at the end of the road.

39 Roanoke River

Key species: Striped bass, largemouth bass, crappie, sunfish, channel catfish, walleye

Overview: The Roanoke River's headwaters begin in the foothills of the Appalachian Mountains. The river ends upon reaching Albemarle Sound. The Roanoke encompasses one of the largest watersheds in the eastern United States. The river was named for the Algonquian word for money. Between the cities of Roanoke and Clarksville, Virginia, the Roanoke is also known as the Staunton River. Before hydroelectric dams tamed the Roanoke, it flooded catastrophically and earned the nickname "River of Death." Now, its nickname is "Rockfish Capital of the World," thanks to the stretch downstream of the last dam at Roanoke Rapids Lake near Weldon. This chapter focuses on that section, where the river flows through and forms part of the borders of Northampton, Halifax, Bertie, and Martin counties.

Best ways to fish: Powerboat, jet-drive boat, kayak

Best times to fish: Spring and summer

Description: The Roanoke River is about 410 miles long. Downstream of the Roanoke Rapids Lake Dam, the river has many oxbows and turns as it flows southeast toward the coast. It is nutrient rich and supports many game fish species.

The fishing: After the river's flow was threatened by the removal of water to another river basin for municipal water supplies in Virginia, a restoration agreement in the 1980s guaranteed a minimum flow to the lower river during the spring spawning runs. Excessive commercial and recreational fishing had by then decimated the striped bass population. Many protection measures have since been put in place to ensure the incredible striped bass fishing that exists today. Anglers can catch and release more than 100 stripers per day during the spring runs. Striped bass are now subject to strict bag and size limits and a closed season. Lures and live-bait rigs with a single barbless hook must be used on certain stretches. Not only have stripers been restored, but the consistent flow may also have had a hand in restoring hickory shad runs.

Sadly, two of the formerly favored striper baits, blueback herring and alewife, collectively called "river herring," declined precipitously and can no longer be used as bait under herring moratorium restrictions. As replacement baits, some anglers use hatchery-raised rainbow trout, shiners, shad, and sunfish. Live redbreast sunfish caught by hook and line and shad caught from Lake Gaston and Roanoke Rapids Lake also make great striper baits.

Some Roanoke River striped bass weigh more than 50 pounds. Besides live minnows and trout, live sunfish, cut baits, jigs, flies, stickbaits, and crankbaits work well for catching stripers. But the large fish are typically caught on some sort of live bait. The run begins in March or April and continues into June.

The river is rocky. Navigation above the U.S. 158/U.S. 301 bridge at Weldon depends upon water flow. The many boulders in the river preclude travel upstream very far unless a jet-drive boat is used. Some anglers travel the river between the dam and the bridge in kayaks or inflatable boats. This may be the most beautiful stretch of the river. The oxbows and coves contain some fantastic fishing for sunfish and largemouth bass. Those with the means to fish this stretch are rewarded with uncrowded fishing, unlike downstream, where striped bass anglers fill the ramps and the river to overflowing. Anglers must be careful on any stretch of the river near Weldon because rocks and submerged stumps and bars are prevalent.

Anglers catch hickory shad by using ultralight tackle to cast small curly-tailed jigs, darts, and spoons. Although redbreast is the primary sunfish species, it is caught along with bluegill and other sunfish. Anglers use jigs, small spinners, worms, and crickets to catch sunfish.

Crappie are usually caught incidentally by sunfish anglers. But some anglers target them in the spring using jigs and minnows in the backwater areas and at deadfalls extending into the water.

The river produces some large catfish. Anglers catch them with live and cut baits, liver, and commercial stinkbaits and dip baits.

For largemouth bass, anglers use spinnerbaits, topwater lures, soft plastics, and jigs. The river offers some exceptional fishing for largemouth bass, but many anglers overlook it because of the striper fishing. Largemouth bass exceeding five pounds are not rare.

N.C. A-G grid: 22, B-4

General information: NCWRC fishing rules and regulations apply. Among the special regulations in effect for striped bass are closed fishing seasons that can change annually. The North Carolina Department of Health and Human Services has issued a limited consumption advisory for carp and catfish in the Roanoke River downstream of Williamston due to dioxins. See the appendix for contact information for NCDHHS fish consumption advisories.

Nearest camping: A few privately run campgrounds are located near the Roanoke River.

Directions: To reach Weldon Boating Access Area from the intersection of U.S. 301 and U.S. 158 near Weldon, travel north on the combined U.S. 301/U.S. 158. The access area is located at the south end of the U.S. 301 bridge.

To reach Gaston Boating Access Area from the town of Gaston, travel south on N.C. 48. The access area is at the north end of the N.C. 48 bridge.

40 Lake Thom-A-Lex

Key species: Largemouth bass, crappie, sunfish, catfish, hybrid bass

Overview: Lake Thom-A-Lex (or Tom-a-Lex), a water supply reservoir for the municipalities of Thomasville and Lexington, was formed by impounding Abbotts Creek. The lake's amenities are operated by the Davidson County Recreation and Parks Department.

Best ways to fish: Canoe, kayak, bank, pier

Best time to fish: March through October

Description: Lake Thom-A-Lex was completed in 1957. The earthen dam is 635 feet in length. The lake drains an area of approximately 73 square miles and has a surface area of nearly 1,100 acres.

The fishing: Lake Thom-A-Lex is a great fishing destination, since most of the larger lakes in the region get very crowded. Although it can become fairly busy on weekends, it is small enough to escape notice and can be fished in relative quiet. No water scooters, water-skiers, or pleasure boats are allowed. The main attractions are crappie, bass, catfish, and hybrid bass.

This is an exceptionally angler-friendly lake for many reasons, including its three fishing piers and the generous availability of bank-fishing opportunities. The lake fluctuates less than two feet annually.

The best bass fishing is early and late in the day. The fishing is best in the spring, before water temperatures rise. The shoreline has some woody cover to attract bass, and the piers provide shady cover. Soft plastics, spinnerbaits, and topwater lures are the best bets for bass. Catching a bass weighing five pounds is possible. In summer, when the bass head deeper during the day, weighted soft plastics and crankbaits are the top lures.

Crappie are very abundant. Anglers catch them from the fishing piers, from the artificial fish attractors, which are marked with buoys, and at the aerators used to control algae. Most crappie anglers fish with live minnows.

Sunfish anglers have excellent luck. Fishing with worms from the bank and the piers is the best way to catch sunfish.

Catfish anglers use worms and liver for bait. Catfish attain weights of up to 15

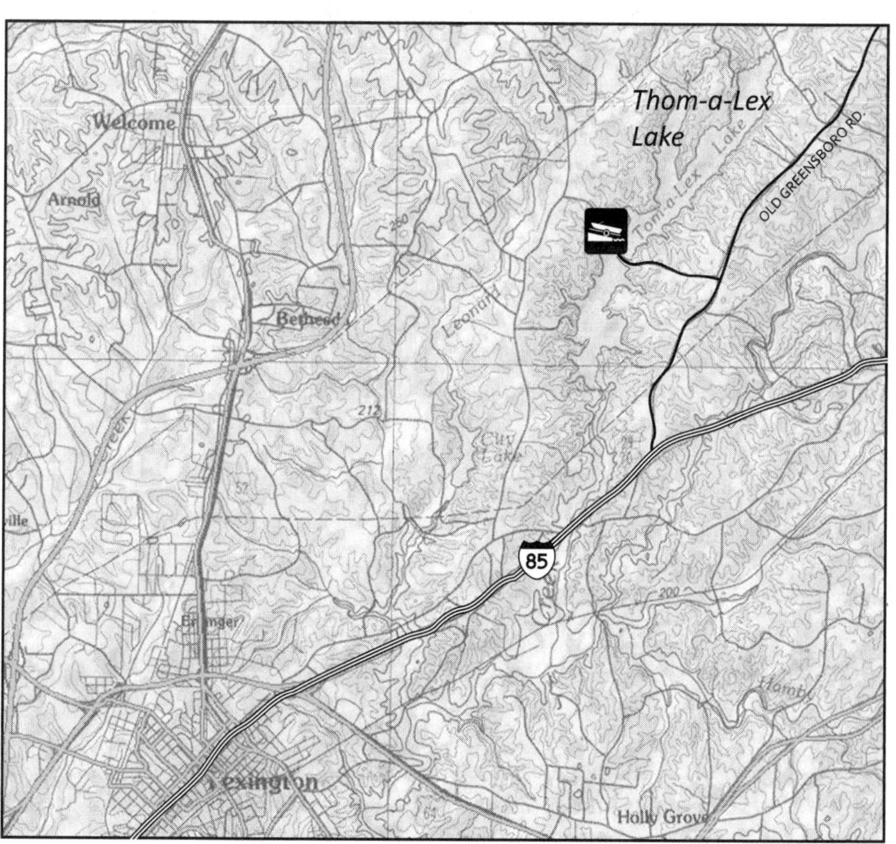

pounds. Blue, flathead, and channel catfish are present in the lake.

The hybrid bass fishing is good. The cold months are the best time to catch the fish. Hybrid anglers troll or cast crankbaits and stickbaits. Live minnows and liver also work well.

N.C. A-G grid: 36, B-4

General information: NCWRC rules apply. The lake has specific hours of operation; longer hours are in effect during the summer months. Fees are charged for launching boats, for fishing, and for reserving picnic shelters. The on-site tackle shop hosts a couple of catfish tournaments each year. See the appendix for contact information for Lake Thom-A-Lex Park.

Nearest camping: Camping is not allowed at Lake Thom-A-Lex.

Directions: To reach the boat access at Lake Thom-A-Lex Park from Lexington, drive north on I-85 Business/U.S. 70/U.S. 29 for approximately 5 miles. Turn right on Old Greensboro Road (S.R. 1798), travel 2.1 miles, and turn left at Yokley Road (S.R. 1819). The access is at the west end of the bridge.

41 Oak Hollow Lake

Key species: Largemouth bass, hybrid bass, striped bass, white perch, crappie, sunfish, catfish

Overview: Oak Hollow Marina opened to the public in 1972. Oak Hollow Park consists of a 1,500-acre park and an 800-acre lake. The lake is located in Guilford County.

Best ways to fish: Powerboat, kayak, canoe

Best time to fish: April through October

Description: Oak Hollow Lake is a reservoir for the city of High Point. Its level is very stable for a water-supply lake.

The fishing: The lake's largemouth bass fishing is good. Anglers catch bass weighing five to seven pounds and occasionally nine pounds or more. The lake doesn't have much structure. Therefore, the best places to fish are the U.S. 311, Centennial Avenue, and Johnson Street bridges, which attract all major game fish species.

Fallen trees extending into the water along the banks are magnets for largemouth bass and crappie. Other structure including Christmas tree attractors and plastic barrel attractors is man-made. Crappie congregate around the fish attractors in the spring. While crappie are present in good numbers, most are stunted. Still, the lake has produced two-pound crappie.

The hybrid bass at Oak Hollow Lake offer some exciting fishing. Many of them grow as large as eight to 10 pounds. Striped bass stockings began once biologists determined the lake could support them along with the hybrids. Anglers catch stripers in the 10-pound range, with an occasional fish topping 20 pounds. The best way to catch striped bass and hybrids is drifting or trolling using live shad baits.

White perch are present in large numbers and readily strike jigs, spinners, and spoons. But the white perch are also stunted. Bluegill sunfish are also abundant but small.

Catfish anglers have little trouble catching the lake's blue and channel catfish, which routinely grow to 10 pounds. Occasionally, the lake gives up a blue catfish

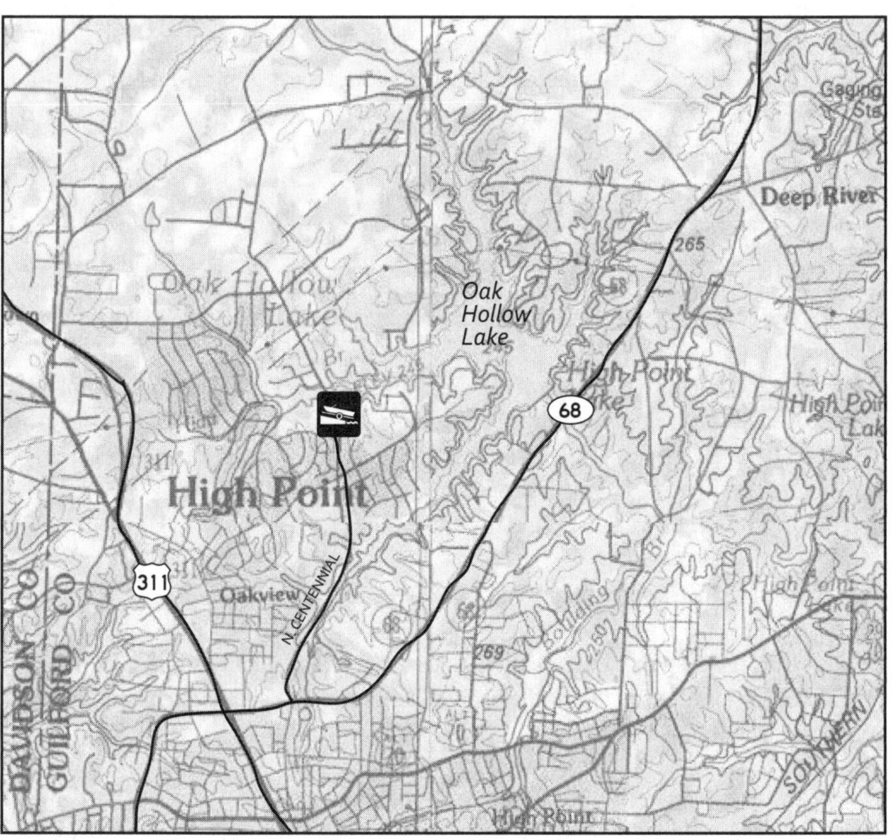

approaching 30 pounds. The best catfish baits are live shad, live bluegill sunfish, chicken liver, and shrimp.

N.C. A-G grid: 37, B-6

General information: NCWRC rules and regulations apply. Bank fishing is allowed adjacent to the large parking area; approximately 300 yards of shoreline is available. The marina has four ramps; see the appendix for contact information for hours of operation. The maximum length allowed is 23 feet for motorboats and 24 feet for pontoon boats. The speed limit is 35 miles per hour. Inflatable boats and water scooters are not allowed. Only Sunfish sailboats are available as rentals. Some night fishing is allowed.

Nearest camping: Oak Hollow Park has campsites for RVs and tents. The campground offers full facilities including shelters and bathhouses. Campsites are offered on a first-come, first-served basis. A fee is charged. See the appendix entry for the High Point Department of Parks and Recreation for contact information.

Directions: To reach Oak Hollow Marina from U.S. 311, take Exit 24, turn left on Johnson Street (S.R. 1818), then turn left on Oakview Road. Continue for 0.5 mile and turn left on North Centennial Street. The access is at the end of the road.

42 High Point Lake

Key species: Largemouth bass, hybrid bass, crappie, sunfish, catfish, carp, bowfin

Overview: Located at Jamestown, High Point Lake, also called High Point City Lake, covers 340 acres in Guilford County. It was formed in 1935 by a dam across the Deep River. It serves as a water-supply reservoir for the city of High Point.

Best ways to fish: Powerboat, kayak, canoe

Best time to fish: April through October

Description: High Point Lake is the site of a park that includes playgrounds and two of the largest swimming pools in the Southeast. It also has an excursion boat and picnic shelters.

The fishing: The lake can become very crowded on weekends. The best opportunity for anglers is fishing from the bank for catfish and sunfish. The bluegill sunfish are extremely aggressive, and the lake is stocked with channel catfish, many weighing between five and 10 pounds.

The lake has fish feeders that attract catfish and sunfish. An aerator system extending from the dam to the two bridges keeps the lake free of algae; the aerators also serve as fish-holding structure. Bank fishing is allowed from a peninsula near the feeders.

The bass fishing is good throughout the warm months. The East Fork and Penny Bend Road bridges attract many fish species, including bass, crappie, sunfish, and catfish. Anglers catch bass early and late in the day by casting soft plastics and topwater lures near the bridges and aerators and along the shoreline. The lake does not have a reputation for producing large crappie. As with many other small lakes, crappie overabundance has led to stunted fish.

N.C. A-G grid: 37, B-6

General information: NCWRC regulations apply. A 10-horsepower restriction applies to powerboats, but anglers can tilt up larger outboards and use electric trolling motors. The park participates in the NCWRC's Tackle Loaner Program, which allows checking out tackle and returning it. Johnboats with motors are available for rent. Fishing is not allowed from rented canoes. The on-site tackle shop sells live baits, including worms and minnows. The park opens at 7 A.M. and closes at varying times, depending on the season. Fees are charged for fishing and launching boats. For contact information for hours of operation, see the appendix entries for the High Point Department of Parks and Recreation and High Point Lake.

Nearest camping: Camping is not allowed at High Point Lake.

Directions: To reach the lake from U.S. 70/U.S. 29 near Jamestown, drive west on West Main Street. The park is on the right.

43 Randleman Regional Reservoir

Key species: Largemouth bass, sunfish, catfish, crappie

Overview: Randleman Regional Reservoir is located on the Deep River in Randolph and Guilford counties in central North Carolina. The lake and dam are named after the town of Randleman, located nearby. Proposed in 1937 by the Corps of Engineers, the lake's construction was postponed because the cost outweighed the potential flood-control benefits. Construction finally started in 2001, and the lake was filled with water beginning in 2007. The Piedmont Triangle Regional Water Authority (PTRWA) administers the lake and its activities.

Best ways to fish: Powerboat, pier, kayak, canoe

Best times to fish: Spring and fall

Description: Randleman Regional Reservoir is located within a 200-foot buffer. The total area of the project including the buffer and dam area is 5,982 acres. The reservoir covers 3,007 acres at its full-pond elevation of 682 feet. The lake opened for fishing in March 2010.

The fishing: The reservoir has been stocked with largemouth bass and channel catfish. Crappie, sunfish, and bullhead catfish were present in the headwaters and ponds that were inundated and therefore have populated the lake. Time will tell if Randleman becomes a good crappie fishing lake, but a few anglers have experienced excellent luck catching crappie during its initial years. The bridges are the best places for crappie. The bass fishing is excellent. Anglers land good numbers of largemouth bass weighing up to eight pounds; catches of four- to five-pounders are very common. The bass fishing should get even better through the years as the bass grow larger. In spring, spinnerbaits and shallow-running stickbaits fished along the shallow shorelines and lipless, fast-vibration crankbaits cast to the points are good choices. The lake has lots of areas with flooded trees and rock outcrops. Some of the shallow, hazardous areas have been marked with buoys. Topwater walk-the-dog lures, buzzbaits, and propeller lures work well through spring; early and late in the day are the best times to fish them along the shoreline. Soft plastics work well for bass at any time. Fishing soft plastics in the deep creek channels, in submerged structure areas such as former roadbeds, and at the U.S. 220 bridge is the best bet for catching summer bass. The park's piers are good places to catch channel catfish and sunfish. The zone where powerboats are not allowed between Groometown Road and N.C. 62 is shallow and filled with flooded underbrush. It is an excellent fishing location that receives lighter pressure than the area where powerboats are allowed.

N.C. A-G grid: 37, C-7

General information: All NCWRC regulations apply. Randleman Regional Reservoir is open Wednesday to Sunday from March 1 through November 30. Boats must be off the water 30 minutes before closing. Hours of operation vary according to the season. All boaters must check out. The launch fee is relatively expensive. Only boats with electric engines, paddleboats, kayaks, canoes, and rowboats are allowed north of the N.C. 62 bridge. South of the bridge, powerboats are allowed; the maximum speed permitted is 25 miles per hour. All boats must register before being launched. Launching is allowed only at designated areas at the two parks. A limit of 100 powerboats is in force in the 2,500-acre area below the N.C. 62 bridge. Some boats may have to wait in line for others to leave the lake during peak fishing months in the spring. All boats must carry a sealed container for sanitary waste and may not touch the shore at any time. Bank fishing is not allowed. Rental canoes, kayaks, and johnboats with trolling motors are available at Southwest Park. Live bait is available at the park offices. Both parks participate in the NCWRC's Tackle Loaner Program.

Nearest camping: Camping is not allowed. Picnic tables and restrooms are available at both parks. Southwest Park has many additional amenities including recreational areas, playgrounds, hiking trails, and scenic overlooks.

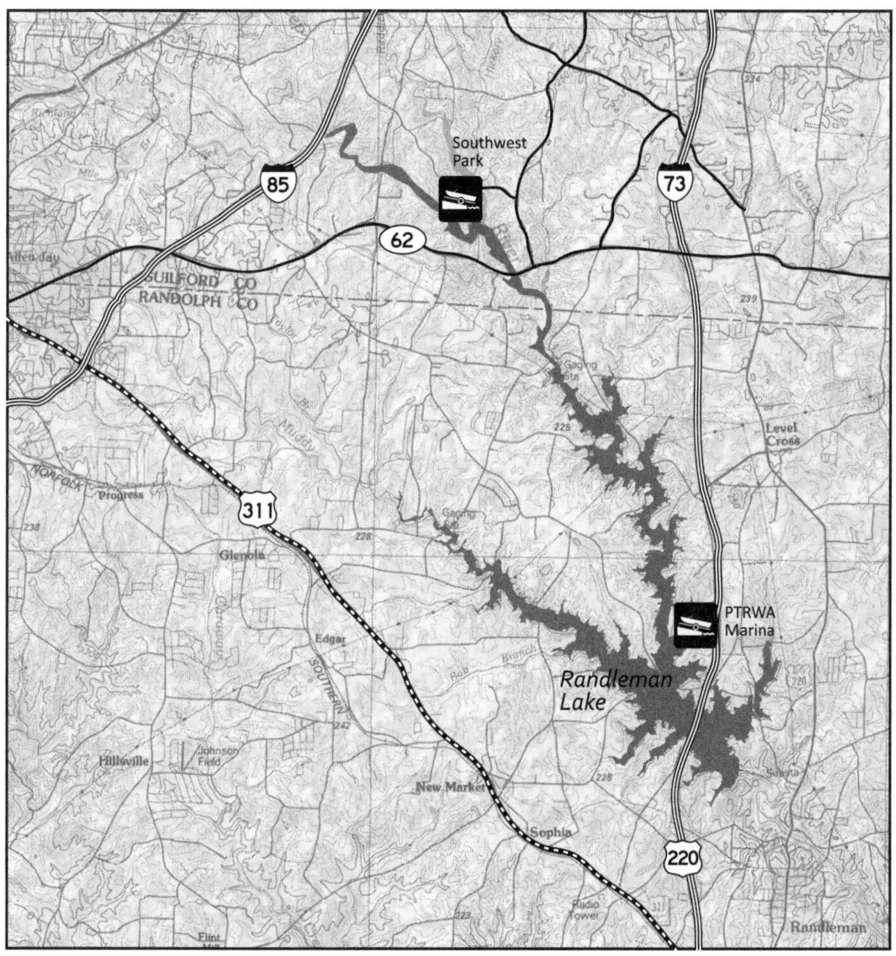

Directions: To reach the PTRWA Marina from U.S. 311 in Randleman, travel north on U.S. 220 for approximately 3.5 miles. After crossing the lake, take the Level Cross exit and turn left on Branson Mill Road. Travel to the stop sign, turn left on Adams Farm Road, drive approximately 1 mile, and turn left at the park entrance.

To reach Guilford County Southwest Park from I-73, take the N.C. 62 exit, turn west, travel 1.8 miles, and turn right on Drake Road. Drive to the stop sign, turn left on Wall Road, go 1.2 miles, and turn left on Southwest Park Drive. The park office and marina are at the end of Southwest Park Drive.

44 Lake Lucas (Back Creek Lake)

Key species: Largemouth bass, crappie, sunfish, catfish

Overview: Lake Lucas is a recreational and water-supply lake operated by the city of Asheboro. Built in 1947, it is called Back Creek Lake on some older maps. A few large, beautiful homes overlook the lake, but no private boat docks are allowed.

Best ways to fish: Johnboat, kayak, canoe, bank, pier

Best time to fish: March through November

Description: Lake Lucas was built by the city of Asheboro to supply drinking water. The simple concrete gravity dam has a length of 375 feet. The lake's surface area is 238 acres.

The fishing: Local anglers are tight-lipped about the lakes at Asheboro. While a significant user fee and a horsepower restriction keep many anglers from visiting Lake Lucas, those who pay the fee and heed the rules will find this lake great for catching panfish, crappie, and largemouth bass.

This is one of the top bass lakes in the state in terms of fish size and abundance. It has produced at least one bass of 12 pounds. The best bass lures are soft plastics fished on Carolina rigs, spinnerbaits, and crankbaits. Live minnows are the top producers in the hot months. The lake boasts picturesque views of the Uwharrie Mountains and is surrounded by trees. Springs feed it, so the water level doesn't fluctuate much. The banks are rocky and steep. Some fallen trees create the best shoreline cover. Water willow in the upper end adds some live structure for bass and crappie in the spring. The Lake Lucas Road bridge across the lake attracts lots of crappie and catfish.

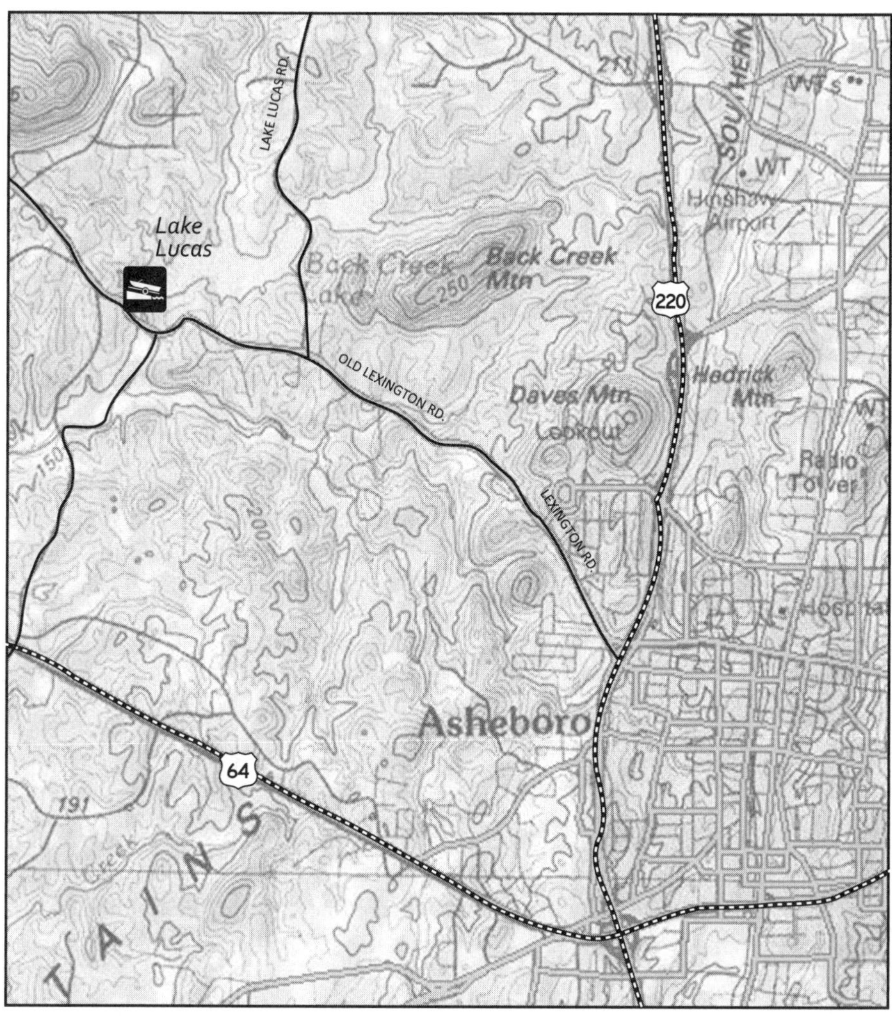

The crappie population is very cyclic. Crappie fishing is best from late February through May. The fishing can be poor for a few years, followed by excellent fishing for a couple of years. Crappie experience a good spawn every five years or so. The state-record black crappie was caught from Lake Lucas. Most anglers use minnows as bait for catching crappie. Inline spinners also work well for casting to the shoreline cover.

A big log cabin serves as the marina. Anglers can fish from the bank and pier at the marina's park, which is located at the dam. Some big channel cats of 10 pounds and up have been caught from the lake. The lake also has bullhead catfish. However, bank fishing is very limited. Live minnows and worms are available at the park's office and tackle shop.

N.C. A-G grid: 37, D-7

General information: All NCWRC regulations apply. Fees are charged for boat launching and fishing. A motor restriction of 15 horsepower and a speed limit are in effect. The marina offers rental canoes and johnboats and also rents slips for privately owned boats. For more information, see the appendix listing for Asheboro Parks and Recreation. The hours of operation are 7 A.M. until sunset. The lake is closed Wednesdays from March 1 through November 15 and Wednesdays and Thursdays from November 16 through February.

Nearest camping: Camping is not allowed at Lake Lucas. A playground and a park with picnic facilities are available.

Directions: To reach Lake Lucas Marina from U.S. 220 in Asheboro, travel west on N.C. 42 for 1 mile, take a slight right onto Lexington Road (S.R. 1004), drive 0.9 mile, and continue for 2.7 miles on Old Lexington Road (S.R. 1004). Lake Lucas is on the right.

45 Lake Reese

Key species: Largemouth bass, crappie, panfish

Overview: Owned by the city of Asheboro, Lake Reese is situated on the Uwharrie River east of town. The lake was named after Robert L. Reese, the longest-serving mayor of Asheboro.

Best ways to fish: Johnboat, kayak, canoe, bank

Best time to fish: March through November

Description: Lake Reese is a 900-acre reservoir built by the city of Asheboro and operated by Asheboro Parks and Recreation. It serves as a municipal reservoir for the city. Completed in 1983, Lake Reese Dam is 135 feet long.

The fishing: Although its shoreline is undeveloped, Lake Reese has a generous amount of underwater structure to fish. Trees that have toppled into the water create the best structure. Rocky submerged islands are the best underwater cover. Some of the islands represent hazards to boating and are marked, making them easy to find and fish. Local anglers routinely pull some very nice crappie from the

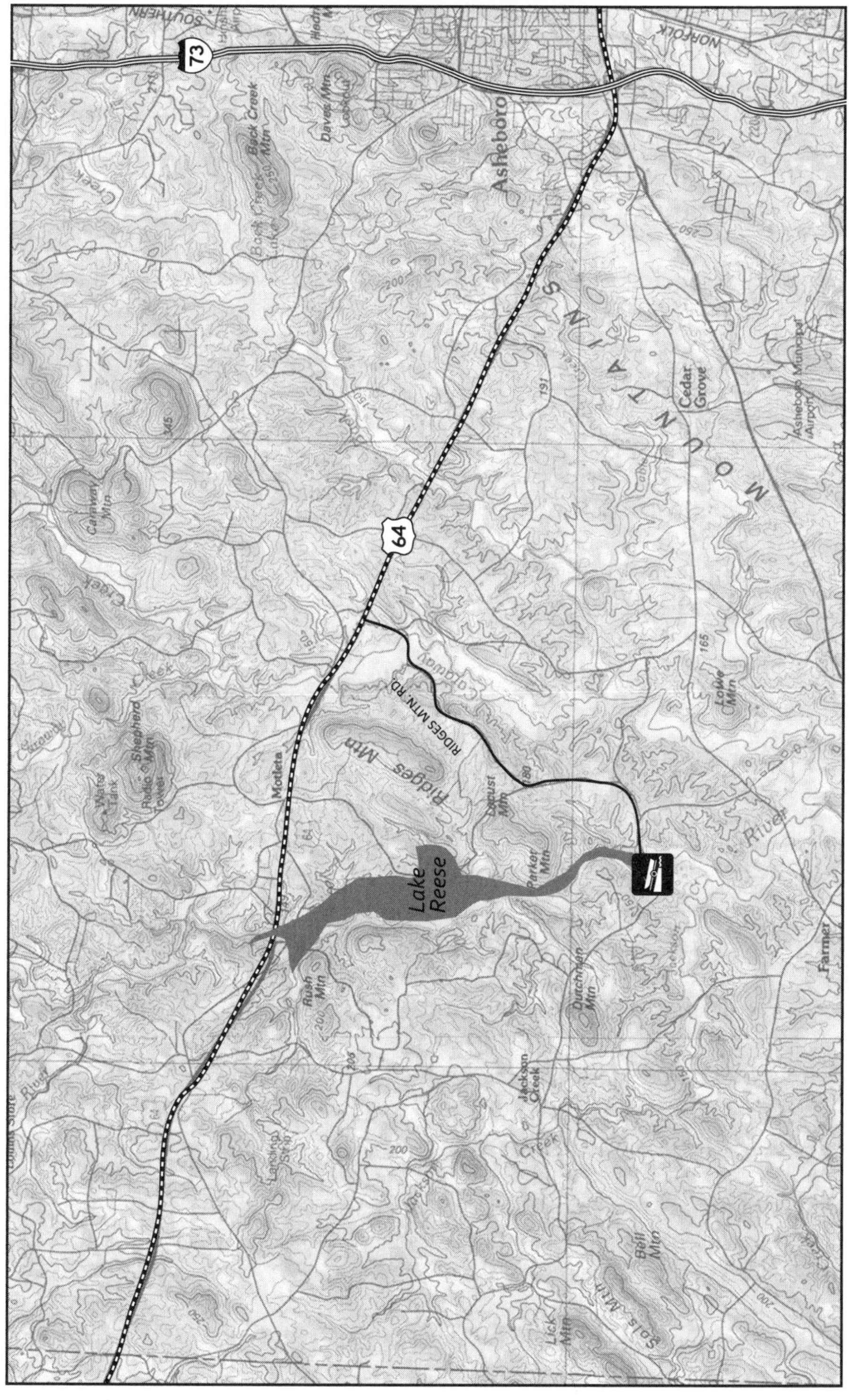
73
64
Asheboro
Lake Reese
RIDGES MTN. RD.
Ridges Mtn
Cedar Grove
Back Creek Mtn
Shepherd Mtn
Parker Mtn
Locust Mtn
Dutchman Mtn
Rush Mtn
Bell Mtn
Lick Mtn
Sols Mtn
Jackson Creek
River
Farmer
NORFOLK
SOUTHERN

lake. Its water is more turbid than that of Lake Lucas, so dark lure colors work best. The bass fishing is very good; anglers catch lots of bass weighing four to five pounds. The crappie fishing is average. Channel catfish weighing five to six pounds are typical catches. Some decent-sized white perch are in the lake, including an abundance of 10-inchers.

N.C. A-G grid: 37, D6

General information: All NCWRC regulations apply. A speed limit of 25 miles per hour is in effect at Lake Reese. See the appendix for contact information for Asheboro Parks and Recreation.

Nearest camping: Camping is not allowed at Lake Reese.

Directions: To reach Lake Reese from U.S. 220 in Asheboro, travel west on U.S. 64 for 6.7 miles, take a left on Moore Road (S.R. 1318), turn right on Ridges Mountain Road (S.R. 1331), and continue for 2.2 miles. Take a left on Garren Town Road (S.R. 1332), drive 1 mile, take a right on Golden Meadow Road (S.R. 1334), go 0.4 mile, turn right on Jackson Creek Road (S.R. 1314), and travel 0.4 mile. Lake Reese is on the right.

46 Lake Mackintosh

Key species: Largemouth bass, sunfish, channel catfish, crappie

Overview: Lake Mackintosh, built in 1991, is located on Big Alamance Creek on the Alamance County–Guilford County line. It serves as a water-supply reservoir for the city of Burlington and also provides recreation.

Best ways to fish: Powerboat, canoe, kayak, rowboat, bank, pier

Best time to fish: February through November

Description: Lake Mackintosh is six miles long, covers 1,100 acres, and has more than 100 miles of shoreline. Its tributaries include Big Alamance and Little Alamance creeks, the sources of the lake's fish.

The fishing: The largemouth bass fishing is excellent; lots of four- to six-pound fish are available. Some really good fishing can be had at the end of the lake south of Huffman Mill Road, where only trolling motors are allowed. The lake has a relatively stable water level. It is turbid, which means it receives plenty of nutrients. That, in turn, is the reason the bass grow so fast and so large. The lake has plenty of woody cover along the shoreline. Rocky outcroppings also serve as bass cover. The outcrops occur primarily as points. The lake also has many man-made fish attractors. Anglers catch bass with soft plastics and crankbaits. In the spring, buzzbaits and spinnerbaits are good bets.

Grass carp have been introduced to eat the vegetation growing in the eastern end of the lake. The crappie fishing is good; the lake produces lots of keeper-sized fish.

N.C. A-G grid: 38, A-2

General information: The lower half of the lake, below Huffman Mill Road, is restricted to boats without fuel-powered motors. Powerboats are allowed on the upper half, above Huffman Mill Road. Anglers should check the website or contact the marinas for exact locations for powerboat use; these areas are also posted at the lake. The marinas include nice parks with playgrounds, picnic shelters, rental clubhouses, bank-fishing access, and rowboat, paddleboat, canoe, and kayak rentals. No swimming, wading, or water scooters are allowed. The lake is closed Monday and Tuesday year-round. It is open in December and January when weather permits; anglers should call before traveling to the lake in those months. The lake

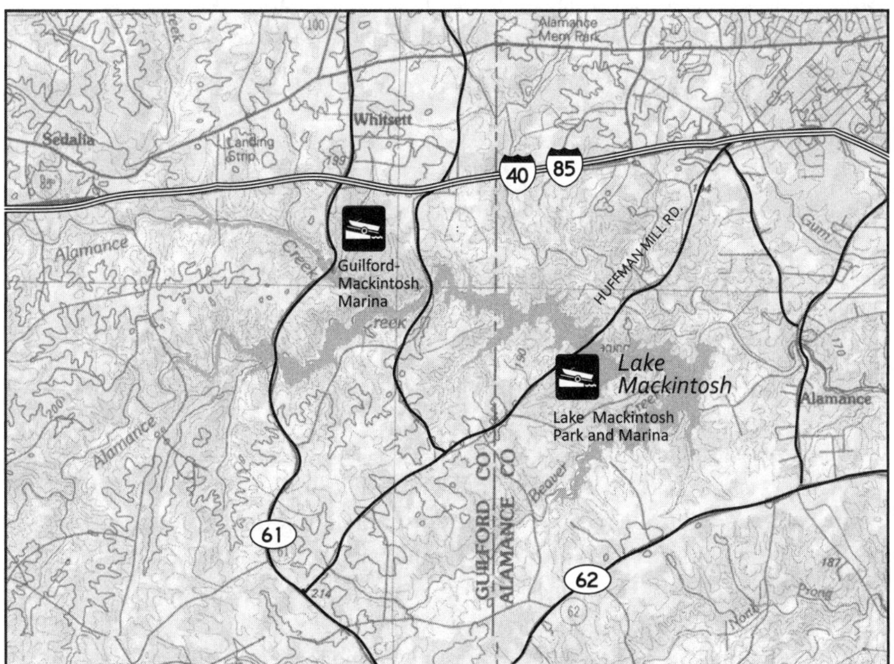

opens and closes at different times, depending on the season; these times are listed on the website. The lake has six boat ramps; launching fees are charged. NCWRC fishing regulations apply. Only paddleboats and boats with electric trolling motors are allowed to launch from Guilford-Mackintosh Marina.

Nearest camping: Camping is not allowed.

Directions: To reach Lake Mackintosh Park and Marina from I-40/I-85, take Exit 141 and travel south for 2.8 miles on Huffman Mill Road. The park and marina are on the left.

To reach Guilford-Mackintosh Marina from I-40/I-85, take Exit 138 and travel south on N.C. 61 for 0.5 mile. The sign and entrance are on the left.

47 Graham-Mebane Lake

Key species: Largemouth bass, crappie, sunfish, catfish

Overview: Graham-Mebane Lake, located in Alamance County east of Burlington, is the drinking-water supply for the towns of Graham and Mebane. It is managed by the NCWRC, which has made this reservoir system one of the top 10 fishing lakes in North Carolina. In order to increase angling solitude, water-skiing and the use of water scooters is restricted to certain parts of the lake. Quaker Creek Reservoir has been incorporated into Graham-Mebane Lake.

Best ways to fish: Boat, pier, bank

Best time to fish: March through October

Description: Graham-Mebane Lake is a 650-acre reservoir. In 1994, it was increased from 150 acres to its present size by joining two lakes.

The fishing: Graham-Mebane Lake offers excellent fishing, thanks to its expansion.

Channel cats provide the best opportunity for catching catfish. Liver, worms, shrimp, and commercial baits work well.

Anglers catch lots of big bass from the lake. The largest thus far weighed more than 12 pounds. The lake receives an extraordinary amount of fishing pressure for its relatively small size. Topwater lures, crankbaits, spinnerbaits, and soft plastics are the best bass lures. The biggest bass are caught in March and April. However, bass fishing is good throughout the warm months.

Although the crappie fishing is poor, the fishing for redear sunfish (shellcrack-

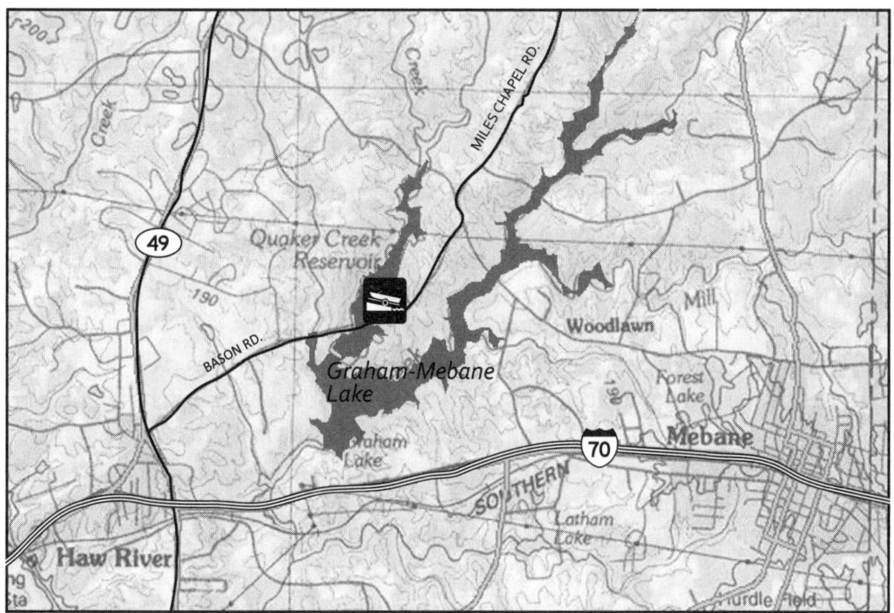

ers) is excellent. Crappie and sunfish can be caught from the pier and at the lake's man-made fish attractors, some of which are located at the bank-fishing areas.

N.C. A-G grid: 38, A-4

General information: All NCWRC regulations apply. The lake is open for fishing and boating from March through November. Hours and days of operation vary depending on the time of year. The lake is closed on Tuesdays. A boat launch is located at the marina; a launch fee is required. An on-site shop offers bait and tackle. The lake hosts a kids' fishing derby and carp/catfish tournaments.

Nearest camping: Camping is not allowed at Graham-Mebane Lake.

Directions: To reach Graham-Mebane Lake Marina from U.S. 70 near the community of Haw River, travel north on N.C. 49 (Roxboro Road), turn right on Bason Road (S.R. 1927), and cross the bridge. The marina is on the left.

48 Cane Creek Reservoir

Key species: Largemouth bass, crappie, sunfish, catfish

Overview: Cane Creek Reservoir is located 25 miles west of Chapel Hill in Orange County. The project was completed in 1988 after several decades of repeated droughts had impacted the Chapel Hill–Carrboro area. The reservoir's recreational facilities were completed in 1993. Limited fishing is available to the public. The Orange Water and Sewer Authority (OWASA) operates the lake.

Best ways to fish: Small johnboat, kayak, canoe, bank

Best times to fish: Although the lake produces fish during all the months it is open, spring and early summer provide the best opportunities.

Description: All the trees were removed from this 540-acre reservoir before the dam was constructed. No attractors or other man-made structure are present. The lake level fluctuates with rainfall and water use.

The fishing: The main attraction is the peaceful, quiet beauty of the lake, which has no shoreline development. But the fishing is also outstanding. The lake is stocked with bass, crappie, catfish, and bluegill sunfish.

Despite a lack of cover, Cane Creek Reservoir has produced exceptional largemouth bass weighing more than 12 pounds. Young bass are overcrowded here, indicating the lake could benefit from increased fishing pressure. Spinnerbaits and soft plastics are the best bets for bass.

Although the crappie fishing is good, anglers will need to explore to find the crappie concentrations. The deep areas, points, and channels are the best places. Trolling along the shoreline contours with jigs and minnows is a good way to find crappie. Anglers catch good numbers of crappie, some weighing more than two pounds.

Bank fishing is allowed at a designated area. Anglers catch bluegills and catfish from the bank. The bluegill fishing is very good, but fishing for cats isn't very popular because the lake is not open at night.

Most anglers rent the facility's canoes or 14-foot johnboats and trolling motors. Some bring their own small boats. No launching ramp is available because trailers are not allowed.

N.C. A-G grid: 39, B-5

General information: All NCWRC regulations apply. Cane Creek Reservoir can be fished only from 6:30 A.M. to 6:00 P.M. on Saturdays from late March through mid-November. It was once open four days per week; that schedule could return, so be sure to visit the website. Powerboats are not allowed. All trolling motors and private boats are inspected for aquatic weeds. Fees are charged for fishing and boating.

Nearest camping: Camping is not allowed at Cane Creek Reservoir.

Directions: Cane Creek Reservoir is about 8 miles west of Carrboro via N.C. 54. The entrance is on the north side of N.C. 54 about a mile west of Stanford Road (S.R. 1100).

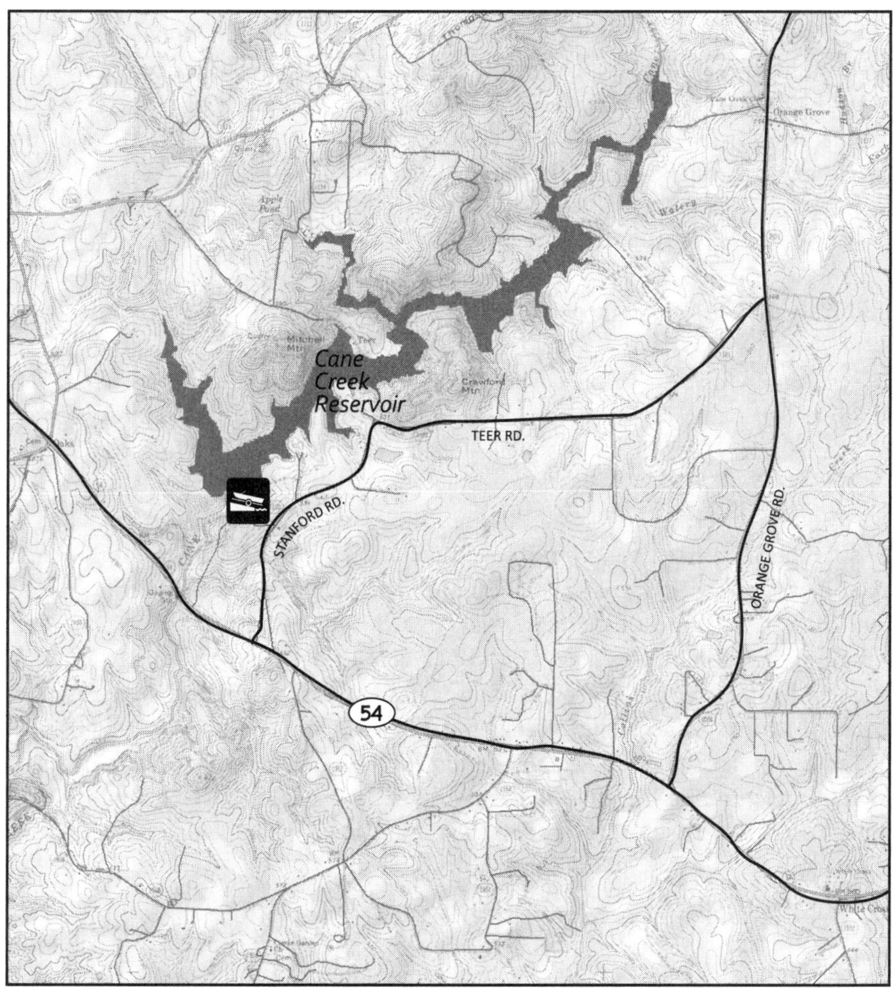

49 University Lake

Key species: Largemouth bass, crappie, catfish, sunfish, warmouth

Overview: Located in Orange County and operated by the Orange Water and Sewer Authority (OWASA), University Lake was created in 1932 to provide drinking water for the Chapel Hill area. It was built by the University of North Carolina at Chapel Hill. Its high water quality is maintained by stringent restrictions on development throughout the lake's 30-square-mile watershed.

Best ways to fish: Canoe, kayak, johnboat

Best time to fish: March through October

Description: University Lake covers 213 acres and is impounded by an 811-foot-long earthen dam. The reservoir impounds Price Creek. Its tributaries include Morgan Creek, Phil's Creek, Neville Creek, Price Creek, and Pritchard's Mill Creek.

The fishing: The lake has been stocked with crappie, sunfish, largemouth bass, and other native species common to Southern lakes and reservoirs. Fees and stringent controls keep most fishermen away. But low angler use makes for a peaceful and rewarding fishing trip. The lake is open only Friday through Sunday, keeping pressure light. It closes the second Saturday in November and opens the first Saturday of spring. Although local anglers catch many largemouth bass, the bass in the lower age classes are typically thin and exhibit slow growth rates. An increase in angler retention of largemouth bass would help the fishing. The crappie fishing is poor and is likely subject to cycles, as in other small lakes.

N.C. A-G grid: 39, B-5

General information: All NCWRC regulations apply. Boats are available for rent, or anglers can launch their own canoes or kayaks. Fees are charged to launch and to fish the lake. Stringent inspections of privately owned boats are conducted. Electric trolling motors are the only propulsion engines allowed.

Nearest camping: Camping is not allowed at University Lake.

Directions: To reach University Lake from N.C. 54 in Carrboro, travel west on

Jones Ferry Road (S.R. 1942) for 0.3 mile, then turn left on Old Fayetteville Road (S.R. 1937). The lake is at the end of the road.

50 B. Everett Jordan Lake

Key species: Largemouth bass, hybrid bass, crappie, sunfish, catfish

Overview: B. Everett Jordan Lake is a reservoir located in Chatham County. The lake, operated by the Corps of Engineers, was created for flood control after several heavy rainfalls from tropical storms flooded the region. Jordan Lake (its abbreviated name) was formed by a dam that impounded the Haw and New Hope rivers. First called the New Hope Lake Project, the reservoir was renamed in 1974 for B. Everett Jordan, a former United States senator from North Carolina.

Best ways to fish: Powerboat, kayak, canoe, bank, dock

Best times to fish: Year-round. January is the worst month. Striper fishing peaks in May, while the fishing for largemouth bass and crappie peaks in April.

Description: The dam at Jordan Lake was completed in 1974 near the mouth of the Haw River. The dam is 1,330 feet long. When it is at full capacity, the reservoir covers 13,940 acres at 216 feet in elevation. The Jordan Lake project also conserves 46,768 acres of wildlife habitat in an expanding urban area.

The fishing: Jordan Lake is one of the state's top lakes for a variety of fishing. Anglers catch largemouth bass, crappie, striped bass, and catfish. The lake was once stocked with hybrid bass (Bodie bass), but that was curtailed in favor of striped bass, due to the potential for the hybrids to travel downstream and dilute the spawning of migratory striped bass in the Cape Fear River. The striper fishing is outstanding. Lots of three- to six-pound fish are caught; some topping 10 pounds have been landed. Striper anglers use all methods, but fishing with live shad is the most popular and productive. Gizzard and threadfin shad are slow-trolled or drifted in the striper schools after anglers have located the fish with electronic depthfinders. Trolling deep-diving lures also works well. Jigging with bucktail jigs and spoons is another good method. Although stripers can be caught all year, the best fishing for them is in early summer; May and June are the peak months.

Largemouth bass congregate around the natural shoreline structure of rocks, clay banks, downed trees, and stumps. Offshore, underwater stumps, logs, rocks, hills, and the channel edges of the former rivers and creeks hold bass. Although

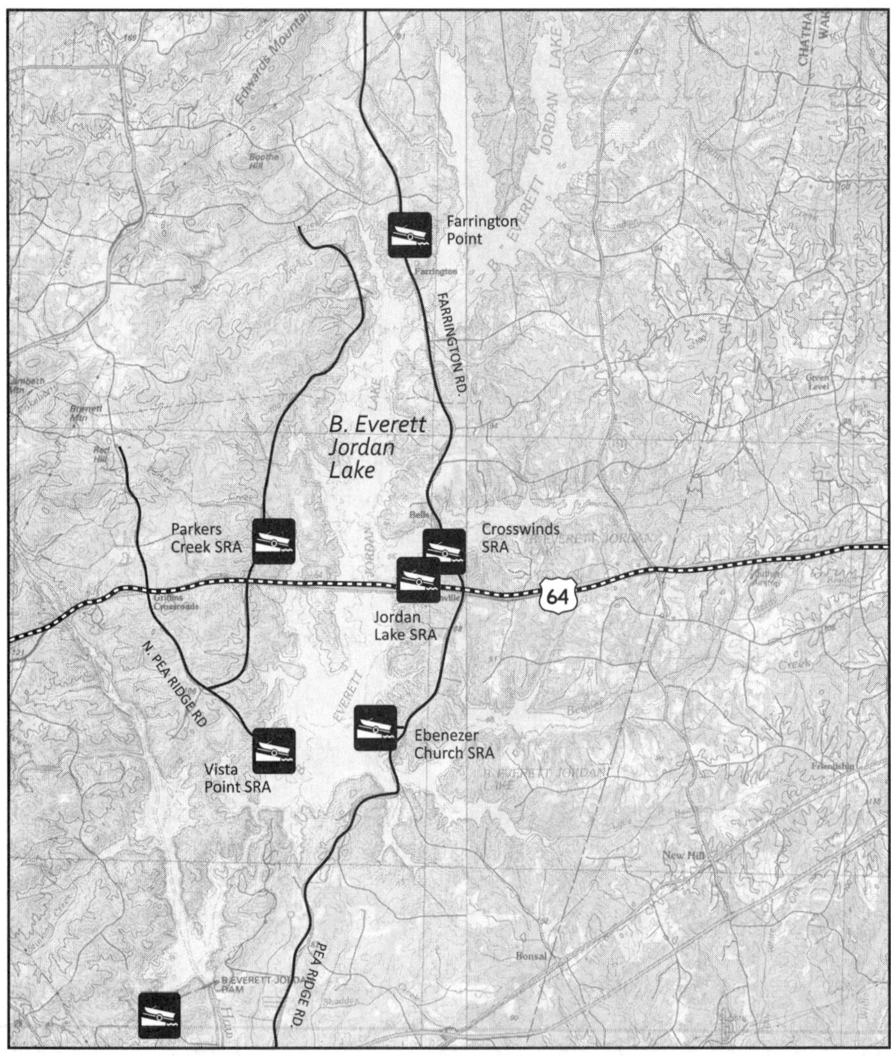

the best period for catching largemouth is February through April, the bass fishing is great all the way through October or even November, depending on the weather. When the fish are in shallow water during the pre-spawn and spawn months, spinnerbaits, buzzbaits, stickbaits, topwater lures, and soft plastics all work extremely well. When the fish are deeper, deep-running crankbaits, weighted soft plastics, and jigs are the go-to lures. The plentiful submerged timber areas and stump fields host excellent bass fishing away from the shoreline. The lake also has lots of artificial fish attractors that hold largemouth bass and crappie.

Jordan is one of the top crappie-producing lakes in the state. Intense fishing pressure is responsible for excellent crappie growth rates. Artificial fish attractors, standing timber, and woody cover along the shoreline and in the coves are the best places to catch crappie when they are in shallow water in April and May. In February and March, crappie congregate along the deeper structure at the creek mouths and points. Trolling or drifting with multiple rods rigged with jigs and minnows is very productive. But most anglers use float rigs baited with minnows, casting them to visible structure. For fishing the attractors, using slip float rigs baited with minnows and jigging with curly-tailed soft plastic jigs are the top methods. The bridges hold crappie year-round. Fishing from the bridges at night using lights to attract crappie is a great method during the warm months.

White catfish, channel catfish, and flathead catfish are all abundant. Anglers often mistake the lake's white catfish for blue catfish, which are not present, at least not in large numbers. Fishing from the banks with liver, worms, cut shad, or shrimp is a great way to catch channel catfish. White catfish school along the channel edges and in the stumps, where they can be spotted with an electronic depthfinder. White catfish and flathead catfish often strike shad baits intended for striped bass. Night fishing from the bank for catfish is popular.

N.C. A-G grid: 39, D-6

General information: NCWRC fishing rules and regulations apply. See the NCWRC website for the locations of the fish attractors and the 24 boat ramps.

Nearest camping: Camping facilities are provided at nine recreational areas around the lake. More than 1,000 campsites are available. The sites include picnic tables, grills, and trash containers. Showers, restrooms, and dump stations are provided at some of the facilities. See the appendix for contact information for Jordan Lake and Jordan Lake State Recreation Area.

Directions: To reach Farrington Point Access Area from U.S. 64, travel 5 miles north on Farrington Road (S.R. 1008). The access area is on the left.

To reach Ebenezer Church State Recreation Area Access from U.S. 64, travel 2.3 miles south on Farrington Road. The entrance is on the left.

51 Falls Lake

Key species: Largemouth bass, white bass, crappie, sunfish, catfish

Overview: Falls Lake is a Corps of Engineers reservoir. Located in Wake, Durham, and Granville counties, it is named after Falls Village, which is just downstream of the dam. The lake project was completed in 1981. Constructed for flood control, the reservoir also provides drinking water for the surrounding Triangle region.

Best ways to fish: Bank, wading, powerboat, kayak, canoe

Best time to fish: February through September

Description: The reservoir covers almost 12,500 acres and is surrounded by 25,500 acres of public land. The earthen dam is 10 miles north of Raleigh. The lake stretches over 22 miles of the Neuse River to the confluence of the Eno, Flat, and Little rivers near Durham. Falls Dam has an elevation of 291.5 feet and an overall length of 1,915 feet. The height above the streambed is 92.5 feet. The lake fluctuates according to water demand and rainfall.

The fishing: Fish attractors have been placed near the shoreline of many of the public fishing areas. The brush has been cleared to allow easy access for those fishing the public areas from the bank.

The bass fishing here is excellent. Many bass tournaments are conducted at the lake. Lots of woody structure from flooded standing timber is in the creeks. The backs of coves are therefore prime areas for targeting bass in late winter and early spring. Spinnerbaits and crankbaits work well during February and March. In April and May, spinnerbaits, crankbaits, topwater lures, and soft plastics work well. During summer, the bass stage along the former creek channels in deeper water. Jigs, weighted soft plastics, deep-diving crankbaits, and spinnerbaits are best for deep fishing. By fall, the fish move to shallow water again. Although the bite isn't as strong as during the spring spawn, the same lures work in the fall. Many largemouth bass of more than five pounds are caught from Falls Lake. The water has low visibility, so anglers go with dark lure colors and gold or copper hammered spinner blades.

The crappie fishing is excellent. Trolling and drifting with multiple rods is popular beginning in February, when the fish stage along the mouths of creeks and in the creek channels before the spawn. As the spawn begins, the fish concentrate at the fish attractors and the woody cover and bushes along the bank. Anglers catch them with float rigs baited with minnows, beetle grub spinners, and feather jigs or jig heads tipped with soft plastic trailers. Good colors are chartreuse, pink, and purple.

The sunfish action is good for a lake of this type. Some large bluegill sunfish are caught from the shoreline cover and woody cover. Although most fishermen use worms and crickets for bait, Falls Lake is a great place for casting a popping bug or sponge spider with a fly rod.

White bass are abundant. Anglers often catch them while fishing for crappie and bass. Trolling with inline spinners and small crankbaits also works well.

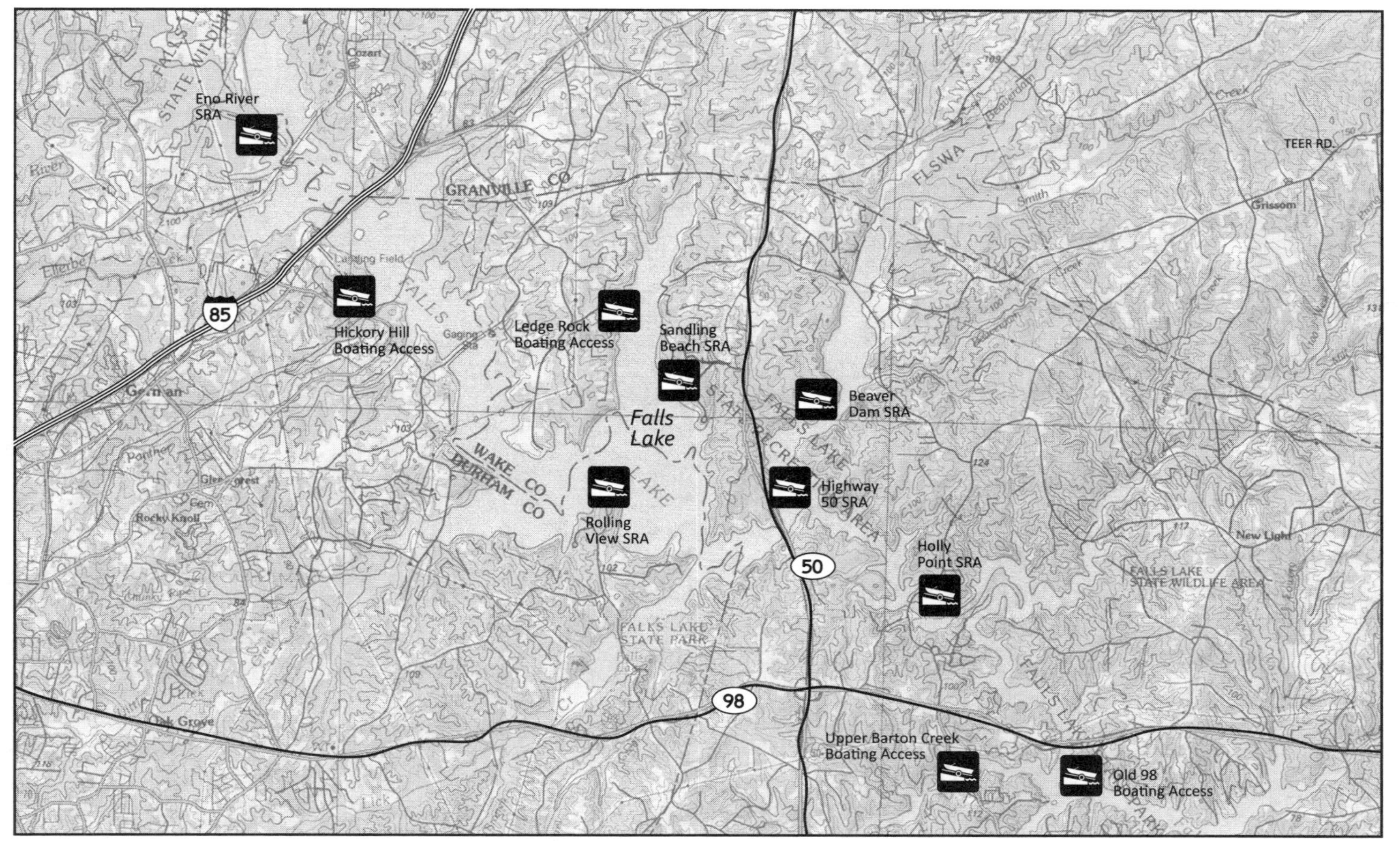

Eno River SRA
85
Hickory Hill Boating Access
GRANVILLE CO
Ledge Rock Boating Access
Sandling Beach SRA
Beaver Dam SRA
Falls Lake
WAKE CO
DURHAM CO
Rolling View SRA
Highway 50 SRA
50
Holly Point SRA
FALLS LAKE STATE WILDLIFE AREA
FALLS LAKE STATE PARK
98
Upper Barton Creek Boating Access
Old 98 Boating Access
TEER RD.
FLSWA
Grissom
New Light

The Piedmont reservoirs are top producers of white crappie. Carol Marsh caught this one by casting a jig in standing timber at Falls Lake.

Schooling white bass are caught with spoons, vibration lures, jigs, and poppers.

The lake offers excellent fishing for bullhead and channel catfish. Fishing from the bank at the public access areas is very popular. The catfish move into the shallow water in the evenings. Fishing from a boat is also productive. In summer, catfish are the most aggressive species in the lake. Worms, shrimp, and chicken liver are the best catfish baits. Most catfish weigh one to six pounds, but larger fish have also been caught here. The catfish are abundant.

N.C. A-G grid: 40, A-2

General information: All NCWRC rules apply. Most of the surrounding area is game land.

Nearest camping: Rolling View and Sandling Beach state recreation areas are located nearby. Both provide restrooms and facilities for camping and picnicking.

Directions: To reach Old 98 Boating Access Area in Wake County from the intersection of N.C. 50 and N.C. 98, travel N.C. 98 East for 3.5 miles. The access area is on the right.

To reach Upper Barton Creek Boating Access Area from the intersection of N.C. 50 and N.C. 98, travel north on N.C. 50 across the bridge. The access area is on the right.

52 Lake Raleigh

Key species: Largemouth bass, black crappie, bluegill, channel catfish

Overview: Lake Raleigh is owned by North Carolina State University and is located on its Centennial Campus. The lake was reopened in 2007 after a dam breach in 1996. It once supplied the drinking water for the city of Raleigh.

Best ways to fish: Canoe, kayak, johnboat

Best time to fish: March through November

Description: Lake Raleigh is a 90-acre lake formed by an earthen dam. Built in 1912, it was used as a water supply until the mid-1980s. A new pier and access were completed in 2007. The lake provides a decent fishing opportunity on the campus of North Carolina State University.

The fishing: Bluegills are the predominant species in the lake. However, plenty of big largemouth bass are also caught here. The best bets are soft plastics and topwater lures. Some anglers use live minnows for bass. The best season for bass fishing is spring, during the spawn and before the lake weeds begin growing. For bluegills, worms, crickets, popping bugs, and spinners are the best bets.

N.C. A-G grid: 40, C-2

General information: All NCWRC regulations apply. It is important for boaters to wash their boats before entering another body of water. Hydrilla, a highly invasive aquatic plant species, is present in Lake Raleigh.

Nearest camping: No camping is allowed around Lake Raleigh.

Directions: To reach Lake Raleigh from I-440, take Exit 297, travel north on Lake Wheeler Road (S.R. 1375), turn left at Centennial Parkway, and turn left on Crump Road.

53 Harris Reservoir

Key species: Largemouth bass, crappie, sunfish, catfish

Overview: Harris Reservoir is located at New Hill. Carolina Power and Light, now Progress Energy, built the lake as a source of drinking water and to provide cooling water to the Shearon Harris nuclear power plant.

Best ways to fish: Bank, powerboat

Best times to fish: Good fishing is available on Harris Reservoir throughout the year, thanks to the warming effects of the power plant's cooling water discharge. The best bass and crappie fishing is in spring and early summer.

Description: Harris Reservoir covers 4,100 acres. It was created by damming Buckhorn Creek in 1982. The following year, the lake was filled to its full-pond elevation of 220 feet above sea level. Harris Reservoir has 40 miles of shoreline and an average depth of 18 feet. The undeveloped shoreline is surrounded by public game land. Duck hunting is popular in the winter months.

The fishing: Harris Reservoir may have the best fishing for crappie and largemouth bass in the state. The water is fertile, and power-plant operations keep it warm through the cold months, allowing bass to grow huge. Limit stringers of five bass weighing more than five pounds apiece have been caught from the lake, and 10-pound fish are always a possibility. The bass get lots of fishing pressure because everyone knows the lake's reputation. Therefore, the best time to fish is on weekdays.

Bass strike well beginning in February and March. Crankbaits and spinnerbaits are the best bets when the water is chilly. Harris Reservoir has many steep drop-offs along the edges, as well as deep creek channels that hold bass during the cold months. As the water warms, the shoreline cover and the pad and hydrilla beds attract bass. Spinnerbaits, topwater lures, floating worms and frogs, jigs, and stickbaits work well when the fish are in the grass. When they move deeper again during the summer, using spinnerbaits, jigs, or weighted soft plastics in depths of eight to 15 feet along the creek channels is a good tactic. Another good bet is fishing a buzzbait, popper, or topwater propeller lure in the shaded coves at dawn. In winter, the bass move to the deep creek channels again, where jigs and soft plastics fished very slowly will catch them.

Crappie are abundant and grow large. Anglers catch them by trolling jigs and minnows along the banks. Casting jigs and beetle grub spinners to the shoreline cover is another good bet. When the fish congregate in the backs of the coves and at the cover offered by submerged stumps, downed trees, and beaver lodge entrances, a float rig with a minnow is the ticket to catching them in large numbers. The three bridges at the upper end of the lake attract bass and crappie. Crappie congregate there all year. During the warm months, the best time to catch crappie at the bridges is at night.

Harris Reservoir has an abundance of channel and flathead catfish. Some of the flatheads grow very large. Bank fishing for catfish is popular. Fishing from a boat is also productive. The best places to fish are near the dam and in the deep creek channels. Shrimp, live and cut panfish, chicken liver, and commercial dough and dip baits work well for Harris Lake catfish. Anglers may experience problems with the hydrilla fouling their hooks. The best bet is to find water deep enough that hydrilla is not present.

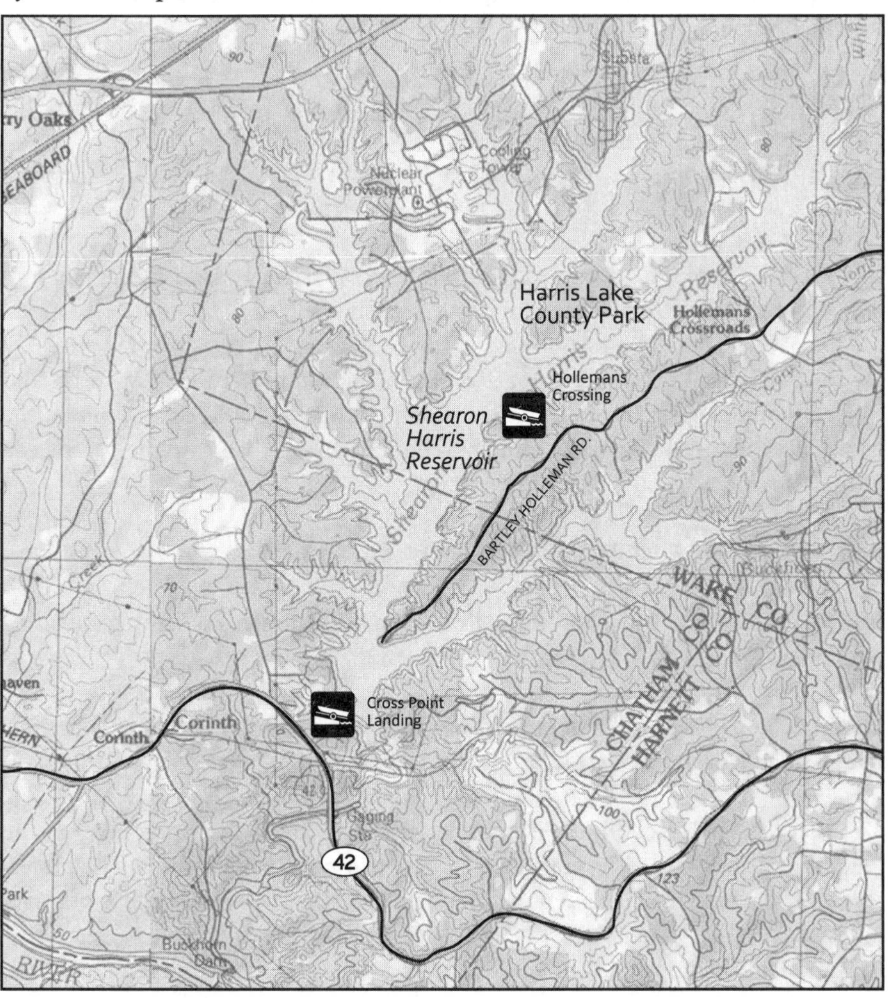

***N.C. A-G* grid: 61, A-7**

General information: NCWRC fishing rules and regulations apply.

Nearest camping: Camping is available at Harris Lake County Park in Wake County. See the appendix for contact information.

Directions: To reach Cross Point Landing Public Boat Access from Corinth, travel 2 miles east on N.C. 42, turn left on Christian Chapel Road (S.R. 1912), drive 0.4 mile, turn right on Cross Point Road, and go 0.4 mile. The access area is at the end of the gravel road.

To reach Hollemans Crossing Boating Access Area from U.S. 1, travel south on New Hill–Holleman Road (S.R. 1127) to Bartley-Holleman Road (S.R. 1130), turn right, and drive 2 miles to the access road, on the right. The access area is at the end of the road.

54 High Rock Lake

Key species: Hybrid bass, striped bass, white bass, largemouth bass, crappie, sunfish, flathead catfish, blue catfish, channel catfish

Overview: High Rock Lake is located east of Salisbury between Davidson and Rowan counties. The lake and dam are named after High Rock Mountain, the largest peak in the Uwharrie Mountains. High Rock Lake begins at the confluence of the Yadkin and South Yadkin rivers.

Best ways to fish: Boat, bank, private dock

Best time to fish: February through November, though something is biting year-round

Description: High Rock Lake covers 15,180 acres and has 365 miles of shoreline. Its full-pond elevation is 655 feet above sea level.

The fishing: High Rock Lake is considered one of the best fishing lakes in the Piedmont. It has hosted several national bass-fishing championships. The professionals confirmed the lake's reputation by producing impressive catches of largemouth bass.

The lake is renowned for the quality and quantity of its largemouth bass.

It has fertile water and all kinds of bass habitat typical of Piedmont impoundments—boat docks, stumps, rocky banks, coves. The lake level is also stable compared to those of most other Piedmont lakes, which translates to great bass-fishing opportunities all year.

While the bass fishing in spring and summer is excellent, anglers also have great opportunities when the fish move to deepwater structure in the heat of summer. Crankbaits are the most popular lures all year long. But anglers also have excellent luck using soft plastic lures and spinnerbaits.

Striper anglers rave over the fishing. Live-bait techniques are the best bets for stripers. Anglers should watch for birds to locate stripers in cold weather. Stripers can also be located with a depthfinder when they suspend over the high spots and along the sloping points.

The crappie fishing is excellent. Trolling with multiple jigs is a standard tactic in January and February. Submerged brush piles, fallen trees, and bushes growing in the backs of the coves attract swarms of crappie in spring. Live minnows fished on float rigs are popular when the fish move to shallow water in March and April.

Anglers use drifting tactics to catch blue catfish in winter. The best technique with migrating schools of blue catfish is to locate shad schools with a depthfinder and drift live shad through the schools. At other times, blue cats stick in the deep holes, where anglers target them with cut and live shad and panfish. In spring, anglers should watch for carp schools to locate blue catfish. The eggs of spawning carp attract blue cats into extremely shallow water. A piece of cut shad tossed near

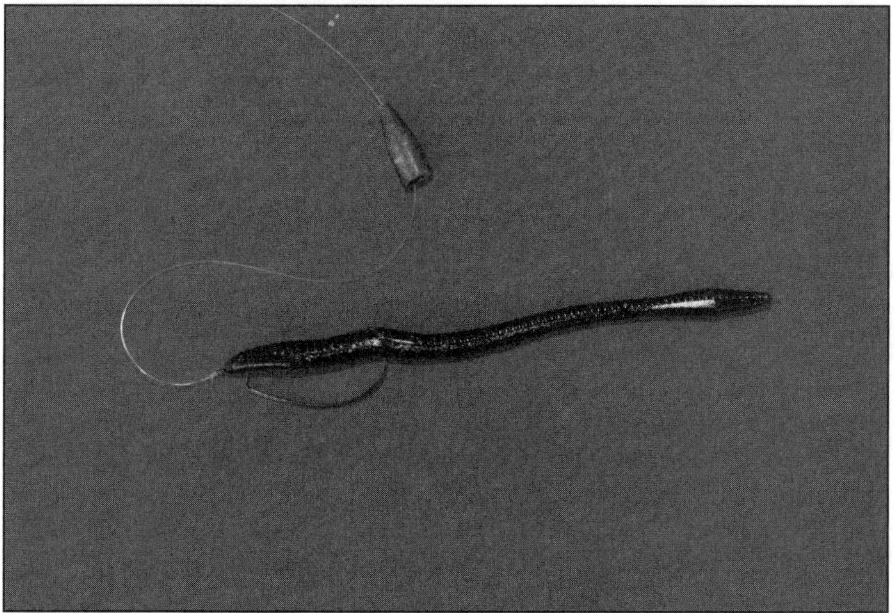

This is a Carolina-rigged plastic worm, one of the most productive bass lures. The slip sinker is threaded onto the line ahead of the hook. The worm is also Texas-rigged, with the hook point embedded slightly into the worm to make it "weedless."

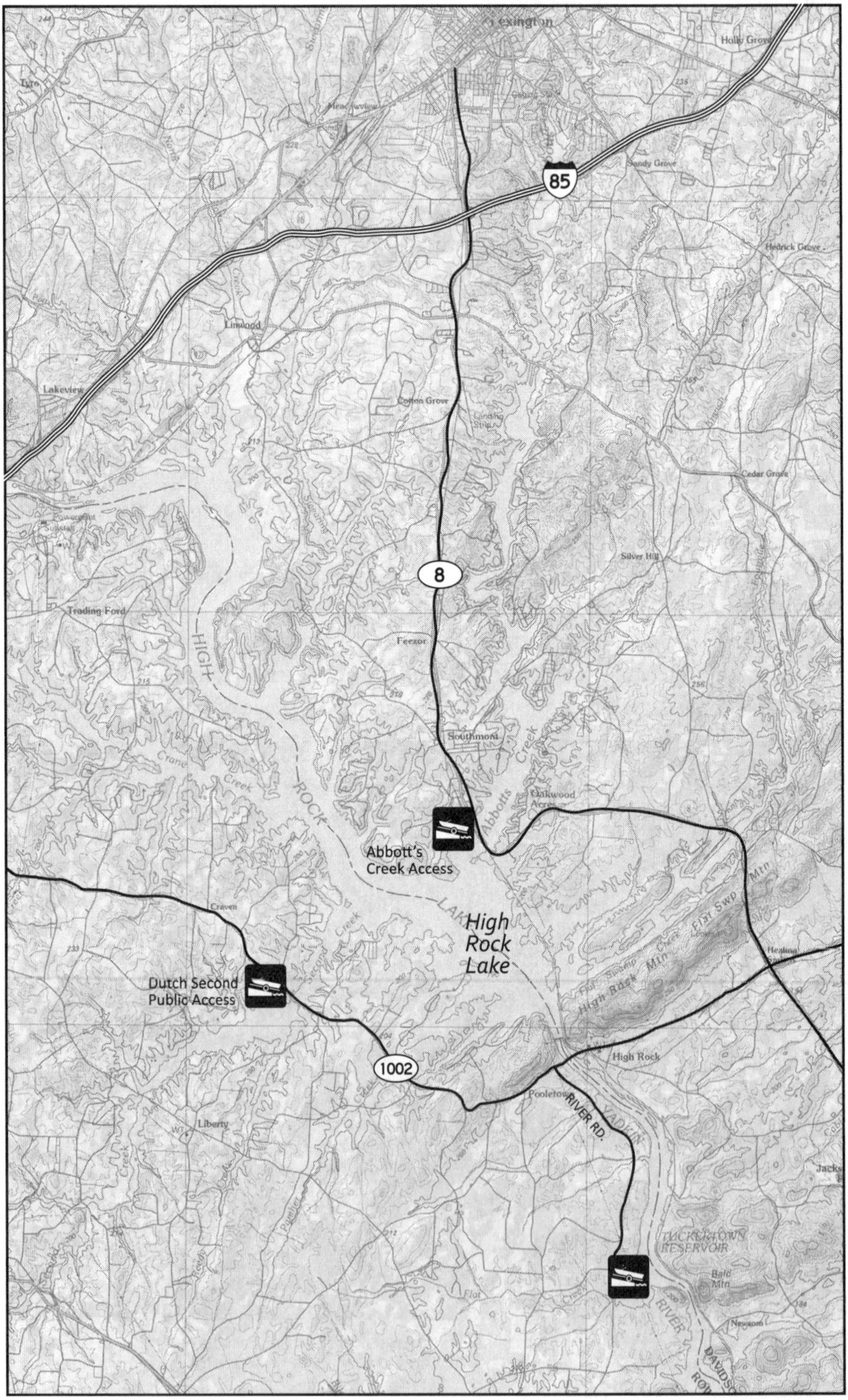
Lexington
Holly Grove
Tyro
Meadowview
85
Sandy Grove
Hedrick Grove
Linwood
Lakeview
Cotton Grove
Landing Strip
Cedar Grove
Silver Hill
8
Trading Ford
Feezor
HIGH
ROCK
LAKE
Southmont
Crane Creek
Abbotts Creek
Oakwood Acres
Abbott's Creek Access
Craven
High Rock Lake
Flat Swp Mtn
High Rock Mtn
Dutch Second Public Access
Healing Springs
High Rock
1002
Pooletown
RIVER RD.
YADKIN
Liberty
TUCKERTOWN RESERVOIR
Bald Mtn
RIVER
Newsom
DAVIDSON

a spot where carp are active is the ticket to a hookup with a blue catfish.

Deep holes in the river channel are excellent places to catch flathead catfish. One of the best holes (because it is easy to find) is at the I-85 bridge. Anglers anchor in the deep holes and fish with live panfish or live shad on float rigs or on light lines to catch flatheads that can top 50 pounds.

N.C. A-G grid: 36, D-4

General information: All NCWRC regulations apply. The lake is owned and operated by Alcoa. See the appendix for contact information for regulations at Alcoa lakes.

Nearest camping: Primitive camping is allowed within the nearby Uwharrie National Forest.

Directions: To reach Dutch Second Public Access from N.C. 8 at Healing Springs in Davidson County, travel 10 miles west on Bringle Ferry Road (S.R. 1002) into Rowan County. After crossing High Rock Lake, turn left into the access area.

To reach Abbott's Creek Access Area from U.S. 70 Business in Lexington, travel south on N.C. 8 for 10.5 miles, turn right on Marvin Hedrick Road (S.R. 1101), drive 0.4 mile, and turn left on Wildlife Recreational Area Access Road (S.R. 1300).

55 Tuckertown Lake

Key species: Largemouth bass, white crappie, sunfish, catfish

Overview: Tuckertown Lake was the last reservoir built along the Yadkin chain by Alcoa. It was completed in 1962 to serve a hydroelectric plant that would provide electricity to the company's Badin operation. Its low dam creates little room for water storage and is therefore considered a "run of the river" dam. Tuckertown Lake is situated on the border of Rowan and Davidson counties.

Best ways to fish: Motorboat, bank, kayak, canoe

Best times to fish: The best fishing is in spring and fall, but something is biting year-round.

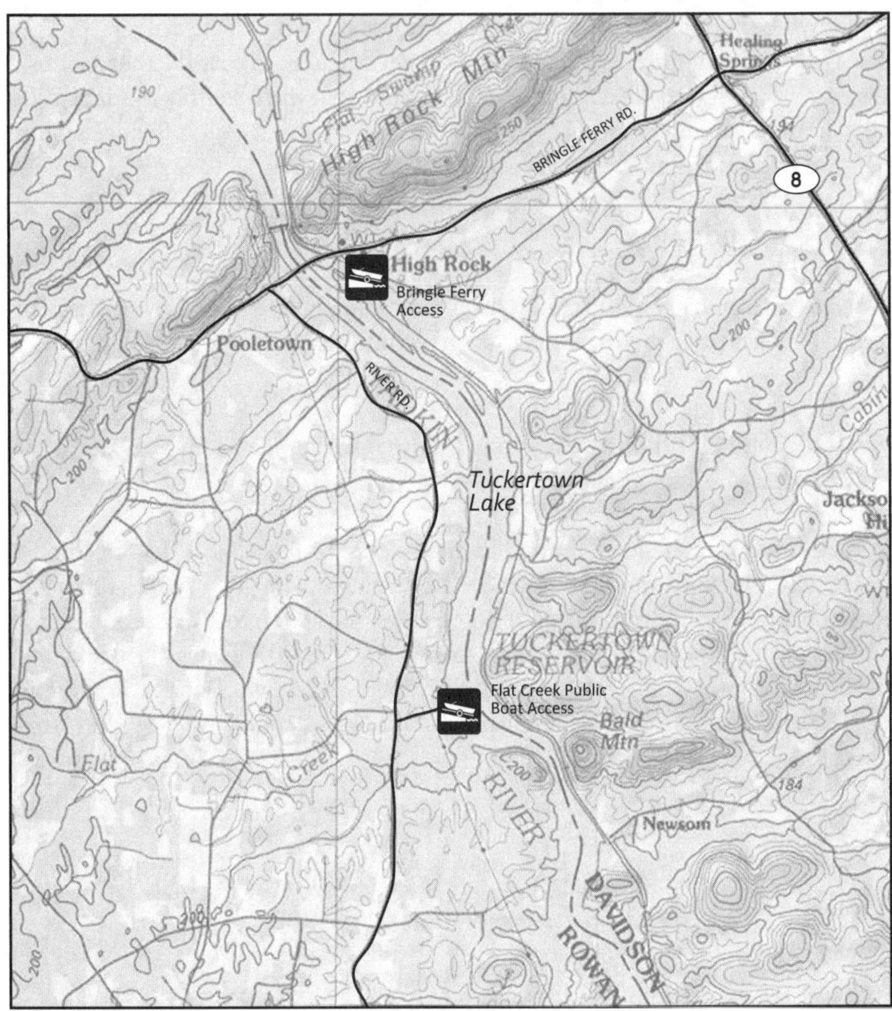

Description: Tuckertown Lake is a 2,500-acre reservoir on the Yadkin River. The surface elevation is 596 feet above sea level.

The fishing: Anglers in boats must be very careful until they become familiar with the area. Although many shallow areas are marked with buoys, some are not well marked. What appears as open water can actually be a shallow stump bed or a high, rocky spot atop a submerged peak. Extra caution is advised, along with careful study of topographic maps of the lake.

Tuckertown Lake is an excellent place to catch bass, crappie, white perch, and stripers. Bass anglers will find plenty of shallow stump fields to probe with soft plastics, spinnerbaits, and topwater lures.

The tailrace of High Rock Dam is an excellent place to catch large catfish, stripers, and white bass. White perch form large schools throughout the lake but are having an adverse impact on white bass and crappie abundance. For schooling fish, topwater lures, spoons, jigs, and small crankbaits are the best bets. Catfish anglers use live and cut baits with success. Crappie anglers have the best success when fish enter the shallows during the warm days of spring. Late March through early May is the peak period for crappie fishing.

N.C. A-G grid: 58, A-4

General information: All NCWRC regulations apply. See the appendix for information about Alcoa lakes.

Nearest camping: Camping is not permitted on the islands within the lake boundaries. It is offered nearby at Morrow Mountain State Park and Badin Lake Campground, which has 37 campsites for tents and trailers.

Directions: To reach Bringle Ferry Access Area below High Rock Dam from N.C. 8 at Healing Springs in Davidson County, drive 3 miles west on Bringle Ferry Road (S.R.1002), then turn left on the access road after the railroad crossing.

To reach Flat Creek Public Boat Access from N.C. 8, drive 3.7 miles west on Bringle Ferry Road, crossing the bridge into Rowan County. Take a left on River Road (S.R. 2152), travel 3.8 miles to Wildlife Access Road (S.R. 2191), turn left, and continue to the access area.

56 Badin Lake

Key species: Striped bass, largemouth bass, white bass, crappie, sunfish, catfish

Overview: A French aluminum company began the construction of Badin Lake. When that venture failed, the Aluminum Company of America (Alcoa) bought the lake in 1915. Badin Lake was completed in 1917 by Alcoa for use in hydroelectric power generation. Formed by impounding the Yadkin River, the lake has shoreline in Stanly, Montgomery, and Davidson counties. The smelting operation ended in 2002. Now, the lake is mainly used for power generation and recreation.

Best ways to fish: Motorboat, canoe, kayak

Best time to fish: Early spring to November, though some species such as striped bass are active year-round.

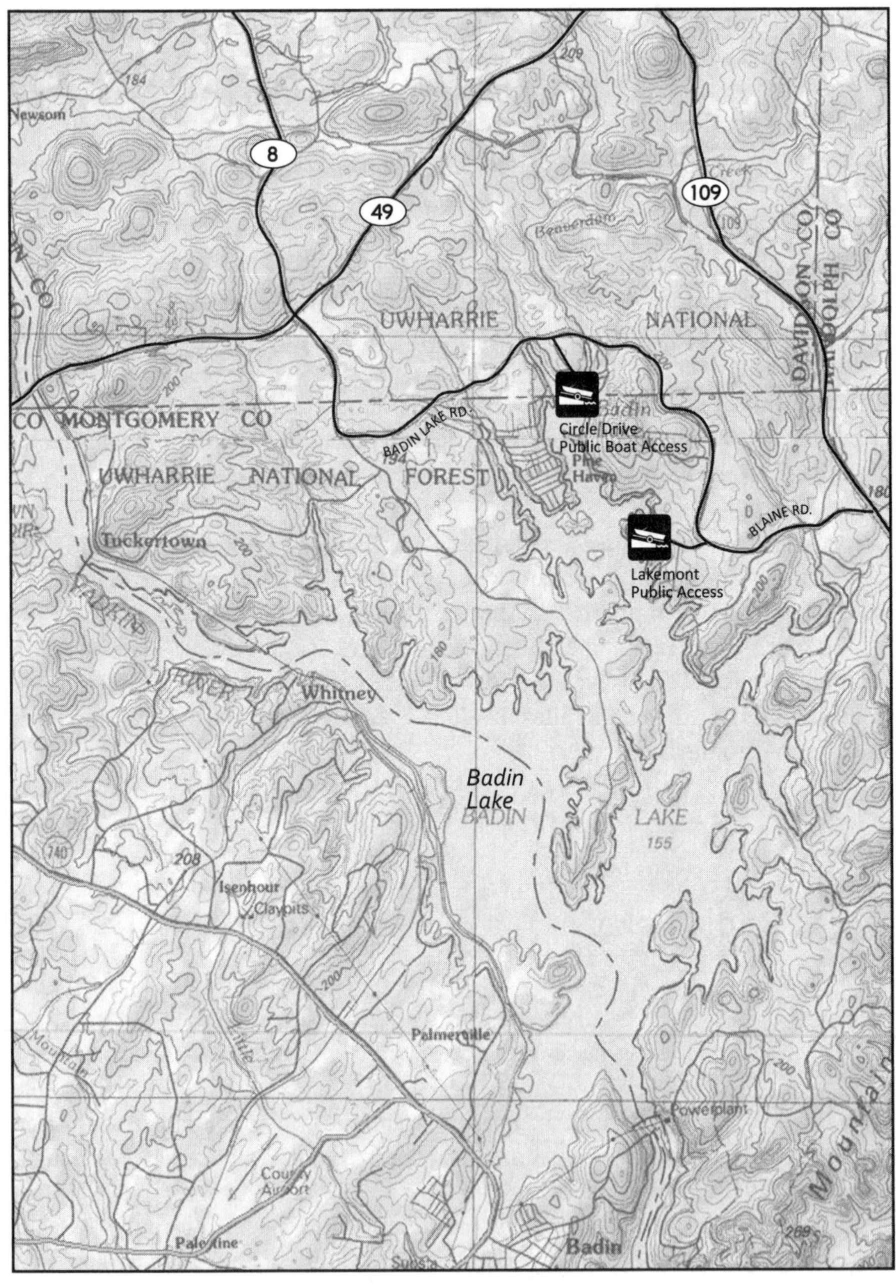

Circle Drive
Public Boat Access
Lakemont
Public Access
Badin
Lake
BADIN LAKE RD.
BLAINE RD.
UWHARRIE NATIONAL FOREST
MONTGOMERY CO
Tuckertown
Whitney
Isenhour
Claypits
Palmerville
Powerplant
County
Airport
Palestine
Badin

Description: Badin Lake covers 5,350 acres and has more than 115 miles of shoreline. It is located in a valley and has a maximum depth of 190 feet. When the reservoir is at full capacity, the surface elevation is 541 feet above sea level. Narrows Dam, or Badin Dam, is located north of the community of Badin. The dam maintains a stable water level, which has led to excellent fishing and other recreational opportunities.

The fishing: The tailrace of Tuckertown Dam at Badin Lake's headwaters produces excellent catches of catfish. The lake is one of the best places in the state for catching heavyweight blue catfish. Cut shad and other cut baits are the best bets for blue catfish. Live bream is the top bait for flathead catfish. Blue catfish typically remain in deep holes day and night. Flathead catfish move from their lairs in undercut banks and deep holes to hunt in the stump beds at night.

The lake has excellent fishing for redbreast sunfish and other panfish. Beetle grub spinners and worms are the best bets for redbreast.

The largemouth bass fishing is above average. Bass anglers target grass beds, points, and stump beds. In winter and early spring, crankbaits are the best bets. As the water warms, soft plastics and topwater lures fished early and late in the day are the top choices. Spinnerbaits are great bass lures anytime.

The best largemouth bass fishing occurs in spring. A peak month is April, when the fish move into the shallows to spawn. The second bass-fishing peak occurs in September and October as the shad move into the backs of the coves.

Although Badin Lake offers excellent crappie fishing, crappie can be hard to find. The best bet is locating underwater brush piles or artificial fish attractors and probing the deep cover with a jig or minnow. Many dock owners place brush piles beneath their docks to attract crappie. Trolling is another good tactic just before the fish move into the shallows for the spring spawn in March and April.

The striper fishing is excellent; the fish bite readily all year long. Anglers catch live gizzard and threadfin shad with cast nets to use for bait. Sometimes, the shad species can be difficult to catch, but it's worth spending as much time as necessary to locate and catch them in order to get the most out of a day or night of striper fishing.

Birds give away the locations of striper schools when the fish are in shallow water during cold weather. But in the warm months, the fish move to deeper water and the birds head back to the coast. When the stripers are deep, trolling deep-diving lures is an excellent tactic. Other good tactics for deep-running stripers include drifting live baits and jigging with lead-head jigs tipped with soft plastic trailers. Green is a great color for artificial striper lures at Badin Lake.

In the spring when stripers run upriver to spawn, one of the best places to catch them is between the railroad trestle and the dam. Since there is not enough flowing water for the eggs to survive, Badin Lake, like other Piedmont and mountain lakes, is stocked with stripers. Other good places to catch stripers at any time of year include Machine Creek and Beaver Creek.

N.C. A-G grid: 58, B-5

General information: All NCWRC regulations apply. A fish consumption advisory is in effect for Badin Lake due to polychlorinated biphenyls (PCBs) in catfish and largemouth bass. See the appendix for contact information for NCDHHS fish consumption advisories, the Alcoa lakes, and Badin Lake Campground.

Nearest camping: Uwharrie National Forest comprises two-thirds of the shoreline of Badin Lake. Primitive camping is allowed in the national forest. Badin Lake Campground offers full facilities, hiking, fishing areas, and many other amenities.

Directions: To reach Circle Drive Public Boat Access from U.S. 52 in Stanly County, travel north on N.C. 49 for 7.7 miles. At the intersection of N.C. 49 and N.C. 8, turn right onto Badin Lake Road (S.R. 2554). Drive 3.1 miles on Badin Lake Road, which becomes Blaine Road (S.R. 1161) in Montgomery County. Turn right at the second entrance to Shoreline Drive (S.R. 2551), travel 0.5 mile, and turn left onto the access road.

To reach Lakemont Public Access Area from N.C. 49 in Davidson County, travel 4.5 miles south on N.C. 109 to Blaine Road (S.R. 1156) in Montgomery County. Turn right on Blaine Road, travel 1.7 miles to Lakemont Road (S.R. 1158), turn left, and continue to the access road, on the left.

57 Lake Tillery

Key species: Striped bass, largemouth bass, crappie, sunfish, white bass, white perch

Overview: Progress Energy, formerly Carolina Power and Light, began construction of the Tillery hydroelectric development in 1926. The project was completed and the plant was placed in service in the spring of 1928. Progress Energy has restricted shoreline development at Lake Tillery. The lake has therefore retained the tranquility that attracts boaters from around the area.

Best ways to fish: Motorboat, kayak, canoe

Best time to fish: February through November

Redbreast sunfish come in a variety of colors depending upon the color of the water they inhabit. This one came from extremely clear water and is therefore light in color. But the red belly and long gill cover remain constant identifiers. Redbreast sunfish are found statewide.

Description: Lake Tillery covers 5,260 acres at full capacity and has 118 miles of shoreline. It is 72 feet deep at the dam. The surface is 278 feet above sea level.

The fishing: For largemouth bass, anglers cast crankbaits, spinnerbaits, and soft plastics in the coves and along the undeveloped shorelines. Woody cover, rocky shorelines, and emergent aquatic vegetation create excellent bass habitat. The best bass fishing occurs in spring and fall, but bass can be caught at any time of year. Tillery has more grassy areas than the other lakes in the Yadkin chain, so anglers take advantage of the opportunity in spring and summer, when the grass beds offer shade and oxygenated water. A floating worm or other topwater lure is the best bet for fishing the grass.

The best crappie fishing occurs where the fish congregate in the tops of fallen trees extending into the water. Brush piles and fish attractors have also been placed in the lake for concentrating crappie. In January and February, trolling with jigs is an excellent way to catch crappie before they enter the coves to spawn. Anglers rig multiple jigs with different colors and sizes of plastic trailers and with live minnows to create a crappie smorgasbord.

Stripers are abundant in the lake. The dam tailrace is an excellent place to fish for them in spring. The main lake points are also excellent sites. Anglers should watch for birds to locate striper schools in winter. As the water warms and the

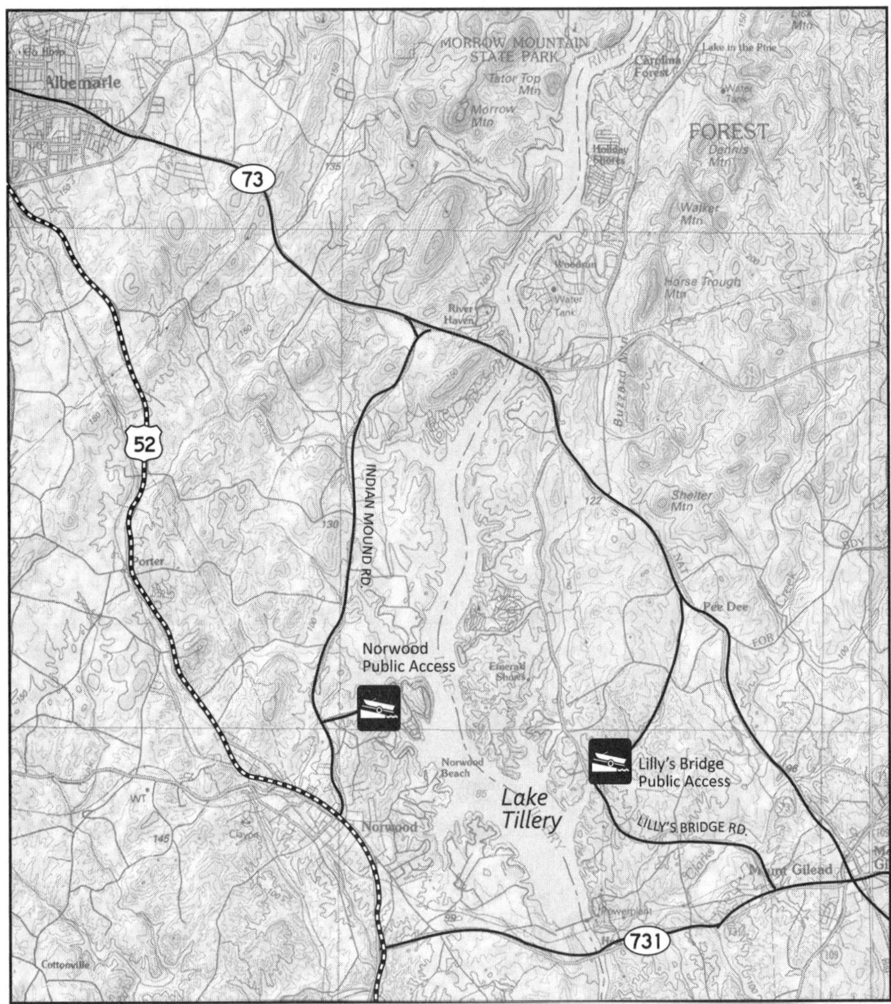

birds disappear, anglers target stripers by slow-trolling or drifting with live baits or by fast-trolling with deep-diving lures or planer rigs. Jigging is also a popular tactic for stripers when they are deep.

Lake Tillery also has excellent fishing for blue catfish and flathead catfish. The best fishing for catfish occurs in the deep holes at night. Live and cut shad and live bream are the best catfish baits.

White perch and white bass are present in Lake Tillery. Anglers have excellent opportunities for catching schooling fish. Spoons, jigs, and small crankbaits are the best lures. The best times to fish are early and late in the day, when the fish often feed at the surface.

The Uwharrie River enters Lake Tillery on the opposite bank from Morrow Mountain State Park. The park offers canoe rentals and other amenities. The Uwharrie River is a great place for fishing from a canoe or kayak above the rapids. It is the state's easternmost water that has smallmouth bass. The river offers excellent fishing for white perch, largemouth bass, smallmouth bass, striped bass, spotted bass, and white bass.

N.C. A-G grid: 59, C-5

General information: All NCWRC regulations apply. Hydrilla is present in Lake Tillery. Herbicides are used in an attempt to combat this nonnative invasive plant. Anglers are advised to wash their boats after fishing Lake Tillery to prevent the spread of hydrilla to other lakes.

See the appendix for contact information for Progress Energy and Morrow Mountain State Park.

Nearest camping: Camping is allowed on the east bank of Lake Tillery in Uwharrie National Forest. Morrow Mountain State Park offers overnight lodging at cabins and campsites; it also offers several historic sites, hiking, canoe rentals, a swimming pool, boating access, and other recreational opportunities.

Directions: To reach Lilly's Bridge Public Access Area from N.C. 73 in Mount Gilead in Montgomery County, travel west on N.C. 731 for 2.3 miles to Lilly's Bridge Road (S.R. 1110). Turn right and drive 2.5 miles to the access area, on the left before the bridge.

To reach Norwood Public Access Area from N.C. 740 in Albemarle in Stanly County, drive east on N.C. 24/N.C. 27/N.C. 73 for 5 miles to Indian Mound Road (S.R. 1740). Turn right and continue 5.4 miles to Lakeshore Drive (S.R. 1797). Turn left and travel 0.5 mile to the access area, on the left.

58 Pee Dee River

Key species: Largemouth bass, crappie, sunfish, blue catfish, flathead catfish, striped bass, American shad, hickory shad

Overview: The Pee Dee River near Wadesboro separates Anson and Richmond counties and hosts unique fishing opportunities. The water discharge from the Blewett Falls hydroelectric power station can change the flow volume and depth quickly.

Best ways to fish: Bank, johnboat

Best times to fish: The Pee Dee has something to catch at any time during the year. The best months for striped bass are May and June. For large blue catfish, the best months are January to June. The best months for catching shad and crappie are March through May. Other species bite from May to November.

Description: The Pee Dee begins as the Yadkin River near Blowing Rock. It is impounded by several dams used for flood control and hydroelectric power, which have created fishing lakes covered in this book. The Pee Dee flows freely downstream of Blewett Falls Dam. It is called the Great Pee Dee River as it enters South Carolina. Some 195 miles downstream of Blewett Falls Dam, the river discharges into the Atlantic Ocean at Winyah Bay, South Carolina.

The fishing: Anadromous fish such as striped bass and shad swim upstream in the Pee Dee from the ocean to spawn. Since the Pee Dee is dangerous to navigate downstream of Blewett Falls Dam, the fishing pressure is minimal. Nevertheless, anglers catch some impressive catfish and striped bass. This section offers unique fishing because it is located in the central part of the state but has no dams downstream to block the sea runs of fish. This leads to catches of some fish species that are otherwise unavailable without driving much farther eastward. The Pee Dee is also the habitat of the robust redhorse sucker, a species of special concern. Anyone who catches one of these rare fish should notify the NCWRC.

The best bets for shad fishing are darts, spoons, and small jigs with soft, curly-tailed trailers, which also work well for crappie and small stripers. For large stripers, live shad, bucktail jigs, and spoons are the best bets.

The boating access areas on either side of the river receive low use. Low-water conditions make launching difficult or impossible, and the parking lots are not well maintained because they receive so little use. A few experts fish the river downstream of the dam for trophy flathead and blue catfish, dropping live and cut baits into the deep holes behind the boulders in the river. Most anglers fish from anchored boats. The best style of anchor is a grapnel. Anglers equip their outboards with special plates to prevent damage to propellers and lower units. The river is a good place for using a jet-drive engine. Other anglers fish from the rocks or wade. Wading anglers must be extremely cautious not to become trapped by rising water.

The trick to fishing the river is learning its moods. Watching the water from the ramp for a few minutes before launching a boat reveals whether it is rising or falling, how fast it is rising or falling, and therefore the status of the discharge from the dam. The best fishing occurs when the water is flowing fairly fast. Most anglers do not venture far from the ramp after launching so they can return if conditions change. Anglers should wear personal flotation devices at all times when fishing the river.

The public fishing area is an eight-foot concrete platform extending the length of the powerhouse wall. For anglers who do not wish to brave the currents or do not have a boat, the public fishing area offers an incredible opportunity for catching all of the river's fish species.

Pee Dee National Wildlife Refuge, located upstream of Blewett Falls Lake, offers some bank-fishing access to the river. Two ponds in the refuge have fishing piers. One is located at the refuge office and the other at Arrowhead Lake. Fish are stocked in Arrowhead Lake through the NCWRC's Community Fishing Program; the lake has a feeder to attract fish.

N.C. A-G grid: 71, A-5

General information: All NCWRC regulations apply. See the appendix for contact information for Pee Dee National Wildlife Refuge.

Nearest camping: Camping is not allowed at Pee Dee National Wildlife Refuge or on Anson County game lands.

Directions: To reach Blewett Falls Public Fishing Access Area from U.S. 220 in Rockingham, travel west on U.S. 74 for 6.3 miles, turn right on S.R. 1748 (Power Plant Road), and go 2.5 miles. The parking lot is on the right just before the entrance to Progress Energy's Blewett hydroelectric plant.

To reach Blewetts Grave Boating Access Area from Rockingham, travel west on U.S. 74 for 4 miles, turn right on Old Charlotte Highway (S.R. 1140), drive 0.9 mile to Blewett Falls Road (S.R. 1141), turn right, and continue 4.5 miles to the access road, on the left.

To reach Rockingham Access Area, travel approximately 6 miles west from Rockingham on U.S. 74 to the bridge over the Pee Dee. The access is under the bridge on the Rockingham side.

59 Blewett Falls Lake

Key species: Largemouth bass, crappie, sunfish, blue catfish, flathead catfish

Overview: Blewett Falls Lake is named after a local family. The former site of the falls is now under the lake. The lake and dam are owned by Progress Energy. Blewett Falls Lake is the last lake on the Pee Dee River before it flows freely to the Atlantic.

Best way to fish: Boat

Randy Willard caught this blue catfish at Blewett Falls Lake.

Best times to fish: Spring and fall

Description: Blewett Falls Lake is a 2,560-acre lake created when the Pee Dee River was dammed for hydroelectric power in 1912. The dam is 50 feet above the riverbed, which brings the lake level to an average of 178 feet above sea level. At full-pond conditions, the lake has approximately 34 miles of shoreline.

The fishing: Blewett Falls Lake is mostly shallow and has an abundance of structure. The best fishing is for blue and flathead catfish. Most catfish anglers fish for both species. Blue catfish prefer cut baits such as cut shad and panfish fished on the bottom. The best areas for blue catfish are the old creek channels and the river channel edges where steep drop-offs occur. Anglers find blue catfish by watching their depthfinders for shad schools orienting to this type of structure. Places where creek channels enter the old riverbed are the best bets for finding blue catfish.

The lake has many stumpy and rocky areas that attract flathead catfish. Flathead catfish are territorial, so catching one or two from a structure means the area is fished out and the angler should move to another location. Using a live sunfish on a float rig at dusk is the best tactic for catching flathead catfish. Both catfish species reach enormous size in the lake.

Anglers can catch sunfish in the river channel. However, the rocky areas can be treacherous, so caution is advised. It is a beautiful area to fish.

Largemouth bass are present in the lake. Spring is the best time to catch them.

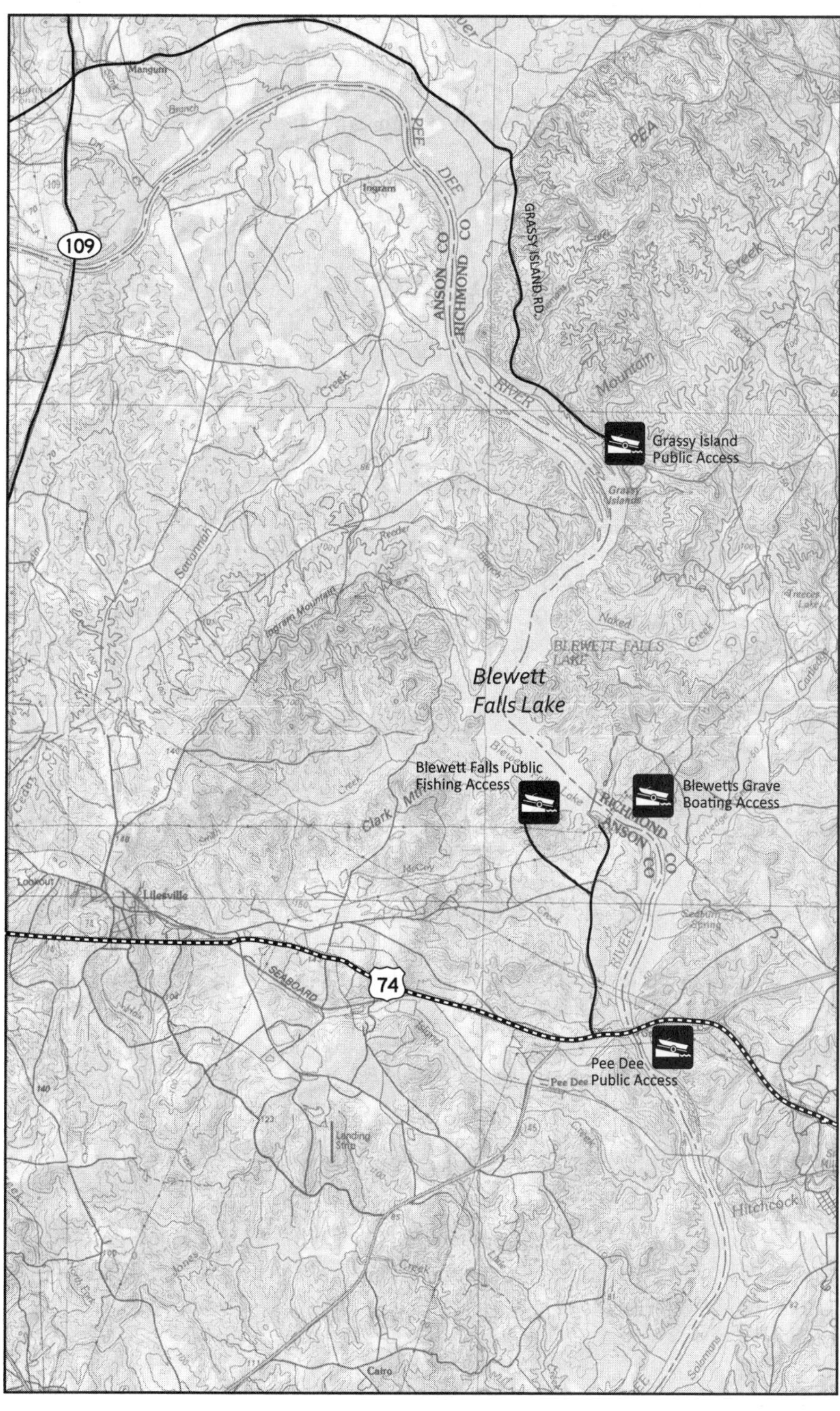
Grassy Island
Public Access
Blewett
Falls Lake
Blewett Falls Public
Fishing Access
Blewetts Grave
Boating Access
Pee Dee
Public Access
109
74
GRASSY ISLAND RD.
ANSON CO
RICHMOND CO
PEE DEE RIVER

All tactics work well. The stumpy areas and rocky points are great places for fishing topwater lures in spring. But any crankbait resembling a shad is also a good bet, particularly in the pre-spawn period in February and March. Spinnerbaits also work well in spring. During the summer, fishing a soft plastic in the deep channels is the best bet.

N.C. A-G grid: 71, A-6

General information: All NCWRC regulations apply. See the appendix for information on Progress Energy lakes.

Nearest camping: Camping is not allowed in Pee Dee National Wildlife Refuge or on Anson County game lands.

Directions: To reach Grassy Island Public Boat Access from N.C. 73 in Mount Gilead, travel 7 miles south on N.C. 109 into Richmond County, take a left on Grassy Island Road (S.R. 1148), and continue 10.5 miles to the access, on the left.

To reach Pee Dee Public Boat Access from the Pee Dee River bridge on U.S. 74 near Rockingham, travel 0.5 mile west to Power Plant Road (S.R. 1745), turn left, continue 0.2 mile to S.R. 1747, and turn left. Drive 0.8 mile to S.R. 1759 and turn right to the access area.

60 Cane Creek Park

Key species: Largemouth bass, crappie, bluegill, catfish

Overview: Canc Crcck is a family-oriented park located in Union County just south of Waxhaw. It was constructed for recreation.

Best ways to fish: Motorboat, canoe, kayak, bank, pier

Best times to fish: Spring and fall are the peak times, but crappie and bass bite all year long.

Description: Cane Creek Lake is a 350-acre lake formed by the impoundment of Cane Creek. The park covers a total of 1,050 acres. The lake's average depth is 11 to 12 feet; the deepest place is 41 feet.

The fishing: Cane Creek Park is one of the most fishing-friendly parks in the state.

It offers some of North Carolina's best largemouth bass fishing and is also a great place for crappie fishing. The lake's forage base is threadfin shad.

A fishing pier is located at the boat ramp, a pier at the activity center, and three piers at the campground. Bank fishing is available at the day-use area and the campground area. Many trails provide good access to the lake for fishing. Bank and pier anglers catch crappie, bluegill sunfish, bass, channel catfish, and bullhead catfish.

The bass fishing is excellent from April until midsummer, when the heat makes the fish lethargic. It picks up again from September through November. Bass anglers use soft plastic lures on Carolina rigs; green and purple are the best colors. Some good spawning areas are located in the upper end where Cane Creek enters the lake. The lake level fluctuates very little. The water is fairly clear, allowing anglers to see the bedding bass in April and May. A few stumpy areas and some old fish attractors set out in the 1980s and 1990s create bass structure, but they are no longer marked with buoys. Anglers can get information on the attractors' locations at the rangers' office. Lots of riprap on the banks also creates bass structure. When the water gets hot in summer, topwater lures fished along the riprap early and late in the day work well for bass. Bass of more than five pounds are caught regularly. A few in the 10-pound range are caught every spring. The lake record for bass is 11 pounds, 15 ounces.

The crappie fishing is excellent in spring and fall, when fish weighing more than two pounds are hauled from the lake. Many anglers catch their limits of crappie. The crappie caught in the fall are usually larger than in the spring. Crappie anglers fish at the old Christmas tree attractors. Several ledges that drop from eight to 18 feet also hold schools of crappie.

Popping bugs cast with fly rods are popular for catching bluegill sunfish. But anglers using worms and crickets also experience great fishing. The first of May is the best time to fish with popping bugs. Anglers can see the spawning beds and smell the spawning fish to find the bedding areas.

Fishing for channel catfish is popular with campers who fish through the night. Catfish of eight to 12 pounds can be caught. Worms and commercial stinkbaits work well for catfish. Catfish bait is available at the campground office; live baits are also available at the park office.

N.C. A-G grid: 80, D-4

General information: All NCWRC regulations apply. Motorboats are allowed, but no water scooters or water-skiing is permitted on weekends. Canoe and rowboat rentals are available. Fees are charged for boat launching and for fishing. Hours of operation vary throughout the year but are typically from dawn until dusk. Shallow-water hazards are marked. The park offers many amenities including playground areas and picnic shelters.

Nearest camping: Cane Creek Park has 108 campsites for primitive camping and recreational vehicles. It also offers rental cabins, swimming areas, miniature golf, hiking trails, and horseback riding.

Directions: To reach Cane Creek Park from N.C. 75 (Waxhaw Highway) in Waxhaw, head south on Old Providence Road (S.R. 1111) for 1.8 miles. Turn right at Providence Road (S.R. 1117), continue for 5 miles, and turn left at Harkey Road (S.R. 1121). The access is on the right.

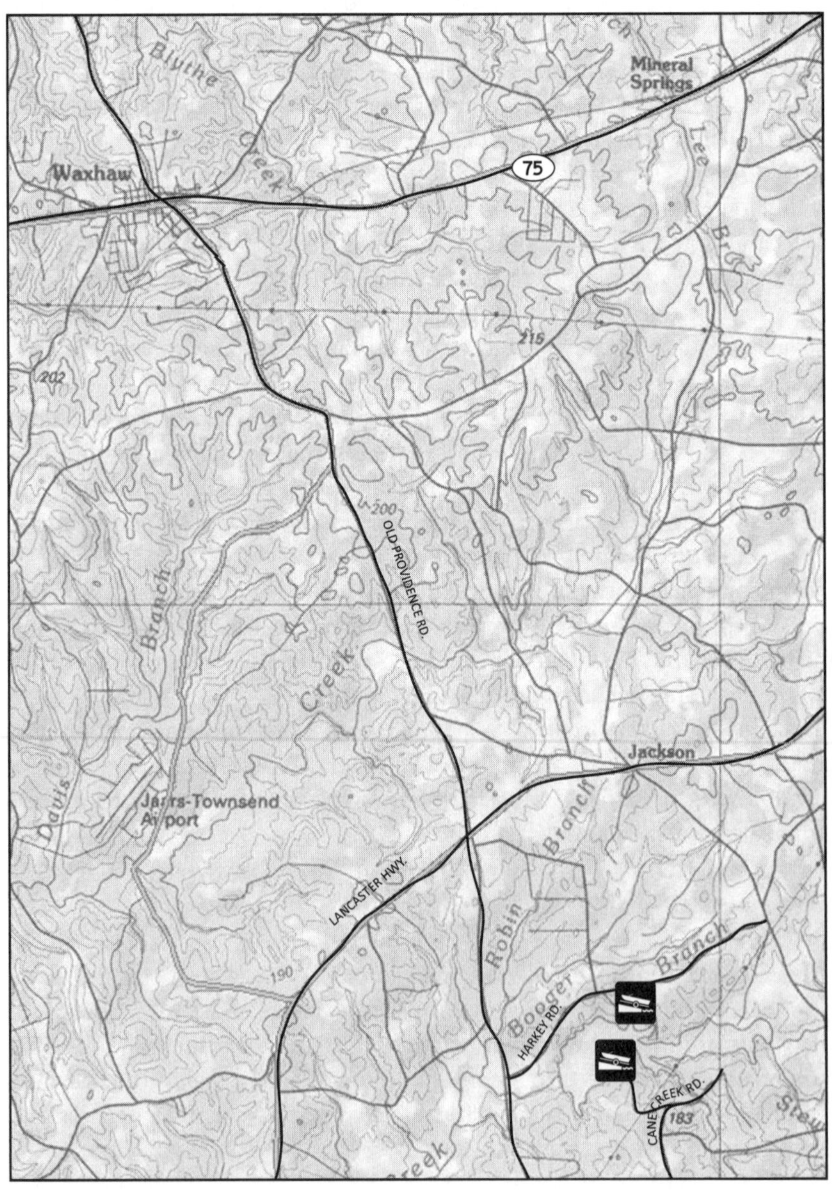

Coastal Region

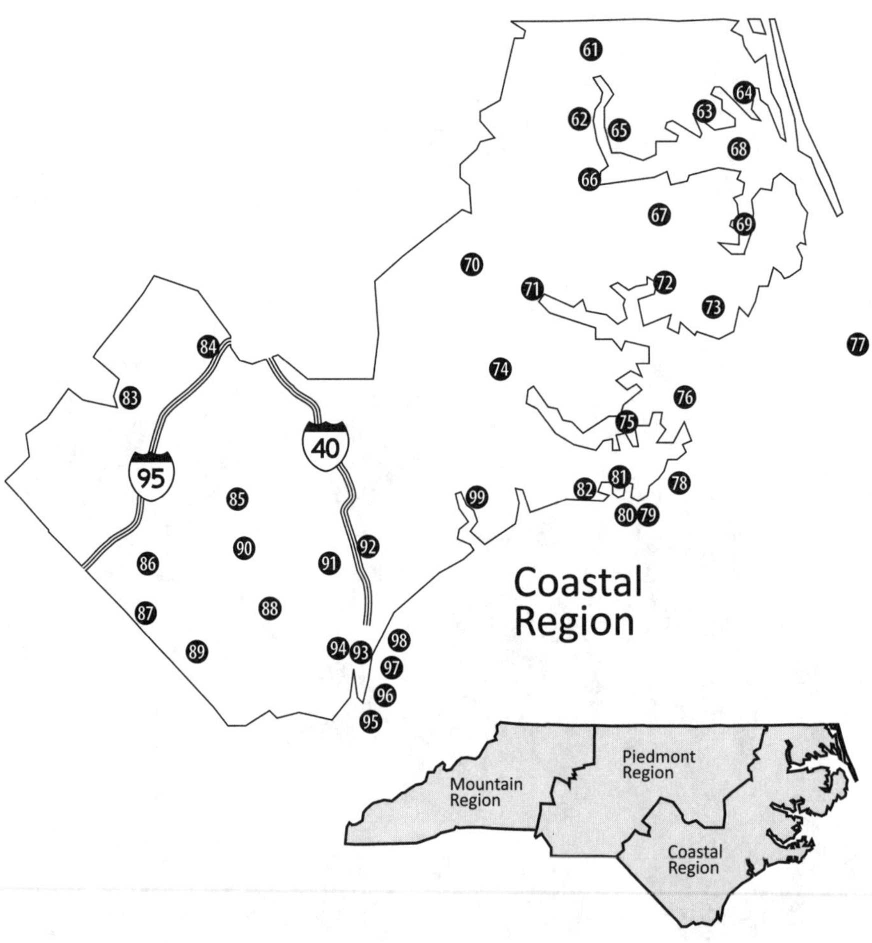

|| Previous page: Trent Evans fishes for pumpkinseed sunfish at the grass beds of Lake Waccamaw.

Basil Watts caught this big bluegill sunfish at Merchants Millpond using a popping bug fished on fly tackle. Huge tupelo and cypress trees make a paddle trip to the state park a unique adventure.

61 Merchants Millpond

Key species: Bluegill, largemouth bass, chain pickerel, black crappie

Overview: Merchants Millpond is part of a state park located in Gates County. Built in 1811 on Bennett's Creek and originally named Norfleets Millpond, the impoundment became a center of economic development for the county. For this reason, it became known as Merchants Millpond.

Best ways to fish: Canoe, kayak

Best time to fish: March through June. During the summer, the weeds make fishing difficult.

Description: Merchants Millpond is about 200 years old. Its total water surface is around 700 acres. The state park contains approximately 3,250 acres and encompasses Lassiter Swamp, which feeds water to Merchants Millpond. Ancient tupelo and cypress trees shade the water and provide a tranquil setting. The black water of the pond reflects the treetops, and the shade keeps boaters cool. This is one of the best places in the state to view a stand of water tupelo with their characteristic buttressed trunks.

The fishing: Fishing around tree trunks and overhangs can yield a largemouth bass or a big bluegill. Other species present are warmouth and pumpkinseed sunfish. In spring, anglers may find some good fishing for black crappie. But the crappie fishing is very cyclic. The bass fishing is poor, though some nice bass are in the millpond. The productivity of the fishing depends upon summer rainfall patterns. The action for all species is fairly good following several years of stable water levels during the summer. Oxygen depletion is a problem in years that have low summer rainfall. However, low water levels also help clear some of the thick aquatic vegetation for better fishing access.

N.C. A-G grid: 24, B-4

General information: All NCWRC regulations apply. The park offers hiking trails, canoe rentals, and marked paddle trails. It is closed on state holidays. Its hours vary depending upon the time of year. See the appendix for contact information for Merchants Millpond State Park.

Nearest camping: The primitive campsites at Merchants Millpond State Park are accessible by foot travel and canoe. The park also has picnic and group camping facilities.

Directions: To reach Merchants Millpond State Park from U.S. 13 in the town of Tarheel, travel east on U.S. 158 for 2.3 miles, take a slight right onto Honeypot Road (S.R. 1400), and continue 1.5 miles. The park is on the left.

62 Chowan River

Key species: Largemouth bass, bluegill, chain pickerel, warmouth, striped bass, black crappie, white perch, yellow perch

Overview: The Chowan River is the main watercourse in the second-largest river basin in the United States; only the Chesapeake Bay basin is larger. However, this is one of the smallest river basins in North Carolina because most of the watershed is in Virginia. The majority of the river's drainage area is undeveloped swampland. The waters and tributaries are free flowing or tidally influenced. The Chowan River is located entirely in North Carolina. It flows from the confluence of the Nottoway and Blackwater rivers at the Virginia line for 50.6 miles before entering Albemarle Sound. The third major tributary, the Meherrin River, empties into the Chowan about 36 miles above the river mouth.

Best ways to fish: Motorboat, kayak, canoe

Best time to fish: Something is biting year-round, but the hottest fishing action occurs in the spring.

Description: It is hard to imagine that only a few decades ago, the Chowan River was declared dead. Today, through the work of concerned citizens, scientists, and conservationists, the Chowan River basin has become a fishermen's paradise. Considering the many species to be caught and the pristine surroundings along its shoreline, the Chowan is an excellent destination for those who want to see coastal scenery. It is a slow-flowing river with a variety of bottom conditions from deep to shallow, vegetated to clear. Lots of deadfalls and snags provide fish-attracting structure.

The fishing: The Chowan is considered some of the best fishing waters in North Carolina. However, the unexplained severe decline in river herring (both the blueback herring and alewife species) has led to the loss of one of the most amazing fisheries on the river. The decline is so severe that fishing for river herring has been severely restricted. River herring are an important forage species for largemouth bass and striped bass.

The Chowan offers excellent fishing for stripers in the spring; April and May are the peak months. The run is spectacular. Individual anglers easily catch more than a dozen fish on most days. Trolling or casting shallow-running stickbaits are the most popular methods for catching stripers. However, they also strike topwater poppers, walk-the-dog lures, and jigs. The best topwater strikes occur at dawn and dusk. Stripers are everywhere. Anglers catch them by trolling the channel and by casting to fallen trees, cypress knees, and other shoreline structure. During the day, shady areas along the banks are good spots for casting. Stripers also congregate in the fall, when October is the peak month. Anglers troll crankbaits and shallow-running stickbaits until they find a school, then stop and cast the same lures or switch to topwater lures and jigs.

The largemouth bass fishing is also outstanding. The Chowan hosts several bass tournaments. Many four- to six-pound bass have been caught. The river has even given up a few 10-pound bass. During spring and fall, topwater lures including buzzbaits, propeller lures, and walk-the-dog lures are excellent bets for largemouth bass. Soft plastic lures fished in the standing timber and stumps also work well. Fast-vibration, lipless crankbaits and swimbaits cast along the edges of the cover areas and to schooling bass in the river channel are good bets during

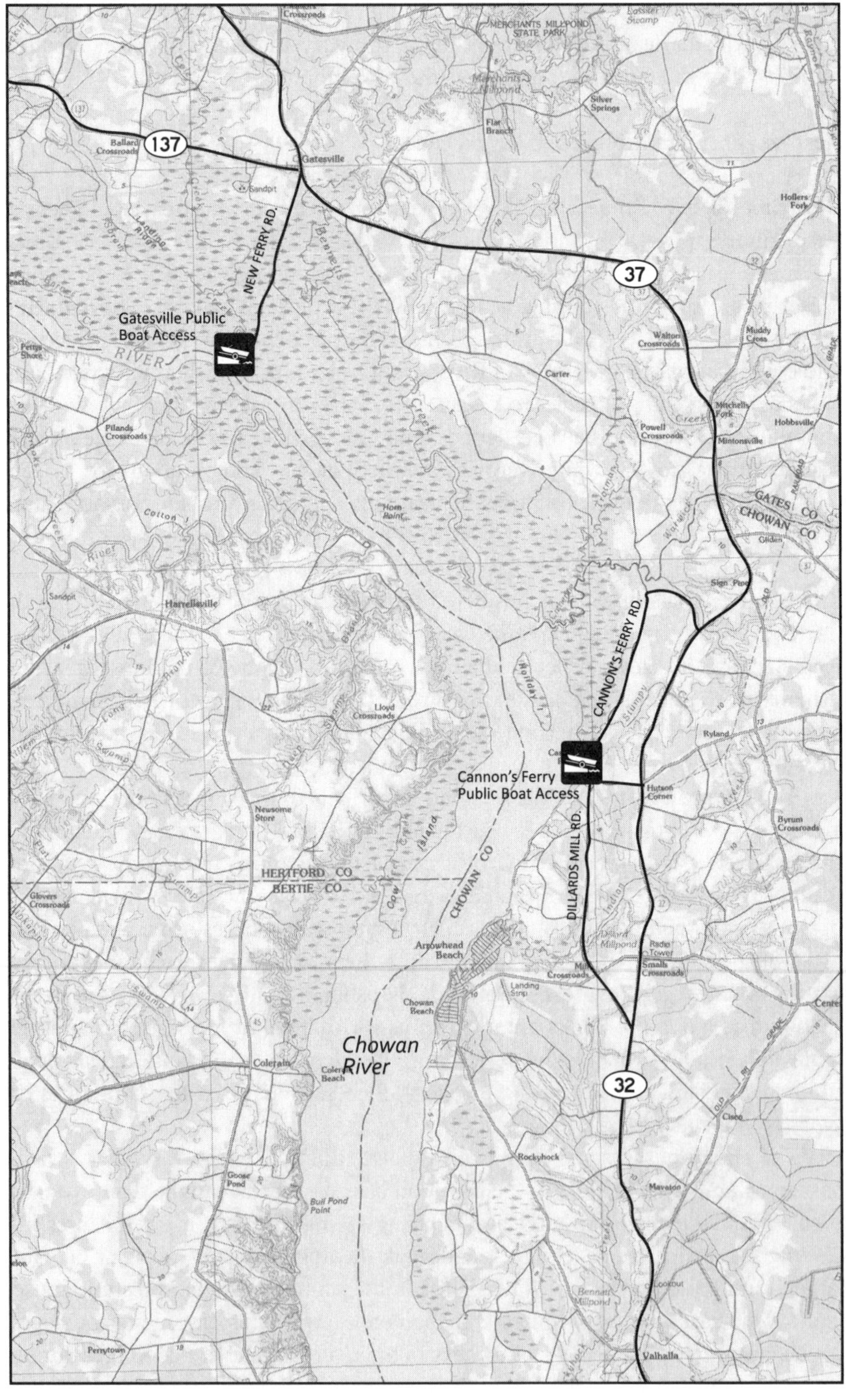
137
37
32
NEW FERRY RD.
Gatesville Public
Boat Access
CANNON'S FERRY RD.
Cannon's Ferry
Public Boat Access
DILLARDS MILL RD.
Chowan
River
Gatesville
Harrellsville
HERTFORD CO
BERTIE CO
CHOWAN CO
GATES CO
CHOWAN CO
Arrowhead Beach
Colerain
Valhalla
Rockyhock
MERCHANTS MILLPOND STATE PARK

the summer months. Spinnerbaits are good choices for working the woody cover areas and swamp edges at any time of year and are especially good for catching bass if the water level is high enough to flood the swamps, when the bass move deep into cover.

Bluegill sunfish grow exceptionally quickly and large in the Chowan and its tributaries. Beetle grub spinners, foam-bodied flies and popping bugs, and live baits such as crickets and worms are the best bets for bluegills. Redbreast sunfish and pumpkinseed sunfish are also abundant. May and June are the best months for catching sunfish. The best places are along the shoreline cover and bars, including bars with pad beds. The small tributaries including Catherine Creek, Bennett's Creek, and the Wiccacon River are good places to catch sunfish.

The swamps are hot and humid during summer, making night the best time for catching catfish in relative comfort. The best places for catfish are the outside bends of channels, where the deepest holes occur. The river has some incredibly deep holes.

The crappie fishing is outstanding in all the feeder creeks during spring and fall. Anglers poke float rigs baited with minnows into downed trees, snags, and other pockets of cover using telescoping fiberglass rods and cane poles. Casting a beetle grub spinner to any woody cover is another good bet for crappie.

A public fishing access was established in 2010 on the east side of the river adjacent to U.S. 17. Chowan River Bridge Access Area, a free public fishing pier, adjoins the original NCWRC boating access area. It consists of 300 feet of the former two-lane road bridge that was replaced by the four-lane U.S. 17 bridge. The site has restrooms and a vending area. Anglers catch striped bass, white perch, catfish, and crappie from the pier.

N.C. A-G grid: 24, D-4

General information: All NCWRC regulations apply. Regulations for striped bass fishing in the waters of northeastern North Carolina are complex and subject to change; they include closed seasons. The NCDHHS has issued an advisory for the consumption of chain pickerel, largemouth bass, and bowfin east of I-95. The NCWRC undertook a restocking effort aimed at restoring largemouth populations to the river system following Hurricane Isabel in 2003, thus establishing a precedent for jump-starting the fishery if and when another heavy rainfall event causes massive oxygen depletion and results in fish kills. Although coastal river fish are capable of recovering on their own, restoration efforts have revived the fishing in impacted rivers like the Chowan at a much faster pace than would naturally occur.

Nearest camping: Primitive campsites are available at nearby Merchants Millpond State Park. Camping platforms for kayakers and canoeists are located along the river in Chowan County. See the appendix for contact information for

Merchants Millpond and the Edenton-Chowan Recreation Department.

Directions: To reach Cannon's Ferry Public Boat Access from U.S. 17 in Edenton, travel north on N.C. 32 for 14.1 miles to Cannon's Ferry Road (S.R. 1231). Turn left and drive 0.9 mile to the access area.

To reach Gatesville Public Boat Access from N.C. 137, travel New Ferry Road (S.R. 1111). The access area is at the end of the road.

63 Perquimans River

Key species: Striped bass, white perch, yellow perch, catfish, flounder, largemouth bass, sunfish

Overview: The Perquimans River is located on the northern shore of Albemarle Sound. Perquimans means "land of beautiful women." The river was named by its earliest inhabitants, the Yeopim Indians, a branch of the Algonquins. It originates in the southern portion of the Great Dismal Swamp and winds slowly south toward Hertford before widening to over a mile and emptying into Albemarle Sound.

Best ways to fish: Canoe, kayak, motorboat

Best time to fish: Year-round

Description: The Perquimans River flows slowly, due to the area's flat topography. The surrounding high ground isn't really very high, reaching an elevation of no more than 10 feet above sea level. Most of the river is surrounded by a cypress-tupelo swamp. It offers more than 64 miles of fishing.

The fishing: Striped bass bring many anglers to the river in spring and fall. But the spring run is short because the stripers head for the Roanoke River to spawn. Trolling shallow-running stickbaits and topwater walk-the-dog lures is the best bet.

The largemouth bass fishing is outstanding; the river hosts several bass tournaments. Bass of four to eight pounds can be expected. Since they feed on menhaden, herring, and shad, casting stickbaits and crankbaits that resemble small baitfish is a good tactic. Lipless vibrating crankbaits are excellent choices. Spinnerbaits cast in the heavy cover areas are another good bet.

Anglers fishing from canoes and kayaks can paddle upstream of the U.S. 17 bridge and catch abundant largemouth bass and sunfish along the swampy shore-

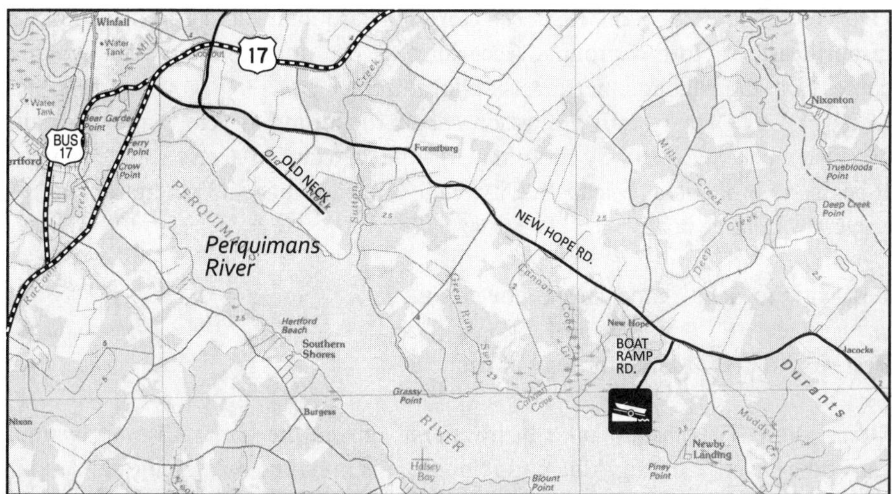

line. When the stripers and shad spawn, anglers crowd the ramps, so be sure to arrive early. The Perquimans has fewer feeder creeks than the Pasquotank. Sutton Creek and Raccoon Creek offer very good bass and bream fishing.

The section of the river between the U.S. 17 bridge and the *S* bridge in Hertford is renowned for its yellow perch fishing in February and March. White perch schools are visible on top in the spring. A good bank-fishing area is located at Missing Mill Park in Hertford.

N.C. A-G grid: 25, D-6

General information: All NCWRC regulations apply.

Nearest camping: Raised camping platforms are available along the Perquimans River and Mill Creek on a first-come, first-served basis. For contact information, see the appendix entry for Paths of the Perquimans.

Directions: To reach Perquimans Public Boat Access from the north end of the Perquimans River bridge on U.S. 17 near Hertford, travel north on U.S. 17 for 0.9 mile, take a right on New Hope Road (S.R. 1300), drive 9.1 miles to Boat Ramp Road (S.R. 1319), turn right, and go 1.2 miles to the access area, on the left.

64 Pasquotank River

Key species: Largemouth bass, striped bass, crappie, white perch, yellow perch, catfish, sunfish, red drum, speckled trout, flounder

Overview: The Pasquotank River runs through Pasquotank and Camden counties in northeastern North Carolina. According to local lore, the name Pasquotank comes from the Algonquian expression for the place "*where the current of the stream divides or forks.*" The river, like most on Albemarle Sound, develops from a small, brackish creek to an estuary more than a mile in width in a very short distance. It begins to broaden at Elizabeth City, which has dockage and entertainment for anglers with large boats.

Best ways to fish: Canoe, kayak, powerboat

Best time to fish: March through November

Description: The Pasquotank's headwaters begin in the Great Dismal Swamp. Like other rivers entering Albemarle Sound, it is impaired by agricultural runoff, which leads to algae blooms, die-offs, decomposition, and oxygen depletion. Rainfall from Hurricane Isabel in 2003 caused massive fish kills, but the river has recovered. Similar events may create the same impact in the future. The wide stretch downstream of Elizabeth City extends 16 miles to Albemarle Sound.

The fishing: The Pasquotank, like other rivers entering Albemarle Sound, flows slowly. The water is fresh to brackish in the upstream stretches and has high salinity in the broader areas near the mouth. Therefore, anglers may catch both saltwater and freshwater fish at the same place and time. Fishing coastal rivers is always an adventure because anglers don't know what will strike next. A topwater lure intended for largemouth bass may attract a strike from a red drum or speckled trout. A live minnow fished on the bottom for flounder, speckled trout, and red drum may catch a largemouth bass or crappie. The most consistent fishing for freshwater species including crappie, sunfish, and largemouth bass is in the narrow reaches upstream of Elizabeth City. Water salinity varies according to wind direction and velocity, as well as rainfall. The wide stretches south of Elizabeth City and close to the sound are the best bets for saltwater fish.

The river is full of striped bass, which may be caught all year. Spring and fall are the best times for catching them; April and October are the premier months. Anglers use stickbaits cast to the shallow flats and shoreline cover. Topwater poppers, propeller lures, and walk-the-dog lures are also good bets.

Soft plastic lures and spinnerbaits cast to the stumps and swamp edges work well for enticing largemouth bass. Schooling fish, whether stripers or largemouth, fall for lipless fast-vibration crankbaits and topwater poppers.

The best bets for crappie and sunfish are the narrow river channel and the creeks above Elizabeth City.

The strength of the saltwater fishing depends on the amount of rainfall during the year. Some years, the water is salty enough that tarpon and speckled trout are

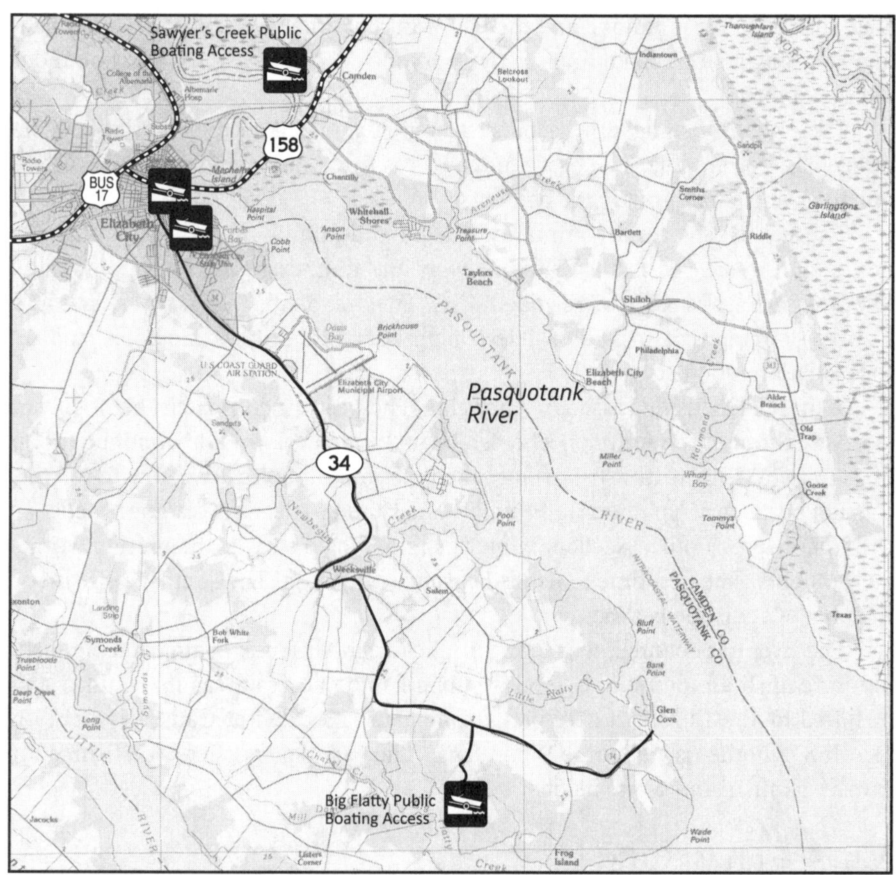

caught all the way upriver to Elizabeth City. During a typical summer, flounder and red drum enter the lower end of the river.

The entire river is a good place to catch stripers in fall and winter. During October and November, stripers school in open water. At that time, trolling crankbaits is a good bet. Once anglers locate a striper school, they stop and cast soft plastic swimbaits. The river is deeper upstream than downstream, which can have an effect on trolling lure depth. Anglers should always watch for surfacing stripers and birds diving on menhaden schools to show the location of stripers.

The largemouth bass fishing is good in the feeder creeks downstream, including Newbegun Creek and Little Flatty Creek. Upstream from Elizabeth City, the Pasquotank turns into a beautiful blackwater stream. Some holes have a depth of 30 feet. Spring and fall are the best times for fishing the blackwater areas. Anything that imitates a juvenile menhaden—including spinnerbaits, small, soft swimbaits, and crankbaits—is a good bet for largemouth bass when cast to woody cover. In warm weather, topwater walk-the-dog lures, lipless fast-vibration crankbaits, and soft plastics fished on the bottom work well. The bass are not nearly as abundant as in the Roanoke and the Chowan, but anglers enjoy some good fishing. Bass anglers can catch four- to five-pound fish. An occasional eight-pounder is a possibility.

The crappie fishing can be outstanding. Juvenile shad and herring are the forage base for crappie. The best time to fish is from late winter into spring. Live minnows and small jigs are the best bets.

The sunfish species are primarily bluegill and pumpkinseed. The panfish action is outstanding in Little Flatty, Newbegun, and Areneuse creeks, as well as any other creek upstream of Elizabeth City. The best panfish baits are crickets and worms. Popping bugs fished on telescoping fiberglass poles, cane poles, and fly rods are also good bets.

White perch fishing is hugely popular. The best time to catch them is from late May through the summer. The fish begin biting at dawn and continue for an hour or two. Anglers drift-fish using cane poles and float rigs baited with worms. Casting beetle grub spinners and small inline spinnerbaits is also a good tactic.

Yellow perch offer excellent winter fishing. Anglers catch them using worms and spinners. The best time to fish is February or March. The stretch upstream of Elizabeth City is the best bet.

The river has channel, white, and bullhead catfish. Bank fishing and pier fishing for catfish are popular at several public fishing access areas maintained and operated by the Elizabeth City parks. One area is located at Causeway Park on U.S. 158. Another is at George Wood Park. The parks' piers offer good fishing for catfish, panfish, and white perch.

N.C. A-G grid: 26, C-2

General information: All NCWRC regulations apply. See the appendix for contact information for the Elizabeth City Parks and Recreation Department.

Nearest camping: Camping is available at Merchants Millpond State Park. See the appendix for contact information.

Directions: To reach the NCWRC's Sawyer's Creek Public Boating Access from U.S. 158 in Camden, drive north on N.C. 343 for 0.7 mile to the Sawyer's Creek bridge. The road to the access area is on the left just north of the bridge.

Two boating access areas are supported by the town of Elizabeth City. Both are located off Water Street. One is in Waterfront Park and the other in Dog Corner Park. To reach these boat ramps from U.S. 17, travel east on U.S. 158 for 1 mile, take a left on Water Street (S.R. 1268), and travel 0.4 mile to the access, on the right.

65 Bennett's Millpond

Key species: Largemouth bass, chain pickerel, panfish

Overview: Built in the 1800s, Bennett's Millpond was the site of a functioning gristmill until the 1960s. Property owners along the shoreline own the bottom of the millpond to its centerline. However, Chowan County has acquired the mill seat, which includes the dam, spillway, millhouse, observation dock, boat dock, and boat ramp. The pond itself is public-trust water, so it is open for public recreational use.

Best ways to fish: Kayak, canoe

Best time to fish: March through June

Description: Bennett's Millpond is an acidic, shallow impoundment covering 180 acres.

The fishing: The millpond's largemouth bass can reach five pounds but are not abundant. The bass fishing ebbs and flows because the water level can get extremely low during drought conditions. Unlike many other small water bodies, Bennett's Millpond remains relatively open at its broadest reaches near the dam and in the center of the pond. Some huge cypress trees grow in the center, but most trees occur in the upstream narrows. Hunting is allowed. Several duck blinds built among the cypress trees provide additional cover for the main attraction, which is the pond's largemouth bass. Soft plastic lures including curly-tailed jigs, lizards, and worms are the top choices for catching bass at any time of year. In the cold months, the best bet for bass is a spinnerbait or live shiner. In the warm months, bass will strike any topwater lure; buzzbaits, propeller lures, and walk-the-dog lures are excellent choices. A floating worm with a very light hook that allows it to sink slowly is one of the deadliest bass lures. An angler will cast into the weed beds or mats of floating duckweed and wriggle the lure along like a snake, letting it pause before dropping into a pocket or the edge of the vegetation. Bass follow the lure's progress, striking it while it moves along on top of the scum or as it falls. The strike is usually spectacular. Gar, bowfin, and chain pickerel strike lures intended for bass.

Bluegill, flier, and redear (shellcracker) are the main panfish species. Yellow perch and black crappie also occur in the millpond's dark, acidic water. The crappie fishing is better in Rocky Hock Creek downstream of the spillway than in the millpond. Anglers often fish for crappie from the footbridge that crosses the creek near the parking area. For crappie, sunfish, and yellow perch, beetle grub spinners and small inline spinners are excellent choices. Fly fishermen using popping bugs and sponge-body ants and spiders will also catch sunfish. But nothing beats a worm or cricket fished on a float rig, whether cast with an ultralight spinning or spincast rig or dangled with a cane pole or telescoping fiberglass pole into a likely looking spot near a tree trunk or fallen limb. The best seasons to fish for panfish are spring and fall. The peak bedding activity runs from April into May and perhaps early June, depending upon water temperature.

N.C. A-G grid: 25, D-4

General information: All NCWRC regulations apply. The site has a good hiking and birding trail. See the appendix listing for the Edenton-Chowan Recreation Department.

Nearest camping: Although camping is allowed, no facilities are available. The best campsite is the level patch of ground near the millhouse.

Directions: To reach the ramp from Edenton, travel N.C. 32 North for approximately 6 miles, turn left on Rocky Hock Road (S.R. 1222), go 200 yards, and watch for the sign for Bennett's Millpond Public Access on the right. Follow the gravel driveway 200 yards to the boat ramp.

66 Cashie, Middle, and Eastmost Rivers

Key species: Largemouth bass, striped bass, crappie, white perch, yellow perch, catfish, sunfish

Overview: The Cashie, Middle, and Eastmost rivers form the closest thing to a true river delta in North Carolina. This area also includes the mouth of the Roanoke River as it enters Albemarle Sound. The Chowan River enters the sound just to the north, creating a unique confluence of five rivers. The shoreline along these rivers is mostly uninhabited and undeveloped because the lowlands are subject to seasonal flooding. The lowland swamps—comprised of old-growth cypress, tupelo, and black gum trees—are beautiful. According to local lore, the Cashie River may have been named after Chief Cashie, the leader of a Tuscarora band that reportedly attacked Edenton in the early 1700s.

Best ways to fish: Kayak, canoe, powerboat

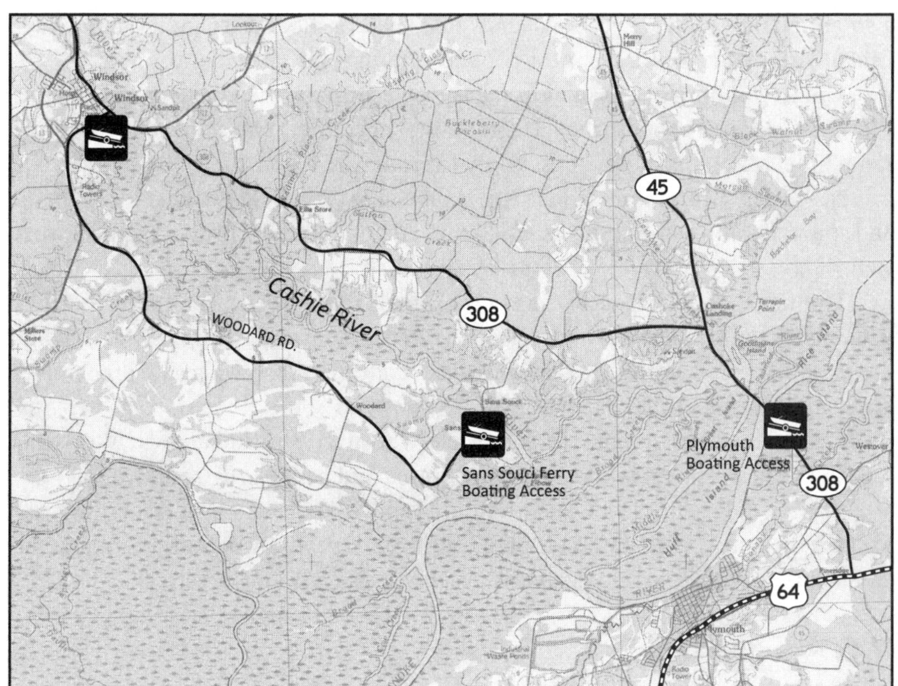

Best times to fish: March through June, October

Description: The Cashie River begins and ends in Bertie County and has some holes as deep as 80 feet. The Middle and Eastmost rivers branch off the Roanoke River in Batchelor Bay, an NCWRC game land.

The fishing: The upper portions of the rivers are freshwater areas with good populations of largemouth bass, crappie, and various sunfish. In terms of variety, size, and numbers, this is one of the best places to fish for many of these species. It is subject to the same oxygen-depletion events following tropical rainfalls that adversely impact other northeastern North Carolina rivers. The region suffered fish kills from Hurricane Isabel, for example. Recovery is assured, thanks to stockings by the NCWRC and the natural reproduction of the surviving fish.

The fishing for black crappie is extraordinary. A good forage base of juvenile menhaden and herring allows crappie to grow quickly and achieve large sizes. Two-pound crappie are not rare. Beetle grub spinnerbaits, jigs, and minnows are the best bets for crappie. Anglers should fish the woody cover along the shoreline. One of the best crappie fishing areas occurs upstream of the Sans Souci ferry landing.

These rivers also offer outstanding shellcracker fishing. The river bottoms are covered with clams that shellcrackers eat. To catch shellcrackers, anglers should fish with worms or shrimp hooked on bottom rigs. Bluegill sunfish are also abundant and large. Worms, crickets fished on float rigs, and popping bugs fished with fly tackle are the most popular offerings for bluegills.

The largemouth bass fishing is fabulous because of the excellent forage base. The area is large enough that it sometimes hosts multiple tournaments at the same time. Many five-pound bass come from the area, and a few 10-pounders are caught. The best lures imitate baitfish. Lipless fast-vibrating crankbaits, stickbaits, and spinnerbaits are the best bets. Early and late in the day, topwater poppers work well.

The fishing for striped bass is good. Small resident stripers are in the river system all summer. The action in the lower Roanoke area picks up in March when the male fish head upriver to spawn. It gets better in April when the big females arrive and continues into early June.

Once the striper season closes, people who want fish to eat switch to white perch. The best bets for white perch are worms and beetle grub spinners.

The lower Cashie is well known for its yellow perch fishing. The best months to catch them are February and March, during the spawning period. Worms, small crankbaits, jigs, and minnows are the best choices for yellow perch.

N.C. A-G grid: 46, B-4

General information: Striped bass regulations in the Roanoke-Albemarle region are complex. Closed seasons are in effect in some areas. All NCWRC regulations apply.

Nearest camping: Multiple campsites are accessible by kayak and canoe along the Cashie River, Broad Creek, and the lower Roanoke River. For information about reserving a campsite, see the appendix entry for Roanoke River Partners. Shipyard Landing is a private campground with cabins and a boat ramp just upstream of the Cashie River mouth; see the appendix for contact information.

Directions: To reach Sans Souci Ferry Boating Access Area from U.S. 13 near Windsor, travel south on U.S. 17 for 1.5 miles to Woodard Road (S.R. 1500), turn left, and drive 10.5 miles. The access area is on the right.

To reach Plymouth Boating Access Area from U.S. 64 east of Plymouth, travel north on N.C. 45 for 3.1 miles. The access area is on the left before the bridge.

67 Lake Phelps

Key species: Largemouth bass, yellow perch, pumpkinseed sunfish, chain pickerel, bullhead catfish

Overview: Lake Phelps is the second-largest natural lake in North Carolina. It is located in Washington County on the Pamlico-Albemarle Peninsula. The lake is named for Josiah Phelps, the first white man to enter its waters. Canoes discovered at Lake Phelps dating from 4400 B.C. are on display at Pettigrew State Park. Artifacts from as early as 8000 B.C. have been found.

Best ways to fish: Wading, powerboat, kayak, canoe, water scooter

Best times to fish: April through June, October

Description: Lake Phelps has a surface area of 16,600 acres. Its depth ranges

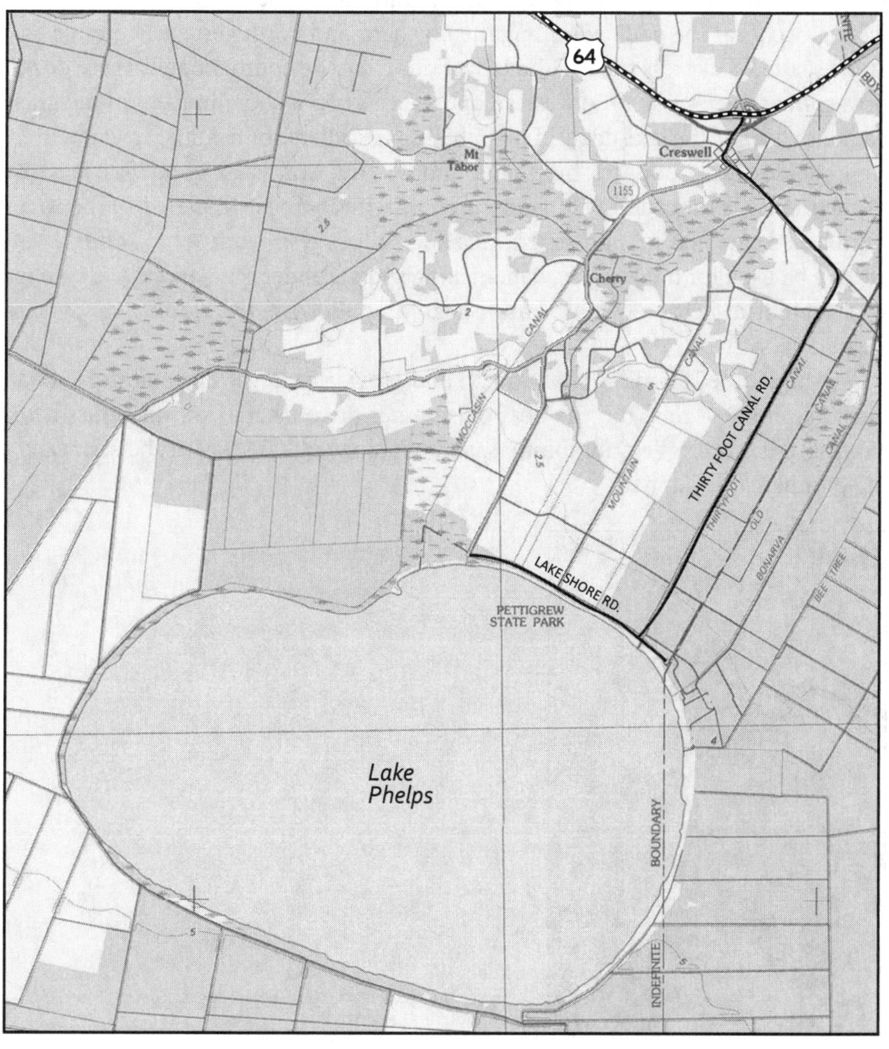

from 4.5 feet to 9 feet. The shallow depth and flat surrounding terrain make the lake prone to wind swell, so anglers must take wind direction into consideration when launching their boats. The lake is very clear. Its level can decline severely during drought conditions. The solid, sandy bottom offers excellent footing for wade fishing.

The fishing: The largemouth bass fishing is excellent at Lake Phelps. Bass are abundant and grow large. Anglers using fly tackle have landed bass weighing more than eight pounds. The water is so clear that anglers can often see the fish before casting to them. The best time to fish is during spring as the water warms and the spawn begins. The bass fishing shuts down during the summer, then picks up again in October. The lake has little shoreline cover, and the edges slope very gradually, making fishing difficult during drought conditions or hot weather. The best bass fishing occurs at the pad beds along the northern and northwestern shoreline and at the scattered cypress trees. Other cover occurs at the approximately three dozen private boat docks along the western and southwestern shoreline and in the grass beds along all of the lake edges. Lake Phelps is excellent for fishing topwater lures; walk-the-dog lures, poppers, buzzbaits, and floating worms are good bets. It is one of the top lakes for catching largemouth bass with fly rods. Anglers fish the edges from bass boats and johnboats. Kayaks and canoes also work well. Water scooters can be used for traveling to wade-fishing spots. Anglers can access the lake for wade fishing at Pettigrew State Park's boat ramp, Pocosin Overlook, and Cypress Point Access Area.

Pumpkinseed sunfish are abundant and grow very large. The colorful sunfish bite well in the spring, but the heat of summer drives them from the grass beds. Worms, crickets, beetle grub spinners, and popping bugs are the best bets for catching pumpkinseed sunfish.

These pumpkinseed sunfish or "grass perch," were caught from Lake Phelps.

Yellow perch school all around the lake. Spring, fall, and winter are the best times to catch them; February and March are the peak months. Anglers locate schools of white perch by drifting with minnows rigged on weighted lines or float rigs and by trolling small spoons, crankbaits, and spinners. Once they find a concentration of yellow perch, anglers cast small jigs, worms, and spoons to the school.

Catfish anglers typically fish from the private docks. Lighted docks are the best places. Bullheads and white catfish are the catfish species in the lake. Worms and liver are the best baits. Anglers also have good luck from the fishing pier at the park's Cypress Point Access Area.

A fish ladder proposed for Bee Tree Canal may reintroduce white perch and herring to the lake. White perch were abundant until a winter kill in the 1980s.

N.C. A-G grid: 47, C-6

General information: All NCWRC regulations apply.

Nearest camping: Pettigrew State Park offers primitive campsites for trailers and tents. The sites have grills and picnic tables and share a bathhouse. Campsites, cabins, and a boat ramp for the sole use of overnight guests are available at Conman's Guide Service and Vacation Rentals. See the appendix for contact information for Pettigrew State Park and Conman's Guide Service and Vacation Rentals.

Directions: To reach Pettigrew State Park from U.S. 64, take Exit 558 (the Creswell exit). Turn left at Main Street (S.R. 1142) and travel 2 miles; the road becomes Spruill's Bridge Road. Turn right on Thirty Foot Canal Road (S.R. 1160) and drive 5 miles. The park is at the end of the road. A boat ramp with a small pier is at the park.

68 Albemarle Sound

Key species: Striped bass, flounder, red drum

Overview: Albemarle Sound is a large estuary in the northeast portion of North Carolina. It is formed at the confluence of the Chowan and Roanoke rivers. The Pasquotank, Perquimans, and Alligator rivers and several other creeks and rivers feed Albemarle Sound. First inhabited in 1586 by Europeans on shoreline plantations, the sound has long been utilized for its fishery. Herring, shad, and striped bass were netted in enough quantities in the past to feed Europe and

New England. However, due to overfishing, herring and other species were almost depleted to extinction.

Best way to fish: Boat

Best times to fish: Spring, fall

Description: Albemarle Sound is a shallow estuary extending 55 miles from the mouths of the Chowan and Roanoke rivers to Pamlico Sound. Albemarle Sound has a maximum depth of 25 feet. It is the largest freshwater sound in North America.

The fishing: Striped bass never leave the area. Trolling is always a good bet for stripers, which can weigh 40 pounds. The biggest stripers come into the sound from the Atlantic in April and May. One of the best places to fish is the N.C. 32 bridge. White perch also school at the bridge. Small jigging spoons are the best bet for the smaller schooling fish. Another good place to catch white perch is Laurel Point Light, located north of the Scuppernong River.

Largemouth bass and crappie can be found in nearly every creek and backwater. The best bets for largemouth bass are crankbaits that resemble menhaden and herring. Crappie anglers use minnows with excellent results.

Anglers fishing for other species routinely catch red drum and flounder, especially when using live bait in the early fall. Soft plastic swimbaits are good lures for catching red drum.

N.C. A-G grid: 48, A-2

General information: All NCWRC and North Carolina Division of Marine Fisheries regulations apply.

Nearest camping: Various camping platforms around the sound are available for rent to paddlers. See the appendix entry for Roanoke River Partners.

Directions: To reach Big Flatty Public Access Area from U.S. 158 in Elizabeth City, travel south on U.S. 17 for 1.1 miles to Halstead Road (S.R. 1152), turn left, and drive 2.1 miles to N.C. 34. Continue on N.C. 34 for 7.5 miles, turn right on Esclip Road (S.R. 1103), travel 2.3 miles to Soundneck Road (S.R. 1104), turn left, drive 1.7 miles to Shadneck Road (S.R. 1108), turn right, and go 1.6 miles. The access road is on the right.

To reach Midway Drive Public Access Area from the north end of the Albemarle Sound bridge on N.C. 32 near Edenton, travel north on N.C. 32 for 1.3 miles to Southside Road (S.R. 1114), turn left, drive 2.8 miles to Midway Drive (S.R.

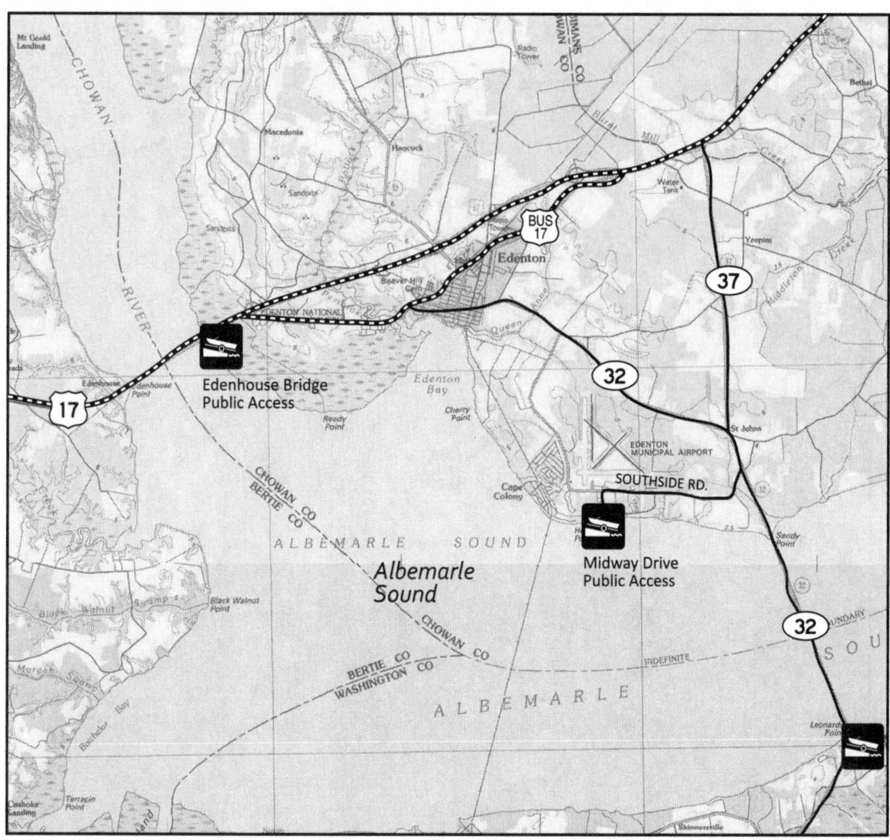

1119), turn left, and go 0.4 mile to the access area, on the right.

To reach East Lake Ferry Public Access Area from the community of Alligator, travel east on U.S. 64, take a left on Old Ferry Dock Road (S.R. 1153), and drive 0.2 mile. The access area is on the left.

To reach Edenhouse Bridge Public Access Area from N.C. 32 in Edenton, travel south on U.S. 17 for 2.7 miles, take Exit 224 for West Queen Extended (S.R. 1204), turn right, go 0.1 mile to Wildlife Access Road, turn left, and drive 0.9 mile to the access area.

69 Alligator River

Key species: Striped bass, largemouth bass, bluegill, crappie, yellow perch, white perch, flounder, red drum, speckled trout, spot, croaker

Overview: The Alligator River is a freshwater tributary of Albemarle Sound. Part

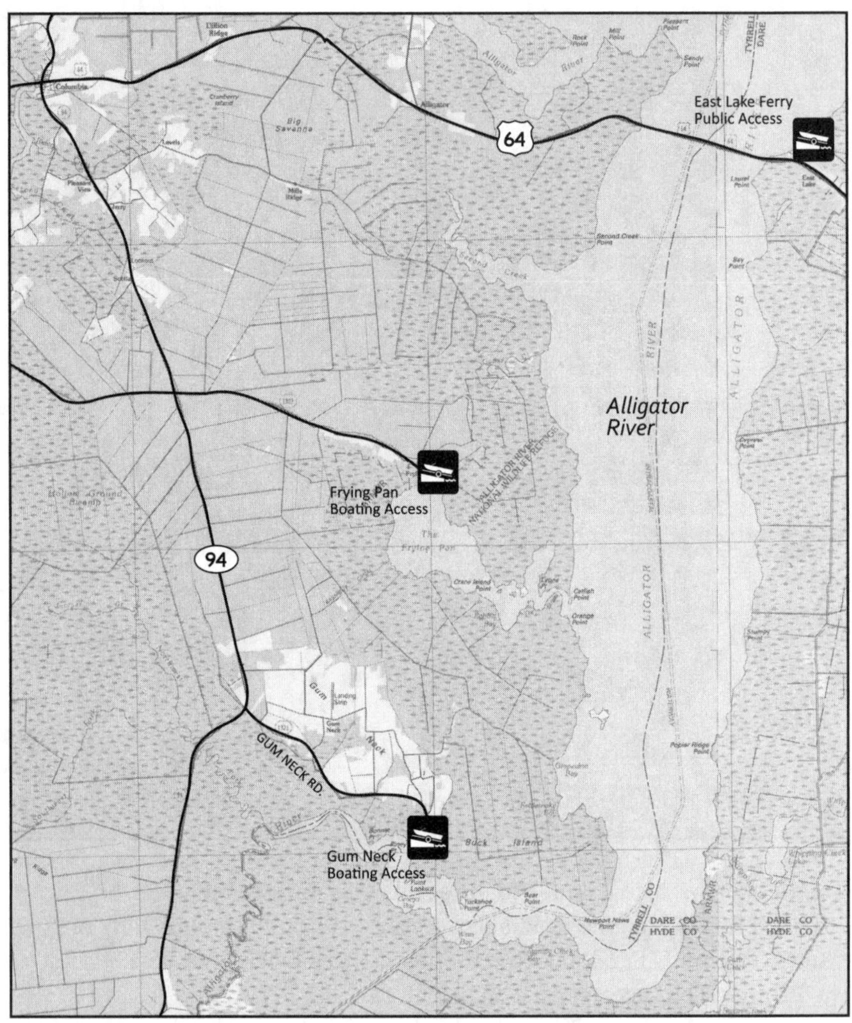

of the Intracoastal Waterway, it connects to the Pungo River via a canal that is 21 miles long.

Best way to fish: Motorboat

Best times to fish: Spring and fall

Description: The Alligator River is surrounded by a pocosin, a Native American word meaning "swamp on a hill." It is located between Pocosin Lakes National Wildlife Refuge on the west and Alligator River National Wildlife Refuge on the east. The water ranges in salinity from fresh to brackish. Some saltwater fishing opportunities are available at the river mouth.

The fishing: Most of the fishing on the Alligator River occurs at the U.S. 64 bridge connecting Dare and Tyrell counties. The bridge is a good place to catch striped bass and white perch, which can be found anywhere in the wide river channel. Striper fishing is subject to a closed season. While some anglers catch and release stripers after the season closes, biologists say the fish are under stress in warm water and have an extremely poor survival rate, so they would like to discourage the practice.

Another good place to fish is "the Frying Pan," a natural bay on the west side of the river. The Frying Pan allows anglers to get out of the wind and provides them a likely opportunity to catch saltwater species.

In the upstream end of the river, freshwater species dominate. Largemouth bass are abundant from approximately Newport News Point to Gum Neck, where the water becomes too acidic for optimum bass habitat. Above Gum Neck, blackwater species like chain pickerel and flier take over from the bass and bluegill. Since this transition area changes with precipitation, anglers should check the water clarity. If the water is stained dark with tannin, it is likely too acidic for good bass fishing.

N.C. A-G grid: 48, B-3

General information: All NCWRC regulations apply.

Nearest camping: No public camping opportunities are available along the Alligator River.

Directions: To reach East Lake Ferry Public Access Area from the community of Alligator, travel east on U.S. 64, turn left on Old Ferry Dock Road (S.R. 1153), and drive 0.2 mile. The access area is on the left.

To reach Frying Pan Boating Access Area from U.S. 64 in Columbia, travel south on N.C. 94 for 6.8 miles to Frying Pan Road (S.R. 1307), turn left, and drive 5.5 miles. The access area is on the right.

To reach Gum Neck Boating Access Area from U.S. 64 in Columbia, travel south on N.C. 94 for 13.1 miles to South Gum Neck Road (S.R. 1321), turn left, and travel 1.6 miles to S.R. 1316.

70 Tar River

Key species: Largemouth bass, striped bass, shad, crappie, white perch, catfish, sunfish

Overview: The Tar River received its name for the same reason that North Carolina came to be nicknamed the Tar Heel State. North Carolina was once a colony that provided naval stores to the British Empire. The vast pine forests provided tar and pitch for the British navy.

Best ways to fish: Powerboat, kayak, canoe

Best times to fish: Spring, summer, fall

Description: The Tar River is approximately 215 miles long. It begins near Louisburg and ends at the Pamlico River. The Tar River was the site of the worst flooding from Hurricane Floyd in 1999. In Greenville, the water crested at 30 feet, exceeding 500-year flood levels.

The fishing: The dark waters of the Tar River are good for freshwater species commonly found in North Carolina's coastal plain. The water level rises and falls dramatically depending upon rainfall. During low water, navigation can be difficult for anglers with powerboats. The best access is at Tarboro.

The largemouth bass fishing is good. Catches of fish weighing four to six pounds are possible. For the best luck, bass anglers cast spinnerbaits and crankbaits in spring. Muddy water conditions dictate the use of vibration lures and rattle inserts in soft plastics to attract the attention of the fish. The best fishing occurs during falling water and at creek mouths, bars, steep banks, and woody cover such as deadfalls and stumps. As the water warms, topwater action picks up. As in most coastal rivers, bass will strike topwater lures and soft plastics all year long. During the hot months, fishing the shady areas and logjams early and late in the day is the best bet for bass.

The Tar River has excellent fishing for American and hickory shad during the spring spawning run, which begins in March and continues into May. Anglers fish in the mouths of feeder creeks and near bridges and bends where the current flow is disrupted. The best tactic is anchoring a boat in the mouth of a creek where clear water enters the muddy river water. This occurs as the river is falling after a rain. Shad strike spoons, curly-tailed jigs, and darts fished at the "wall" created by the two different water chemistries. A popular method is to use a tandem rig consisting of a jig along with a spoon or a dart rigged with a spoon. The best spoon color is gold because of the turbid water.

Some nice channel catfish swim in the Tar River. Fresh and frozen shad, shrimp, liver, worms, and commercial dough or dip baits work well for catching them.

The best sunfish action occurs from April through June. The bite picks up again as the water cools in the fall. Beetle grub spinners, worms, and crickets are the best bets.

The crappie fishing can be good, though concentrations of crappie can be hard to locate. Many crappie are caught by anglers fishing for panfish. Crappie bite through the fall and winter months, but the best bite occurs in April. A minnow fished with a long cane or fiberglass pole and a float rig is the best bet. But jigs and beetle grub spinners cast with ultralight tackle also catch crappie.

N.C. A-G grid: 65, A-6

General information: All NCWRC regulations apply.

Nearest camping: Tent and trailer camping is available at Medoc Mountain State Park, located approximately 21 miles north of Rocky Mount. See the appendix for contact information.

Directions: To reach Falkland Public Boating Access from N.C. 43, take N.C. 222 East. The access is on the east side of the Tar River bridge.

To reach Town Commons Park Access Area from U.S. 264, travel east on N.C. 43 (Martin Luther King Jr. Drive) for 1 mile, turn left on Greene Street (S.R. 1531), drive 0.3 mile, and turn right on First Street. The access area is on the left.

71 Pamlico and Pungo Rivers

Key species: Striped bass, red drum, flounder, speckled trout, cobia, tarpon, black drum

Overview: The Tar River becomes the Pamlico River at the U.S. 17 bridge connecting the towns of Washington and Chocowinity. On the shoreline of the Pamlico River is Bath, the oldest town in North Carolina and once the home port of the pirate Blackbeard.

Best ways to fish: Powerboat, kayak, canoe

Best time to fish: Something is biting year-round.

Description: The Pamlico River has depths of about 12 feet. The river extends approximately 40 miles from Washington to Pamlico Sound.

The fishing: In the upper Pamlico River, the fishing conditions are best for freshwater species. The lower Pamlico holds mainly saltwater species. However, the striper fishing is outstanding throughout the river system. The best striper fishing occurs at Washington, where stripers hold at the U.S. 17 bridge, the railroad trestle, and Chocowinity Bay. Anglers should watch for sea gulls, which reveal the location of feeding stripers. When stripers are feeding at the surface, walk-the-dog lures, poppers, and jigs work well for catching them. The best bets for casting to the bridge pilings are bucktail jigs, lipless crankbaits, live eels, and baitfish. Trolling deep-diving or shallow-running lures around the bridge pilings is another great way to locate stripers. Once anglers locate a school, casting a jig or a soft plastic swimbait is a great way to get fast action.

The upper Pamlico has excellent fishing for largemouth bass. Chocowinity Bay is legendary for producing lots of big bass. Broad Creek, Blounts Creek, Runyon Creek, and Cherry Run Creek are also good places to fish. The topwater action can be very exciting. Floating worms and pencil poppers are excellent bass lures. Walk-the-dog lures and lipless fast-vibration crankbaits also work well for bass.

Downstream beginning at approximately Durham Creek, the speckled trout fishing is excellent. The Pungo River forms a confluence with the Pamlico. The Pungo offers excellent fishing for speckled trout and striped bass all the way upriver to Belhaven. Casting jigs and hard plastic minnow-imitating lures along the shoreline is the best bet for speckled trout.

Above Belhaven, bass dominate. The same lures and techniques that work for Pamlico River bass work well for Pungo River largemouth.

Most saltwater anglers concentrate on speckled trout, so other prevalent saltwater species like flounder and red drum are caught incidentally on speckled trout trips. Fishing with live minnows on float rigs or bottom rigs can also lead to catches of several different saltwater species.

N.C. A-G grid: 66, B-1

General information: All NCWRC and NCDMF regulations apply.

Nearest camping: Primitive camping is available at Goose Creek State Park; see the appendix for contact information.

Directions: To reach the City Boat Docks at Runyon Creek from U.S. 17, travel east on U.S. 264 for 0.4 mile, take a right on North Market Street, go south for 0.2 mile, take a left on East Third Street, drive 0.5 mile, and continue on Park Drive for 0.4 mile. The access is on the left before Runyon Creek.

To reach Mason's Landing Boating Access from U.S. 17 in Washington, travel west on U.S. 264 for 1.6 miles to Clarks Neck Road (S.R. 1403), turn left, and drive 0.5 mile. The area is on the left before the bridge.

To reach the boat ramp at Dinah's Landing in Goose Creek State Park from

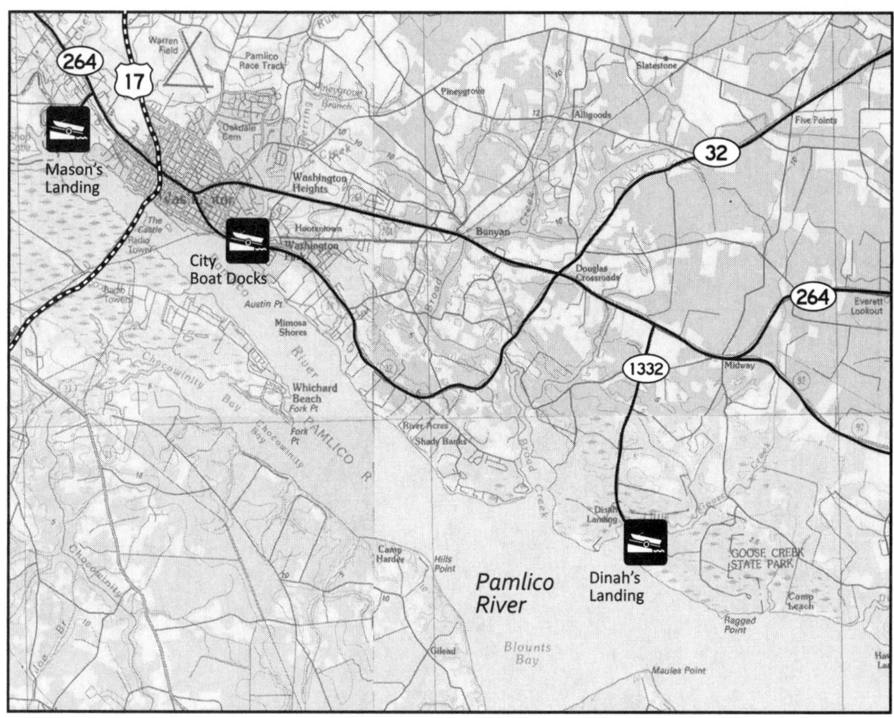

N.C. 32, travel east on U.S. 264 for 1.6 miles, turn right on Goose Creek Road (S.R. 1332), drive 1.2 miles, and continue for 1.5 miles on Dinah's Landing Road (S.R. 1365). The access is at the end of the road.

72 Swanquarter National Wildlife Refuge

Key species: Flounder, croaker, speckled trout, red drum

Overview: In 1932, Swanquarter National Wildlife Refuge became the first refuge formed in North Carolina. It was followed by Lake Mattamuskeet National Wildlife Refuge in 1934. Swanquarter NWR is mainly salt marsh and tidal creeks. Most of the refuge is accessible only by boat. The exception is the amazing Bell Island Fishing Pier.

Best ways to fish: Pier, motorboat, kayak, canoe

Best time to fish: March through November

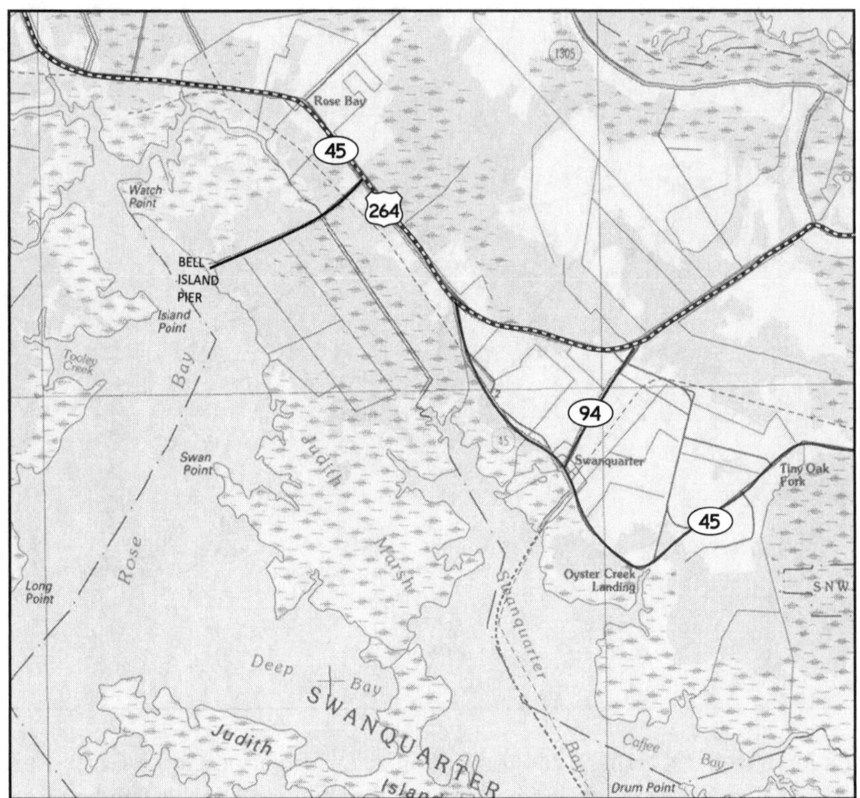

Description: Located on Pamlico Sound in Hyde County, the refuge encompasses approximately 8,800 acres. It is made up of salt marsh islands and forested wetlands interspersed with potholes, creeks, and drains.

The fishing: The 1,000-foot-long Bell Island Fishing Pier is the most popular fishing feature of the refuge. Vehicle access to the pier is via a two-mile dirt road off U.S. 264 just west of the town of Swan Quarter. Croaker, red drum, speckled trout, and flounder are the most commonly caught species. Crabbing is popular during the warm months. Boat ramps allow access to the refuge. The area is best known for its speckled trout fishing.

N.C. A-G grid: 67, B-6

General information: Damaged by hurricanes in the past, the pier has been redesigned to allow the deck planks to come free during stormy conditions and float to the mainland, where they can be recovered and reused. Once the decking is gone, the substructure remains unharmed. All NCWRC and NCDMF regulations apply. Biting midges and mosquitoes can be a problem. An umbrella can bring relief from the sun on warm days.

Nearest camping: Camping is not allowed at Swanquarter National Wildlife Refuge, but private campgrounds are located nearby. See the appendix listings for Osprey Nest Campground and Bayside Marina and Campground.

Directions: To reach Bell Island Fishing Pier from the community of Rose Bay, travel east on U.S. 264 for 1.2 miles, turn right at the sign for Swanquarter National Wildlife Refuge, and continue to the end of the road.

73 Lake Mattamuskeet

Key species: Largemouth bass, crappie, striped bass, white perch, yellow perch, sunfish, catfish

Overview: Lake Mattamuskeet is the largest naturally formed lake in North Carolina. The first Europeans who saw it belonged to a party from Sir Walter Raleigh's Lost Colony of 1585. According to Native American lore, the lake was formed by a peat fire that burned for 13 moons. It is part of the 50,180-acre Mattamuskeet National Wildlife Refuge and is in the middle of the Atlantic Flyway for waterfowl.

Best ways to fish: Powerboat, kayak, canoe, bank

Best time to fish: Fishing is allowed from March 1 to November 1, when waterfowl concentrations are not at their peak.

Description: Lake Mattamuskeet was once 120,000 acres in size. However, due to the great potential agricultural yield of the soil around the lake, attempts were made over the course of many years to drain the lake for farming. In 1837, the Literary Board of North Carolina dug a seven-mile-long canal from Lake Mattamuskeet to Wysocking Bay, reducing the lake's size to its present 40,000 acres. Efforts continued through the 1930s. Lake Mattamuskeet is 18 miles long and seven miles wide. Several water-level control structures maintain its present average depth of three to five feet. Mattamuskeet Lodge, which provides towering views of the lake, was once a pumping facility.

The fishing: The bass fishing can be good or poor, depending on the water level. Since the lake is very shallow, rainfall from tropical events and droughts adversely impacts the fishing. Following Hurricane Isabel in 2003, the NCWRC stocked the lake with largemouth bass several times and will likely do so again following

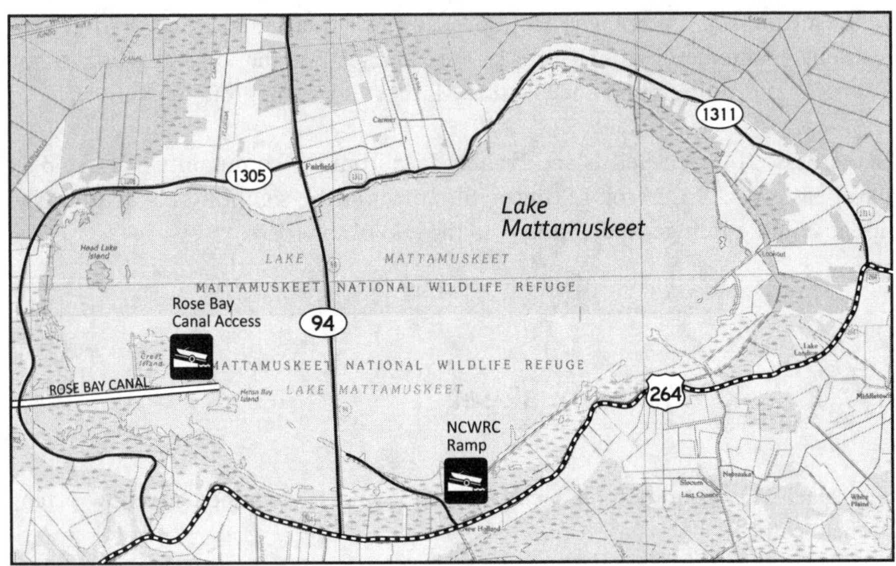

events that disrupt the bass fishing. Channel cats have also been stocked following fish kills. During periods of stable water levels for three years or more, the bass fishing can be extraordinary. Anglers catch lots of 14-inch bass. Bass anglers typically fish from bass boats or johnboats, launching them at the refuge's two ramps. The best time to fish for bass is spring. Topwater action is the best bet. Buzzbaits, floating worms, and rubber frogs are the best choices for fishing the eelgrass and reeds. A few duck blinds offer good structure for catching bass. Cypress trees along the shoreline also attract and hold bass. Anglers who spot bass beds in spring catch the brooding fish by irritating them into striking topwater lures and soft plastics dropped into the beds. Crawfish imitations, jigs, and plastic lizards are excellent for fishing the bass beds.

The canals offer excellent fishing for bass, crappie, and panfish. Spring crappie fishing is the main attraction for canal fishermen. March and April are the best months for crappie. Once the crappie action tapers off, the panfish action begins. That is followed by white perch fishing as hotter weather arrives. The canal at the lodge is a good place to fish. The ramp on the west side provides access to Rose Bay Canal. To reach Jarvis Canal on the east side of the lake, anglers launch at the lodge's boat ramp and travel across the lake. Waupoppin Canal is accessible by vehicle from Lake Landing Road.

Many anglers fish from the bank at the box culverts beneath the causeway dividing the lake. Catfish, sunfish, bass, white perch, and striped bass are common catches at the culverts.

Crabbing is a popular activity at the canals and causeway culverts. Bowfishing for carp and bowfin is encouraged.

N.C. A-G grid: 68, B-1

General information: All NCWRC regulations apply. See the appendix for contact information for Mattamuskeet National Wildlife Refuge. Refuge regulations control fishing and hunting activity, as well as access.

Nearest camping: Osprey Nest Campground offers camping and boat access to the lake. See the appendix for contact information.

Directions: To reach the NCWRC ramp from the N.C. 94 causeway, turn onto the refuge entrance road. The ramp is on Wildlife Drive.

To reach Mattamuskeet National Wildlife Refuge's Rose Bay Canal Access from N.C. 94, travel west on U.S. 264 for 4.7 miles, turn right on Turnpike Road (S.R. 1304), and drive north for 4.7 miles. The access is on the right.

74 Upper Neuse and Trent Rivers

Key species: Largemouth bass, shad, striped bass, crappie, panfish, catfish

Overview: Falls Lake Dam impounds the headwaters of the Neuse River in Wake County. The river starts there and flows eastward through and near many towns including Smithfield, Greenville, Goldsboro, and Kinston before reaching Pamlico Sound. Anglers in all of those towns take advantage of the excellent fishing. The Trent River joins the Neuse at Union Point in New Bern. Both rivers are freshwater bodies upstream and become increasingly brackish as they flow east. The Neuse was one of the earliest rivers to be explored by the English. In 1584, an exploration party from Sir Walter Raleigh's expedition named the river after the Neusiok Indians.

Best ways to fish: Powerboat, kayak, bank

Best time to fish: Something is biting all year.

Description: The city of New Bern sits at the confluence of the Trent and Neuse rivers. The Trent is a small river that flows from the east through swamps and bottom lands. It has better water quality than the Neuse. The Neuse begins in the Piedmont, flows for approximately 275 miles, and has a drainage basin of 5,630 square miles. It is the largest river drainage system contained entirely within North Carolina's borders.

The fishing: The fishing upstream in both the Trent and Neuse rivers is mainly concentrated on freshwater species such as largemouth bass, panfish, and catfish. As the river becomes more brackish near New Bern, saltwater species such as speckled trout, flounder, and striped bass can be caught. Shad and striped bass move far upriver. The removal of a dam at Quaker Neck near Goldsboro was a conservation success story, allowing anadromous fish to complete their spawning runs farther inland. Since the dam was removed, anglers have reported catching stripers all the way upriver to the dam at Falls Lake.

The shad and striped bass fishing is best in the upper rivers during the spring spawning runs in April and May. In Greenville, anglers catch striped bass from the bank during spring. Around New Bern, the bridges offer excellent structure for holding striped bass all year. The best bets for stripers are soft plastic swimbaits, trolling lures, crankbaits, topwater poppers, and walk-the-dog lures. Slow-trolling live eels and live menhaden is another common way to catch striped bass. Shad strike darts, spoons, and curly-tailed jigs all the way upriver to Smithfield.

White perch also school in the Trent and Neuse rivers in spring. Anglers spot the fish surfacing in the large open-water expanses near New Bern and cast small jigs and spoons to the visible schools. Trolling small crankbaits is another way to find schooling white perch. Birds diving to eat baitfish also give away the locations of striped bass and white perch schools.

Red drum, flounder, and speckled trout are also caught around New Bern. Casting live menhaden and mullet on float rigs or bottom rigs works well for saltwater game fish. Scented soft plastics fished with popping cork rigs or on jig heads also work well. The best fishing occurs along shoreline structure such as drop-offs, ditch mouths, boat docks, riprap, stumps, and the roots of downed trees.

Flathead, blue, and channel catfish constitute a major fishing opportunity in the upper Neuse. Blues and flatheads have supplanted native bullhead catfish and most of the former channel catfish population. The best fishing is at night. The river and its tributaries near Kinston and Goldsboro are an excellent area to try. Some flathead catfish exceed 40 pounds; many large fish are caught. Live and cut shad, live and cut panfish, commercial dough and dip baits, worms, liver, and shrimp are all used successfully as catfish baits along the Neuse. Dedicated catfish anglers catch shad in the spring and freeze them for use as catfish bait later in the year. Catfish bite all year long. Late winter and early spring are among the best times for big catfish.

The largemouth bass fishing is good. The best places to catch them are the river bends and oxbows, as well as the feeder streams. The best time to fish for largemouth bass is spring; April and May are the top months. But the river fishing can be good all year. Spinnerbaits are great choices for bass all year. Topwater lures including poppers, buzzbaits, and floating worms work well early and late in the day during the hot months. Weighted soft plastics and rubber jigs are the best bets for fishing logjams, timber blowdowns, and the mouths of feeder creeks. In

Captain Mark Hoff (*left*) and Captain Gary Dubiel caught these stripers from the Neuse River.

October, the bass bite picks up again and continues until the first couple of cold fronts, which usually come in mid- to late November.

The panfish action is also excellent. Most fishermen use live baits such as worms and crickets. Beetle grub spinners and popping bugs also produce well. The best time to catch panfish is April through June. A good panfish bite returns in September or October.

The crappie fishing is fair to good. Live minnows fished along the shoreline are the best bet. The fishing is best in March and early April, but crappie also bite fairly well from November through May.

N.C. A-G grid: 65, D-7

General information: All NCWRC regulations apply. In recent years, the Neuse's water quality has periodically been adversely affected by hurricanes and human impacts. Fish kills are caused by low dissolved oxygen due to the decomposition of algae, which may "bloom" because of agricultural runoff. These events may be historic, with human activities merely a catalyst to the natural cycle. Drought and flood conditions can temporarily have negative impacts on fishing and access opportunities on the upper Neuse.

Nearest camping: Cliffs of the Neuse State Park, located 11 miles southeast of Goldsboro on N.C. 111, offers camping, fishing, boat rentals, and hiking. It also has a boat launch. For contact information, see the appendix listings for the North Carolina Division of Parks and Recreation and Cliffs of the Neuse State Park.

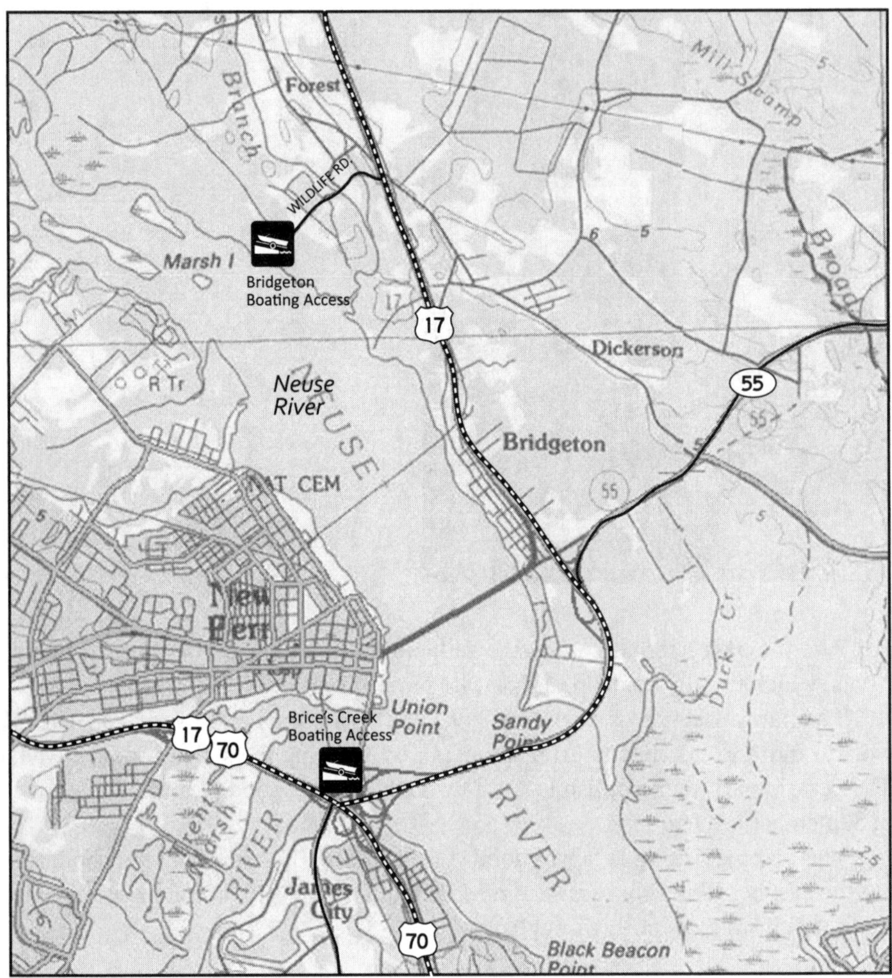

Directions: To reach Bridgeton Boating Access Area from N.C. 55 in Bridgeton, travel north on U.S. 17 for 2.8 miles to Wildlife Road (S.R. 1431), turn left, and drive 1 mile. The access area is at the end of the road.

To reach Brice's Creek Boating Access from the intersection of U.S. 17 Business and U.S. 70 east of New Bern, travel Howell Road (S.R. 1004) for 0.4 mile to Brice's Creek Road, turn right, drive to Perrytown Road, turn left, go 1.5 miles to National Forest Road, turn left, and travel 1.3 miles.

75 Lower Neuse River

Key species: Speckled trout, red drum, striped bass, flounder, tarpon

Overview: The lower Neuse River is a vital estuary that enters and helps form Pamlico Sound. This estuary is one of the most important fish nursery areas in the United States. In a very short distance, the lower Neuse opens from a freshwater river less than a mile wide to a large estuary that is primarily salt water.

Best way to fish: Powerboat

Best times to fish: Something is biting all year. Summer and fall are the best seasons to catch speckled trout, red drum, flounder, and tarpon.

Description: The Neuse flows for about 275 miles from its headwaters to Pamlico Sound. It is a vital area for allowing young fish to develop. The many creeks and streams that flow into the Neuse provide shelter for developing fish.

The fishing: Most of the fishing in the lower Neuse is based out of the town of Oriental in Pamlico County. Other towns along the river including Havelock and New Bern offer access and support for fishermen.

The red drum fishing in the lower Neuse is some of the best in the world. Anglers make night trips for catch-and-release fishing for giant red drum that can top 50 pounds. But the fish are also caught during the day. Large chunks of menhaden, mullet, or croaker are used as drum bait. The baits are cast on bottom rigs in a pattern that spreads them over a large area. Chumming techniques are sometimes used to attract big redfish. The best places to fish are the drop-offs and ledges, which can be very subtle. It takes local knowledge to find the best places. Pamlico Sound and the Neuse River are the only known spawning areas for red drum in the state. Big spawning red drum enter the river in June and stick around until September. A large number of charter captains fish for red drum and tarpon out of Oriental.

The tarpon fishing can be boom or bust. Hookups may occur several times a day or only once every couple of days. Anglers try to spot the fish rolling or showing at the surface, a practice restricted to calm periods during the day. Local anglers say tarpon bite best depending on the moon phase, with moonrise, whether day or night, the optimum time to be in position to catch the fish. Thunderstorms and high winds can grow quickly during July and August, when the best tarpon and red drum fishing occurs, so anglers must have seaworthy boats in the 22-foot-and-up range. Tarpon fishing is essentially the same as fishing for red

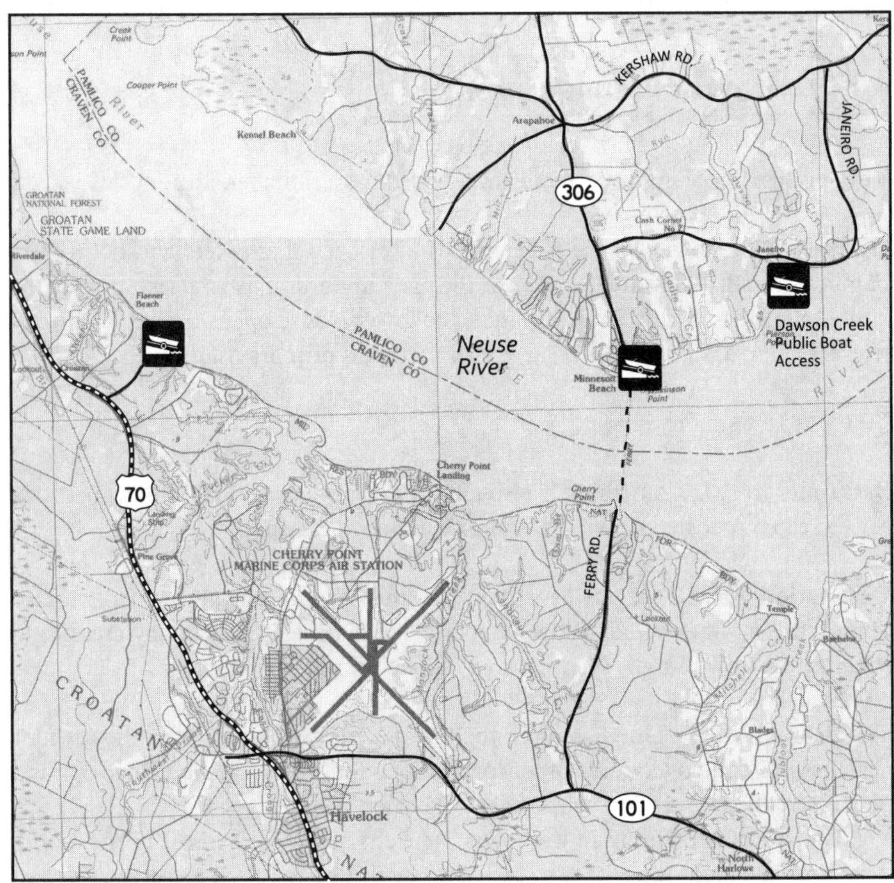

drum. Anglers try to guess which direction the fish are moving and fan-cast baits from anchored boats. Chunking dead baits and tossing them out for chum helps attract tarpon to the baited hooks. Cownosed ray strikes outnumber tarpon strikes at least 10 to 1. Cownosed rays can inflict serious wounds and therefore must be released carefully.

Surface-feeding schooling fish that enter the sound include bluefish and Spanish mackerel. Anglers who spot them cast spoons and jigs to catch the fish.

Puppy drum (the local name for juvenile red drum of up to 27 inches), speckled trout, and flounder occur along the edges and in the creeks off the main river. The fishing for these species can be spectacular beginning in February and continuing into the fall. Slocum, Broad, Goose, Upper Broad, Adams, and Dawson creeks, the South River, and Turnagain Bay are legendary places to catch these species. The best puppy drum bite begins in March and continues into the fall. Flounder begin biting as early as February and continue into September or October. Speckled trout bite all year; some of the best fishing is during the coldest months of winter.

In the upper reaches of the feeder creeks, anglers also catch largemouth bass and striped bass. The best bets for catching multiple species is fishing the edges of the river and the feeder creeks using live shrimp, mullet, menhaden, and mud minnows on bottom rigs and float rigs. Scented soft plastics fished on float rigs, popping cork rigs, or jig heads also work well.

N.C. A-G grid: 79, A-4

General information: All NCWRC and North Carolina Division of Marine Fisheries regulations apply. NCDMF regulations restrict the use of hooks above size 4/0 between 7 A.M. and 7 P.M. from July 1 through September 30 to circle hooks with bent-down or filed barbs and a fixed sinker of not less than two ounces on a leader no longer than six inches. This protects red drum from being deep-hooked. NCDMF recreational fishing regulations change frequently. Anglers are advised to visit the website for current regulations before fishing for saltwater species.

Nearest camping: Primitive camping is available at Neuse River Recreation Area near Flanners Beach. For contact information, see the appendix.

Directions: To reach Dawson Creek Public Boat Access from the intersection of N.C. 306 and Neuse Road (S.R. 1005) in the town of Arapahoe, travel east on Kershaw Road (S.R. 1005) for 4.8 miles to Janeiro Road (S.R. 1302), turn right, drive 2.8 miles to Creek Place Road, turn right, and go 0.3 mile. The access road is on the left.

To reach Oriental Boating Access Area from Grantsboro, travel south on N.C. 55 to Oriental. Turn right on Hodges Street before crossing the N.C. 55 bridge, go 300 feet to Midyette Street, and turn left. The boat ramp is 300 feet along Midyette Street at the foot of the bridge.

76 Pamlico Sound

Key species: Speckled trout, striped bass, flounder, red drum, cobia

Overview: Pamlico Sound is the second-largest estuary in the United States, behind Chesapeake Bay. The name comes from a group of Algonquian Indians called the Pamlico. The first European to discover Pamlico Sound was Giovanni da Verrazano, who mistook the expansive sound for the Pacific Ocean. It is shallow and known to shoal, making it a hazardous body of water for navigation and also making it susceptible to fluctuations anglers call "wind tides." This effect is amplified on the small tributaries, where water levels can change by as much as two feet in a couple of hours during strong winds.

Best ways to fish: Motorboat, kayak

Best time to fish: Something is biting all year.

Description: Pamlico Sound is 80 miles long and 30 miles wide. Its average depth is around 15 feet.

The fishing: The most impressive fishing on the sound is going after tarpon and red drum in June, July, August, and early September. Good jumping-off points are located at Cedar Island. Tarpon and red drum fishing is moon-phase dependent; full-moon times are the best bets. A few oyster reefs and islands hold these large fish and the baitfish that feed on them. The passes, channels, and bars also attract fish. Anglers should watch out for pound nets and pound net stakes in the water. Some experience is required to navigate the shallow sound, which is marked with navigation beacons. Experts go across the sound to Drum Inlet and Ocracoke Inlet for cobia action in summer and red drum action as the big redfish enter and leave the sound in early summer and fall.

Smaller species that offer good fishing include speckled trout, puppy drum (juvenile red drum), flounder, croaker, bluefish, and Spanish mackerel. Puppy drum, flounder, and speckled trout are usually caught on all-purpose lures such as minnow imitations and soft plastics or live bait fished on float rigs or bottom rigs. The best bet is fishing along the shoreline cover, which includes drop-offs, shell beds, stumps, sea walls, bridges, and boating facilities.

Speckled trout offer the best fishing opportunity besides the big red drum and tarpon. Although most anglers prefer fishing for specks in the fall and winter, large speckled trout begin biting in June. One of the best bets for big specks is a popping cork rig with a soft plastic shrimp imitation. The popping cork has a concave top that pops like a topwater popper lure, attracting attention to the artificial shrimp below the cork.

Bluefish and flounder enter the sound in spring and fall. These fish are targets of opportunity for anglers who spot them jumping. Spoons and jigs are the best lures for catching them.

N.C. A-G grid: 79

General information: All NCDMF regulations apply. Special rules apply to red drum and tarpon rigs.

Nearest camping: Primitive camping is available at Neuse River Recreation Area near Flanners Beach. See the appendix for contact information.

Directions: To reach Cedar Island Public Access Area from U.S. 70 near Sea Level, travel north on N.C. 12 for 11.7 miles to Driftwood Road, turn right, and drive 0.3 mile. The access area is at the end of the road.

To reach Rose Bay Marina from N.C. 45 approximately 9 miles east of Belhaven, drive east on U.S. 264 for about 10 miles. The marina is on the right.

77 Cape Hatteras National Seashore

Key species: Red drum, bluefish, striped bass, flounder, croaker, spot, speckled trout, other saltwater fish

Overview: Cape Hatteras National Seashore extends from Whalebone Junction to Ocracoke Island. The first national seashore in the country, it includes historic attractions such as lighthouses and lifesaving stations. The Outer Banks are always in a state of change. Winds, tides, storms, and currents move the sands of the barrier islands constantly. A good fishing spot today can turn into a sand bar tomorrow.

Best ways to fish: Pier, surf

Best time to fish: Something is biting year-round.

Description: Cape Hatteras National Seashore extends 75 miles and covers 30,000 acres. It encompasses several small towns including Buxton, Frisco, and Avon.

The fishing: The fishing along Cape Hatteras National Seashore is some of the best in the world. Among the several major ocean currents that converge on the area is the Gulf Stream, which approaches to within 12 miles of Cape Hatteras. Many species of oceangoing fish are caught from the beach. While surf fishermen can find something to catch all year long, the fall fishing for red drum and bluefish is legendary. In winter, anglers pursue striped bass and whiting. In spring and fall, pompano, flounder, black drum, spot, croaker, and many other species can be caught from the beach.

The best bet is a long surf rod with a conventional revolving spool reel or a spinning reel. Dedicated anglers use four-wheel-drive vehicles to get on the beach. The best fishing occurs in the sloughs that run parallel to the beach. Anglers find these sloughs at low tide and return at high tide to fish them.

When schooling species such as bluefish and striped bass approach close to

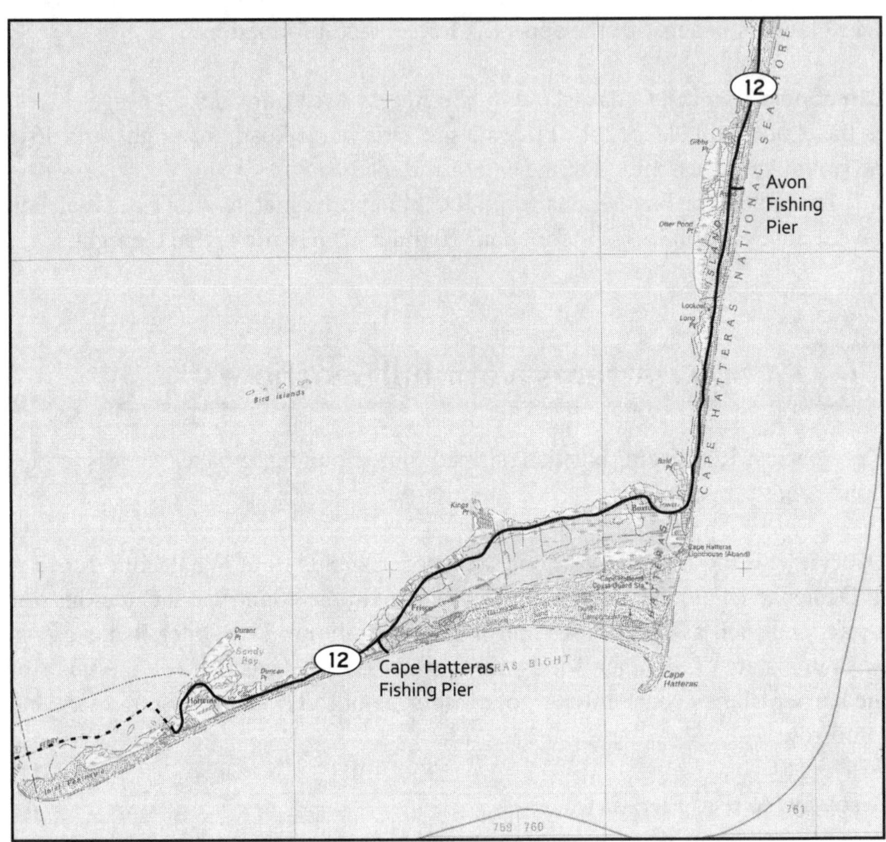

shore, anglers cast spoons, large lures, and bucktail jigs to catch them. Otherwise, the preferred method of surf fishing is to cast cut baits, squid, and shrimp.

The many piers along the Outer Banks provide excellent fishing access, along with amenities. For contact information, see the section of fishing-pier listings in the appendix.

N.C. A-G grid: 69, B-6

General information: All NCDMF regulations apply. Beach anglers must be aware of driving access closures due to nesting shorebirds. They should also note the many park rules regarding beach driving and other activities. A permit is required for beach driving at night. A fee is charged for climbing Cape Hatteras Lighthouse.

Nearest camping: Camping is available at various public campgrounds along Cape Hatteras National Seashore. Advance reservations are recommended during the busy season. Fees are charged for campsites. For contact information, see the appendix listing for Cape Hatteras National Seashore.

Directions: Traveling N.C. 12 will reveal pullovers and beach access points along the length of the shoreline. Many are accessible by walking.

To reach Avon Fishing Pier from the Hatteras-Ocracoke ferry, travel north on N.C. 12 for 16 miles. The pier is on the right.

To reach Cape Hatteras Fishing Pier, better known as Frisco Pier, from the Hatteras-Ocracoke ferry, travel north for 4.2 miles. The pier is on the right.

78 Cape Lookout National Seashore

Key species: Flounder, croaker, speckled trout, red drum

Overview: Cape Lookout National Seashore is located on the lower portion of North Carolina's Outer Banks. Extending from Ocracoke Inlet to Beaufort Inlet, the park encompasses Portsmouth Island, Core Banks, and Shackleford Banks. It has no roads or development.

Best ways to fish: Motorboat, surf

Best time to fish: Something is biting all year.

Description: The 56-mile-long Cape Lookout National Seashore contains Cape Lookout Lighthouse and other historical structures. On the north end is the now-abandoned Portsmouth Village, a historic site.

The fishing: Surf fishing is popular at the Cape Lookout beaches and the inlets at Shackleford Banks and Core Banks. The channels at Barden and Beaufort inlets are the typical way of getting to the banks by private boat. Boats can beach along the interior of the island, but the main landing is at Cape Lookout Lighthouse. The jetty at Beaufort Inlet is an excellent place to catch speckled trout in fall and winter and puppy drum year-round. At times, the beach is lined with vehicles and anglers casting near the jetty. Some winters, if the weather is cold enough, big striped bass come all the way south from Cape Hatteras to Cape Lookout. Giant red drum and tarpon also make their way to the Cape Lookout shoals in spring and fall.

The surf fishing is extremely popular. Pompano, whiting, flounder, red drum, black drum, shark, speckled trout, spot, croaker, bluefish, and many other species are landed by anglers. Those with boats can cruise along the oceanfront casting jigs and spoons for red drum, false albacore, bluefish, and Spanish mackerel.

In the backwaters of Core Sound, anglers fish for speckled trout, red drum, flounder, gray trout, and other species. Spinning rigs with jigs tipped with scented soft plastics, hard plastic lures, and topwater lures are the go-to tackle for sound fishing. Anglers also fish with live mullet and menhaden on bottom rigs and float rigs. Ocracoke Inlet is an excellent place to catch cobia and red drum using live and cut baits fished on the bottom.

N.C. A-G grid: 79, D-5

General information: All NCDMF regulations apply. An excellent charter fleet is located at the Morehead City waterfront. Inshore and offshore charters are available. Wild ponies attract visitors to Shackleford Banks. A few historic buildings at Portsmouth Village are opened seasonally for public visitation. Anglers visiting the national seashore must take everything they need, including water, since there are no facilities available on the islands.

Nearest camping: Primitive camping is allowed at Cape Lookout National Seashore for up to 14 consecutive days. A permit is required for long-term parking in the parking lot. Cabins are available for rent on South Core Banks; reservations may be made by phone. See the appendix entry for Cape Lookout National Seashore.

Directions: The only way to reach Cape Lookout National Seashore is by boat. Several ferry services transport vehicles and passengers. An approved list of ferry services is on the national seashore's website; see the appendix.

79 Beaufort Inlet

Key species: Flounder, croaker, gray trout, speckled trout, red drum, cobia, tarpon, false albacore, bluefish, whiting, black drum

Overview: Beaufort Inlet lies between Shackleford Banks and Fort Macon. It has a rich history. A vessel believed to be the pirate Blackbeard's flagship, *Queen Anne's Revenge*, rests here.

Best way to fish: Motorboat

Best time to fish: Something is biting year-round.

Description: Beaufort Inlet is a deepwater navigable inlet managed by the state port at Morehead City. The maintained shipping channel depth is 45 feet. Beaufort Inlet consists of 463 acres of tidal habitat.

The fishing: The saltwater fishing at Beaufort Inlet is some of the best in the state. Several islands protect the inlet for navigation and fishing during wind conditions that keep anglers in port at most of the other inlets around the state. Speckled trout swarm the beach points and jetties in winter. Puppy drum school on the bars and jetties all year. In spring and fall, bluefish and false albacore form dense schools and chase baitfish to the surface, where birds dive on them. Giant red drum move to the shoals in spring on their way to the northern sounds and Cape Hatteras; they return in the fall. Spanish mackerel swarm the inlet beginning in April or May and stick around until September. Bottom-fishing action for whiting, spot, and croaker is excellent in the channels near the inlet in early spring and fall. Flounder arrive in April and stick around until cold weather moves them offshore by November. King mackerel lurk at the inlet or just outside it.

Picking just one species to catch is difficult, since every fish that swims in nearshore salt water can be caught at the inlet. The cobia fishing, which peaks in May and June, is some of the best in the world. Anglers spot the fish circling the buoys and cast live baits or big soft plastics to entice them into striking. Another technique is fishing with a chunk of fish or a blue crab on the bottom at the edges of the main channels.

The other main draw is the false albacore fishing, which peaks in October or November. A few may stick around all winter. Another smaller run occurs in early spring. False albacore fishermen cast spoons, jigs, and flies. Anglers come from all over the planet to fly-fish for the fast, strong, long-fighting fish.

N.C. A-G grid: 79, D-5

General information: All NCDMF regulations apply. An excellent charter fleet for inshore and offshore fishing is based at the Morehead City municipal docks.

Nearest camping: Camping is permitted on Core Banks. For information, see the appendix entry for Cape Lookout National Seashore.

Directions: To reach Taylor's Creek Public Boat Access from the east end of the U.S. 70 drawbridge in Beaufort, travel east on U.S. 70 for 1 mile to Lennoxville Road (S.R. 1310), turn right, and drive 1.5 miles. The access area is on the right at the waterfront.

To reach the NCWRC's Morehead City Boating Access Area, travel east along U.S. 70 for 2.7 miles past the N.C. 24 intersection and turn right beside the visitor center. The access area is located on the Intracoastal Waterway behind the visitor center.

80 Fort Macon

Key species: Flounder, croaker, speckled trout, red drum, bluefish, black drum

Overview: Fort Macon State Park is located in Carteret County. It lies east of Atlantic Beach on Bogue Banks. The eastern tip of Bogue Banks was selected as the site of a colonial fort to protect the town of Beaufort from pillaging by pirates and foreign powers. Various forts and embankments have been built to protect Beaufort Inlet throughout the area's history. Constructed in 1826, Fort Macon saw service during the Civil War. The fortifications and the surrounding area form the park.

Best way to fish: Surf

Best time to fish: June through November

Description: The state park opened in 1936. Despite being the third-smallest park in North Carolina, encompassing just 389 acres, Fort Macon State Park is the state's most-visited park, boasting an annual visitation of 1.3 million people.

The fishing: Fort Macon State Park is surrounded by the Atlantic, Beaufort Inlet, and Bogue Sound. The park has a generous amount of paved parking area. Anglers can park and walk short or long distances to fish the shoreline of Beaufort Inlet, the Fort Macon jetty, or the oceanfront. Falling tide conditions are typically best for fishing, but anglers can catch fish during any tide stage. The beach along the inlet is wide and flat during the lower tide stages. The best fish-attracting structure is the rock jetty. Speckled trout and black drum are common catches. Anglers can fish with fiddler crabs, mole crabs, cut baits, live mullet, and mud minnows. Casting soft plastic or hard plastic trout lures near the rocks is the best bet for specks. When bluefish or Spanish mackerel show on top, anglers can catch them with spoons or poppers.

Among the many other fish species caught in the Fort Macon area are pigfish, pinfish, red drum, flounder, spot, croaker, whiting, and pompano.

N.C. A-G grid: 79, D-5

General information: All NCDMF regulations apply. Visiting the historic fortifications is a popular side trip. Swimming and sunbathing are also popular pastimes.

Nearest camping: Camping is not allowed at Fort Macon State Park. The park has restrooms and picnic facilities. See the appendix for contact information for the park.

Directions: To reach Fort Macon State Park from U.S. 70 and the Atlantic Beach Causeway (S.R. 1182) in Morehead City, travel south across the causeway, turn left on U.S. 58 (East Fort Macon Road), and drive to the end of the road.

81 Newport River

Key species: Flounder, croaker, speckled trout, red drum

Overview: The Newport River is a small, shallow river that flows southeast from the town of Newport to Bogue Sound. It is popular with kayakers and canoeists. The Northwest Prong and the Southwest Prong begin in the pocosin wilderness. These two tributaries join northwest of Newport.

Best ways to fish: Kayak, canoe, skiff

Best time to fish: April through November

Description: The Newport River opens to two miles wide as it flows toward Bogue Sound. Its many flats and sand bars hold fish. This tidal river takes some exploring, but the effort is worthwhile. Anglers looking for good fishing places enter the river on the low tide as it is rising. That is the best way to spot the sand bars and oyster beds that make the best fish habitat and to discover the best channels into and out of the river.

The fishing: During the cold months, the speck bite is the best bet. But in the spring, specks mix with puppy drum for some fantastic mixed-bag fishing. Anglers always have the possibility of catching a flounder or black drum. Topwater walk-the-dog lures are excellent choices for reds and specks. Jigs with soft plastic grub tails and hard plastic lures are also good choices. Live baits fished on float rigs along the edges of the oyster beds and over the tops of the sand bars are deadly for all species of fish.

The best time to fish the river and other nearby open waters of Bogue Sound is the fall, when the water becomes incredibly clear. Anglers can spot the schools of juvenile puppy drum working the bars and grass beds. Sight-casting for redfish with fly tackle or topwater lures offers some of the most exciting inshore fishing along the coast.

N.C. A-G grid: 78, D-4

General information: All NCDMF regulations apply.

Nearest camping: Privately run campgrounds are located in the area. See the appendix entry for Whispering Pines RV Park and Campground.

Directions: To reach Newport Boating Access Area from N.C. 24 in Morehead City, travel west on U.S. 70 for 3.7 miles to East Chatham Street (S.R. 1247), turn right, and drive 1.4 miles. The access area is on the right.

To reach Taylor's Creek Public Boat Access from the east end of the drawbridge on U.S. 70 in Beaufort, travel east on U.S. 70 for 1 mile to Lennoxville Road (S.R. 1310), turn right, and drive 1.5 miles. The access area is on the right at the waterfront.

82 Bogue Sound

Key species: Flounder, croaker, spot, speckled trout, red drum, sheepshead, black drum

Overview: Bogue Sound is the body of water north of Bogue Banks. Bogue Inlet and the White Oak River border the sound on the west. Beaufort Inlet and the Newport River border it on the east. Bogue Sound is traversed by the Intracoastal Waterway.

Best ways to fish: Kayak, powerboat

Best time to fish: Something is biting all year.

Description: Bogue Sound separates Bogue Banks from the mainland of North Carolina. It is 25 miles long and 2.5 miles wide. The significant sand shoaling that occurs around the sound fluctuates with the tide. Channels can shift after severe weather.

The fishing: Bogue Sound is an amazing stretch of water to fish. The Intracoastal Waterway bisects the sound and provides deepwater habitat as well as access for many species of saltwater fish.

Flounder habitat is everywhere. Man-made structure along the Morehead City waterfront including sea walls, docks, and abandoned or damaged structures creates ideal habitat for big flounder. Flounder topping 10 pounds have come from

Red drum (*top*) and black drum are two of the hardest-fighting coastal inshore game fish.

the area. The best bet for flounder is a live menhaden or mullet fished on a bottom rig. However, smaller fish are fools for scented soft plastics fished on jig heads.

The red drum fishing can be fantastic. The marshy edges of the sound have small islands and hummocks. Red drum work the grassy edges and boat docks on the high tide, then retreat to the flats at the edges during low tide. Topwater walk-the-dog lures offer an exciting way to catch redfish during all tide stages. Jigs and hard plastic lures also work well. The most reliable way to catch redfish is with a live menhaden or mullet fished on a float rig or a live or cut bait fished on a bottom rig.

Speckled trout strike the same lures and baits as red drum. Specks hold in specific areas, hard structure being the main attraction. Oyster beds, sea walls, riprap areas, and marsh edges are the best bets for finding specks.

The U.S. 58 bridges, one at Emerald Isle and the other at Morehead City, offer additional fish-holding structure. At the bridge pilings, anglers can catch whiting, spot, croaker, red drum, gray trout, black drum, flounder, and sheepshead. For multiple-species fishing, nothing beats fresh shrimp for bait. However, anglers also use cut baits and live baits when fishing the bridges. For sheepshead and black drum, fiddler crabs are great baits.

Anglers should also be on the lookout for the bluefish and Spanish mackerel that enter the sound in spring, summer, and fall. A jig, spoon, or topwater popper will catch these schooling fish. Fly fishermen can cast Clouser flies and poppers with equal success.

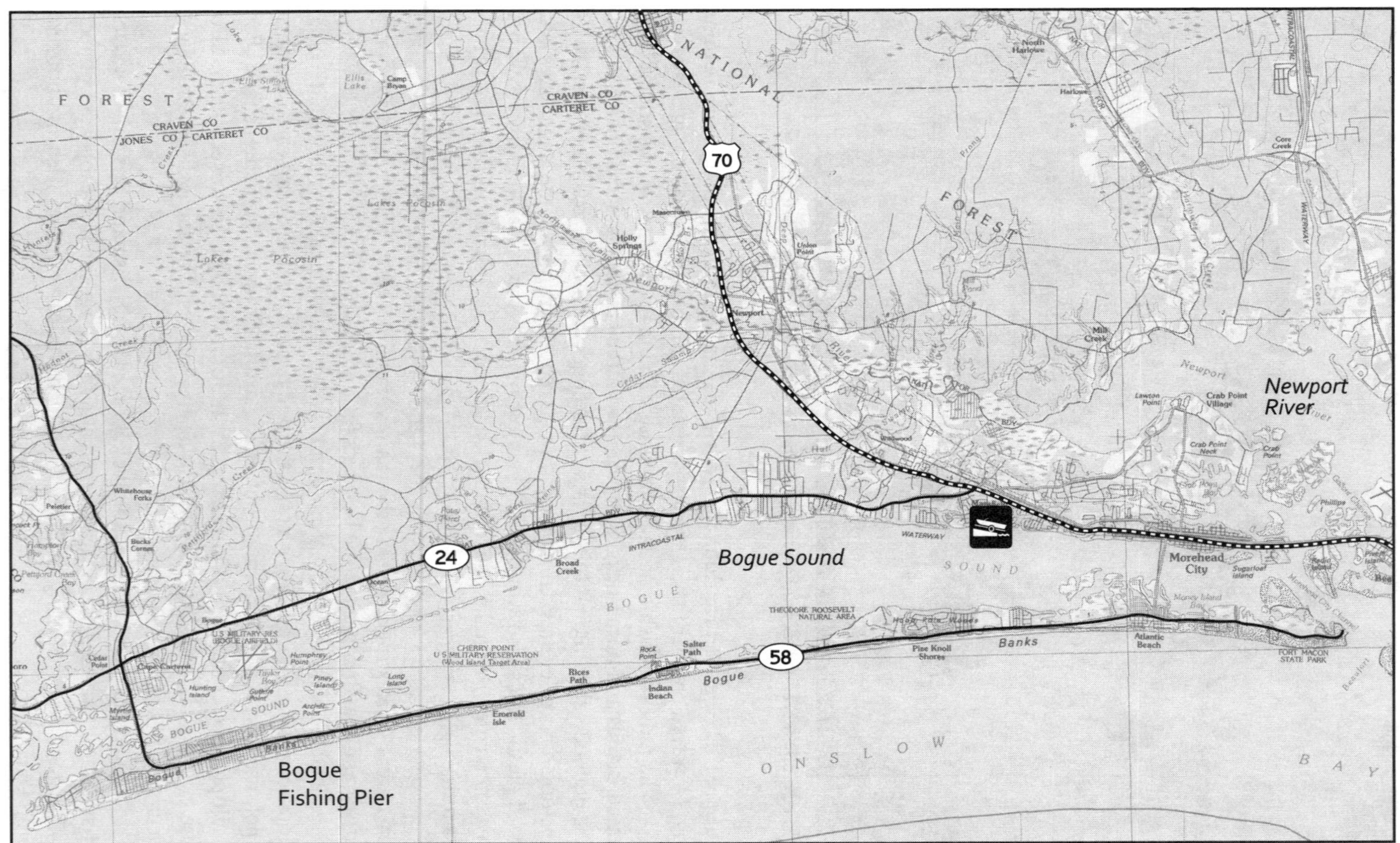
Newport River
Bogue Sound
Bogue Fishing Pier
70
24
58
Morehead City
Atlantic Beach
Broad Creek
Salter Path
Indian Beach
Emerald Isle
Pine Knoll Shores
FORT MACON STATE PARK
CHERRY POINT U S MILITARY RESERVATION
THEODORE ROOSEVELT NATURAL AREA
O N S L O W
B A Y

N.C. A-G grid: 78, D-2

General information: All NCDMF regulations apply.

Nearest camping: Privately run campgrounds are located in the area. For information, see the appendix entry for Whispering Pines RV Park and Campground.

Directions: To reach Crystal Coast Regional Boat Ramp in Morehead City from the intersection of N.C. 24 and U.S. 70, travel east on U.S. 70 for 2.7 miles. Access is on the right.

83 Fort Bragg

Key species: Largemouth bass, bluegill, redear sunfish, channel catfish, black crappie, warmouth, chain pickerel

Overview: Many lakes are located on the Fort Bragg military reservation. They are ranked in three categories: Intensively Managed Lakes, Managed Lakes, and Intensively Managed Catfish Lakes. The categories for individual lakes are subject to change.

The Intensively Managed Lakes include Kiest, Simmons, Boundary Line, McFayden, Hurley, and Holland lakes. These are managed for largemouth bass, bluegill, redear sunfish, and channel catfish to increase the number of quality fish the lakes will sustain.

The Managed Lakes include Texas, McArthur, Mott, Big Muddy, Little Muddy, and Overhills. These maintain the number of fish that would be expected of a normal impounded lake. They are not managed with fertilizer or lime, nor are they stocked.

The Intensively Managed Catfish Lakes include Lower McKellars, Wyatt, Mossgill, and Andrews Church lakes. These are stocked every year at high rates. The fish are fed daily in the warm months in order to support more fish and increase their growth rates. Other fish species may be present in these lakes, but they are not desired, as they may eat catfish fry and compete with catfish for food.

The lakes undergo renovation at times. Anglers should check the status of Deer Pen, Quail, Lindsay, and the other lakes before fishing, since classifications may change and closings and openings may occur. Hutaff, McKeithan, Smith, and Young's lakes are closed.

Best ways to fish: Bank, kayak, canoe, bass boat, powerboat

Best times to fish: Spring, summer, fall

Description: The Fort Bragg lakes exist to support recreational activities for soldiers and their families. However, they are open to the public. The lakes range in size from Mott Lake at 138 acres to Andrews Church Lake at six acres. The larger lakes have ramps, while the others offer bank fishing or primitive launching sites for kayaks and canoes.

The fishing: While some anglers might think it's not worth the trouble to fish Fort Bragg's relatively small lakes with their many regulations, the lakes are ideal for bank fishing and fishing from small watercraft. They also contain some big bass. Many bass weighing more than eight pounds have been caught, and a few in excess of 10 pounds have been reported. The smaller lakes become covered with aquatic plants by summertime, which restricts the available fishing area. They also grow very hot, causing the bass to get lethargic. Therefore, the best fishing occurs before June. March and April are the top months. Before the lake weeds start to grow, crankbaits, stickbaits, and spinnerbaits work well. As the weeds get thicker, topwater lures including floating worms and frogs, poppers, propeller lures, and buzzbaits are the tickets. A weighted soft plastic is a good bet at any time because it can be dropped into a hole in the weeds, along the weed edges, or in deeper water where weeds aren't present. Another good bet is a fly rod with a popping bug or a dragonfly pattern. Bass can be seen chasing dragonflies on the lakes. They come up through the weeds to leap out of the water for an aerial meal. Even the densest weed beds can be fished with a weedless dragonfly pattern all the way through summer.

The larger lakes offer some good bank fishing for sunfish. Worms and crickets are the best bets for bluegill sunfish.

Chain pickerel give thrills to bass anglers. The toothy fish can reach impressive sizes in the large and medium-sized lakes.

The managed catfish ponds have excellent access for fishing from banks and piers. The feeders concentrate the catfish in small areas. Sunfish also congregate around the feeders.

N.C. A-G grid: 61, D-6

General information: All NCWRC fishing regulations apply, as do Fort Bragg fishing regulations. A Fort Bragg fishing permit is required to access the lakes. Bag limits, size limits, and other regulations are posted at all lakes and are listed in the brochure handed out with the purchase of a fishing license. The catfish lakes are closed daily from 6 A.M. to 11 A.M. All lakes are off limits to swimming, Jet Skis, and water-skiing. Motor-size restrictions are not in effect on McArthur and Mott lakes. The other lakes have a maximum 25-horsepower restriction. For contact information, see the appendix entry for Fort Bragg Wildlife.

Nearest camping: Fort Bragg's Smith Lake Recreation Area offers campsites with RV hookups, cabins, swimming, pavilions, bike trails, and other amenities. It is located a mile outside Fort Bragg on N.C. 210 (Murchison Road) near Simmons Army Airfield. It is open to active duty, reserve, and retired military personnel and their families, as well as Department of Defense civilians and contract personnel. See the appendix entry for Smith Lake Recreation Area.

Directions: To reach Fort Bragg Hunting and Fishing Center from the community of Lobelia, head south on Morrison Bridge Road (S.R. 2021) for 2.1 miles. Take a slight left toward Manchester Road (S.R. 2017), then turn left on Manchester Road and continue 6.3 miles. Turn right at Lamont Road, drive 1.6 miles, turn left at McKellars Road, and go 1.8 miles. The center is on the right.

84 Rhodes Pond

Key species: Largemouth bass, crappie, chain pickerel, flier, catfish

Overview: Rhodes Pond was jointly purchased by the NCWRC and the North Carolina Department of Transportation in April 2005 to be used as a game land and as a mitigation area for wetlands destroyed during highway construction. The location had been privately held since the 1700s. The pond is an example of a "mature Sandhills impoundment."

Best ways to fish: Canoe, kayak, small johnboat with electric trolling motor

Best time to fish: March through October

Description: The 455-acre Rhodes Pond is located north of the town of Godwin. An aged earthen dam and spillway built in the 18th century impound the Black River to create the pond. An earthen causeway splits the upper part, which consists of dense cypress swamp, from the lower part, which contains more open water near the dam. The previous owner envisioned a bridge across the narrow remaining gap of the causeway, but it was never built.

The fishing: Rhodes Pond is a blackwater lake. It offers excellent fishing for largemouth bass. The best bet for bass is a soft plastic or topwater lure fished in the expansive pad beds and in the cypress trees. The creek meandering through the trees offers some open water in late summer when the vegetation grows thick. In spring, which is the best time for catching bass, one of the best lures is a floating worm.

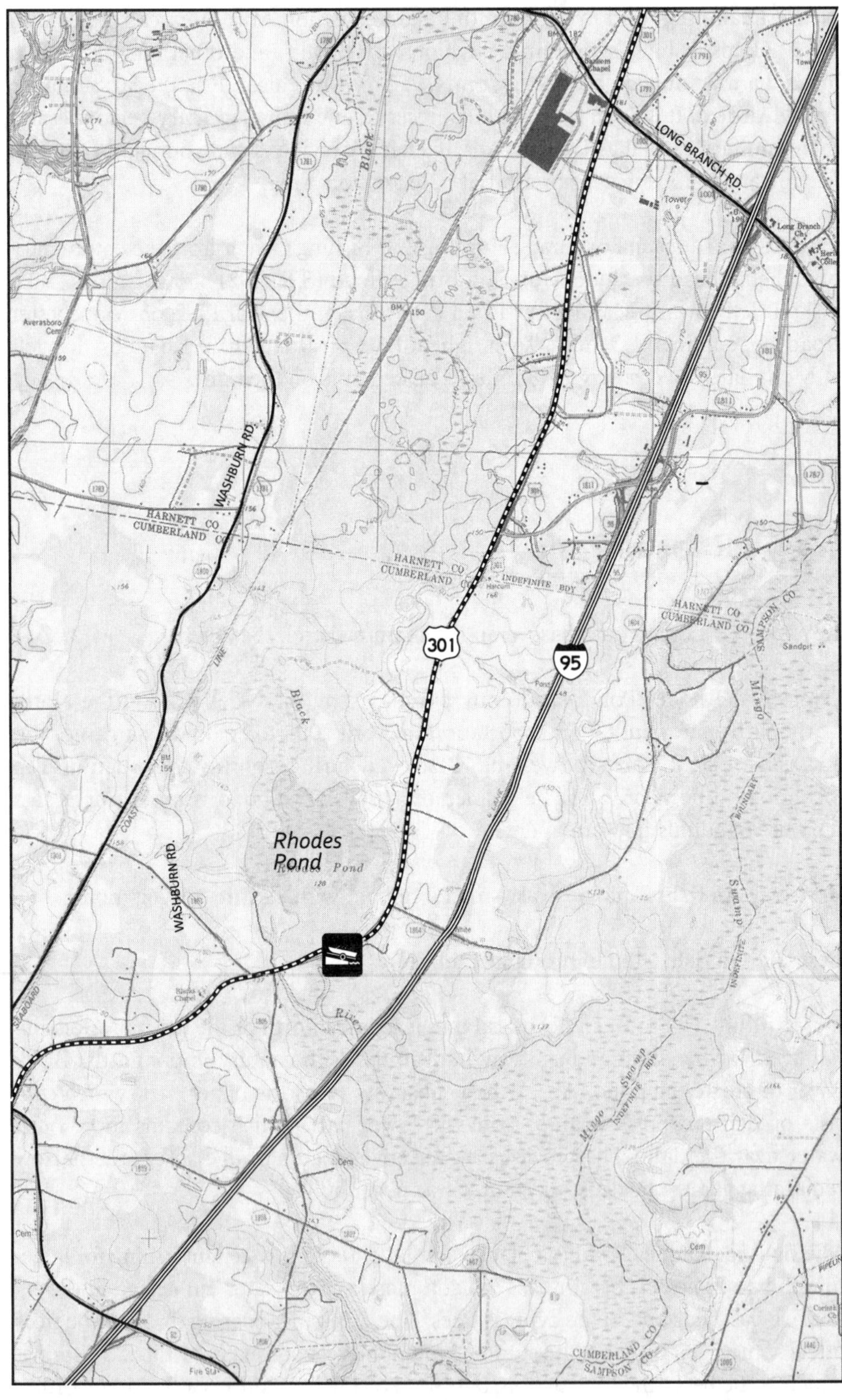
LONG BRANCH RD.
WASHBURN RD.
HARNETT CO
CUMBERLAND CO
301
95
Rhodes Pond
WASHBURN RD.
SAMPSON CO
CUMBERLAND CO
SAMPSON CO
Long Branch
Averasboro Cem
Sandpit
Mingo Swamp
Black River
Fire Sta
Tower

The abundant chain pickerel attack lures intended for bass. The bowfin, another toothy predator, also strikes lures and live baits intended for other fish.

The crappie fishing is good. Live minnows and beetle grub spinners are the best bets. The best place for catching crappie is the open water near the dam, and the best time is spring. But crappie bite all year long back in the shade of the swamp forest. Bank fishermen catch crappie and catfish from the bank at the dam.

Flier and bluegill sunfish are common. Beetle grub spinners and live worms are the best bets for catching panfish. Panfish bite best in the cold months, while other sunfish bite best in spring and fall.

N.C. A-G grid: 62, D-2

General information: NCWRC regulations apply. Motorboats are not allowed. During waterfowl-hunting seasons, when permit hunts for ducks and geese take precedence, fishing boats are not allowed in the area above the causeway.

Nearest camping: Camping is not permitted at Rhodes Pond. Consult the regulations for NCWRC game lands for more information.

Directions: To reach Rhodes Pond from N.C. 82 at Godwin, travel north on U.S. 301. Rhodes Pond is on the right. The ramp is primitive, but the parking area is generous.

85 White Lake

Key species: Yellow perch, largemouth bass, bluegill, warmouth, chain pickerel

Overview: The town of White Lake has been called "the nation's safest beach." Named for its white-sand bottom and clear water, the town's lake offers swimmers, boaters, scooter riders, sailors, and water-skiers an absolutely gorgeous place for summer entertainment. Located east of Elizabethtown, White Lake is a summer resort for many vacationers from the Piedmont and the surrounding area. Although it has no park facilities, it is technically a state park up to the shoreline, like all Carolina bay lakes.

Best way to fish: Motorboat

Best time to fish: Spring

Description: The lake encompasses approximately 1,065 acres and has no inflow

Justin Marsh caught this stringer of yellow perch, or "raccoon bream," at White Lake. Yellow perch thrive in the acid waters of coastal rivers and lakes.

or outflow. The shoreline is highly developed. White Lake is a bit deeper than most other bay lakes and has steeper sides, although they still slope gradually. Wade fishing is not popular here. White Lake has few of the grass beds common to other bay lakes. Its maximum depth is around 11 feet and its average depth five to eight feet. The water is very acidic, with a pH of less than 4. The conductivity is low, so biologists have difficulty sampling the lake using electroshock equipment. A low pH means the water is infertile, in the same way agricultural fields that are not treated with lime to neutralize the pH are infertile. Most plants cannot use nutrients efficiently where the pH is low. But such natural ecosystems have unique species that evolve over millennia. Although White Lake's fish species are similar to those of other Carolina bay lakes, certain lesser-known fish offer the best opportunities.

The fishing: Despite persistent rumors of terrible fishing, White Lake supports reliable populations of some game fish. The top species is yellow perch, which will strike anything that looks like a small minnow and seem especially attracted to yellow perch patterns. Juvenile yellow perch form the major forage base for all predatory fish in the lake. Gold, yellow, hot pink, and bright orange are good lure colors. Anglers cast lures to the edges or troll above the submerged aquatic plant beds. Live baits such as worms and minnows are also good bets. The best months to catch yellow perch are March and April, when the fish are spawning. But the action remains good until the summer water-skiing season arrives. Boat wakes are a problem for summer anglers.

White Lake's largemouth bass grow slowly and are not abundant. However, bass weighing four pounds are routinely caught from the lake. Six-pound fish have been reported; an eight-pounder was reported during an electroshock sampling by NCWRC biologists. Anglers fishing soft plastics and topwater lures from private docks at dawn and dusk have good luck. Others fish the lake from bass boats and johnboats. The best bet for bass is casting medium-depth crankbaits to the ends of the docks. The best months for catching bass are April, May, and October.

Chain pickerel are common catches. The fish strike live minnows, spinnerbaits, and crankbaits.

For multiple-species fishing, nothing beats a beetle grub spinnerbait. Casting the small lures along shoreline structure including boat docks, cypress trees, and stumps can result in catches of every species present, including warmouth and bluegill sunfish. In spring, bluegills bed in the shallow, sandy areas. Anglers can see these beds and fish them with worms on bottom rigs or float rigs.

N.C. A-G grid: 75, D-4

General information: All NCWRC regulations apply.

Nearest camping: Many campgrounds are located around White Lake. See the appendix listing for the town of White Lake for contact information.

Directions: The only public boating access is a pay ramp at White Lake Water Sports and Marina. To reach it from N.C. 87 in Elizabethtown, travel north on U.S. 701 for 6.7 miles and turn right at the marina.

86 Lumber River

Key species: Largemouth bass, sunfish, black crappie, channel catfish, flathead catfish

Overview: The Lumber River is located in southeastern North Carolina. It flows from its headwaters at Drowning Creek southeast of Lumberton into the Little Pee Dee River in South Carolina. The Lumber River was likely named after its use in rafting timber to Georgetown, South Carolina. According to the local Lumbee Indians, the river is properly called the Lumbee River, after their word for "black water." The river is heavily forested in cypress, tupelo, red gum, black gum, and water oak.

Best ways to fish: Motorboat, kayak, canoe, bank

Best times to fish: Spring, fall

Description: The Lumber River flows for 115 miles. It is a free-flowing river with no dams or levees to alter its course. This blackwater river has a slow flow. For 81 of its miles, the Lumber is designated a National Wild and Scenic River, due to its outstanding scenery and lack of human impact. The Lumber meanders more than most other rivers in the coastal plain. Its high bluffs at Princess Ann and High Hill are unusual for a blackwater river.

The fishing: The Lumber River is best known for its panfish action. Redbreast, bluegill, warmouth, flier, redear, and other sunfish species are common catches. The Lumber is navigable in a small skiff or johnboat when the water is at a normal level in spring. But during low-water conditions in summer droughts, anglers have to use canoes and kayaks and drag them across bars and fallen trees. Sunfish anglers use fly rods and popping bugs or cane poles or long fiberglass poles with float rigs baited with worms and crickets.

In the cold months, the crappie bite is very good. The best times to catch crappie are from January through April and again in November. The logjams and fallen trees in the river make great crappie cover. Anglers use small beetle grub spinners and live minnows to catch crappie.

The bass fishing is best in April and May. Soft plastics and spinnerbaits are the best bets for probing woody cover and the areas beneath overhanging limbs. Topwater lures work well in summer, when bass are near the pad beds and along the sand bars.

Flathead catfish have largely supplanted other catfish species and are thought to be having an adverse impact on some sunfish species, especially redbreast sunfish. Flathead anglers fish during the day or at night by casting live sunfish on bottom rigs near the logjams and in the deep holes.

N.C. A-G grid: 81, C-7

General information: All NCWRC regulations apply. Lumber River State Park offers hiking trails, bridle trails, and picnic shelters; see the appendix for contact information.

Nearest camping: Primitive camping is available at Lumber River State Park. Canoe camping areas are located along the river.

Directions: To reach Princess Ann Public Access from the town of Boardman, travel 1.6 miles north on U.S. 74, turn left on N.C. 130 (Woodrow Road), drive 2.4

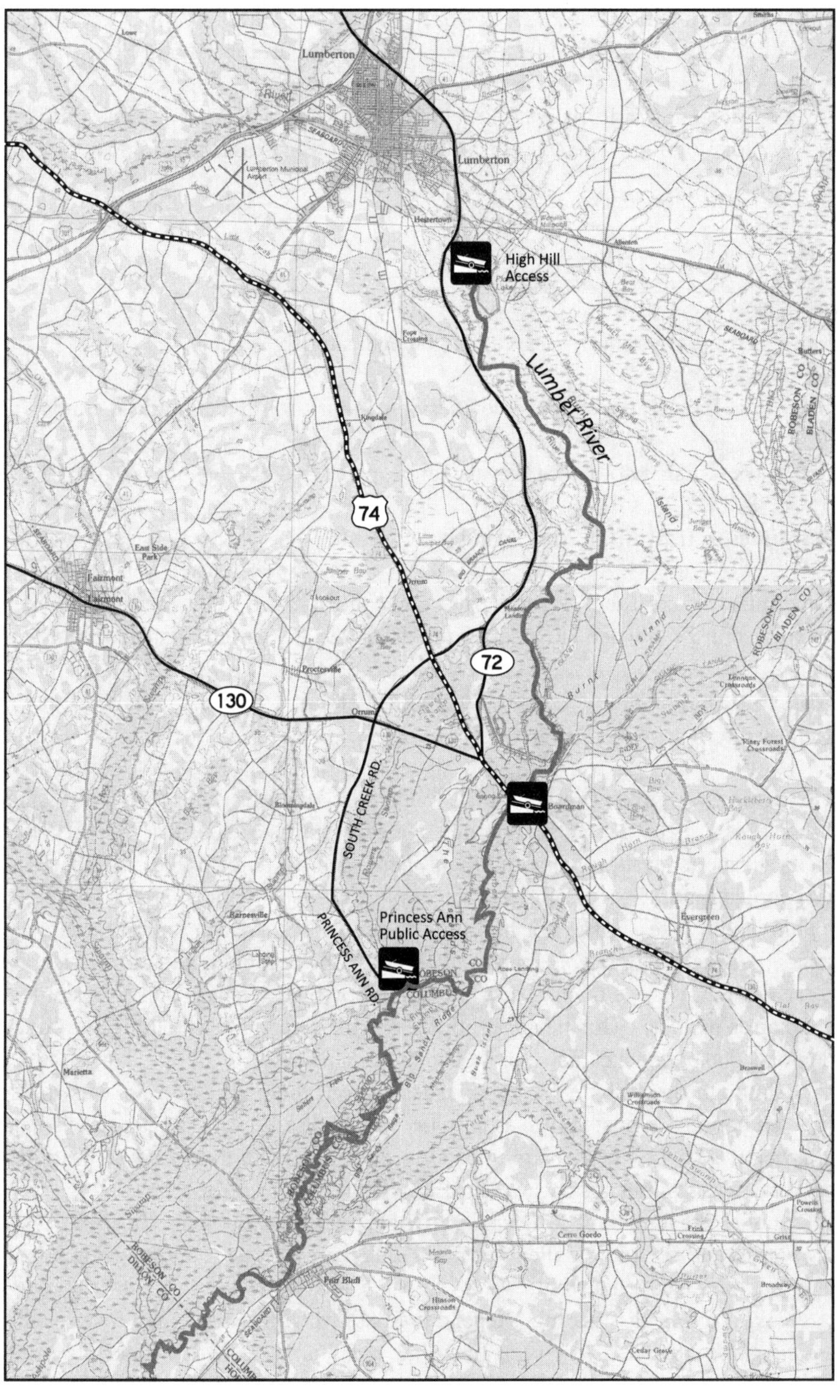
High Hill Access
Lumber River
74
72
130
SOUTH CREEK RD.
Princess Ann Public Access
PRINCESS ANN RD.
Lumberton
Fairmont
Boardman
Evergreen
Cerro Gordo
Fair Bluff

miles, and turn left on South Creek Road (S.R. 2225). Travel 3.6 miles to Princess Ann Road (S.R. 2246), turn left, and drive 2.6 miles. Lumber River State Park is on the left. The access area is at the end of the road.

To reach High Hill Access from N.C. 211 in Robeson County, travel south on N.C. 72 for 1.6 miles. The access is on the right as you cross the bridge.

87 Lake Tabor

Key species: Largemouth bass, catfish, bluegill sunfish, crappie

Overview: Lake Tabor is a reservoir serving Tabor City in Columbus County.

Best ways to fish: Motorboat, kayak, canoe, pier

Best times to fish: April, May, October, November

Description: Lake Tabor was built for flood control in the 1800s. It was completely emptied in 1996 when Hurricane Fran destroyed the dam. Private stockholders owned the lake, so it took legislative wrangling to secure the necessary public funds for rebuilding the dam and restoring the 188-acre lake as the centerpiece of Tabor City.

The fishing: Crappie were not stocked when the lake was refilled in 2000. Lake Tabor is essentially a large farm pond. The early stages of succession are usually the best time for fast-growing and highly reproductive panfish like crappie, since overpopulation and the resulting stunting of adult fish—which happen over time on almost all lakes—have not had time to occur. But even in its former climax stage, the lake was relatively balanced as far as the crappie population was concerned. A wide range of predators including bowfin and chain pickerel kept the population in check. That balance should be maintained, thanks to the reintroduction of 1,000 channel catfish and 1,000 largemouth bass.

Although the crappie fishing is usually good, the population appears to go through boom-and-bust cycles, as in many small lakes. Crappie anglers cast small jigs, beetle grub spinners, or minnows on float rigs to shoreline cover. Another good tactic is trolling jigs in the deep areas of the lake near the dam.

Sunfish are abundant. Anglers catch them by fishing along the shoreline, casting worms and crickets to fallen tree limbs and cypress trees. A popping bug fished on a fly rod is also a good bet.

Lake Tabor's bass fishing is legendary. Bass weighing more than five pounds are caught by anglers every year. In spring, small crankbaits and stickbaits work well. Spinnerbaits also work well until the aquatic vegetation begins growing in late spring. Topwater lures and soft plastics are the best bets as the water warms in early summer and the vegetation makes fishing difficult. The fishing shuts down in the heat of summer, then picks up again in the fall. Determined summer anglers have luck fishing at dawn and dusk from the pier and in the deep water near the dam.

The long pier is an excellent place for catching all species of fish. The shelters on the pier make it a great lounging area.

N.C. A-G grid: 82, D-1

General information: All NCWRC regulations apply. Lake regulations apply to crappie limits.

Nearest camping: Although camping is not allowed at Lake Tabor, picnic facilities and a tackle shop are on the site. Yogi Bear's Jellystone Park at Daddy Joe's offers camping and stocked fishing ponds in Tabor City; see the appendix entry for Yogi Bear's Jellystone Park.

Directions: Fees are charged for fishing and launching at Lake Tabor. To reach the access ramp from U.S. 74 West, take the Whiteville exit and travel south on U.S. 701 for 15 miles. The access is on the right at the intersection with U.S. 701 Business.

88 Lake Waccamaw

Key species: Largemouth bass, pumpkinseed sunfish, redear sunfish, white perch, yellow perch, channel catfish, bullhead catfish

Overview: Lake Waccamaw is the largest of the Carolina bay lakes in coastal North Carolina. It supports abundant wildlife and endemic species, thanks to the natural limestone deposits on the lake bottom along the northern shoreline. Other bay lakes do not have this natural limestone outcropping, which neutralizes the water's acidity and allows a broader diversity of plants, fish, and mollusks. Located in Columbus County, Lake Waccamaw is the headwaters of the Waccamaw River. The waters of Big Creek and Cove Swamp enter the lake.

Best ways to fish: Motorboat, kayak, canoe, bank

Best times to fish: Spring, summer, fall

Mike Marsh caught this redear sunfish, or "shellcracker," by casting a beetle grub spinner beneath a boat dock at Lake Waccamaw.

Description: Lake Waccamaw measures 8,936 acres and has an average depth of 7.5 feet. Since most of the lake is shallow and the bottom is sandy and offers solid footing, it offers excellent wade-fishing opportunities. The lake is oval in shape and measures roughly five miles by seven miles. It is fed by Big Creek and the surrounding cypress swamps including Cove Swamp. A low dam at the headwaters of the Waccamaw River regulates the level of the lake. The dam is 43 feet above sea level.

The fishing: Of all the state's Carolina bay lakes, Lake Waccamaw offers the best fishing for many species. Bank-bound anglers fish from private piers, by wading, or from the public pier at Lake Waccamaw State Park. Most anglers catch fish from pontoon boats, bass boats, or johnboats. Anglers with small paddleboats, kayaks, and canoes fish along the grass beds lining much of the shoreline.

The largemouth bass fishing is excellent. Some very large bass have come from the lake; it will not be surprising if a state record lurks in its waters. This is a great place for fishing with soft plastics and topwater lures. The grass beds and boat docks offer the best cover. A few cypress trees offer bass good cover, as well as shady areas in summer. Some large pad beds along the northern shoreline also offer excellent cover for bass fishing. Spinnerbaits are good bets for fishing the pad beds. Big Creek offers some good fishing for bass and sunfish species. Other species that attack bass lures include chain pickerel, bowfin, and gar. The lake has some huge bowfin.

Pumpkinseed sunfish, which many Waccamaw anglers call "grass perch," are abundant. These colorful sunfish bed in the grass during spring. Anglers catch them by working the grass beds in small paddleboats and dropping worms or crickets hooked on float rigs into the open pockets. Fly rods with popping bugs also work well for catching pumpkinseed sunfish. Anglers fishing the grass beds with beetle grub spinners and inline spinners also catch yellow perch, redear sunfish, and bluegill sunfish.

The lake offers fair crappie fishing. Anglers catch crappie by fishing beneath the piers or beside the row of no-wake markers all around the shoreline. Although the canals around the lake are mostly private, several access points allow crappie anglers to launch small paddleboats. Once warm weather arrives, the high population of alligators in the canals and the massive blooms of floating duckweed inspire anglers to fish the lake rather than the canals.

White perch, which are native to the lake, offer a better fishing opportunity than crappie. White perch bite all year except December and January. Anglers catch them by trolling with spoons, crankbaits, and small spinners. The fish often break the surface while feeding on baitfish. They can also be spotted with a depth-finder. Upon locating a school, anglers catch white perch by casting spoons, jigs, crankbaits, spinners, and flies that imitate minnows.

Catfish anglers fish from the docks at night. But drifting also works well. Worms and shrimp are excellent catfish baits.

N.C. A-G grid: 82, C-4

General information: All NCWRC regulations apply. A low bridge across the

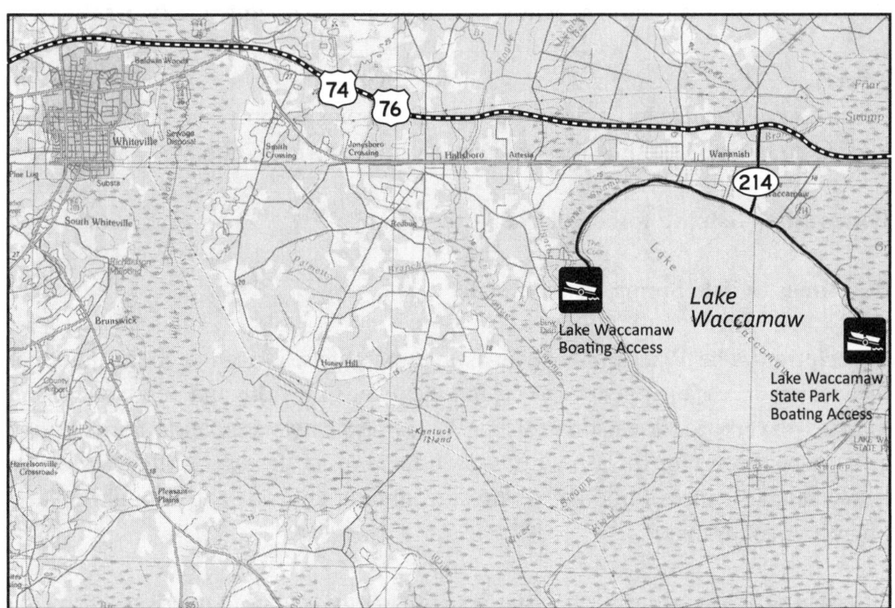

access canal prevents boats with high consoles from entering the lake via the Lake Waccamaw State Park ramp. The state park has hiking trails. One extends from the park to the dam and allows access to the southern shoreline for wading anglers. The park also offers a fishing and swimming pier with a covered area for weather protection. It is a good place to enter the lake for wade fishing.

Nearest camping: Primitive camping is available at Lake Waccamaw State Park; for information, see the park's appendix entry.

Directions: To reach the NCWRC's Lake Waccamaw Boating Access Area from U.S. 701 in Whiteville, travel east on U.S. 74 for 10.5 miles to Chaunceytown Road (S.R. 1735), turn right, drive 0.5 mile to N.C. 214 (Sam Potts Highway), and cross over N.C. 214 to Flemington Drive. Travel 0.3 mile on Flemington Drive to Canal Cove Road, turn right, and go 2.4 miles to the access area, on the left.

To reach Lake Waccamaw State Park Boating Access, follow the above directions as far as Flemington Drive. Travel 0.3 mile on Flemington Drive, turn left on Lakeshore Drive (S.R. 1957), drive 1.9 miles, and turn left on Bartram Lane. Travel 0.1 mile, turn right on Bella Coola Road (S.R. 1947), and drive 1.8 miles. The access is on the right.

89 Waccamaw River

Key species: Sunfish, catfish, yellow perch, white perch, largemouth bass

Overview: The Waccamaw River is a slow-moving blackwater river with headwaters at Lake Waccamaw. It flows through Columbus County and borders Brunswick County before joining the Pee Dee River in South Carolina.

Best ways to fish: Motorboat, kayak, canoe, bank

Best times to fish: Spring, summer, fall

Description: The Waccamaw River is approximately 115 miles long. Its upper reaches are accessible only by canoe, but it expands in width and depth to accommodate powerboats downstream. The Waccamaw flows parallel to the coastline as it passes from North Carolina into South Carolina. It is a moody river where heavy rainfall causes flooding of the surrounding swamps and drought creates low-water conditions.

The fishing: The various sunfish species bring many anglers to the river during the spring spawn. Redbreast, spotted (stumpknocker), redear (shellcracker), bluegill, and warmouth sunfish are abundant in the river. The stumpknocker is indigenous only to the southeastern section of North Carolina. Drab in color and solitary in habits, it guards its territory of a cypress trunk or knee from other sunfish. Sunfish anglers use long poles with float rigs baited with live worms and crickets, lightweight spinning rigs with beetle grub spinners, and fly rods with popping bugs to get in on the action.

Catfish anglers fish from the bank along the Columbus County game land near Pireway or from private property. Many anglers fish for catfish with set-hooks and jug-hooks. Worms, liver, and shrimp are good baits for catfish.

The largemouth bass fishing can be very good. Some bass top six pounds. The best time to catch bass is March through the first of June. Bass anglers cast spinnerbaits and soft plastics to the logjams and the trees that have fallen into the water. As the water heats up, topwater action early or late in the day is the best bet. Propeller lures and buzzbaits are good topwater choices. If the water is high, a floating worm is a good bet for fishing the swampy edges of the river. Bass anglers have to contend with strikes from toothy fish including bowfin, gar, and chain pickerel.

Yellow perch migrate to the foot of the Lake Waccamaw Dam in February and March. Anglers can fish for them by parking at the dam at Lake Waccamaw State Park and walking or wading downstream. The yellow perch action in the lower stretches is also good in February and March. In addition, it's a great time to catch black crappie and white perch. A beetle grub spinner or minnow will catch all three fish species. The best grub colors are green and white.

N.C. A-G grid: 86, A-1

General information: All NCWRC regulations apply.

Nearest camping: Camping is available at Lake Waccamaw State Park but not along the Waccamaw River in North Carolina; see the appendix for contact information for the state park.

Directions: To reach Pireway Boat Access Area from U.S. 17 south of Shallotte, travel west on N.C. 904 (Longwood Road) for 5.3 miles. Turn left to continue on N.C. 904 (Pireway Road). Drive 5.5 miles to the access area, located on the left at the bridge.

90 Upper Cape Fear River

Key species: Striped bass, flathead catfish, blue catfish, channel catfish, black crappie, largemouth bass, spotted bass, American shad, sunfish, chain pickerel

Overview: The Cape Fear River is the largest river system in North Carolina. By the time its waters enter the Atlantic Ocean at Bald Head Island, they have passed through Harnett, Cumberland, Bladen, Pender, New Hanover, and Brunswick counties. The river begins at the confluence of the Deep and Haw rivers in Lee and Chatham counties. This chapter focuses on the Cape Fear above Lock and Dam No. 1, located at Kings Bluff, approximately 39 miles above Wilmington.

Best ways to fish: Motorboat, kayak, canoe, bank

Best time to fish: Something is biting year-round. Above Lock and Dam No. 1, the fishing for blue and flathead catfish is some of the best in the state.

Description: The Cape Fear above Lock and Dam No. 1 has an average depth of eight feet. Consisting of three projects, the lock and dam system provides a navigable channel of 111 river miles extending from Navassa to Fayetteville. The state of North Carolina has expressed an interest in taking over the lock system including the parks and ramps from the Corps of Engineers. A rock rapid has been approved for allowing fish to swim above Lock and Dam No. 1.

The fishing: A favorite fishing hole below the Lock and Dam No. 1 site is where anglers catch shad, catfish, and striped bass. Local groups organize a traditional fish fry at the Lock and Dam No. 1 park during the peak of the shad run at Easter. The American shad run begins in February and continues through May. Anglers use small jigs called darts, curly-tailed grubs on jig heads, and spoons to catch shad. The jigs are cast with light spinning tackle. A few anglers use fly rods. Anchoring near the dam site can be dangerous during heavy flow conditions. Anglers use cinder blocks or other anchors they can cut free if they become stuck on the trees and rocks along the bottom.

Blue catfish gather beneath the shad schools in spring. But the best blue catfish bite occurs during winter. Anglers typically use cut shad to catch blue catfish, which can weigh more than 50 pounds. Between the locks, the river is essentially a deep ditch, its former feeder streams blocked off for navigation uses that no longer apply. Anglers without boats fish at the lock parks or from private property along the banks.

The best way to catch catfish is by fishing the bends with multiple rods. The

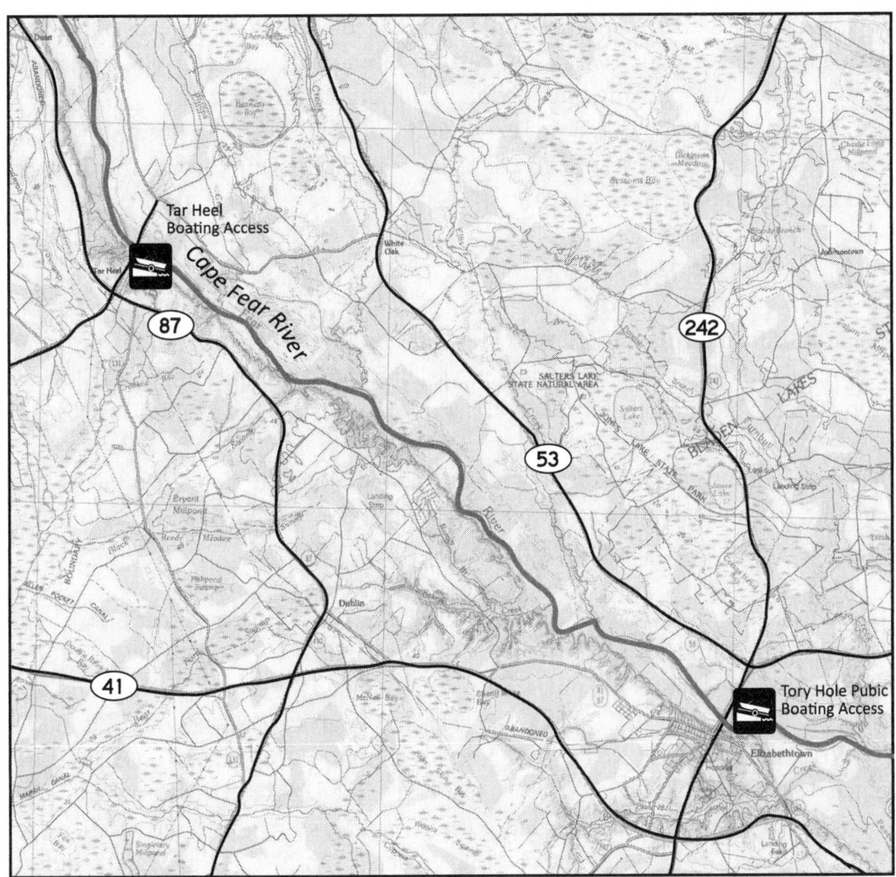

deep holes at the outside areas of the bends hold blue catfish, which migrate to the upstream shallows at night. Anglers spot the catfish using depthfinders, then anchor, cast their baits, and wait.

The logjams hold flathead catfish. More territorial than blues, flatheads come out of the logjams to hunt the shallow bank edges at night. While multiple catches of blue catfish are common, only one or two flathead catfish can be caught from a small area. Daytime anglers target flatheads at the former creek mouths or other areas with deep water and woody cover. State-record flatheads have come from this stretch of the Cape Fear. Live panfish make the best flathead baits. But live eels, shad, cut baits, and liver will catch all of the river's catfish species. A few native bullheads and white catfish may survive, but these species have been all but displaced by the nonnative blue and flathead catfish. Channel catfish, also a nonnative species, were once common but have also been largely displaced by the larger catfish.

To catch crappie, sunfish, and bass, anglers drift along the banks using trolling motors to maneuver while casting to shoreline cover. Drop-offs, sunken logs, logjams, cypress trees and knees, and submerged stumps create excellent cover. Bass anglers have good luck when casting spinnerbaits and soft plastics. Beetle grub spinners and popping bugs are good universal lures for catching all of these species. The best time to fish is late March through May, then again in the fall. During summer, the best time to fish is early in the morning, when the tall trees and high bluffs provide shaded areas.

N.C. A-G grid: 74, 82, 83

General information: All NCWRC regulations apply. Anglers should check current regulations for striped bass, which are subject to a moratorium due to restoration efforts. See the appendix for contact information for Lock and Dam No. 1.

Nearest camping: Public camping is not allowed along the Cape Fear below Fayetteville. Primitive camping is available at nearby Jones Lake State Park; for information, see the appendix entry for the park.

Directions: To reach the COE's Lock and Dam No. 1 Boating Access Area and Park in Kings Bluff from U.S. 74/U.S. 76 in Freeman, turn right on N.C. 11 (General Howe Road), travel 4.2 miles, take a left on N.C. 87, drive 2.2 miles, and turn right on Lock No. 1 Road (S.R. 1734). The access area is at the end of the road.

To reach Tar Heel Boating Access Area from N.C. 131 in Tar Heel, travel north on N.C. 87 for 0.4 mile to Tar Heel Ferry Road (S.R. 1316), turn right, drive 1.6 miles to Wildlife Landing Road, turn left, and go 0.7 mile to the access area.

To reach Tory Hole Public Boating Access from N.C. 87 in Elizabethtown, travel north on U.S. 701 for 0.2 mile to the entrance to Tory Hole Park. Turn left into the park and follow the road to the river front.

91 Sutton Lake

Key species: Largemouth bass, flathead catfish, channel catfish, sunfish

Overview: Sutton Lake is a man-made lake in New Hanover County with a system of dikes that recirculates cooling water for the L. V. Sutton steam electric plant. Sutton Lake was built on Catfish Creek, a tributary of the Northeast Cape Fear River. It was named after Louis V. Sutton, chief executive of Carolina Power and Light, now Progress Energy.

Best ways to fish: Powerboat, kayak, canoe, pier, wading, bank

Best time to fish: February through November

Description: Sutton Lake has 850 acres of surface area. When it was constructed in 1972, lots of woody cover was left in place. That cover provides excellent fish habitat and keeps out pleasure boats and water scooters. Since the bottom has solid, sandy footing, some anglers wade the edges and fish from the bank.

The fishing: Sutton Lake is one of the top destinations for largemouth bass fishing in the southeastern part of the state. Its warm water and trophy management program produce five-pound bass regularly and eight-pound bass occasionally. A few 10-pounders have been reported.

Sutton Lake is warmer than most other lakes because of the closed-loop cooling system. The lake's compartments are called "ponds." In winter, ponds 1, 2, and 3, which are closest to the warm-water discharge, produce the best bass fishing. In summer, the ponds closest to the intake are better bets, with ponds 6 and 7 the coolest. Bass anglers use every technique. The best bets in winter and early spring are spinnerbaits and crankbaits fished along the dikes and the deep holes along their edges that were dug to provide construction material. Soft plastics fished on Carolina rigs are the next-best bet until the algae and pondweed begin to grow

Mike Marsh with a Sutton Lake flathead catfish. Flatheads occur in many lakes and rivers and are voracious predatory fish. They grow to enormous sizes and are powerful fighters.

in late spring. Grass carp and herbicides are used to control aquatic vegetation, but the weeds sometimes get the upper hand temporarily. Bass anglers can find woody cover to fish almost anywhere. The stumps, sunken logs, roots, fallen trees, and cut-and-cabled trees along the shoreline provide excellent bass cover. During warm weather, topwater lures produce well. Propeller lures, walk-the-dog lures, and poppers work best when the algae beds aren't too thick. Floating frogs and worms and buzzbaits are best where and when vegetation covers the water. Since the water is incredibly clear, anglers use small-diameter lines to reduce visibility.

Sutton Lake produces very large flathead catfish. Anglers use live sunfish to catch them. The flatheads are caught at the many fish attractors in the lake, along the dikes and snags, and from the public fishing dock at the boat ramp.

Channel catfish have been stocked in the lake and are abundant. The best time to catch them is early spring; February and March are the peak months. Channel cats are caught at the discharge canal, at the fish attractors, and from the public fishing dock. Shrimp and liver are the most popular channel catfish baits.

Sunfish are plentiful at Sutton Lake. Anglers use float rigs baited with worms and crickets to catch them. Beetle grub spinners and popping bugs also work well. The best time to catch sunfish is when they are bedding in April and May. The main sunfish species is bluegill. A few redbreast sunfish are present as well. The largest species is redear sunfish (shellcracker), but it is much less prevalent than bluegill.

Although anglers land a few crappie, this is not a good lake for catching them. Anglers also land gar, bowfin, chain pickerel, and even an occasional flounder at Sutton Lake.

N.C. A-G grid: 84, C-1

General information: All NCWRC regulations apply. A closed season for keeping largemouth in early spring helps increase the size of Sutton Lake's trophy bass.

Nearest camping: Camping is not allowed at Sutton Lake. Carolina Beach State Park and Lake Waccamaw State Park are nearby. Both offer camping for tents and trailers, picnic facilities, bathhouses, and hiking trails. See the appendix for contact information.

Directions: To reach Sutton Lake Boating Access Area from I-140 west of Wilmington, travel south on U.S. 421 for 0.6 mile to Sutton Lake Road (S.R. 2145), turn right, drive 0.5 mile to the end of the pavement, and continue 1.1 miles on the gravel road to the access area.

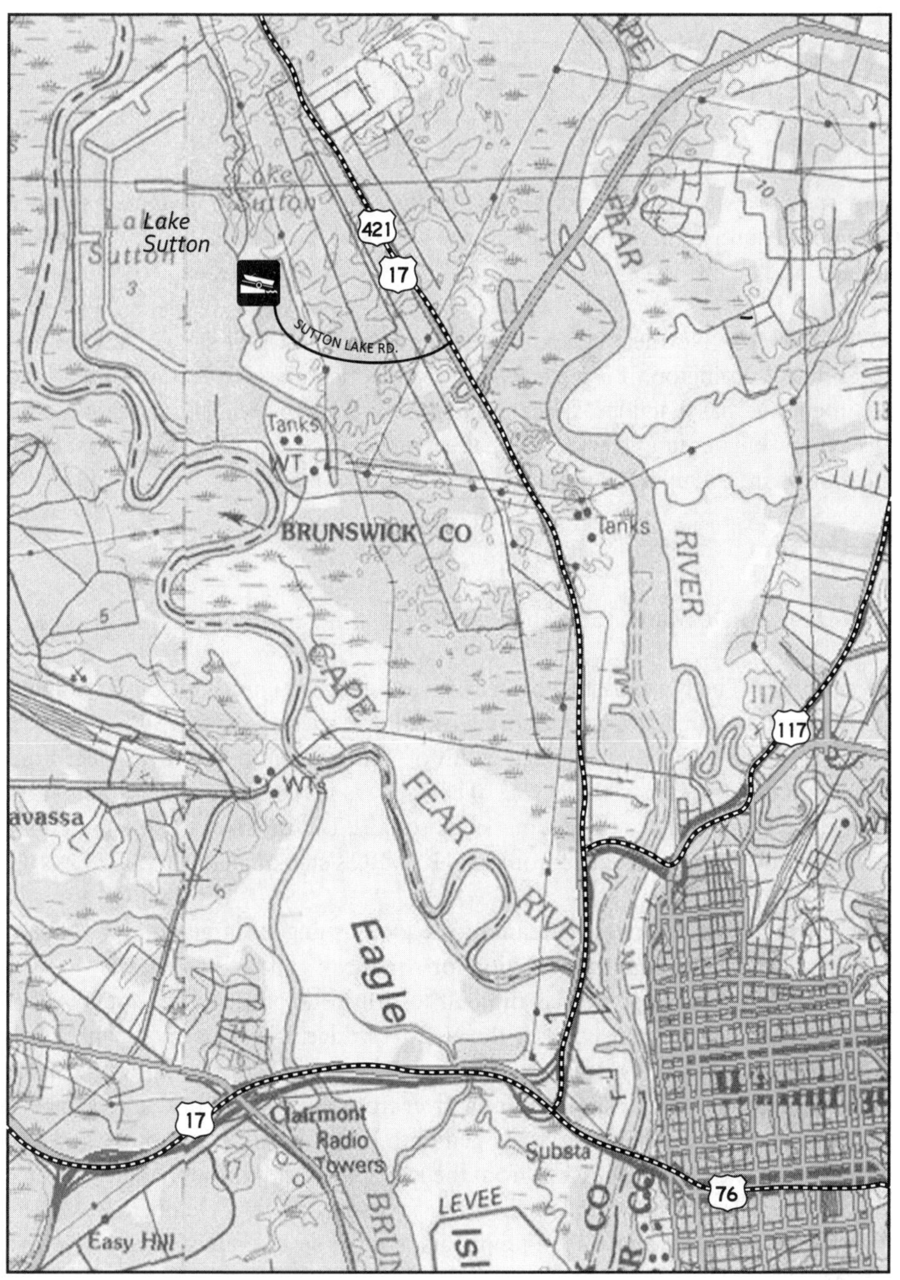
Lake Sutton
421
17
SUTTON LAKE RD.
Tanks
WT
BRUNSWICK CO
Tanks
RIVER
FEAR
CAPE
FEAR
RIVER
Wts
avassa
117
Eagle
17
Clarmont
Radio
Towers
Substa
76
LEVEE
Easy Hill

92 Northeast Cape Fear River

Key species: Largemouth bass, bluegill sunfish, redear sunfish, redbreast sunfish, warmouth sunfish, black crappie, channel catfish, flathead catfish, blue catfish, striped bass

Overview: The Northeast Cape Fear River is a tributary of the Cape Fear that joins it at Wilmington. It is a blackwater river, which means it receives little or no sediment and has a stained appearance from organic matter. The organic matter decays and creates tannic acid, giving the river its black color. The Northeast Cape Fear flows from Duplin County to New Hanover County.

Best ways to fish: Motorboat, kayak, canoe, bank

Best time to fish: March through November

Description: The Northeast Cape Fear River flows from north to south for about 130 miles. It has an average width of 55 feet and an average depth of 4.5 feet above the N.C. 41 bridge and an average width of 150 feet and depth of 8.5 feet from that point downstream to the N.C. 210 bridge. It is subject to severe flooding from tropical events that have caused massive fish kills. But the river's fish populations always recover with assistance from the NCWRC's stocking efforts.

The fishing: This blackwater stream offers good fishing for largemouth bass, sunfish, and catfish and some good action for American and hickory shad.

The Northeast Cape Fear is difficult to fish in Duplin County due to fallen trees and underwater snags. Below the N.C. 41 bridge, it widens and deepens and provides good fishing for largemouth bass and sunfish. The best months to fish for bass are April and May. The section of river from the N.C. 41 bridge to the N.C. 210 bridge offers good fishing for largemouth bass, bluegill, warmouth, and catfish. The peak time for sunfish is from the middle of April through June, but nice catches can also be made throughout the summer and into October. Along the river's upper reaches, anglers use johnboats or other small craft with small electric or gasoline motors.

American and hickory shad can be caught from the middle of March through early May in the lower reaches of the river below Kenansville.

The bass fishing is best in the feeder creeks and oxbows during a falling tide. Soft plastics and spinnerbaits are the best bets. Areas where water is coming into the main river are the best places to fish.

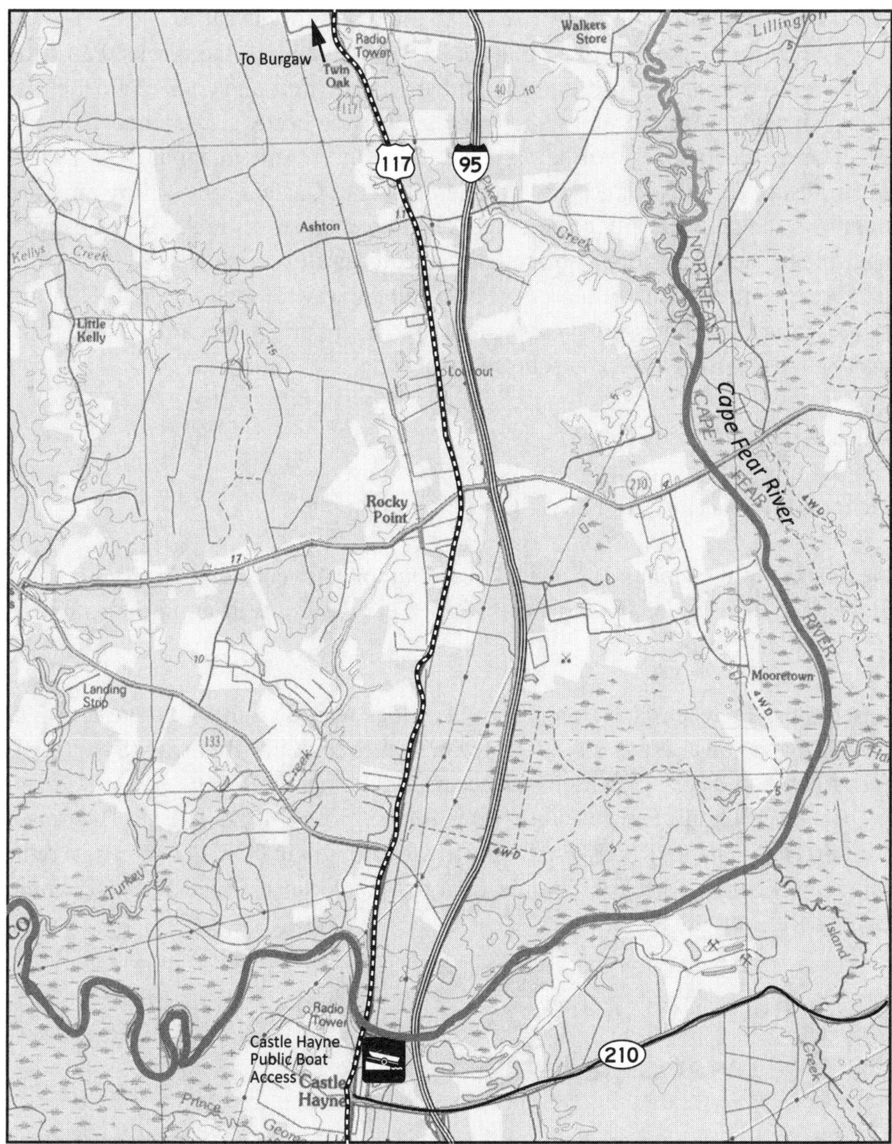

The striper fishing is excellent in the river channel and along all the creeks near Wilmington. The Wilmington waterfront is also a great place for stripers, thanks to all of the structure areas. The river channel offers good places to fish with trolling lures or by casting crankbaits.

Blue catfish and flathead catfish have mostly supplanted channel catfish and bullhead catfish. The blues and flatheads are large, numerous, and aggressive. The best baits for blues include cut shad, eels, minnows, liver, and panfish. Flathead catfish will strike these baits but prefer live panfish or eels. The flats at the creek mouths, the deep holes at the outsides of the river bends, and the logjams and fallen trees extending into the water are all good bets for big catfish.

The panfish action can be fantastic in the river and all the creeks. Pad beds and woody cover are the best bets for panfish. Live worms and crickets are the best baits, but anglers also do well with popping bugs and beetle grub spinners.

The crappie fishing can be excellent. The bite begins in January or February in Prince George, Island, and other creeks from Castle Hayne upstream. Live minnows and spinners are the best bets. The action tapers off in April, but panfish anglers may add occasional crappie to their catches all year long.

Warmouth sunfish are aggressive biters all the way through summer. They are caught from the submerged cypress trunks and knees along the banks. Small spinners and live worms are the best bets for warmouth.

N.C. A-G grid: 84, C-1

General information: All NCWRC regulations apply.

Nearest camping: Holland's Shelter Creek Outdoor Adventures offers RV hookups and cabin rentals along the Northeast Cape Fear River; see its entry in the appendix for contact information.

Directions: To reach Holly Shelter Public Boat Access from I-40, take Exit 398 near Burgaw, travel east on N.C. 53 for 6.3 miles to Shaw Highway (S.R. 1523), turn right, and drive 6.3 miles to the access, on the right.

To reach Castle Hayne Public Boat Access from I-40, take Exit 414, travel west on Holly Shelter Road for 0.8 mile to the stoplight in Castle Hayne, turn right on U.S. 117, drive north for 0.5 mile, turn right on Orange Street, and go 0.2 mile to the access, on the left.

93 Lower Cape Fear River

Key species: Flounder, speckled trout, black drum, red drum, tarpon, sheepshead, spot, croaker, largemouth bass, striped bass, blue catfish, flathead catfish

Overview: This chapter covers the Lower Cape Fear from the vicinity of Wilmington upstream to the first dam and downstream to the river mouth at Southport. The river increases in salinity as it approaches the mouth. It widens and is surrounded by swamps, creeks, and sand ridges. The Black River and the Northeast Cape Fear River join the Cape Fear above Wilmington. The river becomes an estuary that provides habitat for anadromous species. The lower section of the

Steve Laughinghouse caught this 10-pound flounder near Wilmington. Flounder are the most-sought inshore fish along the coast because they are so good to eat.

Cape Fear is dredged to maintain the shipping channel to the state port at Wilmington and to upstream industries. The river was named for Cape Fear, a point of land and an area of dangerous shoals off Bald Head Island.

Best ways to fish: Motorboat, bank, kayak

Best time to fish: Year-round

Description: The Cape Fear is 202 miles long from its headwaters at the confluence of the Haw and Deep rivers below Jordan Lake to the Atlantic Ocean. The shipping channel is dredged to a depth of 45 feet. Most of the river outside the channel is only four to six feet deep.

The fishing: Below the locks and dams, the Cape Fear River system has surprisingly good fishing for largemouth bass. Bass anglers use spinnerbaits and crankbaits cast to pad beds and any woody structure. The creek mouths are the best places to fish. The best time is a falling tide, when baitfish must leave cover. Savvy river anglers "chase the tides," planning their trips around the times of falling tides in the creeks over long stretches of the river.

Blue catfish bite well at Wilmington. The best places to catch them are pilings, bulkheads, and other man-made structure. Striped bass and blue catfish make excellent winter fishing. Both species will strike cut eel, shrimp, and cut shad fished on the bottom. Striped bass also strike trolling lures, jigs, and stickbaits fished in the structure areas.

The saltwater species begin at Wilmington. Speckled trout are a good bet for the cold months. The red drum bite begins in March and continues through November. The flounder bite begins in May and continues through October. This is one of the best places in the state to catch trophy flounder. The state-record flounder was caught in Snow's Cut near Carolina Beach.

The lower river is also a great place to catch red drum and speckled trout. The Elizabeth River marsh complex at Southport and the marsh complexes at Bald Head Island offer excellent fishing. Trophy flounder lurk along the islands and the "junk" around the docks at the Southport waterfront. Black drum, spadefish, and sheepshead are common catches near Southport at the ADM dock and old quarantine station, which is only a set of pilings today.

At Southport, anglers can take advantage of free fishing at a municipal pier that offers good action for all saltwater species. Carolina Beach State Park offers a fishing dock and shore fishing on the river and at Snow's Cut. Snow's Cut Park is another excellent bank-fishing destination. Anglers can find a free public pier and ramp extending into the river at New Hanover County's River Road Park.

The spot and croaker fishing is excellent in the lower river in the fall. Other interesting species in the river include ladyfish, many species of shark, and tripletail, which orient to the buoys of crab pots and other objects.

Sheepshead can be caught at the Snow's Cut bridge and at several channel markers in the creeks of Bald Head Island. For black drum and sheepshead, fishermen use mole crabs and fiddler crabs for bait. The jetties at Bald Head Island Marina are known to hold red drum, speckled trout, and flounder.

Anglers enjoy excellent tarpon fishing on the Cape Fear shoals and in the deep holes at the river mouth. King mackerel, Spanish mackerel, and bluefish enter the river in spring and fall.

N.C. A-G grid: 87

General information: All NCWRC and NCDMF regulations apply. The Cape Fear is a restoration area for striped bass. A moratorium for keeping striped bass exists but may be lifted in the future.

Nearest camping: Camping is available at Carolina Beach State Park; see the park's entry in the appendix.

Directions: To reach Carolina Beach State Park Marina from the U.S. 421 bridge (the Snow's Cut bridge), travel south for 0.5 mile, turn right on North Dow Road (S.R. 1573), drive 0.3 mile, and turn right on State Park Road (S.R. 1628). The marina is at the end of the road.

To reach Snow's Cut Public Boat Access from the U.S. 421 bridge (the Snow's Cut bridge), travel south for 0.5 mile, turn right on North Dow Road, then turn immediately right on Bridge Barrier Road (S.R. 1577). Travel 0.3 mile to Spencer Farlow Drive (S.R. 1532), turn right, and drive 0.5 mile to Pogada Drive. Turn left on Pogada Drive, which becomes Annie Drive. Go 0.2 mile to the access, located at the end of Annie Drive.

To reach Memorial Bridge Access Area in downtown Wilmington from the junction of U.S. 421 and U.S. 17, travel east on U.S. 421/U.S. 17 for 0.7 mile over Memorial Bridge, take the exit for Front Street, merge onto Front, travel north for 0.2 mile, and take a left on Castle Street. Access is at the end of the road.

94 Boiling Spring Lakes

Key species: Largemouth bass, crappie, sunfish, channel catfish, chain pickerel

Overview: The town of Boiling Spring Lakes in Brunswick County is named for a natural spring that "boils" out 43 million gallons of water each day downstream of the dam at Big Lake. The lake, a natural sinkhole filled with water, was dammed to stabilize and increase the water elevation. Periodically, the lake level drops as water moves into the limestone below, which is like a rock formation of Swiss cheese. Various things have been tried to plug the lake, including filling the sinkholes with clay and shoring up the dam. The lake was completely drained for that purpose in 2007. It was restocked after the water level returned. The town has a total of 53 lakes.

Best ways to fish: Powerboat, kayak, canoe, bank

Best times to fish: Spring, summer, fall

Description: Big Lake in Boiling Spring Lakes is impounded by Sanford Dam and is fed by five springs and Allen's Creek. The lake encompasses 275 acres, has 10 miles or shoreline, and is 2.5 miles long. It was built in 1961 as the centerpiece for a residential development. Boiling Spring Lakes also has many smaller lakes. Upstream of Big Lake are Middle Lake, at approximately 10 acres in size, West Lake, at approximately 10 acres, and North Lake, at about seven acres. West Lake and Middle Lake are accessible from Dam Road. North Lake is accessible from East Lakeview Drive. Another popular lake upstream of Big Lake is Pine Lake, which is about six acres in size. Pine Lake is accessible from East Boiling Spring Road.

The fishing: The fishing at the smaller lakes never disappears, as it has at Big

Lake when it experienced problems. The small lakes offer good bass fishing. Some fish exceeding five pounds have been caught, and rumors of 10-pounders abound. The lakes have a variety of structure including boat docks, pad beds, stumps, and emergent vegetation along the shoreline. The fishing at Big Lake should be good also, now that repairs have been made to the lake bottom.

Middle and West lakes are drawn down in winter to control aquatic vegetation. Big Lake is drawn down for flood control when hurricanes threaten. Lowering and raising the water level keeps the ecosystems of these lakes dynamic, increasing their potential for producing large bass and keeping nuisance vegetation at bay.

The bass fishing is best in spring. Most anglers fish Big Lake from a canoe, kayak, or powerboat, casting soft plastic lures and topwater baits. Live minnows are also used for catching bass, especially by anglers fishing from the private docks. Although some of the lakes are shallow enough to wade across, most bank fishermen walk the banks and cast along the shoreline. In summer, algae can create problems in the small lakes. But persistent anglers use floating worms, rubber frogs, and other weedless topwater baits, casting them to the pad beds at dawn and dusk.

Several of the lakes produce crappie; Big Lake is the best bet. The crappie fishing can be good or poor. The best time to catch crappie is February through April. Live minnows and beetle grub spinners are the best bets.

Several species of sunfish are in the lakes. Bluegill sunfish is the most common species. Worms, crickets, spinners, and popping bugs are the best bets for sunfish.

Big Lake and the other large lakes have given up some impressive catfish. Most anglers fish from private docks or the bank using liver, worms, or minnows for bait.

N.C. A-G grid: 87, A-6

General information: All NCWRC regulations apply. Big Lake is the only lake in town where the use of gasoline-powered boats is allowed; the maximum length of boats is 25 feet, but no horsepower restriction is in force. The other lakes with public access from the street rights of way can be fished from the bank or from paddle-powered boats or boats equipped with electric trolling motors. Many of the small lakes are completely surrounded by private property and have no public access. North Lake has a floating dock that serves as a fishing platform. Fishing is allowed along Alton Lennon Drive and from the boat dock at the Big Lake ramp. For contact information, see the appendix entry for Boiling Spring Lakes.

Nearest camping: Camping is not allowed at Boiling Spring Lakes.

Directions: To reach Alton Lennon Boat Ramp from U.S. 17/U.S. 74/U.S. 76 in the town of Leland, take the U.S. 17 South exit toward Myrtle Beach. Travel south on U.S. 17 for 8.5 miles, turn left on N.C. 87 (Boiling Spring Road), drive 8 miles to East Boiling Spring Road (S.R. 1539), turn left, go 2.2 miles, and turn right on Alton Lennon Drive. The access is on the right.

95 Fort Fisher

Key species: Flounder, whiting, croaker, spot, speckled trout, red drum, black drum, sheepshead, shark

Overview: Fort Fisher is the site of the fortifications built to defend the Confederate port at Wilmington from capture by the Union navy. Locally known as "the South End," Fort Fisher State Recreation Area has four miles of drivable sand beach. The beach is also home to sea turtle and seabird nesting areas. Buzzard's Bay, located west of Fort Fisher, is enclosed by a rock sea wall built in the 1890s to curtail shoaling in the Cape Fear River.

Best ways to fish: Surf, kayak, johnboat

Best time to fish: Something is biting all year.

Description: Located at the southern tip of New Hanover County, Fort Fisher was opened as a state park in 1986. Fort Fisher State Recreation Area draws hundreds of thousands of visitors annually.

The fishing: The bay and marsh complex is an excellent place to catch flounder, speckled trout, and red drum. Several inlets to the backwater areas have opened and closed over the years. No inlet is currently open, which has resulted in a great red drum fishery. When Corncake Inlet was open, flounder presented the best fishing opportunity. Any tropical event could open another inlet across the beach strand. These inlets have opened at the northern end of the strand and migrated south until they could no longer be supported by tidal interchange and until tropical events filled them.

Access to the backwater is via the Federal Point ramp. The best bet for fishing is a kayak or johnboat. Fishing from a kayak is extremely popular and productive. Numerous oyster beds and a rock jetty in the marsh pose hazards to other types of watercraft. The hard structure areas including "The Rocks," which connects Zeke's Island to the mainland, hold speckled trout, red drum, black drum, and sheepshead. Anglers fish the rocks with jigs, live crabs, and minnows or troll along the edge with minnow-imitating lures.

The red drum fishing begins in February or March and continues into the fall. April and October are the peak months. Anglers spot the fish working the grass or on the bars and flats. A poling platform is an asset to spotting the fish, and a trolling motor can help anglers stay on the schools.

Speckled trout also occur along the grass beds and in the deep holes. Jigs, minnow-imitating lures, topwater walk-the-dog lures, and live baits are the best bets. The largest fish are usually in the bays during fall and winter, but specks are there all year long.

Although the best flounder fishing occurs in the creek channels, flounder might strike any lure or live bait fished on the bottom at a structure area or in a channel.

Surf fishing is popular for those with four-wheel-drive vehicles. But night closures against beach driving to protect sea turtles hurt the red drum fishing opportunities. Anglers watch for holes, mud lumps, and sloughs at low tide and fish them on the higher tides. Live minnows, cut baits, shrimp, and squid are top baits for surf fishing. Whiting, pompano, spot, croaker, shark, red drum, black drum, pigfish, pinfish, flounder, speckled trout, and bluefish are some of the abundant fish that can be caught in the surf. Tarpon are also hooked but seldom landed by anglers using surf tackle.

N.C. A-G grid: 87, B-7

General information: All NCDMF regulations apply. Access to the southern portion of the park requires a licensed four-wheel-drive vehicle. The fee for access is $10 daily or $40 annually; check for current fees. Park rangers cannot recover stranded vehicles; towing companies are available at the beach towns. Alcoholic beverages are not allowed. For contact information, see the appendix entry for Fort Fisher State Recreation Area. Fort Fisher State Historic Site has a trail complex that accesses the fort. The Civil War museum offers a respite from the weather. The North Carolina Aquarium at Fort Fisher is another great side trip for anglers.

Nearest camping: Camping is not allowed at Fort Fisher but is very popular at Carolina Beach State Park and Freeman Park, alternately called "the North End." See the appendix for contact information for Carolina Beach State Park.

Directions: To reach Fort Fisher State Recreation Area from the U.S. 421 bridge (the Snow's Cut bridge), travel south for 6.5 miles, turn left at Loggerhead Road, drive 0.2 mile, and turn left at Ramsgate Trail.

To reach Federal Point Public Boating Access from the U.S. 421 bridge (the Snow's Cut bridge), travel south for 7.7 miles to the end of the road. The access is on the left.

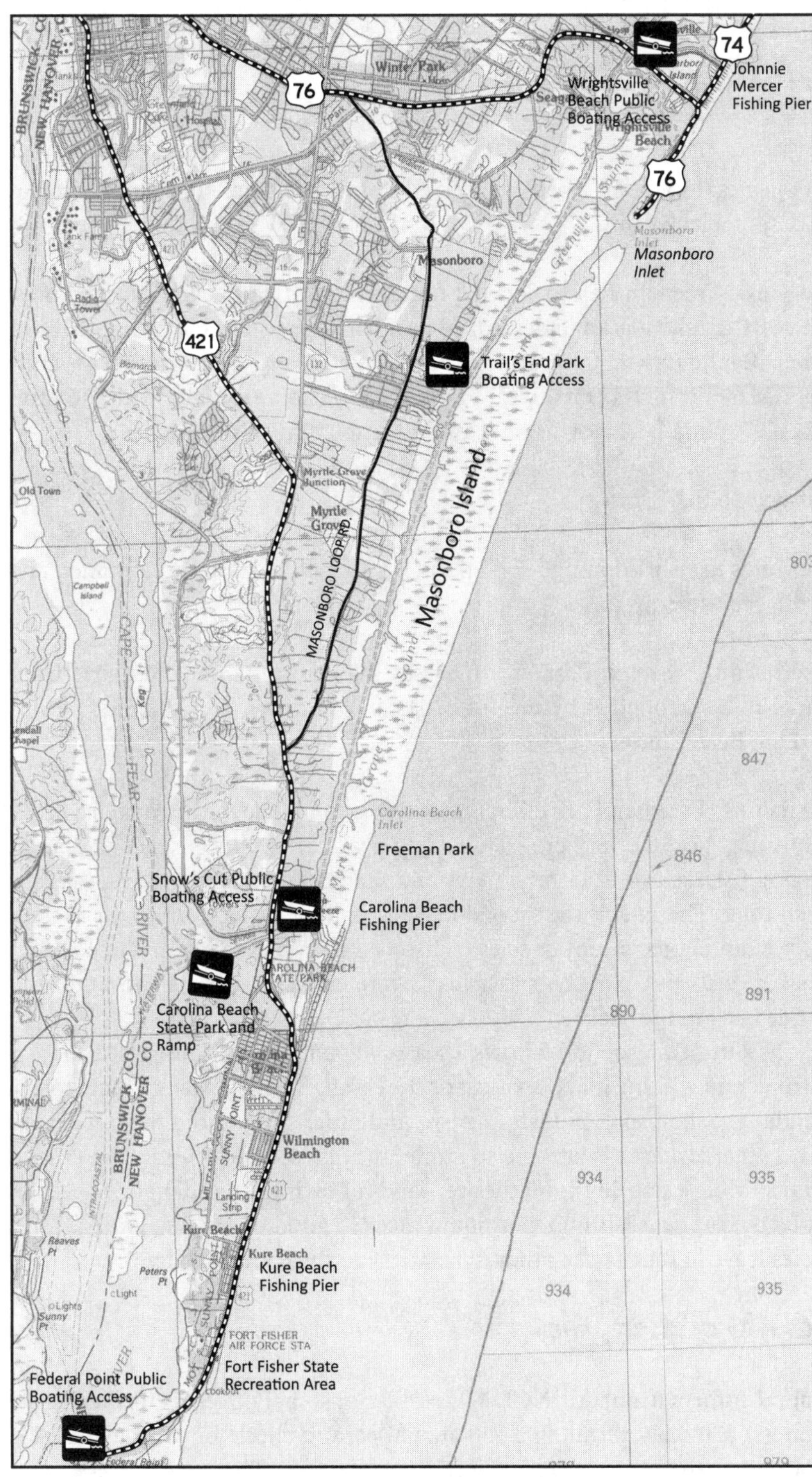

74
Johnnie Mercer Fishing Pier
Wrightsville Beach Public Boating Access
76
Masonboro Inlet
421
Trail's End Park Boating Access
Masonboro Island
MASONBORO LOOP RD.
Freeman Park
Snow's Cut Public Boating Access
Carolina Beach Fishing Pier
Carolina Beach State Park and Ramp
Kure Beach Fishing Pier
Fort Fisher State Recreation Area
Federal Point Public Boating Access

96 Freeman Park

Key species: Flounder, croaker, speckled trout, red drum, bluefish, whiting, pompano, spot, black drum

Overview: Freeman Park is located north of Carolina Beach. Locally known as "the North End," it is an undeveloped beach that provides four-wheel-drive access to the Atlantic Ocean and Carolina Beach Inlet. Long used by residents and visitors, it was recently formed into a park through an agreement with the property owner. Carolina Beach owns only a small strip at the park entrance.

Best way to fish: Surf

Best times to fish: Although something is biting all year, spring, summer, and fall are the peak seasons.

Description: Freeman Park encompasses the peninsula of land above Carolina Beach. It is surrounded by the Intracoastal Waterway, the Atlantic Ocean, and Carolina Beach Inlet.

The fishing: Freeman Park offers surf fishing combined with beach driving. Conditions may become very crowded during peak times on weekends and holidays. The best fishing area is at the sloughs and sand bars on the south end of Carolina Beach Inlet. The inlet is the second-best bet and the beachfront south of the sand bars the last choice. Many species of fish can be caught at all of these areas. Anglers who walk out to the bars to fish at low tide must be careful to beat the incoming tide back to the beach.

The surf-fishing action follows a seasonal pattern. In winter, red drum, speckled trout, and whiting make up most of the catch. Bluefish, black drum, pompano, flounder, croaker, spot, pinfish, pigfish, and other species join them when spring arrives. Sharks and rays become so numerous that they are nuisances in the warm months. Mole crabs dug from the wet sand following a receding tide make excellent baits. Cut baits, shrimp, and squid are also good bets. As fall arrives, the fish species leave in the reverse order in response to the cooling water.

N.C. A-G grid: 87, A-7

General information: All NCDMF regulations apply. Access to Freeman Park requires a $20 daily permit or a $60 annual permit; check for current fees. A kiosk is located at the entrance for collecting access fees. The New Hanover County

Sheriff's Department provides law enforcement. The town of Carolina Beach controls access and provides trash pickup and sanitary facilities. Driving on the dunes is prohibited. For contact information, see the appendix entry for Freeman Park.

Nearest camping: Overnight tent and RV camping is allowed at Freeman Park, but no support facilities except portable toilets are available.

Directions: To reach Freeman Park from the U.S. 421 bridge (the Snow's Cut bridge), travel south for 1.5 miles to Carl Winner Drive, turn left, go 0.1 mile, turn left on Canal Drive, and continue 1.6 miles to the park, located at the end of the road.

97 Masonboro Island

Key species: Flounder, croaker, speckled trout, red drum, bluefish, whiting, pompano, spot, black drum

Overview: Carolina Beach Inlet blasted through the narrow strip of land separating the Intracoastal Waterway from the Atlantic Ocean in 1952, creating Masonboro Island. The Society for the Preservation of Masonboro Island helped accrue private, federal, and state funds to purchase several parcels to complete the reserve, which was dedicated in 1991. Before the inlet was created, the island was part of the north end of Carolina Beach; Freeman Park is now located on the south side of the inlet. Masonboro Island is the largest undisturbed barrier island on the southern portion of the North Carolina coast.

Best ways to fish: Motorboat, surf, kayak

Best time to fish: April through October

Description: Masonboro Island is eight miles long and encompasses 5,046 acres. Approximately 4,300 acres of the reserve are tidal salt marshes and mud flats on Masonboro Sound. The area is included in the North Carolina National Estuarine Research Reserve program. The incredibly beautiful island once had large stretches of maritime forest and high dunes dotted with fishing shacks and cars that had been ferried in by fishermen. But rising sea levels and beach erosion altered the island to the point that several areas are subject to ocean overwash during astronomical or weather-driven high tides. Very little forest remains. Some shacks were removed when the reserve was created, while others simply washed into the sea. Some rusted-out vehicles parked at the island's south end at Carolina Beach Inlet are disintegrating in the salty environment. The sound is a popular area for duck hunting.

The fishing: The surf fishing at Masonboro Island is typically better than at Carolina Beach or Wrightsville Beach. Because access is more difficult, fewer anglers are on the island competing for fish. Another reason for the good fishing is that the island's natural beaches have not been subject to nourishment projects. Natural beaches appear to host a wider variety of the invertebrates that form the base of the food chain. They are therefore likely to attract better populations of predatory fish.

Anglers find drop-offs, coquina outcrops, mud lumps, sloughs, troughs, and shell beds during low tide and fish them at high tide. High tides during full and new moons are good times to catch fish.

Mole crabs caught from the wet sand and mullet caught from the sound with cast nets are the top surf-fishing baits. But any type of cut fish, squid, or shrimp makes an excellent surf-fishing bait. Surf fishermen often overlook the sound behind them, which offers some excellent fishing for red drum during high tides.

Although the fishing here is similar to that at Freeman Park, the red drum action is much better. The surf-fishing action follows a seasonal pattern. In winter, red drum, speckled trout, and whiting make up most of the catch. Bluefish, black drum, pompano, flounder, croaker, spot, pinfish, pigfish, and other species join them when spring arrives. Sharks and rays become so numerous that they are nuisances in the warm months. As fall arrives, the fish species leave in reverse order in response to the cooling water. Anglers also catch flounder and speckled trout in the sound and the Intracoastal Waterway separating the island from the mainland. Surf fishermen occasionally hook large tarpon.

N.C. A-G grid: 84, D-2

General information: All NCDMF regulations apply. Motorized vehicles are prohibited. Some shorebird nesting areas are protected with ropes and signs. The island has no facilities of any type. Some anglers head to the island through the marshes at high tide, allow the tide to fall and strand their boats, then wait for the tide's return to head back to the mainland.

See the appendix for contact information for the North Carolina Coastal Reserve.

Nearest camping: Camping is allowed on Masonboro Island. Weekends can become crowded, especially at the north end. Visitors are advised to clean up all litter, including pet waste.

Directions: The only way to reach Masonboro Island is by boat. Navigating the channels in Masonboro Sound can be tricky depending on the stage of the tide. Except for the northern end at Masonboro Inlet and the southern end at Carolina Beach Inlet, the island is accessible only during the top two-thirds of the tide range. Most visitors anchor along Banks Channel on the north side of the island near Wrightsville Beach.

98 Masonboro Inlet

Key species: Flounder, speckled trout, red drum, bluefish, cobia, Spanish mackerel

Overview: Masonboro Inlet, located at the south end of Wrightsville Beach, separates the town from Masonboro Island. Two rock jetties protect the inlet from shoaling. Masonboro Inlet has been open to the sea and in use since 1733.

Best ways to fish: Motorboat, surf

Best time to fish: April through December

Description: Due to funding limitations, the two jetties at Masonboro Inlet were built at different times. The north jetty was constructed first because the inlet tended to drift northward. The first third of the jetty near the shore has an underwater concrete sea wall, which creates a weir to allow sand to bypass the jetty and prevent shoaling. The north jetty, completed in 1965, is 3,640 feet long. The south jetty, completed in 1980, is 3,450 feet long.

The fishing: Masonboro Inlet is one of the best places to fish on the Southern coast. Anglers in small boats fish on the inside and the outside of the rock jetties, areas protected from the wakes of larger boats and from wind and waves. They also park at the southern tip of Wrightsville Beach and walk to the inlet. Flounder and speckled trout are common catches for surf anglers. Trout prefer the hard structure of the jetty, while flounder prefer the sandy bottom at the deeper part of the channel.

The jetties attract many fish species including red drum, flounder, speckled trout, bluefish, and Spanish mackerel. Anglers cast lures, spoons, and jigs or fish on the bottom with live baits to catch multiple species. Menhaden schools enter the inlet in spring and fall. When bluefish and Spanish mackerel follow them into the inlet, the fishing is extremely good.

Some anglers troll along the jetties using spoons to catch schooling fish. Others drift or cast to the rocks. Hang-ups are frequent until anglers get the knack for casting just close enough to the rocks to entice fish but far enough away to keep their hooks from snagging.

King mackerel, amberjack, and cobia are some of the large species that can be caught at the inlet or along the visible tide line formed where waters of different temperatures and turbidities collide during falling tides. Cobia are attracted to the inlet's buoys. Anglers catch all of these large fish using live baits, especially large menhaden.

In spring, schools of false albacore and Atlantic bonito spice up the fishing. They usually arrive by March or April. Spanish mackerel follow them. Big "chopper" bluefish typically arrive in May and strike topwater lures and live baits fished along the jetties.

The fishing is also excellent in the fall, when all the same species show a renewed bite after the summer doldrums. The exceptions are false albacore and Atlantic bonito, which usually generate good action only in springtime.

The jetties offer some excellent fishing for large speckled trout during the winter months. Live shrimp and scented soft lures are the best bets for winter fishing. Other winter fish include tautog and spottail pinfish (ringtail).

N.C. A-G grid: 84, D-2

General information: All NCDMF regulations apply. The parking at Wrightsville Beach is metered.

Nearest camping: Camping is allowed on Masonboro Island.

Directions: To reach the NCWRC's Wrightsville Beach Boating Access Area from I-40 in Wilmington, travel east on U.S. 74 (Martin Luther King Parkway) for 4.4 miles to the Intracoastal Waterway bridge. After crossing the bridge, turn right at the first intersection and drive beneath the bridge to the access area.

99 New River

Key species: Largemouth bass, sunfish, crappie, catfish, speckled trout, red drum, sheepshead, black drum, flounder

Overview: The New River begins in northwestern Onslow County and flows east-southeast past Jacksonville. The estuary meanders through Camp Lejeune Marine Corps Base and enters the Atlantic at Onslow Bay via New River Inlet. This is the only river in the United States that has its headwaters and mouth in the same county. The river has a marked navigation channel. A boat that misses the

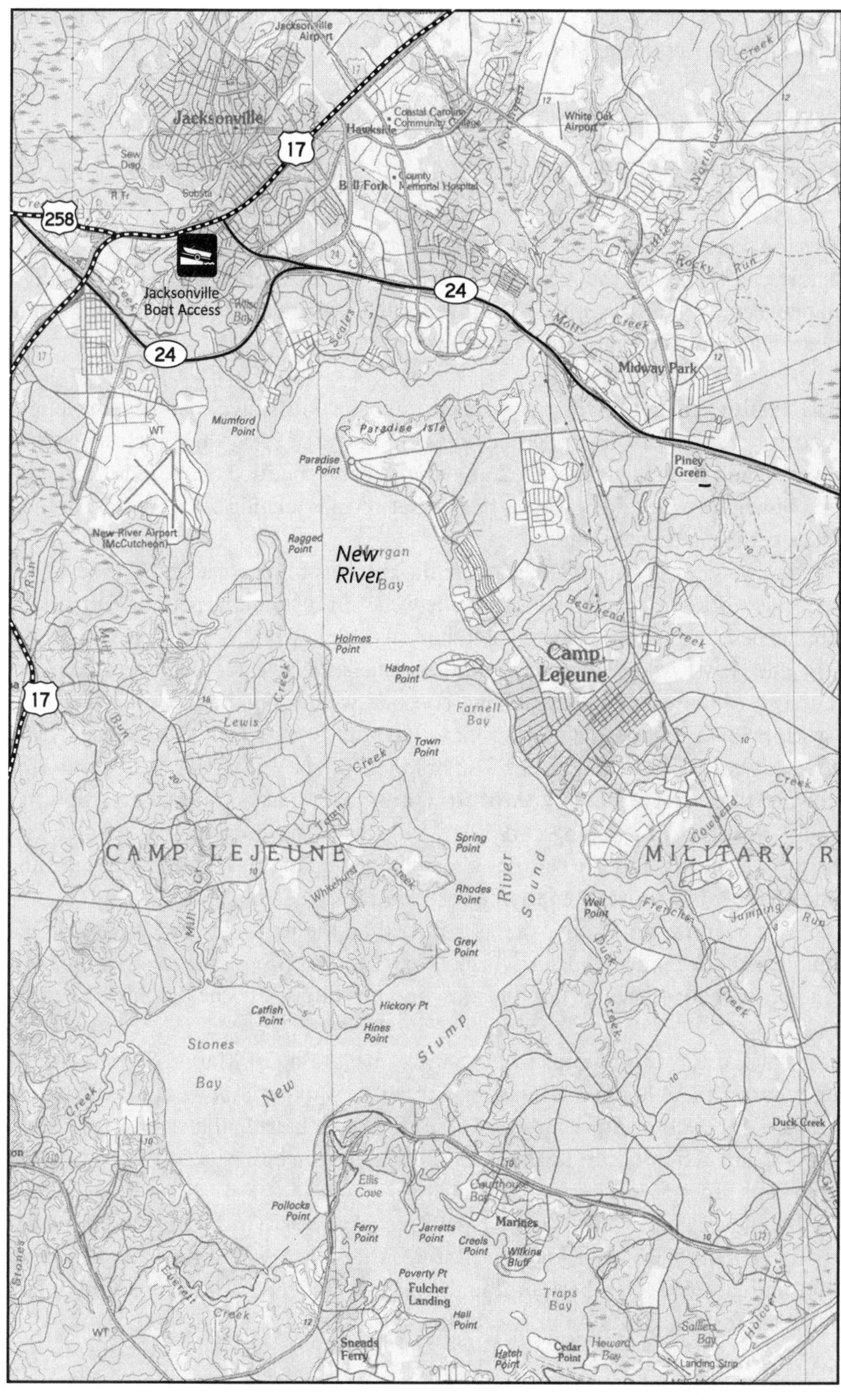
Jacksonville
Jacksonville Airport
Coastal Carolina Community College
Hawkside
White Oak Airport
17
258
24
Jacksonville Boat Access
Bell Fork
County Memorial Hospital
Rocky Run
Mott Creek
Midway Park
Mumford Point
Paradise Isle
Paradise Point
Piney Green
New River Airport (McCutcheon)
Ragged Point
New River
Morgan Bay
Bearhead Creek
Holmes Point
Hadnot Point
Camp Lejeune
Farnell Bay
Lewis Creek
Town Point
CAMP LEJEUNE
MILITARY R
Spring Point
Rhodes Point
Grey Point
Well Point
Frenchs Creek
Jumping Run
Duck Creek
Catfish Point
Hickory Pt
Hines Point
Stones Bay
New
Stump Sound
River Sound
Ellis Cove
Courthouse Bay
Pollocks Point
Ferry Point
Jarretts Point
Creels Point
Marines
Wilkins Bluff
Poverty Pt
Fulcher Landing
Hell Point
Traps Bay
Sneads Ferry
Hatch Point
Cedar Point
Howard Bay
Salliers Bay
Landing Strip
Everett Creek

channel can ground on a sand bar or oyster bed. Although it has the same name as the New River of the Mountain Region, this is an entirely different river.

Best ways to fish: Powerboat, kayak, canoe

Best time to fish: Year-round

Description: The New River stretches 40 miles in southeastern North Carolina before emptying into the Atlantic Ocean. Downstream of Jacksonville, it widens to between two and five miles. The river is shallow and flat and has a soft, sandy bottom and some oyster beds in the lower reaches.

The fishing: In the river's upper reaches above Jacksonville and in the upper reaches of some of the creeks including Southwest Creek, this brackish estuary gives way to freshwater species. Largemouth bass, speckled trout, red drum, gar, and bowfin can be caught. Other freshwater species include bluegill sunfish, flier, black crappie, and warmouth.

Topwater lures and soft plastics are the best bets for bass fishing. The best time to fish is April through June. Panfish bite well during the same period. Full moons are the best bets because that's when the fish are spawning.

The New River is legendary for producing fantastic catches of speckled trout. The fish can be caught all year long and bite well at night. The bridges around Jacksonville are good bets for specks. But Southwest Creek, Northeast Creek, French's Creek, and Duck Creek also hold lots of specks. Oyster beds, sand bars, downed trees, and all other types of structure attract specks. Anglers cast topwater walk-the-dog lures, popping cork rigs with soft plastic shrimp lures, scented soft baits on jig heads, and live shrimp or menhaden on float rigs. March through June and October and November are the best periods for catching big fish.

The shallow, sandy creek areas, rather than the hard structure areas, are the best bets for catching red drum. Anglers can spot the fish moving in the shallows. They cast spoons, scented soft plastics, and topwater walk-the-dog lures to catch them.

Black drum can be spotted in the river beginning in March. Some of them grow larger than 40 pounds. Casting cut bait or small minnows can entice them into striking. But shrimp, clams, and crabs are better baits for black drum. The best black drum action occurs at the N.C. 172 bridge. Sheepshead also bite clam and crab baits dropped beside the bridge pilings.

Anglers catch flounder in the New River channels. The best fishing is toward the river mouth where it joins the Intracoastal Waterway. Live baits fished on bottom rigs are the best bets for flounder. But flounder also strike any lure or bait intended for speckled trout or red drum.

N.C. A-G grid: 77, D-5

General information: All NCWRC and NCDMF regulations apply. Anglers lament the closing of the 14 ramps at Camp Lejeune Marine Corps Base that once were open to civilians through a permit system. The best option remaining is the NCWRC boating access at Jacksonville, which has few parking spaces. The base ramp on Southwest Creek once gave civilian anglers access to some of the best trout fishing in the state. Now, civilians must travel for miles across some wide, dangerous expanses of water in large craft to access the many great fishing areas in the river. Large, seaworthy craft are necessary because the water can get rough when the wind picks up.

Nearest camping: Cabin Creek Campground offers RV camping. For contact information, see the campground's entry in the appendix.

Directions: To reach Jacksonville Boat Access Area from N.C. 24 in Jacksonville, travel U.S. 17 South for 0.4 mile to Riverview Street, turn left, and drive a short distance. The access area is located at the intersection of Riverview and Tallman streets.

100 Ocean Fishing Piers

Key species: Spot, croaker, pompano, black drum, flounder, bluefish, red drum, speckled trout, gray trout, cobia, king mackerel, tarpon, whiting, shark, Spanish mackerel, sheepshead

Overview: North Carolina's ocean piers are renowned for their excellent fishing.

Best ways to fish: Bottom, casting lures, trolley rigs with live bait

Best times to fish: Spring, summer, and fall. Some piers are open in winter, but others are closed.

Description: The piers provide access to ocean fishing for anglers who have physical limitations, who don't have a boat, or who are very young or old. The state once boasted 36 fishing piers. About half remain. The others were victims of hurricanes or economic conditions that made them no longer viable as businesses. The list of piers will continue to change, so anglers should watch for new piers being constructed with state funds. But it will likely be a losing game in which more piers are torn down. All piers charge a fee for fishing. Some are open all year. Others are open free of charge in the winter, when the pier houses are closed.

The fishing: Bottom fishing is the easiest and most popular type of pier fishing. Virtually any rod and reel combination can be used to catch fish on the bottom. A typical pier rig consists of a pyramid or bank sinker on a two-hook rig. Baits can be live bloodworms or artificial bloodworm strips, cut fish, shrimp, or squid. Spot, croaker, flounder, red drum, pompano, whiting, speckled trout, bluefish, and black drum are common fish caught with bottom rigs.

Sheepshead are caught beside the pier pilings. Drop-shot rigs, with the baited hook tied above the sinker, are typically used for sheepshead. The best bait for sheepshead is a mole crab. Anglers can see sheepshead beside the pilings before dropping the bait to them.

The flounder fishing is also unique. Anglers tie wide-bend or Kahle hooks on rigs that may or may not have a float threaded onto the leader. The rig is held to the bottom with an egg sinker or trolling sinker and is baited with a live minnow. The angler walks slowly along, dragging the minnow along the bottom until detecting a strike.

Piers attract schooling fish including Spanish mackerel and bluefish. Anglers catch them using a spinning or bait-casting rod with a spoon, jerk lure, or jig. The best times to catch schooling fish are early and late in the day.

A trolley rig is used to catch large game fish. A trolley rig employs two rods. A long rod, usually a surf rod with either a revolving spool or spinning reel, serves as the "anchor" rod. A short pier rod of about six feet with a revolving spool reel serves as the "fight" rod. A surf sinker with wires sticking from its sides to keep it from being dislodged by wave action is cast with the anchor rod. The angler slides a release mechanism, usually consisting of a clothespin tied with a short piece of rigging wire or monofilament, onto the anchor rod line using a fish-finder slide or other type of release clip. There are many variations on this sliding release clip system, but all of them allow a live baitfish to slide down to the water surface along the anchor rod line on the "trolley" as the line is paid out from the fight rod's reel. The two rods are usually held in surf rod holders attached to the pier railing with stretch cords, but anglers also use much more sophisticated systems. The anchor rod bobs up and down to the rhythm of the Atlantic, while the fight rod stays at the ready, its warning clicker engaged. The baitfish can be almost anything, though most pier anglers prefer bluefish. The bait is hooked on a treble hook rig with a wire leader. A three-way swivel dangling two No. 2 treble hooks on twin wire leaders is the standard rig. Some anglers use more hooks. The hooks can be embedded in the baitfish or dangle free. The trolley rig keeps the bait in place. The angler can adjust the depth or change the bait easily. Another advantage to this system is that it keeps the baitfish and wind from moving the line beneath the pier or fouling the rig of another fisherman. Anglers land small fish by winding them

|| A fall spot run fills Kure Beach Pier with anglers from all across North Carolina and beyond.

in using the reel. They land larger fish with a hoop net or a weighted gaff tied to a rope and lowered to the water.

N.C. A-G grid: See the chart on pages 252-253.

General information: All NCDMF regulations apply.

Nearest camping: See the appendix for contact information for individual campgrounds.

Directions: See the individual pier listings in the appendix for street addresses.

Pier	*A-G* grid	Year built/rebuilt	Overall Length	Live Bait Tank	Unique Characteristics
Avalon Pier	49, A-5	1958	696 feet	No	Live piercam
Nags Head Pier	49, B-6	1939	750 feet	No	Live piercam
Outer Banks Fishing Pier	49, B-6	1959	650 feet	No	Also has a sound pier
Rodanthe Fishing Pier	69, A-7	1960	850 feet	No	Former record redfish landed
Avon Pier	69, D-7	1962	600 feet	No	Record redfish landed
Cape Hatteras Fishing Pier	69, D-6	Being rebuilt			
Bogue Inlet Pier	78, D-1	1960	1,000 feet	No	Observation platform
Oceana Fishing Pier	78, D-4	1958	1,000 feet	No	Family resort
Sheraton Pier	78, D-4		550 feet	No	Full-service resort
Sea View Fishing Pier	85, B-5		1,000+ feet		Will cook your catch
Surf City Ocean Pier	85, B-5	1951/1997	937 feet	No	40-foot octagon at end
Jolly Roger Pier	84, C-4	1954	850 feet	No	Motel complex
Johnnie Mercer's Pier	84, D-2	1937/2000	945 feet	No	Concrete
Carolina Beach Pier	87, A-7	1947/1998	700 feet	No	
Kure Beach Pier	87, B-7	1923	712 feet	Yes	Oldest family-owned pier
Oak Island Pier	87, B-6	1955/1972/1992	965 feet	No	Fenced area at end for king mackerel fishing only
Ocean Crest Fishing Pier	87, B-6		1,000 feet	Yes	T-shaped section at end to increase area for king mackerel fishing
Holden Beach Pier	87, B-5	1960/2001	700 feet	No	Shortened from 1,000 feet following hurricane damage
Ocean Isle Beach Fishing Pier	86, B-3	1958	1,000 feet	No	
Sunset Beach Fishing Pier	86, B-2		900 feet	No	

Appendix

National Parks and Agencies

Appalachian Ranger District
U.S. Forest Service
30 U.S. 19E Bypass, P.O. Box 128
Burnsville, N.C. 28714
828-682-6146
www.usforestcamping.org

Cape Hatteras National Seashore
1401 National Park Dr.
Manteo, N.C. 27954
252-473-2111
www.nps.gov/caha

Cape Lookout National Seashore
131 Charles St.
Harkers Island, N.C. 28531
252-728-2250
http://www.nps.gov/calo/planyourvisit/ferry.htm (ferry)

Cheoah Ranger District
U.S. Forest Service
Route 1, Box 16-A
Robbinsville, N.C. 28771
828-479-6431
www.forestcamping.org

Falls Lake
U.S. Army Corps of Engineers
11405 Falls of Neuse Rd.
Wake Forest, N.C. 27587
919-846-9332
www.saw.usace.army.mil

Fort Bragg Wildlife
Bldg. OT, 9034 McKellar's Rd.
Fort Bragg, N.C. 28310
910-396-7506
www.bragg.army.mil/wildlife/

Grandfather Ranger District
U.S. Forest Service
Route 1, Box 110-A
Nebo, N.C. 28761
828-652-2144
www.forestcamping.org

Great Smoky Mountains National Park
107 Park Headquarters Rd.
Gatlinburg, Tenn. 37738
865-436-1200 or 877-444-6777 (campground reservations)
www.nps.gov/grsm/contacts.htm

John H. Kerr Dam and Reservoir
U.S. Army Corps of Engineers
1930 Mays Chapel Rd.
Boydton, Va. 23917
434-738-6101
www.saw.usace.army.mil

Jordan Lake
U.S. Army Corps of Engineers
2080 Jordan Dam Rd.
Moncure, N.C. 27559
919-542-4501
www.saw.usace.army.mil

Lock and Dam No. 1
996 Lock No. 1 Rd.
Riegelwood, N.C. 28456
910-655-2605 (lock master)
www.saw.usace.army.mil

Mattamuskeet National Wildlife Refuge
Refuge Manager
38 Mattamuskeet Rd.
Swan Quarter, N.C. 27885
252-926-4021
www.fws.gov/refuges

Nantahala Ranger District
U.S. Forest Service
90 Sloan Rd.
Franklin, N.C. 28734
828-524-6441
www.forestcamping.org

Neuse River Recreation Area
Croatan National Forest
141 East Fisher Ave.
New Bern, N.C. 28650
252-638-5628
www.cs.unca.edu/nfsnc/recreation neuse_river.pdf (brochure)

Pee Dee National Wildlife Refuge
5770 U.S. 52 N.
Wadesboro, N.C. 28170
704-694-4424
www.fws.gov/refuges

Smith Lake Recreation Area
Building Q-2812, Smith Lake Rd.
Fort Bragg, N.C. 28310
910-396-5979
www.fortbraggmwr.com/smithlake.php

Tusquitee Ranger District
U.S. Forest Service
201 Woodland Dr.
Murphy, N.C. 28906
828-837-5152
www.forestcamping.org

TVA stream flows (French Broad, Nolichucky, Little Tennessee, and other western N.C. rivers)
800-238-2264
www.lakeinfo.tva.gov/htbin streaminfo

U.S. Coast Guard Headquarters
2100 Second St. SW, Stop 7581
Washington, D.C. 20593-7581
www.usboating.org

U.S. National Forest campground website
www.forestcamping.com

W. Kerr Scott Dam and Reservoir
U.S. Army Corps of Engineers
499 Reservoir Rd.
Wilkesboro, N.C. 27697-7462
336-921-3750
www.saw.usace.army.mil

State Parks and Agencies

Carolina Beach State Park
1010 State Park Rd., P.O. Box 475
Carolina Beach, N.C. 28428
910-458-8206
www.ncparks.gov

Cliffs of the Neuse State Park
345-A Park Entrance Rd.
Seven Springs, N.C. 28578
919-778-6234
www.ncparks.gov

Crowders Mountain State Park
522 Park Office Ln.
Kings Mountain, N.C. 28086
704-853-5375
www.ncparks.gov

Fort Fisher State Recreation Area
1000 Loggerhead Rd.
Kure Beach, N.C. 28449
910-458-5798
www.ncparks.gov

Fort Macon State Park
2300 E. Fort Macon Rd.,
P.O. Box 127
Atlantic Beach, N.C. 28512
252-726-3775
www.ncparks.gov

Goose Creek State Park
2190 Camp Leach Rd.
Washington, N.C. 27889
252-923-2191
www.ncparks.gov

Hanging Rock State Park
2015 Hanging Rock Park Rd.,
P.O. Box 278
Danbury, N.C. 27016
336-593-8480
www.ncparks.gov

John H. Kerr Lake State
Recreation Area
6254 Satterwhite Point Rd.
Henderson, N.C. 27537
252-438-7791
www.ncparks.gov

Jones Lake State Park
4117 N.C. 242 N.
Elizabethtown, N.C. 28337
910-588-4550
www.ncparks.gov

Jordan Lake State Recreation Area
280 State Park Rd.
Apex, N.C. 27523
919-362-0586
www.ncparks.gov

Lake James State Park
P.O. Box 340
Nebo, N.C. 28761
828-652-5047
www.ncparks.gov

Lake Norman State Park
159 Inland Sea Dr.
Troutman, N.C. 28166
704-528-6350
www.ncparks.gov

Lake Waccamaw State Park
1866 State Park Dr.
Lake Waccamaw, N.C. 28450
910-646-4748 or 910-646-1843
www.ncparks.gov

Lumber River State Park
2819 Princess Ann Rd.
Orrum, N.C. 28369
910-628-4564 or 910-628-5643
www.ncparks.gov

Medoc Mountain State Park
1541 Medoc Park Rd.
Hollister, N.C. 27844
252-586-6588
www.ncparks.gov

Merchants Millpond State Park
71 U.S. 158E
Gatesville, N.C. 27938-9440
252-357-1191
www.ncparks.gov

Morrow Mountain State Park
49104 Morrow Mountain Rd.
Albemarle, N.C. 28001
704-982-4402
www.ncparks.gov

N.C. Coastal Reserve
UNC Center for Marine Science
5600 Marvin K. Moss Ln.
Wilmington, N.C. 28409
910-962-2998
www.nccoastalreserve.net

N.C. Department of Health and Human Services fish consumption advisories
www.epi.state.nc.us/epi/fish/

N.C. Division of Marine Fisheries
3441 Arendell St.
Morehead City, N.C. 28557
800-682-2632 or 252-726-7021
www.ncfisheries.net

N.C. Division of Parks and Recreation
1615 Mail Service Center
Raleigh, N.C. 27699
919-733-4181
www.ncparks.gov

N.C. Wildlife Resources Commission
1701 Mail Service Center
Raleigh, N.C. 27699-1701
919-707-0030 (regulations/enforcement), 919-707-0220 (inland fisheries), 919-707-0150 (engineering services/boating access), or 919-707-0391 (license information)
www.ncwildlife.org

New River State Park
P.O. Box 48
Jefferson, N.C. 28640
336-982-2587
www.ncparks.gov

Pettigrew State Park
2252 Lake Shore Rd.
Creswell, N.C. 27928
252-797-4475
www.ncparks.gov

Pilot Mountain State Park
1792 Pilot Knob Park Rd.
Pinnacle, N.C. 27043
336-325-2355
www.ncparks.gov

S.C. Department of Natural Resources
1000 Assembly St., Columbia, S.C. 29201 (street)
P.O. Box 167, Columbia S.C. 29202 (mailing)
866-714-3611
www.dnr.sc.gov

Virginia State Parks
Va. Department of Conservation and Recreation
203 Governors St., Ste. 306
Richmond, Va. 23219
800-933-7275
www.dcr.virginia.gov/state_parks/

County, Municipal, Private, and Other Parks, Facilities, and Agencies

Alcoa lakes
www.alcoa.com/yadkin/en/info_page/lake_access.asp

Almond Boat and RV Park
1165 Almond Boat Park Rd.
Bryson City, N.C. 28713
828-488-6423
www.almondboatpark.com

Asheville–Buncombe County Tourism
www.exploreasheville.com/

Badin Lake Campground
429 Badin Lake Recreation Area Rd.
Troy, N.C. 27371
910-576-6391
http://recreation.gov/campground

Bayside Marina and Campground
480 German Town Rd.
Scranton, N.C. 27875
252-926-6621

Boiling Spring Lakes
9 E. Boiling Spring Lakes Rd.
Boiling Spring Lakes, N.C. 28461
910-845-2614
www.cityofbsl.org/

Cabin Creek Campground
3200 Wilmington Hwy.
Jacksonville, N.C. 28540
800-699-5305 or 910-346-4808
www.campingfriend.com
CabinCreekCampground

Cane Creek Park (Union County)
5213 Harkey Rd.
Waxhaw, N.C. 28173
704-843-3919
www.county.union.nc.us

Cane Creek Reservoir
8705 Stanford Rd.
Chapel Hill, N.C. 27510
919-942-5790
www.owasa.org

Carolina Campin' and Marina
548 Shelton Rd.
Stokesdale, N.C. 27357
800-344-2628 or 336-427-0498
www.carolinamarina.com

Conman's Guide Service and
Vacation Cottages
6693 Shore Dr.
Creswell, N.C. 27928
800-668-7124 or 252-797-7124
http://conmans.homestead.com

Dan River Campground
724 Webster Rd.
Stoneville, N.C. 27048
336-427-8530
www.danrivercampground.com

Duke Energy lakes facts and maps
www.duke-energy.com

Edenton-Chowan
Recreation Department
824 N. Oakum St., P.O. Box 1030
Edenton, N.C. 27932
252-482-8595 or 252-221-4901
www.chowancounty-nc.gov

Elizabeth City Parks and
Recreation Department
200 E. Ward St.
Elizabeth City, N.C. 27909-3658
252-335-1424
www.cityofec.com

Freeman Park
Town of Carolina Beach
Parking Office
1204 N. Lake Park Blvd., Ste. D
Carolina Beach, N.C. 28428
910-458-4614
www.carolinabeach.org

Graham County Travel and
Tourism Authority
15 N. Main St., P.O. Box 575
Robbinsville, N.C. 28771
800-470-3790 or 828-479-3790
www.grahamcountytravel.com

Graham-Mebane Lake Marina
3218 Bason Rd.
Mebane, N.C. 27302
919-563-6544
www.grahamrecreationandparks.com

Harris Lake County Park
2112 County Park Dr.
New Hill, N.C. 27562
919-387-4342
www.wakegov.com/parks

Hickory Parks and Recreation
Department
2000 Sixth St. NW
Hickory, N.C. 28601
828-322-7046
www.hickory.gov

High Point Department of
Parks and Recreation
136 Northpoint Ave.
High Point, N.C. 27262
336-883-3469
www.high-point.net/pr/fees
cfm#marina

High Point Lake
602 W. Main St.
Jamestown, N.C. 27262
336-883-3498
www.high-point.net/pr/citylake.cfm

Holland's Shelter Creek
Outdoor Adventures
8315 N.C. 53 E.
Burgaw, N.C. 28425
910-259-5743

Humphrey's Ridge Family
Campground
435 Humphreys Ridge Dr.
Stokesdale, N.C. 27357
336-427-3949

Hyco Lake Public Access Area
Person-Caswell Lake Authority
P.O. Box 343
Roxboro, N.C. 27573
336-599-4343
www.hycolake.com

Indian Springs Campground
4361 Whitener Dr.
Hickory, N.C. 28602
828-397-5700

Lake Brandt Marina
5945 Lake Brandt Rd.
Greensboro, N.C. 27455
336-545-5333 or 336-373-5888
(shelter reservations)
www.greensboro-nc.gov

Lake Gaston Campground
561 Fleming Dairy Rd.
Littleton, N.C. 27850
252-586-4121
www.gocampingamerica.com

Lake Hickory RV Resort
6641 Monford Dr.
Conover, N.C. 28613
828-256-4303
www.lakehickoryrvresort.org

Lake Higgins Marina
4235 Hamburg Mill Rd.
Summerfield, N.C. 27358
336-643-4295
www.greensboro-nc.gov

Lake James Bridgewater hydro plan schedule and information
828-584-1451

Lake Lucas Marina
3158 Old Lexington Rd.
Asheboro, N.C. 27205-2584
336-629-1639
www.asheboroparksandrecreation.com

Lake Lure Dam daily release schedule
828-625-1599

Lake Lure RV Park and Campground
176 Boy's Camp Rd.
Lake Lure, N.C. 28746
828-625-9160

Lake Mackintosh Park and Marina
2704 Huffman Mill Rd.
Burlington, N.C. 27215
336-538-0896 or 336-449-2078
(Guilford-Mackintosh Marina)
www.ci.burlington.nc.us

Lake Raleigh
Main Campus Dr.,
Centennial Campus
Raleigh, N.C. 27603
919-515-7036
www.ncsu.edu

Lake Reese
Asheboro Parks and Recreation
850 Jackson Creek Rd.
Denton, N.C. 27239
336-241-2570
www.asheboroparksandrecreation.com

Lake Reese Marina
4850 Jackson Creek Rd.
Denton, N.C. 27239
336-241-2570

Lake Tabor
910-653-5814
www.taborcitync.org

Lake Thom-A-Lex Park
700 Yokley Rd.
Lexington, N.C. 27292
336-731-6052
www.co.davidson.nc.us/leisure LakeThom-A-LexPark.aspx

Lake Townsend Marina
6332 Townsend Rd.
Browns Summit, N.C. 27214
336-373-3694
www.greensboro-nc.gov

Latta Plantation Park
5225 Sample Rd.
Huntersville, N.C. 28078
704-875-1724
www.lattaplantation.org

Madison County Visitor Center
72 S. Main St., Box 1527
Mars Hill, N.C. 28754
877-262-3476 or 828-680-9031
www.visitmadisoncounty.com

Nolichucky Gorge Campground
101 Jones Branch Rd.
Erwin, Tenn. 37650
423-743-8876
www.angelfire.com/tn/nolichucky

Oak Hollow Lake Marina
High Point Department of
Parks and Recreation
3431 N. Centennial St.
High Point, N.C. 27265
336-883-3494
www.oakhollowcampground.com

Osprey Nest Campground
6234 Piney Woods Rd.
Fairfield, N.C. 27826
252-926-4491

Paths of Perquimans
P.O. Box 691
Hertford, N.C. 27944
www.pathsofperquimans.org

Person County Lake Authority
P.O. Box 343
Roxboro, N.C. 27573
336-599-4343

Person County Recreation,
Arts, and Parks
425 Long Ave.
Roxboro, N.C. 27573
336-597-1755
http://recreation.personcounty.net/

Ralph J. Andrews Campground
Jackson County Parks and Recreation
88 Cullowhee Mountain Rd.
Cullowhee, N.C. 28723
828-293-3053
www.rec.jacksonnc.org/html/
campground.html

Randleman Regional Reservoir
Piedmont Triad Regional
Water Authority
2216 W. Meadowview Rd.,
Wilmington Bldg., Ste. 204
Greensboro, N.C. 27407
336-547-8437
randlemanlake.com

Randleman Regional
Reservoir Marina
7123 Adams Farm Rd.
Randleman, N.C. 27317

River Bend Park
6700 N.C. 16 N.
Conover, N.C. 28613
828-256-9157
http://www.catawbacountync.gov
depts/parks/riverbend.asp

River Creek Campground
217 River Creek Dr.
Rutherfordton, N.C. 28139
866-287-3915 or 828-287-3915
www.rivercreeknc.com/

Roanoke River Partners
P.O. Box 488
Windsor, N.C. 27983-0488
252-792-3790
www.roanokeriverpartners.org/

Salem Lake Fishing Station
1001 Salem Lake Rd.
Winston-Salem, N.C. 27107
336-650-7677
www.cityofws.org/Home/Departments/RecreationAndParks SalemLake/

Singing Waters Campground
Trout Creek Rd.
Tuckasegee, N.C. 28783
828-293-5872
www.kiz.com/campnet/html/zpnc/0363/0363evnt.htm

Town of Lake Lure
P.O. Box 255
Lake Lure, N.C. 28746
828-625-9983
www.townoflakelure.com

Town of White Lake
1879 White Lake Dr.
P.O. Box 7250
White Lake, N.C. 28337
910-862-4800
www.whitelakenc.com/

Transylvania County Tourism Development Authority
35 W. Main St.
Brevard, N.C. 28712
800-648-4523
www.visitwaterfalls.com

University Lake
919-942-8007
www.owasa.org/whatwedo/recretion.aspx

Whispering Pines RV Park and Campground
2791 N.C. 24
Newport, N.C. 28570
252-726-4902
www.ncpines.com/

White Lake Water Sports and Marina, Inc.
6548 U.S. 701 N.
White Lake, N.C. 28337
910-872-5253
www.whitelakewatersports.com/

Winston-Salem Recreation and Parks
Bryce A. Stuart Municipal Bldg.
100 E. First St.
Ste. 407
Winston-Salem, N.C. 27101 (street)
P.O. Box 2511
Winston-Salem, N.C. 27102-2511 (mailing)
336-727-8000
www.cityofws.org/Home Departments/RecreationAndParks

Yogi Bear's Jellystone Park
626 Richard Wright Rd.
Tabor City, N.C. 28463
910-653-2155
www.taborcityjellystone.com

Piers

Avalon Pier
2111 N. Virginia Dare Trail
Kill Devil Hills, N.C. 27948
252-441-7494
www.avalonpier.com

Avon Pier
41001 N.C. 12
Avon, N.C. 27915
252-995-5480
www.avonpier.com

Bogue Inlet Pier
100 Bogue Inlet Dr.
Emerald Island, N.C. 28594
252-354-2919
www.bogueinletpier.com/

Cape Hatteras Fishing Pier
4221 Cape Hatteras Pier Dr.
Frisco, N.C. 27936
252-986-2533

Carolina Beach Pier
1810 Canal Dr.
Carolina Beach, N.C. 28428
910-458-5518

Holden Beach Pier
441 Ocean Blvd.
Holden Beach, N.C. 28462
910-842-6483

Johnnie Mercer's Pier
23 E. Salisbury St.
Wrightsville Beach, N.C. 28480
910-256-2743

Jolly Roger Pier
803 E. Ocean Rd.
Topsail Beach, N.C. 28445
910-328-4616

Kure Beach Pier
100 K Ave.
Kure Beach, N.C. 28449
910-458-5524
www.kurebeachfishingpier.com

Nags Head Pier
3395 S. Virginia Dare Trail
Nags Head, N.C. 27959
252-441-5141
www.nagsheadpier.com/

Oak Island Pier
705 Ocean Dr.
Oak Island, N.C. 28465
910-278-6464

Ocean Crest Fishing Pier
1409 E. Beach Dr.
Oak Island, N.C. 28465
910-278-6674
www.oceancrestpier.net/

Ocean Isle Beach Fishing Pier
7276 Seashell Ln. SW
Ocean Isle Beach, N.C. 28469
910-579-3095

Oceana Fishing Pier
Fort Macon Rd.
Atlantic Beach, N.C. 28512
252-762-4111
www.oceanana.com

Outer Banks Fishing Pier
8901 Oregon Inlet Rd.
Nags Head, N.C. 27959
252-441-5740
www.fishingunlimited.net/
OuterBanksPier.html/

Rodanthe Fishing Pier
24251 Atlantic Dr.
Rodanthe, N.C. 27968
252-987-2323
www.hatterasislandresort.com/

Sea View Fishing Pier
124 Fishing Pier Ln.
North Topsail Beach, N.C. 28460
910-328-3172

Sheraton Pier
2717 W. Fort Macon Rd.
Atlantic Beach, N.C. 28512
252-240-1155
www.sheratonatlanticbeach.com/

Sunset Beach Fishing Pier
101 W. Main St.
Sunset Beach, N.C. 28468
910-579-6630

Surf City Ocean Pier
112 S. Shore Dr., P.O. Box 2582
Surf City, N.C. 28445
910-328-3521
www.surfcityoceanpier.com/

Index